SECOND EDITION

BASIC SKILLS AND STRATEGIES FOR
COLLEGE READING
A TEXT WITH THEMATIC READER

—JANE L. McGRATH—

COMPANION WEBSITE™
www.prenhall.com/mcgrath

IORE CONT
REA READI
equal
COLLEGI
READINC
SUCCE

WELCOME

to the Second Edition of **BASIC SKILLS AND STRATEGIES FOR COLLEGE READING.** The new edition is updated to include even more content area material with numerous text excerpts and three complete college textbook chapters, stressing the importance of transferring skills and strategies to all types of readings and, most importantly, to other classes.

The Second Edition's expansion of content area reading is important for developing and improving students' reading skills, a fundamental skill for college success. Selections have been thoughtfully and carefully chosen and consider student interests, current affairs, readability level, and writing style.

Hold On to Your Positive Attitude

"It's hard to stay positive under pressure."

Thought for the Day: If your attitude has thorns, you cannot expect others to want to get close to you.

IS IT TIME FOR AN ATTITUDE ADJUSTMENT?

*Barbara K. Bruce
and Denise Foley*

[1]You got your blue eyes from Dad and your strawberry blond hair from Mom. The tiny bump on the bridge of your nose definitely is from Grandpa William. However, did you also inherit your pessimistic attitude or your sunny outlook? Are you genetically programmed to see the glass as half empty or half full?

[2]Recent research suggests that some personality traits and attitudes indeed may be part of your genetic blueprint. In 1996, scientists announced they had located genes linked to anxiety, addiction, happiness, and pessimism. Their studies provocatively suggest that you may have been born to be grumpy, hostile, a worrier, outgoing, or cheerful. You even may be one of those people who is born to be wild because you carry a thrill-seeking gene.

[3a]If you have struggled all your life with chronic worry, dark moods, or a short fuse, does this research mean you are a born loser in a biological game of chance? [3b]The answer is "no." [3c]Biology is not destiny, nor is your attitude entirely a matter of luck. [3d]Part of your personality is inherited, but, at most, only half is. [3e]That leaves a lot of room for self-improvement. [3f]Even more encouraging, the genes for personality aren't like those for eye color or height. [3g]Your blue eyes... ...

With an emphasis on authentic, multi-disciplinary college reading material, the Second Edition includes readings from texts, magazines, newspapers, and journals. Text excerpts include readings from government, history, art, biology, business, career exploration, computers, criminal justice, environmental science, economics, English, geography, health, and much more.

read-ing (red'in) *adj.* **1** inclined [ ]d or study **2** ma
reading n. **1** the act or practic[ ]person who read
of books **2** a public entertainm[ ]which literary [ ]
aloud **3** the extent to which a [ ]n has read **4** ma[ ]
meant to be read **5** the amoun[ ]asured as by a ba[ ]
thermometer **6** the form[ ]specified word, senten[ ]

CHAPTER 6

Reading Multiparagraph Selections

AN IDEA TO THINK ABOUT

Think about all the reading you do during a routine day. For example, you might locate a specific piece of information in a ten-page report for your boss, catch up on the day's events in the newspaper, surf the Internet, read a text assignment for class, make a casserole from a new cookbook, and spend some time with your favorite author's latest novel.

READ ACTIVELY

Did you ever fall asleep while you were playing a game or watching your favorite television comedy? Probably not. Did you ever fall asleep while you were reading an assignment for class? Probably.

The difference is in how mentally and physically involved you are in the activity—whether you are an active or passive participant. For example, when you are actively involved in an activity—playing a game, laughing at a comedy—your mental and physical energy are focused on the task.

Unfortunately, students often view reading as a passive task that doesn't require attention or action. Passive readers are content to sit back and let the words pass by their eyes as their mind slips into neutral or considers what to have for lunch. They "wake up" a few pages later and wonder if they've

Use Your Strategies 3

**COURTLAND BOVÉE, JOHN THILL,
AND BARBARA SCHATZMAN**

Prepare to Read

Courtland Bovée is professor of Business Communication, C. Allen Paul Distinguished Chair at Grossmont College. John Thill is chief executive officer of Communication Specialists of America. Barbara Schatzman is with the Keller Graduate School of Management and president of Summit One Global Business Solutions. This selection is excerpted from Chapter 2, "Communicating in Teams and Mastering Listening and Nonverbal Communication Skills," of their text Business Communication Today, *seventh edition.*

AN IDEA TO THINK ABOUT

Do you ever communicate your feelings without saying a word? For example, do you smile to show you agree, wave your hand to say goodbye, or shrug your shoulders to say, "I don't know"? *As you read*, find out how the various types of nonverbal communication impact our lives.

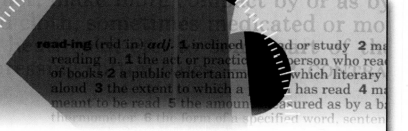

THEME 1 It's All About Attitude

*Some people are always grumbling because roses have thorns;
I am thankful that thorns have roses.*

Alphonse Karr

When you look at this glass, do you see it as half full or half empty?

How you answer may tell a lot about your view of the world and your chances for happiness and success.

This is because people who are optimistic—those who see the glass as half full—expect great things, work hard for those things, and are likely to achieve them. People with a positive attitude look for the "can do" side of every situation. On the other hand, pessimists—those who see the glass as half empty—seem to search for the "cannot do" side of a situation.

AN IDEA TO THINK ABOUT

How do you typically react when your plans don't work out the way you thought they would? *As you read,* try to answer Ziggy's "what if" question.

Selection 4 Questions

1. What does Ziggy want us to think about?

   Ziggy wants us to think about how often we miss the real lessons of

   life because we are too busy being frustrated and impatient that

   things aren't going the way they are supposed to go.

The Second Edition organizes the reading pedagogy into three thematic reading units and six instructional chapters for reading. These chapters provide instruction in reading skills and progress to strategies for reading more critically and effectively, helping students meet the demands of their other courses.

All themes now include an editorial cartoon.

INSTRUCTOR SUPPORT

Prentice Hall is committed to helping every instructor, whether a new adjunct or a seasoned professional, by offering the following Instructor Support Items. Ask your Prentice Hall sales representative for more information.

▼ **Instructor's Edition, Second Edition** (0-13-184903-4)
Includes answers to exercises and an Instructor's Guide with teaching tips in the back.

▼ **Instructor's Manual and Test Bank, Second Edition** (0-13-184901-8)
Provides additional material including exercises and a test bank.

▼ **Prentice Hall Reading Skills Test Bank** (0-13-041249-X)
Offers over 1,000 exercises in eleven different reading skills. Available in print or electronic format.

STUDENT SUPPORT—Customize Your Classroom!

Enrich your classroom with the following Student Support Packages designed to provide additional practice and offer resources to master reading and writing. Ask your Prentice Hall sales representative for more information.

▼ **Text-specific Companion Website™** at *www.prenhall.com/mcgrath*

The open-access Companion Website™ allows students to gain a richer perspective and a deeper understanding of the concepts and issues discussed in BASIC SKILLS AND STRATEGIES FOR COLLEGE READING, SECOND EDITION. Features of the site include the following:
—Additional readings with specific vocabulary, comprehension, and Web activities.
—Online quizzes for each chapter with instant scoring and coaching.
—Essay questions that test students' critical thinking skills.

▼ **The Prentice Hall Textbook Reader**
The PRENTICE HALL TEXTBOOK READER includes eight complete college textbook chapters from a variety of disciplines. Edited by Tim Brown of Riverside Community College, each chapter includes instructions on a reading strategy, a textbook chapter, and various exercises after the selection. Available free when packaged with any McGrath text.
To order THE PRENTICE HALL TEXTBOOK READER, use ISBN 0-13-184895-X. Use this ISBN to order BASIC SKILLS AND STRATEGIES FOR COLLEGE READING, SECOND EDITION, with free PRENTICE HALL TEXTBOOK READER: 0-13-162721-X.

▼ Basic College Vocabulary Strategies

BASIC COLLEGE VOCABULARY STRATEGIES approaches vocabulary development with a unique and proven systematic strategy called **SSCD—See and say** the word, use **Structural analysis**, apply **Context clues** and incorporate **Dictionary knowledge**. The text addresses the need for identifying learning styles and reinforces the system with techniques to develop a repertoire of memory steps to improve retention of information.

To order BASIC COLLEGE VOCABULARY STRATEGIES, use ISBN 0-13-049385-6. Use this ISBN to order BASIC SKILLS AND STRATEGIES FOR COLLEGE READING, SECOND EDITION, with BASIC COLLEGE VOCABULARY STRATEGIES: 0-13-151809-7.

▼ The Prentice Hall Florida Exit Test Study Guide for Reading

This self-paced study guide reinforces the skills students need to demonstrate on the Florida College Basic Skills Exit Test for reading. To order THE PRENTICE HALL FLORIDA EXIT TEST STUDY GUIDE FOR READING use ISBN 0-13-184899-2. Use this ISBN to order BASIC SKILLS AND STRATEGIES FOR COLLEGE READING, SECOND EDITION, with free THE PRENTICE HALL FLORIDA EXIT TEST STUDY GUIDE FOR READING: 0-13-162722-8.

▼ The New American Webster Handy College Dictionary

This updated and expanded edition contains more than 115,000 definitions, covering current phrases, slang, and scientific terms, and includes advice on usage and grammar, notes on etymology, foreign words and phrases, and a world gazetteer. Use this ISBN to order BASIC SKILLS AND STRATEGIES FOR COLLEGE READING, SECOND EDITION, with free dictionary: 0-13-126887-2.

▼ Roget's Thesaurus

The easiest to use and most up-to-date word-finder available. Over 12,000 main entries, 400,000 synonyms and antonyms, and thousands of sentence examples! Use this ISBN to order BASIC SKILLS AND STRATEGIES FOR COLLEGE READING, SECOND EDITION, with free ROGET'S THESAURUS: 0-13-126890-2.

To order BOTH free dictionary and free thesaurus with BASIC SKILLS AND STRATEGIES FOR COLLEGE READING, SECOND EDITION, use package ISBN 0-13-126886-4.

▼ The Prentice Hall Journal

This 150-page, spiral-bound journal provides plenty of space for students to draft essays, complete homework assignments, or just write creatively. Quotations are integrated throughout to inspire students (ISBN: 0-13-184900-X). To package THE PRENTICE HALL JOURNAL available free with this, or any, Prentice Hall text, contact your local Prentice Hall sales representative for ordering details.

ABOUT THE AUTHOR

Jane L. McGrath

earned her undergraduate degree and M.A. in education and mass communications and her Ed.D. in reading education from Arizona State University. During her more than twenty-five years with the Maricopa Colleges, McGrath taught a variety of reading, English, journalism, and computer applications courses. She was named *Innovator of the Year* by the Maricopa Colleges and the League for Innovation in Community Colleges for Project Read-Aloud, a college-community service program, and has received *Outstanding Citizen* awards from the cities of Tempe and Phoenix, Arizona for her community service activities. In addition to her work in reading education, McGrath and her husband Larry write for the high performance automotive industry. Their work has appeared in magazines such as *Drag Racing Today* and *Circle Track*, and their monthly column appears in *Performance Racing Industry*.

ALSO AVAILABLE BY JANE L. MCGRATH:

BUILDING STRATEGIES FOR COLLEGE READING:
A TEXT WITH THEMATIC READER, FOURTH EDITION
Student Edition: 0-13-184889-5
Instructor's Edition: 0-13-184894-1

STRATEGIES FOR CRITICAL READING:
A TEXT WITH THEMATIC READER
0-13-048875-5

PEARSON
Prentice
Hall

To learn more about these titles, please contact your local Prentice Hall sales representative, e-mail us at *english_service@prenhall.com*, or visit our online catalog at *www.prenhall.com/english*.

BASIC SKILLS AND STRATEGIES FOR
COLLEGE READING
A TEXT WITH THEMATIC READER
— SECOND EDITION —

INSTRUCTOR'S EDITION

Jane L. McGrath
Professor Emerita
Paradise Valley Community College

PEARSON
Prentice
Hall

UPPER SADDLE RIVER, NEW JERSEY 07458

Editorial director: Leah Jewell
Senior acquisitions editor: Craig Campanella
Editorial assistant: Joan Polk
Project liaison: Fran Russello
Permission specialist: Connie Golden
Director of Marketing manager: Beth Mejia
Prepress and manufacturing manager: Nick Sklitsis
Prepress and manufacturing buyer: Ben Smith
Creative design director: Leslie Osher
Art director: Carmen DiBartolomeo
Cover/interior design: PreMediaONE, A Black Dot Group Company
Cover art: The Image Bank
Photo researcher: Kathy Ringrose
Image permission coordinator: Debbie Hewitson
Composition/full-service project management: Pine Tree Composition, Inc.
Printer/binder: Von Hoffman Press, Inc
Cover printer: The Lehigh Press, Inc.

Credits and acknowledgments borrowed from other sources and reproduced, with permission, in this textbook appear on page 367.

10 9 8 7 6 5 4 3 2 1

Student Edition:
ISBN 0-13-184898-4
Instructor's Edition:
ISBN 0-13-184903-4

CONTENTS AT A GLANCE

CONTENTS

Basic Skills and Strategies for College Reading, Second Edition, is for college students in a first-level reading course. This edition maintains its focus on the reading skills necessary for effective literal comprehension.

This text, like the next-level text *Building Strategies for College Reading, Fourth Edition,* encourages students to see themselves as active participants in the reading process—readers who can set and accomplish reading and study goals and objectives. Therefore, *Basic Skills and Strategies for College Reading*

- presents detailed instruction in and examples of the basic reading skills students must master to be successful in college;

- provides abundant *authentic* practice with complete articles, essays, and textbook chapters;

- encourages students to develop a repertoire of reading and study strategies and provides guided activities as they learn to select and use different strategies for different tasks;

- stresses the importance of transferring skills and strategies to other readings and other classes;

- encourages students to realize that expanding their vocabulary is fundamental to college success;

- provides extensive practice opportunities in three topical thematic units so that as students broaden their conceptual background knowledge, they see themselves as successful readers; and

- persuades students to plan, monitor, and evaluate their own learning.

ENDURING FEATURES OF THE TEXT

The basic organization remains the same in this second edition: six instructional chapters, three thematic reading units, appendices, glossary, and topic index. The text continues to offer an array of authentic reading tasks—including three complete text chapters—to help prepare students to meet the demands of the texts and tasks they will encounter in future classes.

Chapters

The six chapters provide instruction in reading skills necessary for effective comprehension: previewing textbooks, understanding vocabulary, understanding main ideas, understanding implied main ideas, identifying supporting details and using relationships among ideas, determining a thesis, and reading multiparagraph selections.

The development of each chapter is true to instructional design principles: concise explanations with a constant emphasis on application to college material, examples clearly related to the explanations, and practice—abundant practice. The sequence of development and instructional language encourages students to connect and integrate the new skills and information they are learning with what they already know.

Each chapter begins with An Idea to Think About to help students place the topic and the skill in an understandable context before they begin to work. The At a Glance chapter outline and the Chapter Focus ask students to look at the "big picture" before they begin to work on the parts.

The paragraphs and multiparagraph expository pieces come from texts, magazines, newspapers, and government publications. Subject areas include American government, American history, art, biology, business communications, career exploration, computers, criminal justice, earth science, English, environmental science, geography, health, health occupations, history, human relations, the Internet, interpersonal communications, music, personal development, personal finance, psychology, sociology, and stress management.

Each chapter ends with a Summary of Key Ideas and the opportunity for more practice or skill assessment in the Use Your Strategies sections. A variety of questions and activities to extend thinking are available in Reflect and Connect, Log On to the Web, and the Crossword Puzzle.

Themes

The three thematic reading units—Theme 1, personal development; Theme 2, health and wellness; Theme 3, business communications—each include a full textbook chapter plus related articles and cartoons on the unifying topic. There are more readings than needed for a quarter or even a semester course. However, an abundant collection of authentic material allows instructors to select topics and readings to best meet the needs of students.

Each theme begins with an introduction to the topic and the readings. Each selection in the theme begins with information about the author, definitions for unusual vocabulary, an idea to think about, and one concept or idea for students to find as they are reading. Each selection is followed by vocabulary, comprehension, and reflect and connect questions. Each theme ends with a Log On to the Web activity and Reflect and Connect questions to encourage students to continue reading and thinking about the topic.

Because the thematic approach supplies multiple exposures to a topic, it provides a scaffolding of knowledge that allows students to handle more sophisticated material than isolated readings. This approach also encourages a more meaningful and connected understanding of a topic and promotes thinking as students view a topic from several perspectives.

CHANGES IN THE SECOND EDITION

Instructors who used the first edition will find a variety of small modifications and several major changes in this second edition:

A new format and look.   This edition has a more inviting appearance. The use of color throughout the book should make students more comfortable with transferring skills to other texts and assignments.

Inside the cover. I have added *Strategies for Becoming a Successful Student* inside the front cover for two reasons: First, it is important information students can use immediately; and second, because most college textbooks now include important, general information inside the front cover, this feature helps prepare students for other texts.

New chapter element. Each chapter opens with *An Idea to Think About* to help students place the topic and the skill in an understandable context before they begin to work. In addition, I'm hopeful that this element will help students realize that the "chapter-opening" features in their other texts—case studies, theoretical scenarios, narratives, anecdotes—are useful.

Expanded instruction and practice on understanding main ideas. Although it may be impossible to ever provide "enough" main idea exercises, I have expanded both the discussion and practice of this important skill in Chapter 3.

Concentrated emphasis on making inferences and understanding implied main ideas. It is unfair to assume students have certain underlying skills such as the ability to make inferences. Thus, Chapter 4 helps students develop the skill of making inferences before asking them to infer a main idea.

Chapter readings. Factors such as student interests, current affairs, readability level, and writing style influence my selection of readings. About half of the examples and exercises are new to this edition.

Themes. In Theme 1, "It's All About Attitude," half of the readings are new or revised. Theme 2, "A Healthy Environment," and Theme 3, "Speaking with Confidence," are new to this edition and were developed with our students' needs and interests in mind. In addition, all the themes include a cartoon to lighten the mood and encourage students to begin thinking about reading graphics.

New appendix material. Instruction and practice in distinguishing among *Facts, Opinions, and Reasoned Judgments* has been revised and moved into the Appendix. A new section on strategies for *Using Textbook Design Clues* has been added. *Preparing for and Taking Standardized Reading Tests* has been updated from the first edition.

IN APPRECIATION

Although my name appears on the cover, many, many wonderful people contributed to the development and production of this second edition. First, I am very grateful to my students. Their enthusiasm and perseverance have always been vital to our classroom successes. My thanks to my colleagues across the Maricopa Community Colleges and across the United States for sharing your ideas and expertise to make this text more useful for students.

For their invaluable reviews of the first edition as I prepared my revision plan for the second edition, I am indebted to

Ted Walkup	Clayton College and State University
Miriam A. Kinard	Trident Technical College
Shirley Carpenter	Richard Daley Community College
Meribeth Allman	Anne Arundel Community College
Linda S. Edwards	Chattanooga State Community College

I am thankful for the cadre of dedicated professionals at Prentice Hall, especially Craig Campanella, Senior Editor English, and Joan Polk, Editorial Assistant, who provided unfailing optimism and support for this three-book revision extravaganza. My sincere thanks to Larry McGrath, my partner in all of life's adventures—without his wisdom, good humor, technical expertise, and encouragement, this book would not exist.

And, thank *you* for inviting me into your classroom. I welcome your suggestions and will be delighted to hear your comments at Jellenjay@aol.com.

Jane L. McGrath earned her undergraduate degree and M.A. in education and mass communications and her Ed.D. in reading education from Arizona State University. During her more than twenty-five years with the Maricopa Colleges, McGrath taught a variety of reading, English, journalism, and computer applications courses. She was named Innovator of the Year by the Maricopa Colleges and the League for Innovation in Community Colleges for Project Read-Aloud, a college-community service program, and has received Outstanding Citizen awards from the cities of Tempe and Phoenix, Arizona, for her community service activities. McGrath's other books include *Building Strategies for College Reading: A Text with Thematic Reader* (fourth edition) and *Strategies for Critical Reading*. In addition to her work in reading education, McGrath and her husband Larry write for the high-performance automotive industry. Their work has appeared in magazines such as *Drag Racing Today* and *Circle Track,* and their monthly column appears in *Performance Racing Industry.*

Previewing Textbooks

Have you ever noticed that a skilled carpenter has a toolbox filled with hammers, screwdrivers, and chisels of every size and description, plus an assortment of specialized tools most of us wouldn't even recognize? This is because a carpenter who only knows how to use a large hammer or who has only one small chisel could not do all the tasks required to complete a project. Carpenters need a variety of tools so they can select the best ones for each task.

To be a skilled student, it's essential for you to assemble a toolbox filled with reading and study tools. You need to have and to be able to use a variety of tools so you can select the best ones for each part of a reading assignment. In reading we call these tools *strategies*. A **strategy** is a tool or technique you consciously select in order to complete a task accurately and efficiently.

What strategies do you have in your toolbox?

CHAPTER 1 AT A GLANCE

Chapter Focus
Previewing a Textbook
    Table of Contents
    Preface
    Author Information
    Index
    Appendix
    Glossary

Looking Ahead
Summary of Key Ideas
Use Your Strategies
Reflect and Connect
Log On to the Web

CHAPTER FOCUS

One of the first strategies you need to be a successful reader is to know when and how to preview. The word *preview* means "to look at or see in advance." As used in reading, preview means to survey, or examine, reading material in an orderly way *before* you begin to read. Previewing provides an overall picture of what you are going to read. It's like looking at a completed jigsaw puzzle before you try to fit the individual pieces together. In this chapter you'll work on previewing a textbook before you begin to read a textbook's first chapter.

PREVIEWING A TEXTBOOK

Previewing a textbook is not a random activity. When you **preview**, you systematically read key organizers like the title page, table of contents, and preface. Previewing gives you information about the text and its author and time to make connections between what you know and what you are going to read. It takes only a few minutes, yet previewing the text before you start to read the first chapter can give you a head start on successful reading. To preview a text, look at structural organizers such as the following:

FRONT OF THE TEXT	BACK OF THE TEXT
Title page	Glossary
Table of contents	Appendix or appendices
Preface	Index
Author information	Answer key

The exercises in this chapter will help you practice your previewing skills.

Table of Contents

A **table of contents** is located in the first few pages of a textbook. It lists the titles and often the subtitles of the chapters and the page numbers on which they begin. Reading a table of contents gives you an overview of the topics and a picture of how they relate to one another.

Exercise 1

Use the excerpt on the left, from the Contents of *Student Resource Guide to the Internet* by Cynthia B. Leshin, to answer these questions.

1. On what page would you begin reading to find out what it means to be "on the Internet"?

page 6

2. In which chapter would you look for information on how to use an Internet browser?

Chapter 2

3. On what page does the glossary (Geek Speak) begin? page 209

4. List the titles of the appendices.

Two appendices:

Finding Web Sites That Have Moved

What to Look for When Purchasing a

Computer

5. List the titles of the first three major sections in Chapter 2.

First three major sections in chapter:

Internet Navigation Using Browsers

Learning Adventure Using Browsers

to Surf the Net

Multimedia-Oriented Web

Environments

Exercise 2

Use the Contents in *this* textbook to answer these questions.

1. Where did you find the Contents? (List the page numbers.) pages v–vii

2. On what page does the glossary begin?

page 360

3. List the titles of the thematic reading units.

Three thematic reading units:

It's All About Attitude

A Healthy Environment

Speaking with Confidence

Contents

4. On what page would you begin reading to learn how to find the thesis of a multiparagraph reading selection? <u>page 157</u>

PREFACE

Within the first few pages of some textbooks is an introductory letter from the author called the **preface**. Reading a preface gives you information about the book such as who it is written for, what the author hopes readers will accomplish, and how the book is organized.

Exercise 3

Use the excerpt on the right, from the preface of Leshin's *Student Resource Guide to the Internet*, to answer these questions.

1. Leshin says the Internet is a powerful medium for

   Leshin says the Internet is a powerful medium for "finding information, sharing information, and interacting with others."

2. Leshin lists ten ways you will find the Internet a valuable tool. List the two most important to you today.

   Answers will vary; please see Answer Key.

3. In addition to helping you succeed in school, how does Leshin think understanding the Internet will help you?

   In addition to helping you succeed in school, Leshin thinks understanding the Internet "provides you with important skills that employers value."

Exercise 4

Use the preface in *this* textbook to answer these questions.

1. For whom is this book written?

   This book is for college students in a first-level reading course.

2. How does McGrath want students to see themselves as they work through the text?

   McGrath hopes students will see themselves as active participants in the reading process and will work at becoming independent learners able to set and accomplish reading and study goals and objectives.

3. How is the book organized?

   The book has six chapters, three thematic reading units, and three appendices.

REFACE

The Internet is a powerful medium for finding information, sharing information, and interacting with others. These capabilities offer new ways to access resources for school, college preparation, career planning, and finding a job. Some of the ways that you will find the Internet valuable as a tool for success in school, for improving your grades, and in preparing for a career include:

- finding the latest information on a subject for research papers;
- collecting data from others online;
- collaborating with others who share your research interests;
- cross-cultural exchanges with Netizens worldwide;
- meeting and learning from subject matter experts on virtually any topic;
- access to resources such as dictionaries, encyclopedias, and library catalogs worldwide;
- access to literature such as the classics and novels;
- access to news publications and electronic journals with resources for researching their databases for past articles or stories;
- access to databases of diverse information at universities, and government agencies; and
- learning about companies by visiting their Web sites.

In addition to helping you succeed in school, your understanding and knowledge about how to use the Internet provides you with important skills that employers value. In a time of rapid global change, companies realize that the Internet has an important role in their future. Most companies do not totally understand how the Internet will or can fit into their success, therefore they are looking for bright, knowledgeable, and enthusiastic individuals who will help pioneer this new electronic frontier. Many companies, in fact, are turning to the Internet to find

Author Information

The author's name and school affiliation are often listed on the first page of the book, called the title page. Additional information about the author is sometimes included in a special About the Author section. Reading about the author can give you information about his or her credentials to write the book.

Cynthia Leshin is an educational technologies specialist with her doctorate in educational technology from Arizona State University. Dr. Leshin has her own consulting company—XPLORA. She consults with businesses and schools interested in learning about and implementing technology-rich environments for student success, improved learning, and customer support.

She has authored ten books for Simon and Schuster including *Internet Adventures—Step-by-Step Guide to Finding and Using Educational Resources; Netscape Adventures—Step-by-Step Guide to Netscape Navigator and the World Wide Web; Management on the World Wide Web;* and seven discipline-specific Internet books with Internet-based learning activities. She has also written a book, *Instructional Design: Strategies and Tactics.* Her expertise in educational psychology and theories of learning provides her with a unique background for translating complicated technical information into an easy-to-use, easy-to-understand, and practical learning resource.

Dr. Leshin has taught computer literacy and Internet classes at Arizona State University West and Estrella Mountain Community College. She has taught college-accredited Internet classes using distance learning technology for Educational Management Group, a Simon & Schuster company. The Internet serves as a tool for teaching and communicating with her students.

In Dr. Leshin's "other life" she rides mountain bikes and races for Cannondale's HeadShok team. She also enjoys organic gardening, hiking, skiing, scuba diving, and exploring southwestern trails with her three dread-locked Puli dogs and her husband, Steve.

Exercise 5

Use the excerpt on the left, from the About the Author of Leshin's *Student Resource Guide to the Internet*, to answer these questions.

1. What subjects has Leshin taught? Where has she taught?

   Leshin taught computer literacy and Internet classes at Arizona State University, Estrella Mountain Community College, and on the Internet.

2. In what field is Leshin's doctorate?

   Leshin's doctorate is in educational technology.

Exercise 6

Use the About the Author in *this* textbook to answer these questions.

1. In what field is McGrath's doctorate?

   McGrath's doctorate is in reading education.

2. What information about McGrath did you find most interesting?

   The information about McGrath students find most interesting will vary.

INDEX

An **index** is an alphabetical list of the topics covered in the book and their page numbers. Names and titles of readings are sometimes included. If a text has an index, it is located at the end of the book. Using the index can save you time when you need to locate specific information.

Exercise 7

Use the excerpt on the right, from the index of Leshin's *Student Resource Guide to the Internet*, to answer these questions.

1. On what page will you find information about importing bookmarks?

   pages 33–34

2. If you want to find information on *address*, what other topic must you see?

   For information on address, see URLs.

Exercise 8

Use the index in *this* textbook to answer these questions.

1. On what page will you find information on using context clues?

   page 15

2. If you want to find information on *transition words*, where must you look?

   For information on transition words, see signal words.

APPENDIX

An **appendix** is a special section that contains extra or supplemental information. If a text has an appendix, it is located toward the end of the book. The plural of appendix is appendices. Always check the appendices to see if the information is useful to you.

FINDING WEB SITES THAT HAVE MOVED

The Internet is a dynamic and rapidly changing environment. Information may be in one place today and either gone or in a new location tomorrow. New sites appear daily; others disappear. Some sites provide forwarding address information; others will not. As you travel in cyberspace and find that a resource you are looking for can no longer be found at a given Internet address, there are several steps you can take to find if the site has a new address.

• Check for a new Internet address or link, often provided on the site of the old address.

• Shorten the URL.

  The format for a URL is: **protocol//server-name/path**

  Try deleting the last section of the URL (path), so that the URL ends with the domain name or server name (com, edu, net, org). For example, you may be looking for NASA's links to astronomy sites. Take the original URL provided for the site, in this case **http://quest.arc.nasa.gov/lfs/other_sites.html,** and delete the last part of the address. **lfs/other_sites.html** leaving **http://quest.arc.nasa.gov.** You will most likely get to NASA's Home Page and can navigate to the specific topic or category you are looking for.

• Type in a company name for the URL.

  Companies usually use either their name, some part of their name, or an abbreviation as their domain name that becomes their URL. Netscape 2.02 and 3.0 accept abbreviated Net addresses, without the **http://www.** prefix. If you type a single word as your URL, Netscape adds the prefix **http://www.** and the suffix **.com.** For example, to connect to Netscape's Home

Exercise 9

Use the excerpt on the left, from the appendix of Leshin's *Student Resource Guide to the Internet*, to answer these questions.

1. What information is in this appendix?

   The appendix contains information on how

   to find Web sites that have moved.

Exercise 10

Use the appendices in *this* textbook to answer these questions.

1. How many appendices does this text contain? List the titles:

   Three appendices:

   Facts, Opinions, and Reasoned Judgments

   Preparing for and Taking Standardized

   Reading Tests

   Using Textbook Design Clues

GLOSSARY

If a text has its own dictionary—called a **glossary**—it is located toward the back of the book. Using the glossary is helpful because it gives the meanings of words specific to the context.

Exercise 11

Use the excerpt on the right, from the glossary of Leshin's *Student Resource Guide to the Internet*, to answer these questions.

1. What does the word *bookmark* mean?

    A feature providing the user with the

    opportunity to mark favorite pages for

    fast and easy access.

2. What does the word *cookie* mean?

    Cookie technology allows the storage of

    personal preferences for use with Inter-

    net information and communication

    tools. A text file is created of a user's

    preferences, saved in their browser's

    folder, and stored in RAM while the

    browser is running.

Exercise 12

Use the glossary in *this* textbook to answer these questions.

1. What does the word *paragraph* mean?

    A group of related sentences that

    support and explain one main idea.

2. What does the word *inference* mean?

    The best reasoned conclusion based on

    the information given.

GEEK SPEAK

ActiveX: Microsoft's response to Java was the *ActiveX* development platform. This technology makes it possible for Web programmers to create and for Web surfers to view moving and animated objects, live audio, scrolling banners, and interactivity. The *ActiveX* technology—available in Microsoft Internet Explorer—allows viewing of many plug-in applications without first downloading and installing the required plug-in. *ActiveX* lets desktop applications be linked to the World Wide Web, for example, programs such as Word can be viewed directly from Explorer.

administrative address: The email address used for sending requests to list-servs for either text documents or subscriptions to a mailing list.

anonymous FTP: The method used in file transfer protocol that allows Internet users to log into an FTP server as an unregistered user. Before browsers were used for FTP, users connecting to an FTP server would have to log in by entering a login name and password. The login name was anonymous; the password, your email address.

bit: A single-digit number, either a 1 or a 0, that represents the smallest unit of computerized data.

bookmarks: A feature providing the user with the opportunity to mark favorite pages for fast and easy access. Netscape's bookmarks can be organized hierarchically and customized by the user through the Bookmark List dialog box.

Boolean operators: Phrases or words such as "AND," "OR," and "NOT" that limit a search using Internet search engines.

browser: A client program that interprets and displays HTML documents.

client: A software program assisting in contacting a server somewhere on the Net for information. Examples of client software programs are Gopher, Netscape, Veronica, and Archie. An Archie client runs on a system configured to contact a specific Archie database to query for information.

compression: A process by which a file or a folder is made smaller. The three primary purposes of compression are to save disk space, to save space when doing a backup, and to speed the transmission of a file when transferring via a modem or network.

cookie: Cookie technology allows the storage of personal preferences for use with Internet information and communication tools. A text file is created of a user's preferences, saved in their browser's folder, and stored in RAM while the browser is running. For example, a popular Web audio site, Timecast, allows users to select their personal audio preferences to be played with RealAudio. These personal preferences are saved in a browser folder called a *cookie file*. When the user connects to the site, the server at that site looks for the cookie file on the user's computer to find their specifications.

delayed-response media: Internet communication tools that require time for an end-user to respond (e.g., electronic mail, listservs, and newsgroups).

digerati: A community of diverse professionals—computer scientists, film makers, designers, engineers, architects, artists, writers, musicians—who are becoming increasingly wealthy through their creative and innovative use and exploration of digital technology. Louis Rossetto and Jane Metcalfe (*Wired* magazine) were the first to give a name to these digital elite whom they believed were becoming the most powerful people on earth.

domain name: The unique name that identifies an Internet site. Names have two or more parts separated by a dot such as **xplora.com.**

finger: An Internet software tool for locating people on the Internet. The most common use is to see if an individual has an account at a particular Internet site.

LOOKING AHEAD

Strategies you can use to preview a multiparagraph reading assignment such as a text chapter or a magazine article are included in Chapter 6.

SUMMARY OF KEY IDEAS

- To be a skilled student, you need to have and be able to use a variety of tools so you can select the best ones for each part of a reading assignment. In reading we call these tools *strategies*. A strategy is a tool or technique you consciously select in order to complete a task accurately and efficiently.

- To preview means to survey, or examine, reading material in an orderly way *before* you begin to read.

- Previewing gives you an overall picture of what you are going to read and gives you the chance to make connections between what you know and what you are going to read.

- During preview, you examine a text's features and aids that can give you a head start on good comprehension, such as the title page, table of contents, preface, author information, glossary, appendix, index, and answer key.

Use Your Strategies

Use a textbook from another class or a text you borrow from your college's learning center to answer these questions.

1. List the title and author of the text. _____

   Answers for questions 1 through 10 will vary. _____

2. List the page numbers of the table of contents. _____

   _____

3. List the title of each chapter.

   _____

   _____

   _____

   _____

   _____

   _____

   _____

4. List the aids the book contains, such as preface, glossary, index, and answer key, and the page numbers on which they appear.

_____

_____

_____

_____

5. For whom is this book written? If there is no preface, write your prediction about the book's purpose.

_____

_____

6. What does the author hope readers will accomplish?

_____

_____

_____

_____

7. List two pieces of information about the author.

_____

_____

8. How many appendices does the text contain? List the titles.

_____

_____

_____

9. When do you think you might use the information in the appendix?

_____

_____

10. If there is a glossary, list the first and last word entries. If the text uses another method, such as margin notes, to define words, please describe it.

_____

_____

REFLECT AND CONNECT

A. Visit your college learning center and interview a tutor or staff member to discover his or her best advice on how to be successful in your classes. Describe how you can use the advice.

_____

_____

_____

_____

B. List and explain the skills, attitudes, and behaviors you think are most important to college success.

_____

_____

_____

_____

LOG ON TO THE WEB

A variety of Internet sites give readers an opportunity to preview books before they buy them. For example, e-bookstores such as Amazon.com and bn.com (Barnes & Noble) often post a summary of a book's content, reviewers' comments, and even a sample chapter. College textbook publishers like Prentice Hall post information about their books. The Web pages typically include the table of contents, a description of the intended reader, information about the author, and a description of print and electronic supplements.

For the purpose of this Web assignment, assume you are a member of a committee assigned to find out what textbooks are available in one of your favorite subject areas, such as psychology, general business, or computer applications. To begin your search, log on to Prentice Hall's academic catalog at *<http://www.prenhall.com/list_ac/index.html>*.

Go to the list of texts available in your subject area and select one text to preview. Go to that textbook's homepage and read all the available information about the text and the author.

Write down: (1) the name of the text, (2) who the text is written for, (3) how many chapters the book contains, (4) a description of any aids the book contains, such as a glossary, (5) a description of any print and electronic supplements for the book, such as a companion Website or CD, and (6) what you discovered about the author.

Understanding Vocabulary

AN IDEA TO THINK ABOUT

People who study languages estimate that there are over a million words in the English language. However, some of today's words are different from yesterday's words, and a few of tomorrow's words will be different from today's. Every day a few new words are created and used for the first time, a few are transformed into English from other languages, and a few unused words are deleted. As a result, you often run into unfamiliar and confusing words.

What strategies do you use to find a definition for a word you don't understand?

CHAPTER 2 AT A GLANCE

Words are important. They are the raw material we use to write everything from e-mail messages and memos to letters, essays, and textbooks. Therefore, when you don't understand a word an author uses, you may not understand what he or she is writing about.

When you don't understand a word, you can use several strategies to help you define it. However, just finding a definition isn't always enough. To understand an author's specific meaning of a word, you must look at the word in context—how it is used with the other words in the sentence and surrounding sentences. This is because words take on meaning from their context.

For example, *run* is a common, everyday word. However, if a friend asks you to define *run,* you need to know which *run* she means: for example, *run* as in "the player hit a home run," or "she had a run in her pantyhose," or "he was going to run to the store," or "she was going to run for office." Once you know the context—the situation or the rest of the words—you can give a good definition.

Like *run,* many words have multiple meanings.

EXAMPLE   Think about the definitions of the word *medium* in these sentences.

1. The Internet is a powerful <u>medium</u> for finding information.
2. Copper is a good <u>medium</u> for conducting heat.
3. I asked for my hamburger to be cooked <u>medium</u>—more than rare, but less than well done.
4. At the state fair we saw a fortuneteller and a <u>medium</u> to try to communicate with my dead uncle's spirit.
5. The artist used watercolors on cloth as the <u>medium</u> for her work.

Explanation   Understanding the way the word is used with the other words in the sentence helps you understand the specific meaning of *medium.*

In sentence 1 *medium* is a means of communication.

In sentence 2 *medium* is something that carries energy.

In sentence 3 *medium* is an intermediate amount.

In sentence 4 *medium* is a person who channels communication between the earthly world and spirits.

In sentence 5 *medium* is the technique and material used by an artist.

Whatever strategy you use to define a word, always make sure the meaning you select makes sense in the author's context. The more words you understand, the more accurately you will understand the author.

USING CONTEXT CLUES TO DEFINE WORDS AND PHRASES

Authors often provide clues in their writing to help you understand words and phrases. Unless a sentence is very difficult, using **context clues** to understand an unfamiliar word can be a quick and efficient way to ensure a correct definition. Sometimes authors directly state the **definition** of an unfamiliar word.

EXAMPLE   A <u>liquid asset</u> is cash or any other asset that can be converted to cash with a minimum amount of trouble and no loss in market value. (Winger & Frasca, *Personal Finance*)

Explanation   In this sentence Winger and Frasca directly state that the definition of *liquid asset* is "cash or any other asset that can be converted to cash with a minimum amount of trouble and no loss in market value."

Sometimes authors help you understand a word or phrase by giving an **example** or an **explanation.**

EXAMPLE   <u>Ordinary contractions</u>—can't, haven't, isn't—can be used in most current magazine articles. (McGrath, *Magazine Article Writing Basics*)

Explanation   To help writing students understand what is meant by *ordinary contractions,* three examples are given.

EXAMPLE   Using <u>Hypertext Markup Language</u> (HTML), the programming language used to create a Web page, formats the text of the document and specifies links to other documents. (Leshin, *Student Resource Guide to the Internet*)

Explanation   In this sentence Leshin uses commas to set off her explanation that Hypertext Markup Language is "the programming language used to create a Web page."

Occasionally, authors use the **opposite** of the unfamiliar word as a clue.

EXAMPLE   The expensive, high-end recreational vehicles (RVs) that roam today's highways offer luxuries most <u>stationary homeowners</u> would envy. (Kronemyer, "Living on the Road," *Active Times*)

Explanation   In this sentence Kronemyer makes it clear that "stationary homeowners" are the opposite of those who own RV homes. Since RVs move from place to place, stationary homes are houses and apartments built to stay in one place.

Authors also combine context clues to help you understand the meaning of a word or phrase.

EXAMPLE   <u>Nonverbal behavior</u> plays a strong, necessary role in interpersonal relationships. So much can be "said" by a smile, hug, or handclasp that words are often not needed. (Barker and Barker, *Communications*)

Explanation   To help define *nonverbal behavior*, Baker and Baker give examples, "a smile, hug, or handclasp," and an explanation, "words are often not needed."

In addition, authors often use **punctuation marks,** such as a dash, a colon, parentheses, or commas, to call attention to their word clue.

EXAMPLE   <u>Portamento</u>—sliding or gliding from one tone to the next—is extensively used in American Black music, both vocal and instrumental. (Brooks, *America's Black Musical Heritage*)

Explanation   In this sentence Brooks defines the musical term *portamento* as "sliding or gliding from one tone to the next" and sets it off with dashes.

Word meanings that you figure out using context clues are not wild guesses. They are the logical result of combining all the information about the word an author provides. We call this process *making an inference*. An **inference** is a sensible, reasoned conclusion based on the information you are given.

> **Exercise 1**   **Using the Context to Help Define Words and Phrases**

Use the author's context clues to discover the meaning of the underlined words and phrases in these sentences. Circle the best definition.

EXAMPLE   The tornado left only <u>devastation</u> in its path. The town—homes, buildings, cars—was completely destroyed.

   a. flooding   **c.** construction

   b. total destruction   **d.** trees

Explanation   From the statement that "homes, buildings, and cars" were completely destroyed, we can infer that *devastation* means destruction.

1. A decision to <u>terminate</u>—fire—an employee should never be made on the spur of the moment.

   a. limit   **c.** fire

   b. confine   **d.** hire

2. <u>Aseptic</u> means germ free, or without disease-producing organisms.

   a. disease germs   **c.** a cut or injury

   b. bacteria   **d.** without germs

3. A <u>savvy</u> consumer, one who shops around, can often find remarkably good buys on clothing.

    a. lazy   **c.** foolish

    (b.) sharp   **d.** unaware

4. In gaming <u>meccas</u> such as Las Vegas, Atlantic City, and Reno, the gambling options are unlimited.

    a. casinos   **(c.)** centers of activity

    b. buildings   **d.** churches

5. The Central Library offers a monthly lecture series in <u>conjunction</u> with the college to make the best use of expert speakers and facilities.

    (a.) working together   **c.** cultural

    b. working separately   **d.** competition

6. Employees who think products are more important than customers <u>hinder</u>, rather than help, sales.

    a. increase   **c.** help

    (b.) hurt, decrease   **d.** assist

7. Before making a large purchase, consumers should make sure they are dealing with a <u>reputable</u> company, one that is known for good products and customer service.

    a. famous   **c.** large

    b. dishonest   **(d.)** honest

8. In addition to providing meaning and purpose in our lives, spending time helping others may have a <u>positive effect</u> on our health.

    (a.) good influence   **c.** harmful result

    b. unknown result   **d.** limiting outcome

9. Early hunter-gatherer settlements were never large and were of <u>relatively short duration</u> because, as one area was "picked over," the tribe was forced to move on.

    a. family-oriented   **c.** inferior

    b. clean   **(d.)** for a brief time

10. As farmers left the countryside in search of work in new factories, whole villages were <u>abandoned</u>, while nearby factory towns swelled into big cities.

    a. looted   **(c.)** deserted

    b. defended   **d.** full

Exercise 2 **Using the Context to Help Define Words and Phrases**

Use the author's context clues to discover the meaning of the underlined words and phrases in these sentences. Write the definition.

1. <u>Leadership</u> (the process of influence) can originate from a number of sources. (Manz and Neck, *Mastering Self-Leadership*)

   leadership: the process of influence
   _____

2. There is some form of <u>measurement</u> or evaluation for every job. (Chapman and O'Neil, *Your Attitude is Showing*)

   measurement: evaluation
   _____

3. "Although we have not received many complaints about Internet scams, they are <u>abundant</u>," she said. (Holstein, "How to Avoid Con Artists," *The Arizona Republic*)

   abundant: plentiful
   _____

4. <u>Acculturation</u> is the process by which a certain people are influenced by a foreign culture. (Brown, *The Art of Rock and Roll*)

   acculturation: the process by which a certain people are influenced
   by a foreign culture

5. In Tanzania, women and girls in rural villages may have to walk miles to collect the water—often polluted—that they will use for drinking, cooking and washing. Similar <u>treks</u> of increasing length must be taken to collect the firewood for cooking. (Nebel and Wright, *Environmental Science*)

   treks: walks of increasing length
   _____

6. At the end of the glacier, tidal action causes '<u>calving</u>': A slab of ice breaks off, and an iceberg is born. (Whelan, "Ice Police Cry, 'Stop That Berg!'" *The Wall Street Journal*)

   calving: A slab of ice breaks off, and an iceberg is born.
   _____

7. A variety of <u>domestic</u> and business applications form the foundation of personal computing. Domestic applications include maintaining an up-to-date inventory of household items; storing names and addresses for a personal mailing list; maintaining records for, preparing, and sending

personal income tax returns; creating and monitoring a household budget; keeping an appointment and social calendar; handling household finances. . . . (Long and Long, *Computing*)

domestic: home or household

8. Some Internet search engines permit the use of <u>Boolean operators</u> (words such as "and," "or," and "not") to restrict the search. (Leshin, *Student Resource Guide to the Internet*)

Boolean operators: words such as "and," "or," and "not"

9. A loan's <u>balloon payment</u> is usually the last installment payment, and it is for an amount much greater than the other monthly payments. (Winger and Frasca, *Personal Finance*)

balloon payment: the last installment payment, and for an amount

much greater than the other monthly payments

10. The meals you eat away from home generally contain more fat and less fiber, iron and calcium. Thus, they tend to be <u>less nutritious</u>. (Heilman, "Health Tips," *Active Times*)

less nutritious: meals that contain more fat and less fiber, iron and

calcium

11. It all started with the "smiley" figure that shows someone is happy or telling a joke. Now a new language is developing as clever people use computer keystrokes to create <u>emoticons</u>, symbols that convey thoughts and emotions. (Macionis, *Sociology*)

emoticons: symbols that convey thoughts and emotions created with

computer keystrokes

12. When you understand the <u>primitive</u> beginnings of medicine, you appreciate the advances made during the past 5,000 years. (Badasch and Chesebro, *Introduction to Health Occupations*)

primitive: simple, original

13. Because Earth is related to all other objects in space, the science of <u>astronomy</u>—the study of the universe—is very useful in probing the origins of our own environment. (Lutgens and Tarbuck, *Foundations of Earth Science*)

astronomy: the study of the universe

14. Identifying an object, act, or person by name so that she, he, or it can be referred to in communication is known as <u>labeling</u>. (Barker and Barker, *Communication*)

labeling: identifying an object, act, or person by name

15. For now, reaching 100 is still considered news. Of the 273 million people in the United States, only 70,000 are <u>centenarians</u>. But in the next 50 years, as science extends the span of human life, 100th birthdays will become more common. (Warshofsky, "The Methuselah Factor," *Modern Maturity*)

centenarians: people who are 100 years old

Exercise 3 ▶ **Using the Context to Help Define Words and Phrases**

Using one of your texts, identify five sentences with unfamiliar words where the author provides a context clue. Copy the sentences onto a sheet of notebook paper, underline the unfamiliar words, and write the definitions.

The five words and definitions will vary.

USING PARTS OF A WORD TO HELP DEFINE IT

Another strategy you can use to help understand a word is to examine the parts of the word. For example, some words are made by combining two components that are words themselves—*commonplace, headache, policeman.* You can often define these compound words by defining each individual word.

You can also look for a **root word** and any prefixes and/or suffixes. The root is the basic part of a word. A **prefix** can be added to the beginning of a root word and/or a **suffix** can be added at the end of a root word to make other words.

Prefixes and suffixes change the meaning of the root word. A suffix can also change the way a word can be used in a sentence and its part of speech.

Knowing the meanings of word parts—roots, prefixes and suffixes—helps you unlock and understand the meanings of whole families of words. For example, knowing the Latin root *manus* means "hand" can provide a clue to the meaning of the words built with the root, such as *manual* (doing physical work with the hands) and *manuscript* (written by hand).

However, because many of our roots, prefixes, and suffixes come from the ancient Latin, Greek, and Anglo-Saxon languages, the changes in spelling and meaning over the years can make using this strategy a challenge. For example, since the word *manufacture* is made from the root *manus*, manufacture should mean "make by hand." Although that definition was accurate many years ago, today manufacture generally means "making something by any means, but especially with machinery."

Nevertheless, knowing even a few word parts can help unlock the meanings of many unknown words.

(JEFF STAHLER, reprinted by permission of Newspaper Enterprise Association)

EXAMPLE

Everyone agrees that hiring an employee is a <u>multistep</u> process.

The college offers an excellent <u>multicultural</u> program for future teachers.

Before you can experience <u>multimedia</u> Web sites, you need to install some basic plug-ins.

Explanation   Knowing that the prefix *multi* means "many," you are better able to understand the sentences.

The following table lists some common word parts and their definitions.

Word Part	Definition	Example Word
a, an	without, not	amoral
able, ible	able to	visible
aminus, halare	breath	animate, exhale
ance, acy, ency	action, quality, state of	privacy
annu, anni	year	annual
ante, pre	before	antechamber, prepared
anthrop	humankind	anthropology
anti, contra	against	antidote, contradict
aqua	water	aquarium
archi	chief, first	archbishop
aster, astro	star	astronomy
audi, aur	hear	auditorium
auto	self	autobiography
bene	good	beneficial
bi, di	two, both	biannual, dichotomy
bio	living organisms	biology

Word Part	Definition	Example Word
carcin	cancer	carcinogen
cardio	heart	cardiology
cent, hecto	hundred	century
chrono	time	chronograph
circum, peri	around	circumvent, perimeter
con, com, co	with, together	congregate
crede	belief	credibility
de	down or away	depose
deca	ten	decade
demo	the people	democracy
derm	skin	dermatologist
dict	speak	diction
dis	not or away	dislike
divers	different	diverse
duc, duct	lead, make, shape	reproduce
ec, eco	habitat	ecology
ence, ency	action, quality of	competency
er, or, st	one who, thing which	actor
ex	out	exhale
flect, flex	bend	reflect, flexible
ful, ose	full of	careful, verbose
fy, ify, ize	make, form into	magnify
gene, gen	origin, type	genetics
geron, geras	aging, old age	gerontology
grad, gress	to go, take steps	graduate, regress
graph, graphy	writing, record	autobiography
halare, aminus	breath	exhale, animate
helio	sun	heliotrope
hemi	half	hemisphere
hemo	blood	hemoglobin
hetro	different	heterosexual
homo	same	homosexual
hyper	excessive, more than normal	hyperthermia
hypo	low, less than	hypothermic
il, in, im, ir	in/into or not	illogical, inactive
inter	among, between	intermural

Word Part	Definition	Example Word
intra	within, inside	intramural
ism	quality or doctrine of	conservatism
kilo	thousand	kilometer
less	without	homeless
lingua	language	bilingual
literate, literatus	able to read/write	illiterate
locu, loqu, log	speak	loquacious
logy	study of	anthropology
macro	large	macroeconomics
mal	bad	malfunction
manu	by hand	manual
mega	large	megastore
meter	to measure	thermometer
micro	small	microeconomics
milli	thousand	millimeter
miss, mitt	send	transmit
mono, uni	one, single	monotone, unity
mor, mort	die	mortician
morph	form	amorphous
multi	many	multifaceted
neo	new	neophyte
non	not	noncooperation
nym, nomen	name	synonym
ology	study of	biology
omni	all, everywhere	omnipresent
para	beside, beyond	paranormal
pathy	feeling	empathy
ped, pod	foot	pedestrian
peri, circum	around	perimeter, circumvent
phobia	fear	claustrophobia
phono	sound	phonograph
poly	many	polygamy
port	carry	portable
post	after, behind	postscript
pre, ante	before, in front of	prepared, antechamber
pro	in favor of, ahead of	progress
proto	original, chief	prototype

Word Part	Definition	Example Word
pseudo	false	pseudonym
psych	mind, soul	psychology
quad, tetra	four	quadruplets, tetrad
quint, penta	five	quintuplet, pentagram
re	again	reproduce
retro-	backward	retrospective
scribe, script	write	prescription
sect, seg	cut	dissect
semi	half	
soph	wise	philosophy
spect	look at, see	inspect
sub	under, below	subway
super, supra	above	supervisor
tact, tang	touch	tactile, tangible
tele, trans	across, over a distance	telegraph, transport
therm	heat	thermometer
ultra	beyond, excessive	ultraism
un, non	not	uncooperative
uni, mono	one	unity, monotone
vid, vis	see	video, visible

Exercise 4   Using Parts of a Word to Help Define It

Use your understanding of common word parts to discover the meaning of the underlined words in these sentences. Circle the best definition.

EXAMPLE   It's possible to be <u>hypersensitive</u> to anything in your diet.

   a. dislike   (**c.** oversensitive)
   b. undersensitive   **d.** enjoy

Explanation   The prefix *hyper* means more than normal. Therefore, you can be more sensitive than normal, or *oversensitive*, to anything in your diet.

1. Although many considered his actions old-fashioned, he lived by a strict <u>creed</u>.

   a. aging   **c.** perfection
   (**b.**) set of beliefs   **d.** set of mistakes

2. During her second year of medical studies, she decided to specialize in geriatrics.

   a. problems of aging people   **c.** problems of the skin
   b. problems of children   **d.** problems of the eyes

3. There was much fear and excitement at the start of the new millennium.

   a. year   **c.** thousand year period
   b. century   **d.** golden age

4. The college encouraged intramural sports activities.

   a. team games   **c.** games played with teams from other colleges
   b. contact sports   **d.** games played among teams within the college

5. Recent legislative actions have targeted certain sweepstakes promoters and telemarketers. Telemarketers are people who

   a. sell products by mail   **c.** sell products at flea markets
   b. sell products over the phone   **d.** sell products door-to-door

6. The business owner hired a new accountant when he discovered thousands of dollars had been misappropriated.

   a. wrongly used   **c.** hidden
   b. given away   **d.** saved

7. She thought cigar smoke was quite disagreeable.

   a. sweet-smelling   **c.** pleasant
   b. harmful   **d.** unpleasant

8. Many children throughout the world are malnourished.

   a. poor   **c.** in foster homes
   b. without enough to eat   **d.** without access to education

9. In the future we will see more proactive approaches to the way diseases are detected and treated, such as early detection and prevention.

   a. using technology to help   **c.** acting before a problem happens
   b. fearful   **d.** limited

10. Behavioral techniques have proved successful in treating phobias, especially simple and social phobias.

    a. temptations   **c.** fears
    b. a fondness for   **d.** accidents

Exercise 5 **Using Parts of a word to Help Define It**

Use your understanding of common word parts to unlock the meaning of the underlined words in these sentences. Write the definition.

1. Experts would tell baby boomers that the only thing they have to fear is <u>gerontophobia</u> itself. (Lague, "The Longevity Masters," *Modern Maturity*)

   gerontophobia: fear of aging

2. Goals are generally more effective for managing our immediate behavior if they are specific and challenging, yet <u>achievable</u>. (Manz and Neck, *Mastering Self-Leadership*)

   achievable: able to be achieved or attained

3. Psychosocially healthy people recognize that there are others whose needs are greater than their own. They <u>enrich</u> the lives of others. (Donatelle and Davis, *Access to Health*)

   enrich: make richer, better

4. Because geographers are trained in a broad range of topics, they are particularly well equipped to understand <u>interactions</u> between people and their environment. (Rubenstein, *An Introduction to Human Geography*)

   interactions: connections between

5. We cannot determine if someone is <u>chronologically</u> 80 years old, yet biologically 60. There is no one-size-fits-all span for human life. (Warshofsky, "The Methuselah Factor," *Modern Maturity*)

   chronologically: according to the number of years lived

6. Although prominent public figures may have great <u>credibility</u>, their statements should not keep us from asking our own questions. (Davis and Palladino, *Psychology*)

   credibility: trustworthiness

7. Ill-timed self-disclosures (telling about ourselves, our values, attitudes and beliefs) can result in others seeing us as <u>maladjusted</u>. (Bittner, *Each Other*)

   maladjusted: unstable, not well adjusted

8. The inventory of e-mail devices is growing as more people, even techies, seek fast and <u>portable</u> ways to e-mail. (Dreyfuss, *Simply e-mail*)

   portable: easily moveable

9. To strive for something difficult, to go beyond what's called for in every-day life, becomes <u>empowering</u>. . . . (Beckley, director of Alpine Ascents International travel company)

  empowering: authorizing, giving power to

10. In the late 1960s, jeans acquired an image of youthful independence in the United States, as young people adopted a style of clothing previously associated with low-status <u>manual</u> laborers and farmers. (Rubenstein, *An Introduction to Human Geography*)

  manual: doing work with your hands

Exercise 6   Using Parts of a Word to Help Define It

Using a text from one of your other classes, identify five unfamiliar words where your understanding of common word parts helps you unlock the meaning. Copy the sentences containing the words onto a sheet of notebook paper, underline the unfamiliar words, and write the definitions.

The five words and definitions will vary.

USING A DICTIONARY TO DEFINE WORDS AND PHRASES

We often use a dictionary to check the spelling of a word. It's also a good source for definitions. That makes using a dictionary another good strategy for finding the meaning of an unfamiliar word.

In addition to definitions, a dictionary includes the pronunciation, history, and parts of speech of the word. A word entry may even include synonyms and antonyms. **Synonyms** are words and phrases that have the same or nearly the same meaning. **Antonyms** are words that mean the opposite.

Dictionaries are not all the same. The more familiar you are with the content and layout of yours, the easier it will be to use.

The excerpt on page 28, from *Webster's New World Dictionary, Third College Edition*, contains the words from *Corpus Christi* to *Corrode*. Notice how much information beyond the definition is given for the word *Correct*.

Since you usually find several definitions for a word, you must read through the definitions to find the one that best fits the context. Keep in mind, however, that because of writing style differences and language changes, a dictionary definition probably won't fit word-for-word into the sentence you're reading. When that happens, put the definition into your own words and try that in the sentence to be sure it makes sense.

Definitions In this dictionary, definitions are arranged in historical order, so the more recent or common meanings may be near the end of the entry.

Corpus Christi / corrode ← Guide Words at the top of a page give the first and last word entries on that page.

Pronunciation tells how the word is most commonly used by English speakers. Symbols used are explained in a "Key to Pronunciation." (See below)

Word History (Etymology) tells how the word came into English, using symbols such as ME for Middle English and < for "derived from."

Main Entry All main entries are listed in strict alphabetical order. If the word can be spelled more than one way, all variations are listed.

cor·rect (kə rekt') *vt.* ⟦ ME *correcten* < L *correctus*, pp. of *corrigere* < *com-*, together + *regere*, to lead straight, rule: see RECKON ⟧ **1** to make right; change from wrong to right; remove errors from **2** to point out or mark the errors or faults of **3** to make conform to a standard **4** to scold or punish so as to cause to rectify faults **5** to cure, remove, or counteract (a fault, disease, etc.) —*vi.* to make corrections; specif., to make an adjustment so as to compensate *(for an error, counteracting force, etc.)* —*adj.* **1** conforming or adhering to an established standard; proper *[correct behavior]* **2** conforming to fact or logic; true, accurate, right, or free from errors **3** equal to the required or established amount, number, price, etc. —**cor·rect'-able** *adj.* —**cor·rect'ly** *adv.* —**cor·rect'ness** *n.* —**cor·rec'tor** *n.*
SYN.—**correct** connotes little more than absence of error *[a correct answer]* or adherence to conventionality *[correct behavior]*; **accurate** implies a positive exercise of care to obtain conformity with fact or truth *[an accurate account of the events]*; **exact** stresses perfect conformity to fact, truth, or some standard *[the exact time, an exact quotation]*; **precise** suggests minute accuracy of detail and often connotes a finicky or overly fastidious attitude *[precise in all his habits]* See also PUNISH —*ANT.* **wrong, false**

Part-of-Speech Labels When a word is used as more than one part of speech, long dashes introduce each different part of speech.

Synonyms/Antonyms Some dictionaries list words that mean the same as and words that mean the opposite of the main word.

Key to Pronunciation The key at the bottom of a dictionary page shows how the symbols sound.

at, āte, cär; ten, ēve; is, īce; gō, hôrn, look, tool; oil, out; up, fur; ə *for unstressed vowels, as* a *in* ago, u *in* focus; ' *as in* Latin (lat''n); chin; she; zh *as in* azure (azh'ər); thin, *the*; ŋ *as in* ring (riŋ) *In etymologies:* * = unattested; < = derived from; > = from which ☆ = Americanism **See inside front and back covers**

EXAMPLE Which dictionary definition best fits the word *critically* in this sentence? We want you to be able to evaluate <u>critically</u> the information you read and hear in the media and elsewhere. (Davis and Palladino, *Psychology*)

crit|i·cal (krit'i kəl) *adj.* **1** tending to find fault; censorious **2** characterized by careful analysis and judgment *[a sound critical estimate of the problem]* **3** of critics or criticism **4** of or forming a crisis or turning point; decisive **5** dangerous or risky; causing anxiety *[a critical situation in international relations]* **6** of the crisis of a disease **7** designating or of important products or raw materials subject to increased production and restricted distribution under strict control, as in wartime **8** *a)* designating or of a point at which a change in character, property, or condition is effected *b)* designating or of the point at which a nuclear chain reaction becomes self-sustaining —**crit'|i·cal|ly** *adv.* —**crit'|i·cal'|i|ty** (-kal'ə tē) or **crit'|i·cal·ness** *n.*

Explanation Definition 2 is the most appropriate. The authors are saying they want you to think about and objectively judge—consider both the merits and faults—the information you read and hear.

Using a Glossary

A glossary, like the one in the back of this text, is an in-book dictionary. It includes an alphabetical listing of the text's important, difficult, and technical words and phrases. A glossary is a quick, easy-to-use resource because it only lists the specific meaning of the word as it is used in the book. Content area texts often contain glossaries.

EXAMPLE   Assume you are reading Politoske's *Music* text for your Introduction to Music class. You come to this sentence with the unfamiliar word *accidentals.*

> In classical music, at least before Beethoven, <u>accidentals</u> tend to appear as surprising touches or as part of a predictable change of key. (Politoske, *Music*)

Compare the definitions for the word *accidental* in *Webster's New World Dictionary* and in the glossary in Politoske's *Music* text.
The entry in *Webster's New World Dictionary:*

> **ac·ci·den·tal** (ak'sə dent″l) *adj.* ⟦ME < LL *accidentalis:* see prec.⟧ **1** happening by chance; fortuitous **2** belonging but not essential; attributive; incidental **3** *Music* of an accidental —*n.* **1** a nonessential quality or feature **2** *Music a)* a sign, as a sharp, flat, or natural, placed before a note to show a change of pitch from that indicated by the key signature *b)* the tone indicated by such a sign —**ac'ci·den'tal|ly** *adv.*

The glossary entry in Politoske's *Music* text:

> **accidental** sharp, flat, or natural sign before a note indicating that the pitch is not to be played as it normally would be in a given key, but is to be altered according to the sign.

Explanation   The glossary entry is specific to the way Politoske uses the word, whereas the dictionary provides all possible definitions.

However, not all books provide a glossary, and even those that do sometimes won't provide enough information, so you may still need to use a dictionary.

Exercise 7   Using a Dictionary to Define Words and Phrases

Decide which dictionary definition best explains the underlined words. Underline the correct dictionary definition and write the meaning.

EXAMPLE   Up to 90 percent of allergic reactions while eating are <u>triggered</u> by a handful of foods: eggs, soybeans, wheat, milk, fish, nuts, and shellfish.

> **trig·ger** (trig'ər) *n.* ⟦earlier *tricker* < Du *trekker* < *trekken,* to draw, pull: see TREK⟧ **1** a small lever or part which when pulled or pressed releases a catch, spring, etc. **2** in firearms, a small lever pressed back by the finger to activate the firing mechanism **3** an act, impulse, etc. that initiates an action, series of events, etc. —*vt.* **1** to fire or activate by pulling or pressing a trigger **2** to initiate (an action); set off *[the fight that triggered the riot]* —☆**quick on the trigger** [Colloq.] **1** quick to fire a gun **2** quick to act, understand, retort, etc.; alert

Explanation   In the example sentence, *triggered* is used as a verb (action word), not a noun (name of person, place, or thing). Of the two verb definitions given, the second one fits this context. *Triggered* means "caused by."

1. Desert landscapes frequently appear <u>stark</u>. (Lutgens and Tarbuck, *Foundations of Earth Science*)

> **stark** (stärk) **adj.** ⟦ME *starc* < OE *stearc:* see STARE⟧ **1** *a)* stiff or rigid, as a corpse *b)* rigorous; harsh; severe *[stark* discipline] **2** sharply outlined or prominent *[one stark* tree] **3** bleak; desolate; barren *[stark* wasteland] **4** *a)* emptied; stripped *[stark* shelves] *b)* totally naked; bare **5** grimly blunt; unsoftened, unembellished, etc. *[stark* realism] **6** sheer; utter; downright; unrelieved *[stark* terror] **7** [Archaic] strong; powerful —**adv.** in a stark manner; esp., utterly; wholly *[stark* mad] —**stark′ly adv.** —**stark′ness n.**

stark: **3** bleak; desolate; barren [stark wasteland]

2. The <u>angle</u> from which an object is photographed can often serve as an author's comment on the subject matter. (Giannetti, *Understanding Movies*)

> **an·gle**[1] (aŋ′gəl) **n.** ⟦ME & OFr < L *angulus,* a corner, angle < Gr *ankylos,* bent, crooked: see ANKLE⟧ **1** *a)* the shape made by two straight lines meeting at a common point, the vertex, or by two planes meeting along an edge (see DIHEDRAL, SPHERICAL ANGLE) *b)* SOLID ANGLE **2** the space between, or within, such lines or planes **3** the measure of this space, expressed in degrees, radians, or steradians **4** a sharp or projecting corner **5** an aspect, as of something viewed or considered; point of view *[to examine a problem from all angles]* **6** [Colloq.] *a)* a motive *b)* a tricky method for achieving a purpose —**vt., vi. -gled, -gling 1** to move or bend at an angle or by means of angles **2** [Colloq.] to give a specific point of view to (a story, report, etc.) —**SYN.** PHASE[1]

angle: **5** an aspect, as of something viewed or considered; point of

view [to examine a problem from all angles]

3. To be part of the solution to preventing hate and bias crimes you can support educational programs designed to <u>foster</u> understanding and appreciation for differences in people. Many colleges now require diversity classes as part of their academic curriculum. (Donatelle and Davis, *Access to Health*)

> **fos·ter** (fôs′tər, fäs′-) **vt.** ⟦ME *fostren* < OE *fostrian,* to nourish, bring up < *fostor,* food, nourishment < base of *foda,* FOOD⟧ **1** to bring up with care; rear **2** to help to grow or develop; stimulate; promote *[to foster* discontent] **3** to cling to in one's mind; cherish *[foster* a hope] —**adj. 1** having the standing of a specified member of the family, though not by birth or adoption, and giving, receiving, or sharing the care appropriate to that standing *[foster* parent, *foster* brother] **2** designating or relating to such care —**fos′ter·er n.**

foster: **2** to help to grow or develop; stimulate; promote [to *foster* dis-

content]

4. World War I proved a <u>watershed</u> for many aspects of American art and life, and certainly for music. (Politoske, *Music*)

> **wa·ter·shed** (-shed′) **n. 1** a ridge or stretch of high land dividing the areas drained by different rivers or river systems ☆**2** the area drained by a river or river system **3** a crucial turning point affecting action, opinion, etc.

watershed: **3** a crucial turning point affecting action, opinion, etc.

5. If you speak below your listeners' educational level, they more than likely will be not only bored but also angry when they discover they are being <u>patronized</u>. (Baker and Baker, *Communications*)

> **pa·tron·ize** (pā'trən īz', pa'-) *vt.* **-ized', -iz'ing 1** to act as a patron toward; sponsor; support **2** to be kind or helpful to, but in a haughty or snobbish way, as if dealing with an inferior **3** to be a regular customer of (store, merchant, etc.)

patronized: **2** to be kind or helpful to, but in a haughty or snobbish

way, as if dealing with an inferior

6. A <u>compress</u> and a soak are both moist applications in which water touches the skin. They can be either warm or cold. A compress is a localized application. A soak can be either localized or general. (Wolgin, *Being a Nursing Assistant*)

> **com·press** (kəm pres'; *for n.* käm'pres') *vt.* [ME *compressen* < OFr *compresser* < LL *compressare* < L *compressus*, pp. of *comprimere*, to squeeze < *com-*, together + *premere*, to PRESS¹] to press together; make more compact by or as by pressure —*n.* **1** a pad of folded cloth, sometimes medicated or moistened, for applying pressure, heat, cold, etc. to some part of the body ☆**2** a machine for compressing cotton bales —*SYN.* CONTRACT —**com·press'ibil'ity** *n.*

compress: **1** a pad of folded cloth, sometimes medicated or moistened,

for applying pressure, heat, cold, etc. to some part of the body

7. The Chicago Bulls' first shoe deal with Converse, while exceedingly <u>modest</u> in comparison to today's mega-shoe deals, filled a need for our young club. (Colangelo, *How You Play the Game*)

> **mod·est** (mäd'ist) *adj.* [Fr *modeste* < L *modestus*, keeping due measure, modest < *modus*: see MODE] **1** having or showing a moderate opinion of one's own value, abilities, achievements, etc.; not vain or boastful; unassuming **2** not forward; shy or reserved [*modest* behavior] **3** behaving, dressing, speaking, etc. in a way that is considered proper or decorous; decent **4** moderate or reasonable; not extreme [a *modest* request] **5** quiet and humble in appearance, style, etc.; not pretentious [a *modest* home] —*SYN.* CHASTE, SHY¹ —**mod'estly** *adv.*

modest: **4** moderate or reasonable; not extreme [a *modest* request]

8. Poor listening creates <u>friction</u> and misunderstanding in both personal and professional relationships. (Watson in Baker and Baker, *Communications*)

> **fric·tion** (frik'shən) *n.* [Fr < L *frictio* < pp. of *fricare*, to rub: see FRIABLE] **1** a rubbing, esp. of one object against another **2** disagreement or conflict because of differences of opinion, temperament, etc. **3** *Mech.* the resistance to motion of two moving objects or surfaces that touch —**fric'tion·less** *adj.*

friction: **2** disagreement or conflict because of differences of opinion,

temperament, etc.

9. We have <u>ample</u> testimony that artists themselves tend to look upon their creations as living things. (Janson and Janson, *A Basic History of Art*)

> **am·ple** (am'pəl) *adj.* **-pler** (-plər), **-plest** (-pləst) [ME & OFr < L *amplus*, prob. < **amlos* < IE base **am-*, to contain] **1** large in size, extent, scope, etc.; spacious; roomy **2** more than enough; abundant **3** enough to fulfill the needs or purpose; adequate —*SYN.* PLENTIFUL —**am'ple·ness** *n.*

ample: **2** more than enough; abundant
_____

_____

10. The first step in investigating a biotic community may be to simply
<u>catalogue</u> all the species present. Species are the different kinds of
plants, animals, and microbes.

> **cat|a·log** or **cat|a·logue** (kat′ə lôg′, -läg′) ***n.*** [Fr *catalogue* < LL
> *catalogus* < Gr *katalogos*, a list, register < *katalegein*, to reckon, list
> < *kata-*, down, completely + *legein*, to say, count: see LOGIC] a
> complete or extensive list, esp. ☆*a*) an alphabetical card file, as of
> the books in a library *b*) a list of articles for sale, school courses
> offered, items on display, etc., usually with descriptive comments
> and often with illustrations *c*) a book or pamphlet containing such
> a list *d*) a long list, as of warriors, rivers, or ships, characteristic of
> the classical epic —***vt., vi.*** **-loged′** or **-logued′, -log′ing** or **-logu′ing**
> **1** to enter in a catalog **2** to make a catalog of —***SYN.*** LIST[1] —**cat′|a·**
> **log|′er, cat′|a·logu′|er, cat′|a·log′ist,** or **cat′|a·logu′ist** ***n.***

catalogue: a complete or extensive list
_____

_____

> **Exercise 8**   **Using a Dictionary to Define Words and Phrases**

Use your dictionary to define the underlined words. Write the definition that
fits the context.

1. For most high school students, fun is an <u>integral</u> part of their lives.

   integral: necessary for completeness, essential
   _____

2. Other composers developed a percussive rhythmic style with sharp,
   constantly changing <u>accents</u>. (Politoske, *Music*)

   accents: emphasis or stress on a note or chord
   _____

3. A basic difference, however, is that while psychologists focus on the individual, sociologists look at the person's <u>web</u> of social relationships.
   (Macionis, *Sociology*)

   web: interconnection of elements, network
   _____

4. Being aware of the various steps of good listening has little value unless
   we can manage the steps with skill and <u>consistency</u>. (Bittner, *Each Other*)

   consistency: agreement or conformity with previous practice
   _____

5. Computers are very good at <u>digesting</u> facts and producing information.
   (Long and Long, *Computers*)

   digesting: thinking over and absorbing
   _____

6. <u>Matter</u> is all around us. Almost everything we see, touch, taste, or smell
   is matter. (Miller and Levine, *Biology*)

   matter: what things are made of, constituent substance
   _____

7. Maps often are the best way to present information, such as population <u>density</u>. (Rubenstein, *An Introduction to Human Geography*)

   density: quantity or number per unit or area

8. The word "style" is derived from *stilus,* the writing instrument of the ancient Romans. Originally, it referred to <u>distinctive</u> ways of writing: the shape of the letters as well as the choice of words. (Janson and Janson, *A Basic History of Art*)

   distinctive: different, individual

9. From bridge and chess to Trivial Pursuit and Scrabble, games are en-joying a <u>renaissance</u> in digital form. (Arar, *Computer Games for Grownup Kids*)

   renaissance: revival, new popularity

10. Computer technology is having a <u>profound</u> effect on physically chal-lenged people. (Long and Long, *Computers*)

    profound: deeply or intensely felt

Exercise 9 **Using a Dictionary or Glossary to Define Words and Phrases**

Using a text from one of your other classes, identify five sentences with unfa-miliar words. Copy the sentences onto a sheet of notebook paper and under-line the unfamiliar words. Use either the glossary or a dictionary to find the definitions. Write the definitions.

The five words and definitions will vary.

Using a Thesaurus

A thesaurus is a book of words and their synonyms. Synonyms are words and phrases that have the same or nearly the same meaning. A word's syn-onyms can often help you figure out the meaning of the word.

(©2003, The Washington Post Writers Group. Reprinted with permission)

For example, compare this entry in *Roget's 21st Century Thesaurus* for "correct" with the dictionary entry on page 28.

correct *[adj] accurate, exact* according to Hoyle, actual, amen, appropriate, cooking with gas, dead on, equitable, factual, faithful, faultless, flawless, for sure, free of error, impeccable, just, legitimate, nice, okay, on target, on the ball, on the beam, on the button, on the money, on the nose, on track, perfect, precise, proper, regular, right, right as rain, righteous, right on, right stuff, rigorous, stone, strict, true, undistorted, unmistaken, veracious, veridical See INCLINATION, SPECIFICITY, SUPERIORITY proper, appropriate acceptable, becoming, careful, comme il faut, conforming, conventional, decent, decorous, diplomatic, done, fitting, meticulous, nice, okay, punctilious, right, right stuff, scrupulous, seemly, standard, suitable See ATTRIBUTE OF BEHAVIOR, SUITABILITY

correct *[v] fix, adjust* alter, ameliorate, amend, better, change, clean up, clean up act, cure, debug, doctor, do over, edit, emend, fiddle with, fix up, get with it, go over, help, improve, launder, make over, make right, make up for, mend, pay dues, pick up, polish, put in order, reclaim, reconstruct, rectify, redress, reform, regulate, remedy, remodel, reorganize, repair, retouch, review, revise, right, scrub, set right, set straight, shape up, straighten out, touch up, turn around, upgrade See RECTIFY discipline, chastise, administer, admonish, castigate, chasten, chide, penalize, punish, reprimand, reprove See CRITICIZE, PUNISH

Exercise 10 **Log On to the Web**

Several dictionaries and thesauruses are now available online. When you have the time and the access, you can log on and find definitions, synonyms, and antonyms. Use a search engine to locate the resources you need or try these general dictionary sites:

http://www.m-w.com/netdict.htm
http://www.dictionary.com/
http://www.yourdictionary.com/

There are also specialized dictionary sites such as these:

http://whatis.techtarget.com/ (definitions and explanations of Internet terms)
http://www.getty.edu/research/tools/vocabulary/ (fine art and architecture)

Web activities will vary.

DEFINING WORDS AND PHRASES WHILE READING

When you're reading passages other than practice material, strategies for defining unfamiliar words are not as obvious as the ones for the example words in the practice sentences. To understand the variety of material you're required to read, you must use the strategies flexibly: choose the strategy or strategies that best fit the situation.

For example, when you come to a word you don't understand, you might first look for any context clues you can use. On the other hand, if you recognize a part of the word, perhaps that is all the clue you need. Or, you might start by looking it up in the dictionary and fitting the meaning back into the context.

Read this passage from *Computers,* by Long and Long.

Few will argue that we are rapidly approaching the age of automation, an era when invisible computers participate in or help us with nearly all we do. (Long and Long, *Computers*)

How you define the words in this sentence depends on factors such as how many words were unfamiliar, your experience with computers, how much time you have, and your knowledge of word parts such as *auto* and *in*.

The same is true whenever you read. You choose the best way to define each word.

Even familiar words can cause comprehension problems. For example, some words are confusing because they sound like another word.

THE FAMILY CIRCUS ®   By Bil Keane

"That's not a jet. It's just a plain plane."

Exercise 11   **Defining Familiar Words That Are Easily Confused**

In these sentences use the most appropriate strategies to decide which word best fits the context of the sentence. Circle your answer.

1a. Log on to the Web (cite, sight, site) listed on page 2 of your syllabus.

1b. If you want an A on your paper, you must correctly (cite, sight, site) the author's information.

1c. From the balcony the sunset was a magnificent (cite, sight, site).

2a. If I accurately measured each (angle, angel) of the triangle, the answer would be correct.

2b. The gift shop had a wonderful music box with an (angle, angel) on top.

3a. We can leave when (your, you're) ready.

3b. Is this (your, you're) jacket?

4a. To receive your free copy of the book, send a request on company (stationary, stationery).

4b. The art museum's garden exhibit included both (stationary, stationery) pieces and displays with moving pieces called mobiles.

5a. By signing this contract you agree to (accept except) the terms and interest charges.

5b. You can access all of the newspaper's information online (accept, except) the comics.

> **Exercise 12**   **Defining Unfamiliar Words and Phrases**

Using the strategies you decide are most appropriate, define the underlined words and phrases. Write the definitions.

1. Chronic drinkers are more likely than others to have histories of violent behavior. (Donatelle and Davis, *Access to Health*)

    chronic: habitual, confirmed over a long period of time

2. In his inaugural address Herbert Hoover told the American people that the years ahead were "bright with hope." He was expressing the optimism that many Americans felt, and he and they apparently had good reason for their sunny expectations. (Unger, *These United States*)

    expressing the optimism: giving the positive outlook, sunny expectations

3. Throughout the past hundred years, people have lamented that nobody writes letters anymore. ("A Century of Eureka Moments," *The Wall Street Journal*)

    lamented: expressed sorrow, regretted

4. Perhaps the prototypical American composer of the period was the German-trained Edward MacDowell (1860–1908), a man once regarded as America's greatest composer. (Politoske, *Music*)

    prototypical: classic, model

5. During the last decade, the subject of domestic violence has finally grabbed our attention. (Donatelle and Davis, *Access to Health*)

    decade: ten-year period

6. As inevitable as it may seem today, the zipper was anything but an overnight success. (Grunwald and Adler, Introduction to Clarke Sales Company Manager's Letter, *Letters of the Century*)

    inevitable: certain, necessary, inescapable

7. The term ore denotes useful metallic minerals that can be mined at a profit. (Lutgens and Tarbuck, *Foundations of Earth Science*)

    denotes: means

8. This book is about what I believe. Of course, what I (or anyone else) believe is the culmination of many things: family and faith and experience, education and intuition, all mixed together to provide a share of knowledge and—hopefully—a touch of wisdom. (Colangelo, *How You Play the Game*)

culmination: the combined effect of, the result of

9. The earth <u>intercepts</u> only a <u>minute</u> percentage of the energy given off by the sun—less than one two-billionth. (Lutgens and Tarbuck, *The Atmosphere*)

intercepts: catches, stops

minute: small, tiny

10. As a business owner you must be familiar with the growing list of federal laws that <u>supersede</u> state statutes and guarantee various forms of job-security protection. (McGrath and McGrath, "Firing Employees," *Performance Racing Industry*)

supersede: overrule, replace

Exercise 13   Defining Unfamiliar Words and Phrases

Using the strategies you decide are most appropriate, define the underlined words and phrases. Write the definitions.

1. Emotionally unhealthy people are much more likely to let their feelings overpower them than are emotionally healthy people. Emotionally unhealthy people may be <u>highly volatile</u> and <u>prone</u> to <u>unpredictable</u> emotional outbursts and to inappropriate, sometimes frightening responses to events. An ex-boyfriend who becomes so angry that he begins to hit you and push you around in front of your friends because he is jealous of your new relationship is showing an extremely unhealthy and dangerous emotional reaction. Violent responses to situations have become a problem of <u>epidemic</u> proportions in the United States. (Donatelle and Davis, *Access to Health*)

highly volatile: very unstable, erratic

prone: inclined, likely

unpredictable: random, can't be anticipated

epidemic: widespread, far-reaching

2. Popular music—folk, soul, jazz, country, rock—whatever the style, plays an <u>overwhelming</u> part in the daily lives of most Americans. The origins of any popular music are deep in the human spirit, and its history reaches back to the earliest ages. Today, it has a far greater <u>commercial</u>

<u>market</u> in America than does "classical" music, and it has a significant role in the film industry. Through video, popular music is also closely <u>allied</u> to visual arts, and it is at the edge of <u>emerging</u> computer technologies. (Politoske, *Music*)

overwhelming: strong, major

commercial market: sales power

allied: related, associated

emerging: rising, developing

3. <u>Primitive</u> human beings had no electricity, few tools, and poor shelter. Their time was spent protecting themselves against <u>predators</u> and finding food. They were <u>superstitious</u> and believed illness and disease were caused by supernatural spirits. In an attempt to heal, tribal doctors performed ceremonies to <u>exorcise</u> evil spirits. They used herbs and plants as medicines. Some of the same medicines are still used today. (Badasch and Chesebro, *Introduction to Health Occupations*)

primitive: ancient, from the earliest time

predators: preying on, exploiting others

superstitious: belief in the supernatural

exorcise: cast out, rid

4. We might be much better off to try positive <u>adaptations</u> to stress. For example, physical exercise tends to prepare the body for stressful situations and creates a tension-relieving <u>mechanism</u> in some people. Under a doctor's care we might develop a jogging program or a <u>strenuous</u> exercise program. Some form of relaxation may also help us to <u>alleviate</u> stress. Sitting quietly in pleasant surroundings or going for a walk in the park or the country are all ways of alleviating stress. Cutting down on the amount we eat and cutting back or stopping the intake of caffeine or other stimulants may also be solutions to handling stress. (Bittner, *Each Other*)

adaptations: changes and adjustments

mechanism: a system or means of

strenuous: energetic, requiring great effort

alleviate: ease, lessen

5. Communication is <u>central</u> to the learning process. Words, gestures, and other <u>symbols</u>, or things that stand for other things, are used to <u>transmit</u> ideas through symbolic communication. Only human beings have the ability to develop and use symbols with which to

communicate. This ability <u>enables</u> humans to learn ideas from others and to teach them to new generations. Culture, that combination of ideas, inventions, and objects, is both understood and transmitted because of this ability to communicate. (Rose, Glazer, and Glazer, *Sociology*)

central: very important, primary

symbols: things that stand for other things

transmit: convey, pass along

enables: makes possible

6. The year is 2010. Computers are <u>invisible</u>; that is, they are built into our <u>domestic</u>, working, and external environment. Imagine this <u>scenario</u>. Your invisible computer is preprogrammed to awaken you to whatever stimulates you to greet the new day. The wake-up call could be the sound of your favorite music, a vibrating bed, or any of hundreds of video information or entertainment options, such as your favorite network morning program, today's weather, a stock report, a production status report for the evening shift at your place of employment, the movie of your choice, or a to-do list for the day. Suppose your wake up choice is the <u>latter</u>—a to-do list for the day. Besides listing the events of your day, your invisible computer might verbally emphasize important events. . . . (Long and Long, *Computers*)

invisible: very pervasive in the environment and thus not seen

domestic: home

scenario: scene, story

latter: last mentioned

REMEMBERING WORDS

Unless you actively work at remembering new words, you will have to rediscover the meaning each time you see the word.

Understanding

Being able to remember something often depends on how thoroughly you learned it in the first place. You must "get," or understand, something before you can "forget" it. Sometimes when we say, "I forgot," what we mean is "I didn't understand it."

Understanding, in this context, means your ability to translate words and information into ideas that make sense to you. Something that doesn't make sense to you is hard to learn. The more understandable information is to you, the easier it is to learn.

There is not one best method for remembering everything. However, applying several of your senses will help: see it, say it, hear it, write it.

Reviewing and Using

Regular review, spaced over time, is critical to remembering new words and information. Rather than one two-hour study session, plan short but frequent study sessions. Begin a session by reviewing some of the words you've already learned, and then tackle new ones.

You also have to use new information to remember it. In fact, it's been estimated that you must use a new word at least ten times before it's really "yours." Try to use a few new words in your writing and conversations each day.

One Strategy for Learning the Meanings of Words and Phrases

One strategy for learning—understanding and remembering—new words and phrases is to make flashcards. Write the word and sentence (context) on the front of a 3 × 5 index card. Also note the class and/or text page number.

Davis, p. 36

foster

To be part of the solution to preventing hate and bias crimes you can support educational programs designed to foster understanding and appreciation for differences in people.

On the back of the card write the definition (the one that most closely fits the way the word is used in your original sentence). You can also write a sentence with a personally meaningful context.

to help to grow or develop; stimulate; promote

My health class was designed to foster healthier living.

Use the cards at odd moments during the day to review and test yourself. Sometimes, look at the word and try to recall the definition. At other times, look at the definition and try to recall the word.

Once in a while as you go through the cards, sort them into two stacks: *know* and *don't know*. The next time you review, use only the *don't know* stack to concentrate your study.

SUMMARY OF KEY IDEAS

■ Words are the building blocks of everything we write. Therefore, it's important to understand the meaning of words and phrases.

■ Words take on meaning from their context—how they are used with the other words in the sentence and surrounding sentences.

■ To understand an author's specific meaning for a word, you must consider the word's context.

■ Strategies you can use to figure out the meaning of a word include using the author's context clues, breaking the word into parts, looking it up in a dictionary or other resource book, and asking someone for help.

■ To remember information, you must understand it, use it, and review it often.

Use Your Strategies 1

Using the strategies you decide are most appropriate, define the underlined words and phrases. Write the definitions.

1. In previous years, more employees worked alone and therefore did not have to concern themselves with the <u>interpersonal relationships</u> that

are necessary to achieve high standards of excellence in a modern business enterprise. (Chapman and O'Neil, *Your Attitude Is Showing*)

interpersonal relationships: connected relationships among people

2. Jazz, one of the few distinctly American types of music, was <u>derived</u> from a variety of sources. (Politoske, *Music*)

derived: gotten and/or adapted from

3. Nineteenth-century cities looked much more <u>rustic</u> than they would later on, with rural areas rarely more than three miles away. (Hertz and Klein, *Twentieth Century Art Theory*)

rustic: unsophisticated, rough

4. Assume that ten reporters who work for a magazine in San Diego, California, are <u>collaborating</u> on a story about that city's best restaurants. (Macionis, *Sociology*)

collaborating: working together, cooperating on

5. Nonverbal messages usually <u>complement</u> verbal messages. (Barker and Barker, *Communication*)

complement: supplement, complete

6. A <u>sedentary</u> lifestyle, alcohol abuse, tobacco, and caffeine are known contributors to osteoporosis. (Rosenfeld, *Live Now, Age Later*)

sedentary: inactive

7. The earth's atmosphere is unlike that of any other body in the solar system. No other planet is as <u>hospitable</u> or exhibits the same life-sustaining mixture of gases as the earth. (Lutgens and Tarbuck, *The Atmosphere*)

hospitable: friendly, livable

8. Hundreds of studies have sought to identify what it is that <u>differentiates</u> effective managers from ineffective ones. (Robbins, *Training in Interpersonal Skills*)

differentiates: distinguishes between, contrasts

9. A place having two or more local names presents a <u>quandary</u> to <u>cartographers</u> who need to give the place a label on the map. (Rubenstein, *An Introduction to Human Geography*)

quandary: dilemma, problem

cartographers: people who make maps

10. The most striking works of Paleolithic art are the images of animals <u>incised</u>, painted, or sculpted on the rock surfaces of caves, such as the

wonderful *Wounded Bison* from the cave at Altamira in northern Spain.
(Janson and Janson, *A Basic History of Art*)

incised: cut or carved into

Use Your Strategies 2

Using the strategies you decide are most appropriate, define the underlined
words and phrases. Write the definitions.

1. Recent <u>immigrants</u> are <u>not distributed uniformly</u> through the United
   States. One-fourth are clustered in California, one-fourth in New York
   and New Jersey, one-fourth in Florida, Texas, and Illinois, and one-
   fourth in the other 44 states. Coastal states were once the main entry
   points for immigrants because most arrived by ship. Today, nearly all
   arrive by motor vehicle or airplane. California and Texas are the two
   most popular states for entry of motor vehicles from Mexico, and these
   six states have the country's busiest airports for international arrivals.
   (Rubenstein, *An Introduction to Human Geography*)

   immigrants: people who have recently come to the United States

   from another country

   not distributed uniformly: not scattered equally among all 50 states

2. Violence in American society is a topic that <u>garners</u> much interest, concern and debate in this country. How police respond to violence, especially police use of force, is of particular concern to many of us. (Hurtt,
   "Use of force limited")

   garners: collects, accumulates

3. The <u>proceeds</u> from the sale of gifts and raffle tickets for prizes will help
   to fund the wildlife center's mission of <u>rehabilitating</u> injured animals
   and returning them to the wild.

   proceeds: profits

   rehabilitating: helping them recover

4. Cameron Judd's novel *Firefall* is set in 1884. The story begins one night
   as a meteor falls from the sky to <u>demolish</u> a Montana mining town.

   demolish: destroy, wreck

5. Scientists who launched the Galileo probe on its 2.7 billion-mile mission to explore Jupiter may send the craft on a final flight—a <u>kamikaze
   plunge</u>. Yes, NASA may deliberately crash the spacecraft into Jupiter or
   one of its icy moons in 2002.

   kamikaze plunge: deliberate crash

6. Although everyone loves fresh flowers, there's no question that silk flowers can make an impression nearly <u>indistinguishable</u> from the real thing. Best of all, you don't have to spend a fortune to enjoy gorgeous floral arrangements year-round.

   indistinguishable: unable to be differentiated

7. Owning a house requires a lot of work—lawns to mow, roofs to repair and leaky faucets to fix. So, when a job demands most of your time and your schedule is <u>erratic</u>, renting an apartment instead of owning a home may be sensible.

   erratic: irregular, unpredictable

8. The home of the future will be smarter, cleaner, and more <u>serene</u>, thanks to a new generation of stylish appliances and furniture that make use of fresh designs and modern technology. For example, the home office will be upgraded from an extra bedroom where the computer was stored to a <u>sanctuary</u> with comfortable custom furniture in soothing colors, wood tones, and glass. (adapted from Koenenn, "Smart Houses")

   serene: peaceful, calm

   sanctuary: retreat, haven, pleasant place to be

9. Considering all your options means more than taking stock of the <u>pros</u> and <u>cons</u> of any given choice, although that's a good first step. In addition to reviewing the positive and negative points, think about a third one: the <u>neutral</u> reasons. (adapted from Carter and Troyka, *Majoring in the Rest of Your Life*)

   pros: positives

   cons: negatives

   neutral: neither positive or negative, unbiased

10. One of the things the founders of our nation most feared was <u>centralized</u> government power. Indeed, our Constitution and our Bill of Rights were written <u>explicitly</u> to <u>ensure</u> that power rested with the people and that no single branch of government—whether the executive, legislative, or judicial—gains a <u>monopoly</u> of power. (McClenaghan, *Magruder's American Government*)

    centralized: concentrated in one branch

    explicitly: clearly, specifically

    ensure: guarantee

    monopoly: exclusive control

REFLECT AND CONNECT

A. When you look up words in the dictionary, you often find definitions that are labeled <u>old-fashioned</u>, <u>archaic</u>, or <u>obsolete</u>. Although all three terms point out a definition that is not used in today's language, each term has a slightly different meaning. What do the different labels mean?

_____

_____

_____

Why do you think words and definitions become old-fashioned, archaic, and obsolete?

_____

_____

_____

B. Think back over all the words you read this week. Select two words you think are unusual or that you didn't completely understand. Find out all you can about the words, such as meanings, parts of speech, and history. Write down the resources you use and what you discover.

_____

_____

_____

_____

LOG ON TO THE WEB

Another strategy you can use to improve your vocabulary is to work and play with words. For example, these Web sites contain word games, puzzles, and links to information about vocabulary.

Vocabulary University at *http://www.vocabulary.com/*
Learn Vocabulary Syndicate at *http://www.syndicate.com/*
English Word Games at *http://www.nanana.com/wordgames.html*

Log on to one of these sites or use a search engine to locate another site with information about how to improve vocabulary.

Play one word game, complete one puzzle, or read one person's advice on how to improve your vocabulary. Then, write down

1. the complete Web address
2. the name of the person or company who sponsors and maintains the site
3. a sentence describing what you did or read
4. the name of the person or company who wrote the game, puzzle, or advice
5. what you know about the writer
6. the most important thing you learned from the activity about improving your vocabulary

CROSSWORD PUZZLE

Across

1 more than enough

3 household

6 germ free

10 your best reasoned conclusion

13 word part added to end of a root word

15 basic part of a word

16 hinder

17 positive

20 bleak; desolate; barren

22 point of view

23 ten-year period

24 not extreme

Down

2 word part added to beginning of a root word

4 how words are used together in a sentence

5 to terminate

7 study of the universe

8 improve

9 a network

11 to help to grow

12 savvy

14 phobias

18 means

19 set of beliefs

21 journeys

Word List (not all used)

ample	domestic	optimism
angle	enrich	portable
aseptic	fears	prefix
astronomy	fire	primitive
centenarians	foster	root
context	friction	sharp
contractions	glossary	stark
creed	good	stationary
decade	hurt	strategy
denotes	incised	suffix
deserted	inference	treks
disagreeable	modest	web

CHAPTER
3

Understanding Main Ideas

AN IDEA TO THINK ABOUT

Have you ever tried to carry on a conversation with a person who just chattered away with what sounded like random bits and pieces of information? If so, you probably said something like, "What in the world are you talking about?" or, "Get to the point!" In other words, you need the person to give you a general, or main, idea that will tie all the bits and pieces of specific information together.

When you are reading for learning, you need the author to give you main ideas to tie the bits and pieces of specific information together. Identifying and understanding main ideas is essential to comprehending what you hear and what you read.

CHAPTER 3 AT A GLANCE

The basic unit of writing authors use to express their ideas is the sentence. Understanding individual sentences is important. Most of the time, however, you read groups of sentences that have been combined into a paragraph.

A **paragraph** is a group of sentences that fit together to support and explain one main idea. In many expository paragraphs the author directly states the one main idea. An expository paragraph is written specifically to report or explain facts, events, and ideas rather than to narrate a story or describe a scene.

Paragraphs that have a directly stated main idea contain two types of sentences:

1. one general sentence that contains the main idea, and
2. one or more specific sentences that contain details to develop and support the main idea. (We consider these sentences in Chapter 5.)

In this chapter you will first practice strategies for distinguishing among general and specific words, ideas, and sentences and then for locating and understanding the one general sentence in a paragraph that contains the main idea.

DISTINGUISHING AMONG GENERAL AND SPECIFIC WORDS AND IDEAS

Key to understanding the groups of words and sentences you read is figuring out how they relate to one another. One important relationship is the level of specificity: By that I mean, is one word or idea more *general* or more *specific* than another? **General** means broad, comprehensive, including everything. **Specific** means limited, individual, narrow.

To see how these labels apply to everyday words and ideas, consider this list of terms:

Thanksgiving   New Year's Eve   holidays   Labor Day

In this list, the term *holidays* is the most general because it includes all the other terms.

The terms *Thanksgiving, New Year's Eve,* and *Labor Day* are specific terms because they are limited, individual examples of holidays.

EXAMPLE I   Think about these two terms. How are they related to each other? Which term is more general than the other term? Which term is more specific?

basketball player   athlete

The more general term is _____

The more specific term is _____

Explanation   Athlete is the general, or comprehensive, term for people who excel in many kinds of sports. A basketball player is more specific because it is an individual example of one kind of athlete.

EXAMPLE 2   Consider the relationships among these four terms. To decide which term is most general, ask yourself "Who or what is this group of terms about?" Your answer will tell you which term is the most general.

    computer   telephone   office equipment   copy machine

    The most general term is _____

Explanation   In this example, office equipment is the more general term because it covers, or includes, all the other terms. A computer, telephone, and copy machine are more specific because they are individual examples of office machines.

Exercise 1   **General and Specific Words and Ideas**

The words in each group are related. Look at the relationships among the words. Decide which word is more general than the other three. Underline the most general word in each group—the word that answers "Who or what is the word group about?"

EXAMPLE   jazz   rock and roll   <u>music</u>   country

Explanation   Music is underlined because it is the most general word; jazz, rock and roll, and country are specific kinds of music.

1. (animal)   cat   dog   horse
2. dime   quarter   (money)   dollar
3. trout   (fish)   tuna   shark
4. soda   coffee   tea   (drink)
5. (fabric)   silk   wool   cotton
6. basketball   tennis   (sport)   cycling

Exercise 2   **General and Specific Words and Ideas**

The words in each group are specific examples of a general idea. In the space provided, write the general idea that connects them—a word or phrase that can answer the question "Who or what is the word group about?"

EXAMPLE   fear   happiness   love   <u>emotions</u>

Explanation   Fear, happiness, and love are connected because they are each a specific type of emotion or feeling.

1. pie   cake   ice cream   <u>desserts</u>
2. earring   necklace   pin   <u>jewelry</u>
3. cocker spaniel   poodle   golden retriever   <u>dogs</u>

4. runner	boxer	soccer player	athletes
5. dishwasher	blender	microwave	kitchen appliances
6. desk	table	bed	furniture

Exercise 3 **General and Specific Words and Ideas**

Each word listed represents a general idea. In the spaces provided, write two specific examples of the general word.

EXAMPLE   crime   robbery   assault

Explanation   Crime is the general word; robbery and assault are specific kinds of crime. Students need any two examples of the category. These are just samples.

1. vehicle   car, truck, motorcycle

2. occupation   teacher, truck driver, banker

3. food   hamburger, chicken, pizza

4. clothing   sweater, jeans, shirt

5. medicine   aspirin, Tylenol, vitamin

6. drinks   soda, beer, water

Distinguishing Various Levels of Specificity

Unfortunately, figuring out the relationships among a group of words or ideas isn't always as uncomplicated as the previous exercises make it seem. This is because words can change in specificity: words can be general sometimes and specific at other times.

Stated another way, words can play different roles in different sentences. In the same way words take on their definition from their context, words take on their role (whether they are general or specific) from their context.

Also, there are not always an equal number of general and specific terms in a list or paragraph. The number of relationships among groups of words or among sentences in a paragraph can vary greatly. For example, several words or sentences can be at the same level of specificity, each can be at a different level, or there can be a mixture. Therefore, the question you must always ask is "What are the relationships among *this* group of words or ideas?"

EXAMPLE   In the previous example with the terms *athlete* and *basketball player*, you determined that basketball player was the more specific term. But what happens when we add *Michael Jordan* as a third term? What are the relationships among these three terms? Which one is now the most specific term?

basketball player   athlete   Michael Jordan

The most specific term now is _____

Explanation In relation to one another, *athlete* is still the more general, or comprehensive, term for people who excel in many kinds of sports. A *basketball player* is still a specific example of one kind of athlete. However, *Michael Jordan* is the most specific term because he is a specific example of a basketball player.

EXAMPLE What are the relationships among the terms when we add *tennis player*? Arrange them from most general to most specific.

basketball player   athlete   Michael Jordan   tennis player

_____

_____

_____

_____

Explanation In relation to one another, *athlete* is the more general term for people who excel in many kinds of sports; *basketball player* and *tennis player* are at the same level of specificity because they are both specific examples of athletes; *Michael Jordan* is a more specific term because he is an example of a basketball player.

It is often helpful to write the information in a way that shows the relationships. One common way to do this is to use the structure of an informal outline: indent specific information under the more general. An indent is a tab or space from the margin. Using this format, the previous example would look like this:

athlete
  tennis player
  basketball player
    Michael Jordan

Exercise 4 **General and Specific Words and Ideas**

The words in each group are related. Each word is at a different level of specificity. Arrange the words from most general to most specific.

EXAMPLE   soup   liquids   chicken-noodle

liquids
  soup
    chicken-noodle

Explanation *Liquids* is the most general word (it answers the question, "What is the group about?") *Soup* is an example of a liquid, and *chicken-noodle* is an example of soup.

1. round object   baseball   ball

   <u> round object   </u>

        <u> ball   </u>

             <u> baseball   </u>

2. running shoe   athletic shoe   footwear

   <u> footwear   </u>

        <u> athletic shoe   </u>

             <u> running shoe   </u>

3. movie   entertainment   *Star Wars*

   <u> entertainment   </u>

        <u> movie   </u>

             <u> *Star Wars*   </u>

4. food   corn   vegetable

   <u> food   </u>

        <u> vegetable   </u>

             <u> corn   </u>

5. Arabian   horse   animal

   <u> animal   </u>

        <u> horse   </u>

             <u> Arabian   </u>

6. athlete   golfer   Tiger Woods

   <u> athlete   </u>

        <u> golfer   </u>

             <u> Tiger Woods   </u>

IDENTIFYING THE TOPIC

In reading and writing we often call the general word or phrase the **topic**. The topic answers the question, "Who or what is the author writing about?"

EXAMPLE   This group of sentences shares one general topic. After reading the group of sentences, underline the word or phrase that best expresses the topic—who or what the author is writing about.

1. Harriet Beecher Stowe wrote *Uncle Tom's Cabin,* a forceful book against slavery.

2. Several romantic novels, short stories, and religious poems were written by Harriet Beecher Stowe.

3. Harriet Beecher Stowe was born in 1811 and died in 1896.
   a. writers
   b. <u>Harriet Beecher Stowe</u>
   c. *Uncle Tom's Cabin*

Explanation   The term writers (a) is too general because the three sentences talk about only one writer, Harriet Beecher Stowe. The title of her book, *Uncle Tom's Cabin* (c), is too specific because it is only one of her writings.

Exercise 5   **Identifying the Topic**

In this exercise each group of sentences shares one general topic. After reading a group of sentences, underline the word or phrase that best expresses the topic—the who or what the author is writing about.

Group 1

1. The Strait of Dover separates England from France and the European continent.

2. One of the busiest maritime routes in the world is the Strait of Dover, which connects the English Channel and Atlantic Ocean with the North Sea.

3. The Strait of Dover is about 34 km (about 21 mi.) wide.
   a. ocean shipping routes
   b. you can't drive from England to France
   c. the Strait of Dover

Group 2

1. Armistice Day, now called Veterans Day, was proclaimed in 1919 to commemorate the end of World War I.

2. We now observe Veterans Day in the United States to honor all, living and dead, who served with the armed forces in wartime.

3. Veterans Day is known in Canada as Remembrance Day and in Great Britain as Remembrance Sunday.
   a. World War I
   b. Veterans Day
   c. holidays

Group 3

1. A primary example of Art Deco design in the United States is the interior of Radio City Music Hall in New York City, designed by Donald Deskey in 1931.

2. Art Deco is a style of design used in furniture, jewelry, textiles, and interior decor that was popular in the 1920s and 1930s.

3. Art Deco declined in popularity in the late 1930s, but it is now enjoying a comeback.
   - a. Art Deco design
   - b. popular design styles
   - c. Radio City Music Hall

Group 4

1. Sir Edmund Hillary, with his Nepalese Sherpa guide, was the first mountain climber to reach the summit of Mount Everest, the world's highest peak.
2. The sport of mountain climbing began in eighteenth-century Europe when people wanted to climb Mont Blanc, the highest peak of the Alps.
3. World-class climber Chris Bonington describes several major mountain-climbing expeditions in his book *The Climbers: A History of Mountaineering.*
   - a. popular mountains to climb
   - b. Sir Edmund Hillary
   - c. mountain climbing

Group 5

1. Steven Spielberg's early movies include *Jaws* (1975), *Close Encounters of the Third Kind* (1977), *E.T.* (1982), and, of course, the Indiana Jones series *Raiders of the Lost Ark* (1981), *Indiana Jones and the Temple of Doom* (1984), and *Indiana Jones and the Last Crusade* (1989).
2. Hollywood's Academy of Motion Picture Arts and Sciences produces the Academy Awards show each year to recognize people who create the best movies.
3. Movies, also called feature films, are produced in three stages: preproduction, production, and postproduction.
   - a. movies
   - b. Steven Spielberg
   - c. Oscars

Group 6

1. Recent research indicates that the cholesterol in eggs is not as harmful as once thought.
2. The number of eggs eaten by Americans hit an all-time low in 1991.
3. Scrambled eggs are once again a popular breakfast item.
   - a. scrambled eggs
   - b. eggs
   - c. cholesterol in eggs

Exercise 6   **Identifying the Topic of a Paragraph**

After reading each paragraph, underline the word or phrase that best expresses the topic of that paragraph. Remember, the topic answers the question, "Who or what is the author writing about?"

E XAMPLE   If you've ever been on a roller coaster, you know what it's like: you go up, you go down, maybe you go upside-down, and then suddenly it's over. The first true roller coaster in America was built in 1884 at Coney Island in New York. It was called the Gravity Pleasure Switchback, and it moved at a blazing 6 mph. Today's roller coasters have a bit more zip. The Superman coaster at Six Flags Magic Mountain in Valencia, California, reaches a top speed of 100 mph.

  a. the Superman coaster
  b. the first roller coaster in America
  c. <u>roller coasters</u>

Explanation   The topic of this paragraph is c, roller coasters. Answers a and b are too specific.

 1. Medicare and Medicaid are two different government programs that greatly influence health care. Medicare is a federal U. S. government program funded by Social Security and available to all individuals over age 65, regardless of income. It also covers the health care of some disabled or handicapped persons of all ages. Medicaid is a separate program, funded by each state to help meet the medical and health care needs of low-income individuals or families. Medicaid programs and eligibility vary from state to state. (Wolgin, *Being a Nursing Assistant*)
  a. Medicare
  b. Medicaid
  (c.) Medicare and Medicaid

 2. Happy people are optimists. Optimists tend to have lower stress levels and better coping skills because of how they see the world and their positive outlook. Optimists are not necessarily unrealistic or unwilling to accept or face negative circumstances; rather, they choose to focus on what is right rather than bemoaning all that is wrong. They look for evidence that life is good and that they are doing all right. When misfortune strikes, as it does in everyone's life at some point, optimists recover more quickly. (Abascal, Brucato, and Brucato, *Stress Mastery*)
  a. coping skills
  (b.) optimists
  c. stress mastery

 3. In a recent survey of Fortune 1000 executives, 83 percent said their firms are working in teams or moving in that direction. Why are teams so important in today's workplace? One reason is performance. A recent study of 232 organizations across 16 countries and more than eight industries revealed that organizations working in teams experience the highest improvement in performance. Creativity is another reason that teams are important. Teams encourage creativity in workers through participative management—involving employees in the company's decision making. (Bovée, Thill, and Schatzman, *Business Communication Today*)
  a. today's workplace
  b. improving performance
  (c.) working in teams

4. Drinking appears to be most frequent among younger men at higher socioeconomic levels and least frequent among older women at lower levels. Members of the higher socioeconomic classes drink to excess less often; heavier drinking is found at lower socioeconomic levels and among young people (Kandel, 1991). When drinking is analyzed by occupation, however, a different pattern emerges: Business and professional men are most likely to be heavy drinkers, whereas farmers are less likely to drink heavily. Among women, service workers drink most heavily. (Kornblum and Julian, *Social Problems*)

(a.) patterns of drinking

b. youth drinking

c. drug use

5. Everyone copes with stress in different ways. For some people, drinking and taking drugs helps them cope. Others choose to get help from counselors. Still others try to keep their minds off stress by engaging in positive activities such as physical exercise or relaxation techniques. (Donatelle and Davis, *Access to Health*)

(a.) coping with stress

b. drinking and taking drugs

c. mental health

6. Today, probation is the most common form of criminal sentencing in the United States. The number of persons supervised yearly on probation has increased from slightly over 1 million in 1980 to over 3.4 million today—more than a 300% increase. Specifically, data show that 58% of all persons under correctional supervision in the United States as of January 1, 1999, were on probation. Even violent offenders stand about a 1-in-5 chance of receiving a probationary term. (Schmalleger, *Criminal Justice Today*)

a. criminal sentencing

(b.) probation

c. criminal justice

IDENTIFYING THE MAIN IDEA

A main idea is more than just a topic; it is more than just who or what the author is writing about. A main idea includes a **controlling thought**. A controlling thought is the most important point the author makes about the topic. The controlling thought answers the question, "What does the author want me to know or understand about the topic?"

Therefore, a main idea contains two parts:

1. The one general subject the whole paragraph is about, called the topic.
2. The most important point the author makes about that topic, called the controlling thought.

Together, the topic and the controlling idea—the **main idea**—tie all the sentences in the paragraph together. In fact, a main idea is often called the *umbrella idea* because it covers everything in the paragraph.

Identifying the Controlling Thought

Consider these two paragraphs. The topic in each paragraph is the same, but the controlling thoughts—what the author wants the reader to understand about the topic—are very different.

PARAGRAPH 1

> I found my first gray hair this morning. Clerks and cashiers are starting to call me "Ma'am." I didn't recognize half of the musicians nominated for this year's Grammy Awards and I actually blushed at the language in the movie we saw last night. Getting older is better than the alternative, but it certainly isn't any fun.

Explanation   Who or what is the author writing about? *Getting older* is the topic. What does the author want the reader to understand about getting older? *That it's no fun* is the controlling idea. Therefore, the main idea—the combination of the topic and the controlling idea—is *getting older isn't any fun.*

PARAGRAPH 2

> Whoever said "The best is yet to come" was certainly right. From a never-ending list of people to see, places to go, and things to do, I now have the freedom to choose what to do and when to do it. The friends I've made over the years are truly wonderful. Every day is a gift just waiting for me to enjoy it. Getting older has so many advantages.

Explanation   Who or what is the author writing about? *Getting older* is the topic. What does the author want the reader to understand about getting older? *That it has many advantages* is the controlling idea. Therefore, the main idea—the combination of the topic and the controlling idea—is *getting older has many advantages.*

To fully understand a paragraph, it is important to identify and understand the main idea, not just the topic.

Exercise 7   Identifying the Controlling Thought

In each paragraph the topic is underlined. Circle the controlling thought—what the author wants you to know or understand about that topic. When you combine the topic and the controlling thought, you have the main idea of the paragraph.

EXAMPLE   A variety of over-the-counter products are now available to help people stop smoking. One product is a special filter that reduces the amount of nicotine from each cigarette. There is also chewing gum that contains nicotine. It helps quitters slowly cut down on cigarettes. In addition, patches that slowly release nicotine into the body are available.

Explanation   The topic—what the paragraph is about—is *stopping smoking.* The controlling idea—what I want you to know about the topic stopping smoking—is that *a variety of over-the-counter products are now available to help.* Therefore, the main idea—the combination of the topic and the controlling idea—is that *many over-the-counter products are available to help people stop smoking.*

1. (Many people find it very hard to stop) smoking. Some are addicted to the nicotine. Others find it difficult just to break the habit of smoking. Still others are caught up in the social aspects of smoking. They want to fit in with their friends.

2. Weather (has a big influence on our lives.) It affects our everyday activities, our jobs, and our health and comfort. The weather often controls what we wear. Sometimes, it even influences where we can and can't go.

3. Looking for a *Star Wars* action figure or something to brighten up your living room? No problem. Just log on to your computer, join an auction, and bid for it. (There are hundreds of general and specialized) online auction sites.

4. The 2000 Arena Football League season (will be played) after all. Last week the owners canceled the season because of problems with the players' organizing committee. However, this week owners and players have decided to work out their differences. They will begin to negotiate an agreement next week.

5. Some say you see a bigger variety at the mall. Others prefer the supermarket. A few think the library is the best place. You also hear a lot about airport lounges and art galleries. The fact is, no matter where you are, people-watching (is fun.)

6. Technology (is rapidly changing the way we communicate.) In fact, the present era is called the Information Age because so many changes are happening so rapidly. In the nineteenth century, people began developing new forms of communication—the telegraph, the telephone, and the radio. In the last few decades, the invention of many more ways to store, retrieve, and transmit information has created an information explosion.

7. In Salzburg, Austria, (you can still visit the) places that were used in the movie version of *The Sound of Music* in 1964, starring Julie Andrews and Christopher Plummer. For example, you can walk through the Mirabell Gardens where Maria and the children danced around the statue of Pegasus, the winged horse, as they sang "Do-Re-Mi." You can also visit the Leopoldskron Castle that was used as the setting for the von Trapp family home, and you can see the Mondsee Cathedral where scenes of the marriage of Maria to the Baron were shot.

8. Today's households seem to have one thing in common: Nobody wants to make dinner. The stay-at-home soccer moms, the two-career couples, and the army of singles are too busy, too tired, or too unmotivated to spend hours each week shopping, planning meals, and cooking. But everyone has to eat. That is why deli, restaurant, and grocery takeout meals (are the food industry's fastest growing segment.)

9. Willie Morris's autobiographical novel, *My Dog Skip*, (is a nearly perfect piece of bedtime reading for kids and their parents.) Each chapter is a self-contained story. The descriptions of World War II–era Mississippi are lush and dreamlike. The activities of the central canine character, who is smarter, faster, and just plain better than any other dog, will capture the attention of readers of all ages.

10. The salt cedar, or tamarisk tree, (is a serious threat to native plants and wildlife across much of the Southwest.) One way it forces out other

plants and animals is by using large amounts of water. For example, one salt cedar alone can use 200 gallons of water a day, more than the amount used by a small family. It also adds large amounts of salt to the soil and rivers. The trees now cover more than 1 million acres.

Identifying Stated Main Ideas

In writing designed to inform, such as a textbook, an author often states the main idea in the first sentence of the paragraph. This is helpful because it clearly focuses your attention on the author's message and prepares you for the rest of the paragraph.

However, the main idea sentence—also called the topic sentence—can appear anywhere in a paragraph. It can be in the middle of the paragraph, tying the beginning and ending together; at the end of the paragraph, as a summary; or even split between two sentences in the paragraph.

No matter where the main idea sentence is located, your strategy for identifying and understanding the main idea is the same:

1. Identify the topic by answering the question, "Who or what is the author writing about?"
2. Clarify the controlling thought by answering the question, "What does the author want me to know or understand about the topic?"
3. Combine the topic and controlling thought and identify the main idea/topic sentence.

EXAMPLE 1   Read this paragraph and then practice the three steps: (1) identify the topic, (2) clarify the controlling thought, (3) combine them and identify the main idea or topic sentence.

> [1]A well-balanced diet contains all the necessary vitamins. [2]This means that most people do not need to take vitamin supplements in order to stay healthy and keep their body working well. [3]In fact, the body quickly eliminates many of these high-dosage supplements without using them.

Who or what am I writing about? (the topic): _____

What do I want you to understand about the topic? (controlling thought):

_____

Therefore, the main idea of this paragraph is stated in sentence(s): ____

Explanation   Who or what am I writing about? *Vitamins*. What do I want you to understand about vitamins? *A well-balanced diet contains the ones we need*. Therefore, in this paragraph, the main idea is stated in sentence 1.

EXAMPLE 2   Read this paragraph and determine the main idea.

> [1]Vitamins are organic compounds the body requires to work effectively, to protect health, and to assure proper growth in children. [2]Vitamins help us form hormones, blood cells, nervous-system chemicals, and genetic material. [3]They also help produce hundreds of important chem-

ical reactions throughout the body. ⁴Without vitamins, many of these reactions would slow down or stop. ⁵However, the complex ways in which vitamins act on the body are still unclear.

Who or what am I writing about? (the topic): _____

What do I want you to understand about the topic? (controlling

thought): _____

Therefore, the main idea of this paragraph is stated in sentence(s): ____

Explanation   Who or what am I writing about? *Vitamins.* What do I want you to understand about vitamins? *They are important, but we don't know how they work.* Therefore, in this paragraph, the main idea is split between sentences 1 and 5.

Exercise 8   Identifying a Stated Main Idea

Each of these paragraphs contains a stated main idea. The main idea answers "Who or what is the author writing about?" *and* "What does the author want me to know about the what or who?" For each paragraph, write the number of the sentence that contains the main idea.

1. ¹Adobe is an ancient building material. ²Peruvians and Mesopotamians knew at least 3,000 years ago how to mix adobe—three parts sandy soil to one part clay soil—and box and mold it into bricks. ³The Walls of Jericho, the Tower of Babel, Egyptian pyramids, and sections of China's Great Wall are adobes. ⁴So are more modern structures like Spain's Alhambra, the green mosques of Fez and Marrakech, and the royal palace at Riyadh. (Steinhart, *Dirt Chic*)
    The main idea is stated in sentence(s) _____1_____.

2. ¹The earliest device created to measure the passage of time was the sundial. ²It measured the sun's shadow. ³The water clock was an improvement over the sundial since it didn't depend on the sun. ⁴Once the art of glass making was perfected, the hourglass was created to mark the passage of time with sand. ⁵People created several ways of keeping track of the passage of time before the invention of the modern clock.
    The main idea is stated in sentence(s) _____5_____.

3. ¹Parents don't have total control over a child's life. ²They don't produce little robots who act on adult wishes at the press of a button. ³Children are also socialized by their peers, those of their own age group with whom they share experiences. ⁴In their peer group, children learn to play, compete, and fight. ⁵They practice grown-up roles, exchange secrets, interact with others, and explore the world. (Rose, Glazer, and Glazer, *Sociology: Understanding Society*)
    The main idea is stated in sentence(s) _1 and 3_.

4. ¹Drugs differ in the ways in which they affect the body. ²Some drugs kill bacteria and are useful in treating disease. ³Other drugs affect a particular system of the body, such as the digestive or circulatory system.

[4]Among the most powerful drugs, however, are the ones that affect the nervous system in ways that change behavior. (Miller and Levine, *Biology*)

The main idea is stated in sentence(s) ____1____.

5. [1]Eating healthy is easy. [2]Increase your intake of fruits, vegetables, and whole grains and reduce your intake of fatty meats and whole-milk dairy products. [3]Choose small portions of veal, skinless poultry, and fish instead of high-fat beef. [4]Make meats the side dish to pasta, beans, and veggie-based main dishes. [5]Also, steam or broil food instead of frying. (Lincoln Health Network, *Well Worth It*)

The main idea is stated in sentence(s) ____1____.

6. [1]Physical attractiveness greatly influences the early impressions that others form of us. [2]Physically attractive people are viewed more positively than are less attractive people, a phenomenon referred to by psychologists as the halo effect. [3]In a study by Bersheid and Walster (1972), subjects were shown pictures of men and women of varying degrees of physical attractiveness and were asked to rate their personality traits. [4]The physically attractive people were viewed as more sensitive, kind, interesting, strong, poised, modest, sociable, intelligent, witty, honest, more sexually responsive, happy, successful, and less socially deviant than were the average-looking people. [5]Although beauty is a factor in initial acquaintance, more substantial personal qualities become important later in a relationship. (Alexander, *Adjustment and Human Relations*)

The main idea is stated in sentence(s) __1 and 5__.

Exercise 9 ▶ Identifying a Stated Main Idea

Each of these paragraphs contains a stated main idea. The main idea answers "Who or what is the author writing about?" *and* "What does the author want me to know about the what or who?" For each paragraph, write the number of the sentence that contains the main idea.

1. [1]Communication occurs in many forms. [2]You can pick up the phone and have a conversation with your supervisor or leave her a voice-mail message if she's unavailable. [3]You can choose, instead, to write her a memo and send it by e-mail. [4]In turn, she can respond to your message in the form of her choice. [5]Your supervisor may decide to forward your message to other employees or managers, and they may communicate it to customers or outsiders. (Bovée, Thill, and Schatzman, *Business Communication Today*)

The main idea is stated in sentence(s) ____1____.

2. [1]Many things make a difference in a patient's behavior and attitude during an illness. [2]Some factors or influences are the diagnosis, seriousness of the illness, age, previous illness, past experience in hospitals, and mental condition. [3]Other things that might make a difference are the patient's personality, disposition, and financial condition. (Wolgin, *Being a Nursing Assistant*)

The main idea is stated in sentence(s) ____1____.

3. [1]Coffee, black tea, chocolate, and many soft drinks (especially colas) are very high in caffeine. [2]Caffeine is a stimulant that chemically induces

the fight-or-flight response in your body. ³If you are already having trouble coping with stress or with sleeping, caffeine will just make it worse. ⁴Limit or eliminate your intake of caffeinated beverages if you are under stress or if you have difficulty sleeping, or coping with the pressures in your life. ⁵However, low to moderate caffeine consumption (for example, one or two cups of coffee daily) can certainly help boost alertness and concentration. (Abascal, Brucato, and Brucato, *Stress Mastery*)

The main idea is stated in sentence(s) ___3 and 5___.

4. ¹The United States revolted to escape from the British Empire and turn its back on European power politics. ²However, in order to win the war, the new nation had to strike bargains with those same European powers. ³These alliances and treaties set the stage for national and international struggle well into the nineteenth century as Americans tried to establish a place for themselves in the new world political and economic order. ⁴Successful diplomatic relations with British and European powers were critical to the success of the American political economy, for they would make possible the new nation's survival and its prosperity. (Boydston, Cullather, Lewis, McGerr, and Oakes, *Making A Nation*)

The main idea is stated in sentence(s) ___4___.

5. ¹Spending for personal health care accounts for almost 88 percent of total national health-care expenditures, and hospital charges account for almost 41 cents of every dollar spent on personal health care (*Statistical Abstract*, 1996). ²As the population continues to age, the costs of nursing-home care and related services will continue to escalate. ³These escalating cost trends combine to make health-care expenditures an urgent national priority (White House Domestic Policy Council, 1993). (Kornblum and Julian, *Social Problems*)

The main idea is stated in sentence(s) ___3___.

6. ¹During the late 1800s, immigrants tended to concentrate in certain industries and occupations by nationality. French Canadians crossed the border from Quebec to the nearby New England textile towns, where they displaced many of the Irish. Jews from Russia and Poland entered the garment industry of New York, Rochester, and Chicago. Italians concentrated in the construction industry; Slavs entered mining and heavy industry; the Portuguese moved into the New England fishing industry. (Unger, *These United States*)

The main idea is stated in sentence(s) ___1___.

RESTATING THE MAIN IDEA IN YOUR OWN WORDS

To be sure you understand the author's meaning, it is a good idea to rephrase the main idea or topic sentence using your own words. For example, in one of the paragraphs about vitamins, you determined the main idea was a combination of these two sentences: "Vitamins are organic compounds the body requires to work effectively, to protect health, and to assure proper growth in children," *and* "However, the complex ways in which vitamins act on the body are still unclear." To be sure you understand the meaning of the sentences, you could rephrase them like this: *Although we aren't sure how vitamins work, we know our bodies must have them to stay healthy.*

EXAMPLE   Rephrase this topic sentence using your own words.

A well-balanced diet contains all the necessary vitamins.

Rephrase: _____

Explanation   One possibility is, We can get all the vitamins our bodies need with a well-balanced diet.

Exercise 10   Restating the Main Idea in Your Own Words

Each of these paragraphs contains a stated main idea. For each paragraph, write the number of the sentence that contains the main idea. Then, rephrase the main idea using your own words.

How students rephrase the main idea will vary.

1. [1]A variety of domestic and business applications form the foundation of personal computing. [2]Domestic applications include such things as maintaining an up-to-date inventory of household items; storing names and addresses for a personal mailing list; maintaining records for, preparing, and sending personal income tax returns; creating and monitoring a household budget; keeping an appointment and social calendar; and handling household finances. [3]The variety of business applications available today is almost endless. (Adapted from Long and Long, *Computing*)

    The main idea is stated in sentence(s) __1__.

    Rephrase: _____

2. [1]The Great Depression was a human disaster of colossal proportions. [2]Despair spread through every part of the country and penetrated every walk of life. By the winter of 1932–33 a quarter of those Americans willing to work were without jobs. [3]The plight of blue-collar wage earners, who had few resources to cushion them against adversity, was the worst. [4]Millions of factory hands and construction workers tramped the streets looking for jobs or waited in lines for handouts from charity organizations. [5]But hard times did not respect class lines. [6]Small business owners went bankrupt as their customers dwindled. [7]Lawyers had fewer clients; doctors and dentists discovered that their patients put eating before health care. [8]The sharp decline in building and construction left architects without commissions. (Unger, *The United States*)

    The main idea is stated in sentence(s) __1__.

    Rephrase: _____

3. [1]Firearms are the weapon of choice in most murders. [2]Ours is a well-armed society, and guns accounted for 65% of all killings in 1998. [3]Handguns outnumbered shotguns 18 to 1 in the murder statistics, while rifles were a distant third. [4]Knives were used in approximately 13% of all murders. [5]Other weapons included explosives; poisons; nar-

cotics overdoses; blunt objects, such as clubs; hands; feet; and fists. (Schmalleger, *Criminal Justice Today*)

The main idea is stated in sentence(s) ___1___.

Rephrase: _____

4. [1]As the twenty-first century began, it became increasingly clear that federal departments and agencies were having a hard time recruiting talented individuals, partly because of the lower wages and financial incentives paid by government, as opposed to the private sector. [2]There is a pay gap of 20–25 percent between comparable federal and private jobs. [3]Moreover, unlike the private sector, federal work rules provide few rewards for performance. [4]And, of course, stock options are nonexistent in the federal government. (Burns, Peltason, Cronin, Magleby, and O'Brien, *Government by the People*)

The main idea is stated in sentence(s) ___1___.

Rephrase: _____

5. [1]The forty to sixty nutrients necessary for maintaining good physical and emotional health include vitamins; minerals; amino acids from proteins; essential fatty acids from vegetable oils and animal fats; and sources of energy from carbohydrates, proteins, and fats. [2]Most foods contain multiple nutrients. [3]However, because no one food supplies all the essential nutrients in the needed amounts, the greater the variety in your diet, the less likely you are to develop either a deficiency or an excess of any single nutrient. (Abascal, Brucato, and Brucato, *Stress Mastery*)

The main idea is stated in sentence(s) ___3___.

Rephrase: _____

6. [1]We might be much better off to try positive adaptations to stress. [2]For example, physical exercise tends to prepare the body for stressful situations and creates a tension-relieving mechanism in some people. [3]Under a doctor's care we might develop a jogging program or a strenuous exercise program. [4]Some form of relaxation may also help us to alleviate stress. [5]Sitting quietly in pleasant surroundings or going for a walk in the park or the country are all ways of alleviating stress. [6]Cutting down on the amount we eat and cutting back or stopping the intake of caffeine or other stimulants may also be solutions to handling stress. (Adapted from Bittner, *Each Other*)

The main idea is stated in sentence(s) ___1___.

Rephrase: _____

LOOKING AHEAD

Unfortunately, authors do not always directly state the main idea of a paragraph. When this happens, the author wants you to add together the information from all the sentences and infer, or put together, the main idea. In Chapter 4, you'll gain strategies for making valid inferences and identifying implied (not directly stated) main ideas.

SUMMARY OF KEY IDEAS

- The basic unit of writing authors use to express their ideas is the sentence. Understanding individual sentences is important. Most of the time, however, you read groups of sentences that have been combined into a paragraph.

- A paragraph is a group of sentences that fit together to support and explain one main idea.

- Paragraphs typically have two types of sentences:
  1. one general sentence that contains the main idea
  2. one or more specific sentences that contain details to develop and support the main idea

- Key to understanding groups of words and sentences is figuring out how they relate to one another. One important relationship is the level of specificity—whether one word or idea more general or specific than another.

- The one general subject the whole paragraph is about is called the topic. The most important point the author makes about that topic is called the controlling thought. Together, the topic and controlling thought are called the main idea. A main idea ties all the sentences in the paragraph together.

- An author often states the main idea in the first sentence of the paragraph. However, the main idea can appear anywhere in a paragraph. In addition, authors do not always state the main idea of a paragraph.

- To be sure you understand the author's meaning, it is a good idea to rephrase the main idea or topic sentence using your own words.

Use Your Strategies 1

Answer the questions following each paragraph.

1. [1]AIDS is a global <u>epidemic</u>. [2]The World Health Organization (WHO) estimates that more than 7.7 million cases of AIDS have occurred since the beginning of the epidemic and that almost 22 million people are infected with the HIV virus. [3]It is estimated that 7 million to 8 million women of childbearing age have been infected with HIV; in fact, women represent 40 percent of all new cases, compared to 10 percent a decade ago. [4]About 1.6 million children have been infected, WHO estimates, mainly through <u>perinatal</u> transmission. (Kornblum and Julian, *Social Problems*)

   epidemic means ___widespread disease_____

   perinatal means ___before birth_____

   main idea ___sentence 1_____

2. [1]Your body movement and posture can send powerful <u>nonverbal</u> clues. [2]For instance, how you walk is often a strong <u>indicator</u> of how you're feeling. [3]When you have a problem, you may walk very slowly with

your head down and your hands clasped behind your back. [4]You may even pause to kick a rock on the ground. [5]On the other hand, when you feel especially proud and happy, you may walk with your chin raised, your arms swinging freely, and your legs somewhat stiff—with a bounce in your step. (Adapted from Barker and Barker, *Communication*)

nonverbal means _unspoken, body language_

indicator means _guage_

main idea _sentence 1_

3. [1]The population in the American colonies grew at a rate <u>unprecedented</u> in human history during the eighteenth century. [2]In 1700 there were just over 250,000 people living in all of the colonies, but by 1750 the population had grown more than 300 percent to more than 1 million. [3]The rate of growth was highest in the free population in the most <u>prosperous</u> farming regions. [4]It even grew rapidly among the slaves, in spite of the harsh conditions of their lives. (Boydston, Cullather, Lewis, McGerr, and Oakes, *Making A Nation*)

unprecedented means _record, more than ever before_

prosperous means _wealthy, thriving_

main idea _sentence 1_

4. [1]A mentally healthy person is likely to respond in a positive way even when things do not go as expected. [2]For example, a mentally healthy student who receives a *D* on an exam may be very disappointed, but she will try to assess why she did poorly. [3]Did she study enough? [4]Did she attend class and ask questions about the things she didn't understand? [5]Even though the test result may be very important to her, she will find a constructive way to deal with her frustration: [6]She may talk to the in-structor, plan to devote more time to studying before the next exam, or hire a tutor. [7]In contrast, a mentally unhealthy person may take a <u>distorted</u> view and respond in an <u>irrational</u> manner. [8]She may believe that her instructor is out to get her or that other students cheated on the exam. [9]She may allow her low grade to provoke a major crisis in her life. [10]She may spend the next 24 hours getting wasted, decide to quit school, try to get back at her instructor, or even blame her room-mate for preventing her from studying. (Donatelle and Davis, *Access to Health*)

distorted means _unrealistic, untrue_

irrational means _unreasonable_

main idea _sentence 1_

5. [1]E-mail can be as informal and casual as a conversation between two old friends. [2]But it can also <u>emulate</u> "<u>snail mail</u>" by using conventional business language, a respectful style, and a more formal format—such as a traditional greeting, formalized headings, and a formal closing sig-nature. [3]As with any business communication, how formal you make

your e-mail depends on your audience and your purpose. (Bovée, Thill, and Schatzman, *Business Communication Today*)

emulate means ___imitate, be like___

snail mail means ___traditional mail sent by postal service___

main idea ___sentence 3___

6. [1]The geographic setting can greatly influence the temperatures experienced at a specific location. [2]For example, a coastal location where <u>prevailing winds</u> blow from the ocean onto the shore (a windward coast) experiences considerably different temperatures than does a coastal location where prevailing winds blow from the land toward the ocean (a leeward coast). [3]In the first situation, the windward coast will experience the full <u>moderating influence</u> of the ocean—cool summers and mild winters—compared to an inland station at the same latitude. (Lutgens and Tarbuck, *The Atmosphere*)

prevailing winds mean ___main, dominant___

moderating influence means ___tempering___

main idea ___sentence 1___

7. [1]The Europeans who came to this country in the 1600s and 1700s settled in small communities where families and neighbors took responsibility for assisting the poor. [2]As farmers trying to survive in a new and uncertain world, most people expected hard times and saw both poverty and charity as normal parts of life. [3]Some colonists—especially the early Puritans in New England—looked down on the very poor, seeing poverty as a sign of <u>moral weakness</u>. [4]But, on the whole, early U. S. society held that people in need were <u>entitled</u> to a helping hand. (Macionis, *Social Problems*)

moral weakness means ___a human flaw___

entitled means ___it was their right___

main idea ___sentence 1___

8. [1]Some personality traits appear to be inborn. [2]They are acquired by <u>heredity</u>, passing from parent to offspring just as hair color and eye color do. [3]Other personality traits are shaped by a person's physical and social <u>environment</u> or surroundings. [4]Most personality traits, however, are influenced by a combination of both heredity and environment. (Pruitt, Crumpler, and Prothrow-Stith, *Health Skills for Wellness*)

heredity means ___what you are born with; genetic___

environment means ___your surroundings___

main idea ___sentence 4___

9. [1]The last quarter of the seventeenth century was a time of great violence throughout the colonial regions of the continent. [2]Much of the warfare was between colonists and Indians, but <u>intertribal</u> warfare and <u>intercolonial</u> rivalry greatly contributed to the violence. [3]It extended from Santa Fé—where the revolt of the Pueblos was the single most effective instance of Indian resistance to colonization—to the shores of Hudson's Bay, where French and English traders fought for access to the rich region of the north. (Faragher, Buhle, Czitrom, and Armitage, *Out of Many*)

   intertribal means ___between tribes___

   intercolonial means ___between colonies___

   main idea ___sentence 1___

10. [1]A strong self-concept leads to <u>self-confidence</u>, which has many important <u>implications</u> for job performance. [2]People who are confident in themselves are more effective in leadership and sales positions. [3]Self-confident workers are also more likely to set higher goals for themselves and persist in trying to reach their goals. (DuBrin, *Human Relations*)

   self-confidence means ___feeling of self-worth___

   implications means ___consequences, influences on___

   main idea ___sentence 1___

Use Your Strategies 2

1. [1]Life expectancy has increased <u>dramatically</u> in the United States over the course of the last two centuries. [2]Looking back to the earliest hunting and gathering societies, most people never survived childhood, and living to twenty meant reaching a "ripe old age." [3]Today, people in the United States think of twenty-year-olds as just reaching adulthood. [4]The government reports that males born today can expect to live seventy-four years while females can expect to live eighty years (U. S. Census Bureau, 2000). [5]By contrast, life expectancy in poor societies is much lower. In the poorest nations of central and eastern Africa, life expectancy is about forty. (Macionis, *Social Problems*)

   dramatically means ___significantly___

   main idea ___sentence 1___

2. [1]Between the ages of 18 months and 2 years, toddlers begin to produce words in two- or three-word combinations ("Mama here," "my toy") with a common quality: They are <u>telegraphic</u>. [2]When people had to pay for every word in a telegram, they quickly learned to drop unnecessary articles (*a, an,* or *the*) and auxiliary verbs (such as *is* or *are*), but they still conveyed the message. [3]Similarly, the two-word "telegrams" of toddlers omit articles, auxiliary verbs, other parts of speech, and word

endings, but they are still remarkably accurate in conveying meanings. (Wade and Tavris, *Invitation to Psychology*)

telegraphic means ___in the manner of a telegram___

main idea ___sentence 1___

3. [1]The United States was <u>predominantly</u> rural and agricultural in 1800. [2]According to the census of 1800, 94 in 100 Americans lived in communities of fewer than 2,500 people and four in five families farmed the land, either for themselves or for others. [3]Farming families followed centuries-old traditions of working with hand tools and draft animals, producing most of their own food and fiber. [4]Crops were generally intended for home use. [5]As late as 1820, only 20 percent of the produce of American farms was consumed outside the local community. (Faragher, Buhle, Czitrom, and Armitage, *Out of Many*)

predominantly means ___mainly, mostly___

main idea ___sentence 1___

4. [1]"You rotten, no-good, little punk, you never do anything right." [2]"I wish you had never been born." [3]A child who is constantly exposed to negative statements like these is likely to suffer from emotional abuse. [4]Emotional abuse, the nonphysical mistreatment of a person, can destroy a person's sense of worth. [5]When parents' attitudes are <u>hostile</u> and threatening much of the time, children do not receive the warmth and security they need. (Pruitt, Crumpler, and Prothrow-Stith, *Health Skills for Wellness*)

hostile means ___unfriendly, unpleasant___

main idea ___sentence 5___

5. [1]Despite the many advantages of goals, they can create problems. [2]A major problem is that goals can create <u>inflexibility</u>. [3]People can become so focused on reaching particular goals that they fail to react to emergencies. [4]Another problem is that goals can contribute to a narrow focus, thus neglecting other worthwhile activities. [5]For example, students who have established goals for achieving a high grade might be tempted to concentrate their efforts on the details they think will appear on a forthcoming test and neglect to review other beneficial aspects of the course. (Adapted from DuBrin, *Human Relations*)

inflexibility means ___inability to change when necessary___

main idea ___sentence 1___

6. [1]As a result of technological change, the building of machinery, and the <u>acquisition</u> of knowledge, societies learn to produce new things and to produce old things better. [2]For example, in the early days of the U. S.

economy, it took nearly half of the population to produce the required food supply. [3]Today less than 2.5 percent of the country's population works in agriculture. (Case and Fair, *Principles of Economics*)

acquisition means ___gaining___

main idea ___sentence 1___

7. [1]The health care required most by poor developing-world communities is not high-tech bypass surgery or chemotherapy; rather, it is the basics of good <u>hygiene and nutrition</u>. [2]It is simple activities such as boiling water to avoid the spread of disease, and properly treating infections and common ailments such as diarrhea. [3]It is helping mothers feed their starving children. (Adapted from Nebel and Wright, *Environmental Science*)

hygiene and nutrition mean ___cleanliness and proper diet___

main idea ___sentence 1___

8. [1]The term *cole crop* refers to several cool-season crops related to cabbage and having similar cultural requirements. [2]All cole crops <u>thrive</u> under cool temperatures and will survive light frosts. [3]Included are broccoli, Brussels sprouts, cabbage, cauliflower, collards, and kale, as well as several less common vegetables. (Rice and Rice, *Practical Horticulture*)

thrive means ___flourish, do well___

main idea ___sentence 1___

9. [1]Human beings are <u>not distributed uniformly</u> across Earth's surface. [2]Approximately three-fourths of the world's population live on only 5 percent of Earth's surface. [3]The balance of Earth's surface consists of oceans (about 71 percent) and less inhabited land. [4]In addition, the world's population is clustered in five regions: East Asia, South Asia, Southeast Asia, Western Europe, and Eastern North America. (Adapted from Rubenstein, *Human Geography*)

not distributed uniformly means ___don't live in equal proportions___
___across Earth___

main idea ___sentence 1___

10. [1]One strategy for reducing wage <u>inequity</u> that has been used for almost 100 years in many countries is the minimum wage. [2]The first minimum wage law was adopted in New Zealand in 1894. [3]The United States adopted a national minimum wage with the passage of the Fair Labor Standards Act of 1938, although many individual states had laws on the books much earlier. (Case and Fair, *Principles of Economics*)

inequity means ___inequality___

main idea ___sentence 1___

REFLECT AND CONNECT

A. Write a paragraph with at least four sentences on the topic "one way to be successful in college." Circle your main idea.

_____

_____

_____

_____

_____

_____

_____

_____

_____

B. List three tasks or activities you consider to be "active."

_____

_____

_____

List three tasks and activities you consider to be "passive."

_____

_____

_____

Consider the differences in your behavior when you complete activities on the two lists. What is one reason that effective reading must be an active rather than a passive activity?

_____

_____

_____

LOG ON TO THE WEB

Educational institutions often post instructional information on their Web site. For example, individual instructors often make lecture notes, study guides, and handouts available, and learning centers post general study strategy guides.

These sites have information about finding main ideas in paragraphs. Log on to one of these sites or use a search engine to locate an educational site with information about finding main ideas in paragraphs.

http://english.glendale.cc.ca.us/topic.html

http://www3.cerritos.edu/bettino/study_skills/main_idea.html

http://usfwebdev.admin.usf.edu/odt_dev/clast/topics/skills/literal/main.htm

http://www.public.asu.edu/~ickpl/Main_Idea.htm

Read the advice about how to find the main idea of a paragraph and/or complete the exercises.

Write down (1) the complete Web address, (2) the name of the institution that sponsors and maintains the site, (3) what you read and/or did, and (4) something you learned or something you knew that the information on the site reinforced.

CROSSWORD PUZZLE

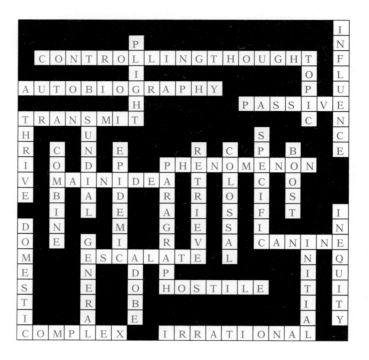

Across

3 most important point about topic

5 story of your life

6 sedentary

7 communicate

15 incident, unusual event

16 topic and controlling idea

20 dog

22 intensify

24 unfriendly, aggressive

25 complicated

26 unreasonable

Down

1 persuade

2 difficulty

4 general subject of paragraph

7 prosper

8 early device to measure time

9 limited, narrow

10 unite

11 widespread

12 recover

13 huge

14 increase

15 group of sentences with one main idea

17 imbalance

18 household

19 comprehensive

21 preliminary

23 ancient building material

Word List

adobe

autobiography

boost

canine

colossal

combine

complex

controlling thought

domestic

epidemic

escalate

general

hostile

inequity

influence

initial

irrational

main idea

paragraph

passive

phenomenon

plight

retrieve

specific

sundial

thrive

topic

transmit

CHAPTER
4 Understanding Implied Main Ideas

AN IDEA TO THINK ABOUT

You are walking down the street and you see smoke coming from the windows of a building. You see a fire truck approaching. What do you think is happening?

As you head into the movie theater, you notice that all the people coming out of the movie are smiling and laughing. How do you think they liked the movie?

In each situation you reach your decision about what to "think" by making an inference. An inference is a logical, reasoned conclusion about what you do *not* know for certain based on the information you do know. Some people call this an educated guess.

So, based on the smoke and fire truck, you can logically *infer* there is a fire. Based on the smiles and laughter, you can reasonably *infer* people enjoyed the movie.

You also make inferences when you read. Although you don't have clues like smoke or smiles, you do have the author's word and punctuation clues. What kinds of clues have you used to help you understand what you read?

CHAPTER 4 AT A GLANCE

In Chapter 3 you worked with paragraphs in which the authors stated the main idea: you could find one sentence or combine two sentences that accurately stated the main idea.

In this chapter you will practice strategies for finding the main idea of a paragraph when it is not clearly or directly stated. You will learn to add together all the information in a paragraph to reach a logical, reasoned conclusion about the main idea. You will *infer* the main idea.

First, let's sort out the meanings of two often-confused words: **imply** and **infer** . To imply means to express indirectly—to hint at, to suggest. To infer means to arrive at a conclusion from information—to arrive at a logical conclusion, to make an educated guess. Therefore, an author implies; you infer.

MAKING INFERENCES WHILE READING

You make several types of **inferences** when you read. For example, you discovered in Chapter 2 that you often infer the meaning of unfamiliar words. In this sentence from *Environmental Science,* Nebel and Wright do not state the meaning of *treks,* but they do give you information that suggests its meaning.

EXAMPLE   In Tanzania, women and girls in rural villages may have to walk miles to collect the water—often polluted—that they will use for drinking, cooking and washing. Similar <u>treks</u> of increasing length must be taken to collect the firewood for cooking.

Explanation   When you use the author's clue, "may have to walk miles to collect the water," you can infer that in this sentence *treks* means "long walks."

Using similar skills, you can infer an author's main idea. You can use what the author does say to arrive at a logical inference about the main idea.

You Must Be Careful

An inference is a *reasonable* conclusion—a logical guess based on what the author says. To increase your chances of making valid, appropriate inferences,

1. Be sure you understand what is stated. It's almost impossible to make a statement about what *is not known* if you are uncertain about what *is known.*
2. Make certain your inferences are based on and supported by the information the author provides.
3. Check that your inferences are not contradicted by any of the author's stated information.

UNDERSTANDING IMPLIED MAIN IDEAS

Like defining a word through context, to infer a main idea, you combine what the author says with your own knowledge. Inferring a main idea is not a wild guess. It is a reasonable conclusion based on the information you are given.

The following is a basic strategy for identifying an **implied main idea**.

1. Identify the topic. Answer the question, "Who or what is the author writing about?"
2. Identify the controlling thought. Answer the question, "What does the author want me to know about the topic?"
3. Combine the topic and controlling thought into a main idea statement.

Remember, the main idea is the overall or umbrella idea of the paragraph. So, if you aren't sure you have identified the main idea of a paragraph, try this: After each sentence of the paragraph, read your main idea sentence. If you have the main idea, your sentence will be more general than all the other sentences. Your main idea will tie together all of the sentences of the paragraph.

Consider these two paragraphs.

EXAMPLE 1   In this paragraph the main idea is not stated in any one sentence. However, when you add together what is stated—the topic and controlling thought—you can infer the main idea.

> [1]In the vast, dry Arizona desert, it's not easy to come by a cool drink of water, a natural swimming pool and a fishing hole all in one place. [2]But for thousands of birds, the area surrounding the Colorado River—the Imperial National Wildlife Refuge—provides just that. (Jones, *Taking Refuge*)

Who or what is Jones writing about (the topic)? _____

What does Jones want you to understand about the topic (controlling

thought)? _____

_____

Therefore, the main idea of this paragraph is _____

_____

Explanation   Who or what is Jones writing about? *Arizona's Imperial National Wildlife Refuge.* What does Jones want you to understand about the Imperial National Wildlife Refuge? *It provides a wonderful natural habitat for birds.* Thus we can infer the main idea is that *Arizona's Imperial National Wildlife Refuge provides a wonderful natural habitat for birds.*

EXAMPLE 2   Read this paragraph. Identify the topic and the controlling thought. Then, state the main idea in your own words.

¹It is estimated that the average American who enters the workforce today will change careers, not just jobs, five to seven times. ²This means that training for work should emphasize transferable skills, not simply specific knowledge and particular skills. ³Examples of nonspecific, and thus transferable, skills include time management, personnel management, and self-management skills. ⁴A specific skill, such as the ability to take dictation, can become outdated. (Alexander, *Adjustment and Human Relations*)

Who or what is Alexander writing about (the topic)? _____

What does Alexander want you to understand about the topic (controlling thought)?_____

_____

Therefore, the main idea of this paragraph is _____

_____

Explanation   Who or what is Alexander writing about? *Americans can plan on changing careers several times.* What does Alexander want you to understand about Americans changing careers several times? *The best preparation is learning general skills that can be applied to several careers rather than learning only job-specific skills.* Thus, we can infer the main idea is that *because Americans are likely to change careers several times, the best preparation is to learn general skills that can be applied to several careers rather than learn only job-specific skills.*

Exercise 1   Identifying an Implied Main Idea

The main idea in these paragraphs is implied. Following each paragraph are three possible main idea statements. Circle the number of the sentence that best expresses the main idea. Remember, the main idea answers both "Who or what is the author writing about?" *and* "What does the author want me to know about the who or what?"

1. The biggest challenges facing small businesses have traditionally been taxes, government regulations, and access to money. But a recent study finds a bigger problem in this day of low unemployment rates— a labor shortage. The Small Business Administration (SBA) study found that about half of small businesses are looking to hire someone and most of them are having trouble finding good people. (Small Business Administration, *Labor Shortages and Related Issues in Small Businesses*)

   a. Small businesses often have problems with taxes, laws, and money.

   b. The unemployment rate is at an all-time low.

   c. Currently, the biggest problem for small businesses is finding good workers.

2. Although quite reduced from previous years, Mexico still has a small population of wolves. Somewhat larger populations—perhaps twenty to twenty-five thousand—remain in Alaska and Canada. The largest concentrations of wolves still in the lower forty-eight states are in northeastern Minnesota (about one thousand) and on the Isle Royale in Lake Superior (about thirty). There is a very small wolf population in Glacier National Park in Montana and a few in Michigan's Upper Peninsula. Occasionally lone wolves show up in the western states along the Canadian border. . . . (Adapted from Lopez, *Of Wolves and Men*)

   (a.) The number of wolves in North America has gotten smaller over the years.

   b. The largest concentration of wolves in the lower forty-eight states is in northeastern Minnesota.

   c. About twenty to twenty-five thousand wolves remain in Alaska and Canada.

3. There's no question that word-processing programs streamline the writing process. But there's a tendency to give those programs more credit than they deserve. After all, a computer is pretty stupid. It's just a tool, kind of like a screwdriver. A good screwdriver does the hard work, but you still have to pick out the right screw for the job. It's the same when you use the computer as a tool to help you write. You still have to supply the key ingredient for good writing—the thinking that underlies it. (Chan and Lutovich, *Can a Computer Improve Your Writing?*)

   (a.) Although a computer can help in some ways, good writing still requires good thinking.

   b. A computer is just a tool like a screwdriver.

   c. A word-processing program makes some parts of the writing process easier.

4. Employees should have clear goals for what they are trying to accomplish in their jobs. Further, managers have the responsibility for seeing that this is achieved by helping employees to set work goals. These two statements seem obvious. Employees need to know what they're supposed to do, and it's the manager's job to provide this guidance. Simple? Hardly! (Adapted from Robbins, *Training in InterPersonal Skills*)

   a. Employees need to know what they're supposed to do in their jobs.

   b. A manager's job is to help employees know what they're supposed to do.

   (c.) Employees and managers both have a responsibility to set work goals, but it isn't always as simple as it sounds.

5. Individuals and companies are purchasing small, inexpensive microcomputers for a variety of business and domestic applications. The growth of this general area, called personal computing, has surpassed even the most adventurous forecasts of a decade ago. Some high-tech companies actually have more personal computers than telephones. (Long and Long, *Computing*)

a. Personal computing uses for home and business are more popular than ever imagined.

b. Companies are purchasing microcomputers for a variety of business applications.

c. The personal computer is more popular than the telephone.

6. Six billion is an enormous number, impossible to imagine in any context. Yet sometime during 1999 the human population on Earth reached and began surpassing 6 billion people. The United Nations projects continued population growth well into the twenty-first century, and there is no reason to doubt that our numbers may well reach 9 billion before the middle of the century—a 50% increase in 50 years. Virtually all of the increase will be in the developing countries, which are already densely populated and straining to meet the needs of their people for food, water, health, shelter, and employment. (Nebel and Wright, *Environmental Science*)

a. In 1999 the human population on Earth reached and began surpassing 6 billion people.

b. The human population is growing rapidly, and developing countries are growing so fast it is becoming difficult to meet the needs of all the people.

c. There will probably be 9 billion people on Earth before the middle of this century—a 50% increase in 50 years.

Exercise 2   Identifying an Implied Main Idea

The main idea in these paragraphs is implied. For each paragraph, write its topic and controlling idea. Remember, the topic answers, "Who or what is the author writing about?" and the controlling idea answers, "What does the author want me to know about the what or who?"

1. [1]At least 25 percent of the people in the United States suffer from stress overload at work. [2]According to a 1995 Gallup poll, 37 percent of American workers report daily job stress, while 75 percent reported significant stress at least once weekly. [3]A study by the National Center of Health Statistics revealed that more than half of forty thousand workers surveyed reported experiencing moderate to severe job stress in the previous two weeks. [4]A 1998 Gallup poll strongly suggested that stress continues to mount for American workers, as fully 80 percent reported being significantly stressed at work. (Abascal, Brucato, and Brucato, *Stress Mastery*)

Topic   stress

Controlling idea   Many people suffer stress at work.

2. [1]Death comes early in poor societies, where families lack adequate food, safe water, secure housing, and access to medical care.

[2]Organizations combating child poverty estimate that at least 100 million city children in poor countries beg, steal, sell sex, or work for drug gangs to provide income for their families. [3]Such a life almost always means dropping out of school and puts children at high risk of disease and violence. (Macionis, *Sociology*)

Topic   <u>poverty</u>

Controlling idea   <u>Poverty always has a negative impact on children.</u>

3.   [1]Some fruit trees—citrus, olive, and avocado, for example—require no pruning to change their shapes. [2]Most nuts also do not require pruning, and indeed many are so tall that it is impractical to do so after the first few years. [3]Most deciduous fruits—those that drop their leaves in the winter—should be pruned, however. (Rice and Rice, *Practical Horticulture*)

Topic   <u>trees</u>

Controlling idea   <u>Different trees require differing amounts of pruning.</u>

4.   [1]The loss of a job, a serious illness, a family breakup, or other family circumstances can lead to financial problems in the family. [2]If money problems are serious or long-lasting, a family may be unable to afford such necessities as adequate food, health care, and a place to live. [3]A growing number of families in the United States today have become homeless due to financial crises. (Pruitt, Crumpler, and Prothrow-Stith, *Health Skills for Wellness*)

Topic   <u>family financial problems</u>

Controlling idea   <u>Serious or long-lasting financial problems can have serious consequences.</u>

5.   [1]Many of us have fired off a blistering memo, made an angry phone call, or spouted off in a meeting while upset. [2]And many of us have had to eat our words. [3]If a situation prompts you to send an emotionally charged message, write or draft your thoughts but hold on to them for a day or two. [4]Letting the message ferment and then editing it carefully can help you avoid embarrassment and serious credibility damage. (Bienvenu and Timm, *Business Communication*)

Topic   <u>responding when angry</u>

Controlling idea   <u>To avoid problems, always take time to "cool off" before responding.</u>

6.   [1]It is wise to drink fluids if you are exercising or exposed to hot weather because dehydration can lead to irritability and fatigue. [2]Water also

helps aid digestion and flush toxins out of your system more quickly, including toxins built up by stress. ³All weight-loss programs recommend drinking four to eight 8-ounce glasses of water daily. (Adapted from Abascal, Brucato, and Brucato, *Stress Mastery*)

Topic   <u>drinking fluids</u>

Controlling idea   <u>Drinking fluids has many positive effects.</u>

Exercise 3   Identifying the Main idea

The main idea in these paragraphs may be stated, or it may be implied. Read each paragraph, write its topic and controlling idea. Remember, the topic answers, "Who or what is the author writing about?" and the controlling idea answers, "What does the author want me to know about the what or who?"

1. ¹A hockey player rushing up ice travels at more than twenty-five miles per hour; a slap shot hurls a frozen rubber disc toward a goalie at one hundred miles per hour. ²Everything that happens in hockey—passing, stickhandling, checking, shooting—happens fast. (Greenfield, "The Iceman Arriveth")

   Topic   <u>hockey</u>

   Controlling idea   <u>is a very fast-played game</u>

2. ¹Acadia National Park in Maine offers visitors a variety of wonderful scenery. ²For example, it includes a rugged coastal region of great natural beauty with the highest land on the eastern seaboard. ³It also includes most of Mount Desert Island, parts of Isle au Haut, and a number of other islets, as well as the tip of the Schoodic Peninsula. ⁴Wave-eroded granite cliffs characterize the coast. ⁵The inland portion of the park is forested with spruce and fir, and contains lakes and mountains carved by glacial action. (McGrath and McGrath, "Travel Treasures")

   Topic   <u>Acadia National Park in Maine</u>

   Controlling idea   <u>offers visitors a variety of wonderful scenery</u>

3. ¹Of all the skills we are taught in high school and college, few receive less emphasis than listening skills. ²Instead, we concentrate most of our time on speaking and becoming good senders of communication. ³But our success as senders is directly tied to our ability to understand the total communication process, and that involves listening. ⁴Listening

involves much more than just "hearing" what someone is saying. [5]In fact, being a good listener often requires greater skill than being a good speaker. (Bittner, *Each Other*)

Topic good listening skills

Controlling idea are very important to successful communication, yet we spend very little time learning the skills

4. [1]When you set a purpose for reading, you focus your attention on the specific parts of the assignment you need to understand. [2]Without setting goals you are saying that everything in the assignment is of equal value and that you want to learn it all in complete detail. [3]Although this total-mastery approach may be necessary in a few reading assignments each term, most times it will just lead to frustration and information overload. [4]Setting a purpose each time you read can make you more effective and efficient. (McGrath, *Understanding Diverse Viewpoints*)

Topic setting a purpose each time you read

Controlling idea can make you more effective and efficient

5. [1]There seems to be no limit to the number of individuals a single person is capable of recognizing. [2]An adult living in a large city probably sees millions of faces over a lifetime, and can recognize thousands of them, even if he cannot assign names to them. [3]Not even the passage of decades clouds the memory for faces. [4]Psychologists have shown people photographs cut from their high school yearbooks 15 years after graduation, and they were able to match 90 percent of the faces with the correct names. [5]Nearly fifty years after graduation the accuracy only dropped to 70 percent. (Brownlee, "What's in a Face")

Topic number of individuals a single person recognizes

Controlling idea seems to be unlimited

6. [1]What is a budget? [2]Put very simply, a budget is any plan—simple or complex—that expresses your financial goals and how you will allocate your limited resources to achieve them. [3]A budget can be so simple that you keep it on the back of an envelope and monitor your monthly progress with checkmarks. [4]Or it can be as complex as the one the federal government prepares each year, detailing how almost $2 trillion will be spent. (Winger and Frasca, *Personal Finance*)

Topic a budget

Controlling idea is any plan that expresses your financial goals and how you will allocate your limited resources to achieve them

Exercise 4   Identifying the Main Idea

The main idea in these paragraphs may be stated, or it may be implied. For each paragraph, combine the topic and controlling idea and write the main idea. Remember, whether the main idea is stated or implied, it answers both "Who or what is the author writing about?" *and* "What does the author want me to know about the what or who?"

1. [1]Led Zeppelin was an incredibly important band from 1968 until 1983. [2]The two most important members were probably Jimmy Page, recognized by everyone for his influence on rock guitar players, and the vocalist Robert Plant. [3]While Jimi Hendrix may be credited as rock's most significant guitar player and the first influence leading toward heavy metal, Led Zeppelin should be considered the first great heavy metal band. [4]Led Zeppelin has also influenced the mythology of heavy metal, since Jimmy Page believes in exotic philosophies; this clearly comes through in their song lyrics and playing style. (Brown, *The Art of Rock and Roll*)

   Led Zeppelin should be considered the first great heavy metal band.

   _____

   _____

2. [1]Tornadoes and hurricanes are nature's most awesome storms. [2]Because of this status, they are logically the focus of much well-deserved attention. [3]Yet, surprisingly, these dreaded events are not responsible for the greatest number of weather-related deaths. [4]That distinction is reserved for lightning and flash floods.

   Although tornadoes and hurricanes are nature's most awesome

   storms, lightning and flash floods are responsible for the greatest

   number of weather-related deaths.

3. [1]Online investing is fast, easy, cheap and puts you totally in charge—which gives it the appeal of a good video game. [2]If you use it sensibly, you'll invest more efficiently. [3]But if you forget that each mouse click is a real financial decision, you quickly can dig yourself into a hole. (Brenner, "The Smart Way to Invest Online," *Parade*)

   You can manage your investments efficiently online, but you can also

   lose your money quickly.

   _____

4. [1]A well-known proverb states, "The best potential in 'me' is 'we.'" [2]The underlying message in this proverb is critical for good team work: For you to reach your ultimate potential at school and/or at work, you must work with your team and not against it. [3]If team members focus only

on themselves and the credit they receive rather than focusing on the success of the team as a whole, both the team member's performance and the team's overall performance will suffer. (Adapted from Manz and Neck, *Mastering Self-Leadership*)

> For you to reach your ultimate potential at school and/or at work, you must work with your team and not against it.

5. [1]You are unique. [2]No one in the world likes exactly the same music, food, movies, books, clothes, colors, or people as you do. [3]While you may find a lot in common with others, you alone possess your unique personality. (Carter and Troyka, *Majoring in the Rest of Your Life*)

> While you may find a lot in common with others, you alone possess your unique personality.

6. [1]The *curve of forgetting,* discovered by German psychologist Hermann Ebbinghaus in the late 1800s, shows that our memory for learned material is best right after the learning session. [2]As time passes, we forget more and more. [3]This basic finding has been reproduced numerous times since Ebbinghaus discovered it. [4]For example, Jenkins and Dallenbach (1924) found that subjects recalled the most when they were tested immediately following learning. [5]In their experiment, the subjects learned a list of 10 nonsense syllables and then were asked to recall the list ½, 2, 4, and 8 hours later. [6]One-half hour following the initial training session, the subjects were able to recall half of the list; their performance became worse as time passed. [7]The *curve of forgetting* research is clear: You can expect your best recall shortly after a learning session. (Adapted from Davis and Palladino, *Psychology*)

> You can expect your best recall shortly after a learning session.

SUMMARY OF KEY IDEAS

■ You make a variety of inferences when you read.

■ An inference is a sensible, reasoned conclusion about what we do not know based on the information we do know. Some people call an inference an educated guess.

■ To increase your chances of making valid, appropriate inferences,

1. Be sure you understand what is stated. It's almost impossible to make a statement about what *is not known* if you are uncertain about what *is known.*

   2. Make certain your inferences are based on and supported by the information the author provides.

   3. Check that your inferences are not contradicted by any of the author's stated information.

■ Authors do not always state the main idea of a paragraph. When this happens, you must infer the main idea.

■ Use the following strategy for identifying and understanding an implied main idea:

   1. Identify the topic by answering the question, "Who or what is the author writing about?"

   2. Clarify the controlling thought by answering the question, "What does the author want me to know or understand about the topic?"

   3. Combine the topic and controlling thought into a main idea statement.

■ To be sure you understand the author's idea. It is helpful to rephrase the main idea using your own words.

■ If you aren't sure you have identified the main idea of a paragraph, try this: After each sentence of the paragraph, read your main idea sentence. If you have the main idea, your sentence will be more general than all the other sentences. Your main idea will tie together all of the other sentences of the paragraph.

Use Your Strategies 1

The main idea in these paragraphs may be stated, or it may be implied. For each paragraph, define the underlined vocabulary words and then combine the topic and controlling idea and write the main idea.

1. ¹You may think of communication only in terms of conversations with friends. ²But communication goes far beyond that. ³Communication is the <u>transmission</u> of information and meaning from one individual to another. ⁴The <u>central concept</u> here is meaning. ⁵Communication is only successful when both parties understand not only the information communicated but also the meaning of that information. (Donatelle and Davis, *Access to Health*)

Transmission means   transfer

A central concept is   primary idea

Main idea   Communication is only successful when both parties

   understand the information communicated and the meaning of that

   information.

2. ¹American artist Mary Cassatt (1844–1926) possessed both <u>superb</u> technical skill and great talent. ²Her dedication and devotion to the highest standards for her art helped her overcome the "handicap" of being a woman. ³As an American in Paris, at a time when Paris was the center of the art world, she absorbed the best innovations in her <u>contemporary</u> world of painting. [4]Cassatt developed an independent style based on precise draftsmanship, refined color sensibility, and a gift for creative compositions. (Slatkin, *Women Artists in History*)

Superb means ___excellent___

Contemporary means ___fashionable, present-day___

Main idea ___Even though she was a woman, Mary Cassatt was a___ ___distinguished American artist.___

3. [1]No matter how much we look at the events of our lives with <u>optimism</u>, we all find that troubles will at times dim our path. [2]Part of life involves dealing with disheartening events from loneliness, depression, or unfair treatment at the hands of others, to the loss of a loved one. [3]It is to our advantage to learn how to face these troublesome times in our lives. [4]Most important is for us to get past them and not to let their pain <u>hinder</u> us in such a way that we are too discouraged to go on. (Alexander, *Adjustment and Human Relations*)

Optimism means ___hopeful enthusiasm___

Hinder means ___stand in the way, block___

Main idea ___It's important to learn how to deal with and move past___ ___life's problems.___

4. [1]People travel for a variety of reasons: study, work, leisure, and to volunteer. [2]Regardless of the motivation, experiencing the world offers <u>immense</u> personal and professional rewards. [3]By <u>venturing</u> out of your safe, familiar environment, you gain insights about humanity and about yourself. [4]Your understanding of other cultures expands along with your self-awareness, important elements in developing a healthy worldview. (Carter and Troyka, *Majoring in the Rest of Your Life*)

Immense means ___huge___

Venturing means ___adventuring, going___

Main idea ___Travel enriches our lives in many ways.___

5. [1]A quiet but powerful revolution is reshaping the United States. [2]The number of elderly people—women and men aged sixty-five and over—is increasing more than twice as fast as the population as a whole. [3]Between 1970 and 1996, while the overall U.S. population rose 31 percent, the number of seniors climbed by 69 percent, and the number over age eighty-five <u>soared</u> by 167 percent. [4]This "graying" of the United States promises <u>profound</u> effects. (Macionis, *Sociology*)

Soared means   climbed, increased

Profound means   significant, extreme

Main idea   The United States will experience significant changes as

the number of people over sixty-five continues to increase.

6. [1]You can have the best coach in the world, someone who knows the game [tennis] inside out and is an excellent teacher. But he or she can only help to a certain point. After that, it's up to you to produce the <u>mental side</u>, to carry out what the coach has said. My dad taught me how to play the game, but I taught myself to win. <u>Embracing</u> his belief that the one who works the hardest will do the best started me on the road to success. (Evert Lloyd, *Chrissie: An Autobiography*)

Mental side means   psychological attitude

Embracing means   wholeheartedly accepting

Main idea   Although a good coach is important to an athlete's success,

the player must follow through mentally as well as physically.

7. [1]Understanding what someone is saying often involves much more than listening and speaking. [2]It is often what is *not* actually said that may speak louder than any words. [3]Rolling your eyes, looking at the floor or ceiling when speaking rather than <u>maintaining</u> eye contact, body movements, hand gestures—all these nonverbal clues influence the way we interpret messages. [4]Researchers have found that only 7 percent of the meaning of a message comes from the words spoken. [5]An <u>astounding</u> 93 percent of the meaning comes from nonverbal cues. (Donatelle and Davis, *Access to Health*)

Maintaining means   keeping, sustaining

Astounding means   amazing, incredible

Main idea   Understanding what someone is saying involves

interpreting nonverbal clues as well as listening and speaking.

8. [1]Vote-by-mail elections have stirred a growing <u>controversy</u>. [2]<u>Critics</u> fear that the process threatens the principle of the secret ballot. [3]They worry about fraud, and especially the possibility that some voters may be subjected to undue pressures when they mark their ballots. [4]Its supporters say that it can be as fraud-proof as any other method of voting. [5]They also cite this fact: The process increases voter turnout in local elections and, at the same time, reduces the costs of conducting them. (McClenaghan, *Magruder's American Government*)

Controversy means   debate, argument

Critics are   opponents

Main idea   Vote-by-mail elections have stirred a growing controversy.

9. ¹In the very distant past, life on Earth was far different from what it is today. ²Most people lived in small tribes and family groups that hunted animals and gathered plants for food. ³Because these groups were small and almost always on the move, their effects on the environment were minimal. ⁴Natural processes could easily <u>restore</u> <u>depleted</u> food sources and break down wastes once the humans moved on. (Miller and Levine, *Biology*)

   Restore means _rebuild, revive_____

   Depleted means __consumed, used up_____

   Main idea _Because of their lifestyle, ancient peoples had very little im-

   _pact on the environment._____

10. ¹Word processing is the perfect example of how automation can be used to increase productivity and <u>foster</u> creativity. ²It reduces the effort you must devote to the routine aspects of writing so you can focus your attention on its creative aspects. ³As a result, most word processing users will agree that their writing styles have improved. ⁴The finished product is less <u>verbose</u>, better organized, without spelling errors, and, of course, more visually appealing. (Long and Long, *Computers*)

    Foster means __encourage, promote_____

    Verbose means __wordy_____

    Main idea __Word processing is the perfect example of how automation

    _can be used to increase productivity and foster creativity._____

Use Your Strategies 2

The main idea in these paragraphs may be stated, or it may be implied. For each paragraph, define the underlined vocabulary word and then combine the topic and controlling idea and write the main idea.

1. ¹Because two of every three deaths and one of every three hospitalizations in the United States today are linked to largely <u>preventable</u> behaviors—tobacco use, alcohol abuse, sedentary activities, and overeating, for example—primary and secondary prevention are essential to reducing the incidence (number of new cases) and prevalence (number of existing cases) of diseases and disabilities. (Donatelle and Davis, *Access to Health*)

   Preventable means __can be avoided_____

   Main idea __Because many of today's diseases and disabilities are pre-

   _ventable, we need a concentrated prevention effort._____

2. ¹Throughout history, sports have been oriented primarily toward males. ²The first modern Olympic Games held in 1896, for example, excluded women from competition; in the United States, until recently, even

Little League teams in most parts of the country <u>barred</u> girls from the playing field. ³Such exclusion has often been defended by unfounded notions that girls and women lack the strength or the stamina to play sports or that women risk losing their femininity if they do. (Macionis, *Sociology*)

Barred means __kept from participating__

Main idea __For a variety of erroneous reasons, sports have traditionally__

__been oriented primarily toward males.__

3. ¹Not getting enough sleep can make a child distracted, easily frustrated and, in some cases, hyperactive. ²This last behavior might seem <u>counterintuitive</u>: When most of us get tired, we wind down, our emotions get quieter. ³But fatigue makes some adults and children more active, more intense. ⁴In kids, this behavior sometimes gets treated with drugs like Ritalin when trying to help them stay rested would be a better first step. (Wilkoff, *Getting Serious About Sleep*)

Counterintuitive means __contrary to what seems logical__

Main idea __of sleep can make a child distracted, easily frustrated, and__

__in some cases, hyperactive.__

4. ¹Americans today expend much less energy than did previous generations, perhaps as much as a few hundred calories per day less. ²All the "advances" that make our life easier—like e-commerce, drive-up teller machines and automatic doors—contribute to the current <u>epidemic</u> of obesity and related diseases. (Krucoff and Krucoff, *Healing Moves*)

An epidemic is a __widespread problem__

Main idea __Because technology makes our lives so much easier, we are__

__becoming inactive and overweight, with all the associated problems.__

5. ¹Safeguarding the world's diversity of species is <u>integral</u> to a sustainable future. ²Yet, as humans dominate and alter increasing portions of the planet, increasing numbers of species are threatened with extinction for various reasons, one of which is simple monetary gain. ³Illegal trade in wildlife is an estimated $2–3 billion a year business, with profits comparable to the drug trade. (Nebel and Wright, *Environmental Science*)

Integral means __vital, essential__

Main idea __Safeguarding the world's diversity of species is essential to__

__our survival.__

6. ¹When a university I was associated with faced hiring a new president, it hired an <u>interim</u> president to run the university during the search process. ²The person hired in the interim did not bring to the job the traditional credentials of a Ph.D. and academic experience. ³The individual had spent his career in business, not education. [4]But during the time he spent as interim president, *he listened.* [5]He listened to every level of the university from janitor to dean. [6]He listened to every constituent of the university from alumni to student. [7]He listened to every friend of the university from business executive to local civic leader. [8]A quiet person who dressed casually and undertalked every conversation, the interim president kept the university running smoothly. [9]Because of his ability to listen to others, the university experienced a tremendous "calming" effect during his tenure. That effect lasted long after he left. (Adapted from Bittner, *Each Other*)

Interim means   temporary, short-term

Main idea   The interim president's ability and willingness to listen had

a long-term positive effect on the university.

7. [1]A type of stereotyping that is <u>subtle</u> and rarely mentioned is physical attractiveness. [2]Psychological research shows that many people in our society equate character with looks. [3]According to the attractiveness stereotype, we view people who are attractive as "more sensitive, kind, interesting, strong, poised, modest, sociable, outgoing, exciting, and sexually warm." [4]Furthermore, we tend to assume that they will "hold better jobs, have more successful marriages, and lead happier and more fulfilling lives." (Adapted from Bucher, *Diversity Consciousness*)

Subtle means   restrained, understated

Main idea   Many people in our society equate good character with

physical attractiveness.

8. [1]The Civil War cut off the Texas cattle industry from its major markets. [2]During these <u>fallow</u> years the cattle ran wild on the Texas grasslands, and by 1866 there were an estimated 5 million head. [3]Meanwhile, the rest of the country, having depleted its cattle stock to meet the Union army's needs, was starved for beef. [4]In Texas cattle were selling for $4 a head, while in the eastern cities they were worth as much as $40 and $50 a head. (Unger, *These United States, Vol. II*)

Fallow means   barren

Main idea   When the Civil War cut off Texas' cattle industry from major

markets, Texas had a surplus of cattle and the price of beef dropped, while

the eastern cities had a shortage and the price of beef increased sharply.

9. [1]In a recent survey of Fortune 1000 executives, 83 percent said their firms are working in teams or moving in that direction. [2]Why are teams so important in today's workplace? [3]One reason is <u>performance</u>. [4]A recent study of 232 organizations across 16 countries and more than eight industries revealed that organizations working in teams experience the highest improvement in performance. [5]Creativity is another reason that

teams are important. [6]Teams encourage creativity in workers through participative management—involving employees in the company's decision making. (Bovée, Thill, and Schatzman, *Business Communication Today*)

Performance means _work output, productivity_____

Main idea _For a variety of reasons teams are increasingly important_

_in today's workplace._____

10. [1]"No higher-level job can be <u>obtained</u> without a good command of the language," says Steven Harwood, chief of nuclear medicine at the Veterans Administration Hospital in Bay Pines, Florida. [2]"Writing skills are the most important skills you can develop—especially for obtaining higher-management-level jobs. [3]You must be able to clearly communicate your ideas to others." (Carter and Troyka, *Majoring in the Rest of Your Life*)

Obtained means _gained, attained_____

Main idea _Being able to clearly communicate your ideas, especially_

_in writing, is vital to job advancement._____

REFLECT AND CONNECT

A. Select a paragraph from one of your other textbooks. List the clues the author uses to help you understand the paragraph.

_____

_____

_____

_____

B. In the past two days, how many times have you smiled at someone? How many positive thoughts have you enjoyed? How many times have you said something like "thank you" or "I appreciate your help," and how many times have you done something for someone else so that they could make a comment like that to you?

_____

_____

_____

Behaviors like these reflect your attitude. How important do you think a positive attitude is to your success in school, work, and life?

_____

_____

_____

LOG ON TO THE WEB

The federal government posts many consumer publications on its various Web sites. Log on to *<http://www.consumer.gov/health.htm>*, a resource on consumer health information about such diverse topics as aging/elder care, buying smart, choosing quality health care, outdoor recreation, and dieting and weight control.

Or, log on to one of these other consumer information sites:

http://www.consumer.gov/food.htm

http://www.consumer.gov/productsafety.htm

http://www.consumer.gov/yourhome.htm

http://www.consumer.gov/yourmoney.htm

http://www.consumer.gov/transportation.htm

http://www.consumer.gov/children.htm

http://www.consumer.gov/education.htm

http://www.consumer.gov/Tech.htm

Select one article and read the first paragraph.

Write down (1) the complete Web address, (2) the title and author of what you read, (3) the main idea of the first paragraph, and (4) one piece of information you predict the article will include.

CROSSWORD PUZZLE

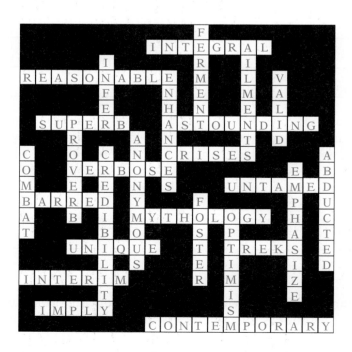

Across

2 essential

5 sensible

8 excellent

10 amazing

14 major problems

16 wordy

18 wild

19 prohibited

21 legends, fictional stories

23 one of a kind

24 long walks

25 temporary

26 to express indirectly

27 of that period in time

Down

1 agitate

3 illnesses

4 arrive at a logical conclusion

6 improves

7 well-founded

9 an old saying

11 unknown

12 fight

13 reliability

15 kidnapped

17 to stress or highlight

20 promote

22 positive outlook

Word List

abducted	emphasize	optimism
ailments	enhances	proverb
anonymous	ferment	reasonable
astounding	foster	superb
barred	imply	treks
combat	infer	unique
contemporary	integral	untamed
credibility	interim	valid
crises	mythology	verbose

read-ing (red´in) *adj.* **1** inclined ... ad or study **2**
reading n. **1** the act or practic ... erson who r
of books **2** a public entertainm ... which litera
aloud **3** the extent to which a ... n has read **4**
meant to be read **5** the amoun ... asured as by a
thermometer **6** the form of a specified word, sent

CHAPTER
5

Identifying Supporting Details and Using Relationships Among Ideas

AN IDEA TO THINK ABOUT

If authors wrote only main idea statements, paragraphs would be one sentence long. For example,

> A falling star is not a star at all.

If we could read only main ideas, we would have a lot of questions. For example, if a falling star is not a star, what is it?

Fortunately, authors add a variety of details to explain, expand, and support their main ideas. For example,

> A falling star is not a star at all. A falling star is a meteor. A meteor is usually the size of a grain of sand but weighs even less. A star, on the other hand, is a huge ball of burning gas that sends off great amounts of energy in the form of light and heat. Our sun is a star. Stars do not fall.

Details help us to understand a main idea. But, are all details equally important? Do you always need to remember all the details? If you answer no to either question, how do you decide what is important to remember?

CHAPTER FOCUS

As you know, a well-written expository paragraph has one main idea that is either directly stated or implied. The main idea is the general idea that unifies, or ties together, all the ideas and sentences in a paragraph.

In addition to the main idea, paragraphs have one or more specific sentences that contain details to develop and support the main idea. However, the number of sentences and the number of details vary from paragraph to paragraph. Therefore, to understand a paragraph, you must understand how each of the details and sentences relate to the main idea and/or to the other details and sentences.

To help you develop strategies to understand these important relationships, this chapter has two major, interconnected sections: first, understanding how the ideas and sentences in a paragraph relate to one another—in other words, differentiating among the main idea, major supporting details, and minor supporting details—and second, understanding how those ideas and details fit together, that is, identifying how the paragraph is organized or structured.

UNDERSTANDING HOW IDEAS AND SENTENCES IN A PARAGRAPH RELATE TO ONE ANOTHER

Early in Chapter 3 you discovered how important it is to understand the relationships among words and sentences. Specifically, you found that distinguishing among general and specific words and ideas helped you identify an author's main idea. Now, let's consider another important aspect of the relationships among groups of words and sentences: how details support and explain a main idea.

Because a paragraph can have any number of sentences, it can have any number of details. There are two general categories of details that support main ideas: **major supporting details** and **minor supporting details**.

A major detail is a specific piece of information that directly supports and explains the main idea.

EXAMPLE   In a previous exercise you determined that sentence 1 is the main idea of this paragraph about Acadia National Park. Now, consider how the other sentences in the paragraph support and explain the main idea "Acadia National Park offers visitors a variety of wonderful scenery."

¹Acadia National Park in Maine offers visitors a variety of wonderful scenery. ²For example, it includes a rugged coastal region of great natural beauty with the highest land on the eastern seaboard. ³It also includes most of Mount Desert Island, parts of Isle au Haut, and a number of other islets, as well as the tip of the Schoodic Peninsula. ⁴Wave-eroded granite cliffs characterize the coast. ⁵The inland portion of the park is forested with spruce and fir, and contains lakes and mountains carved by glacial action.

Explanation   Sentence 2, 3, 4, and 5 contain specific examples to directly support and explain the main idea that Acadia National Park offers visitors "a variety of wonderful scenery." Thus, they are called major details.

A minor detail is a very specific piece of information that supports and explains a major detail.

EXAMPLE   Consider the relationships among the ideas in the three sentences in this revised paragraph about the park.

¹Acadia National Park in Maine offers visitors a variety of wonderful scenery. ²For example, it includes a rugged coastal region of great natural beauty with the highest land on the eastern seaboard. ³The park's Cadillac Mountain is 1,530 feet above sea level.

Explanation   Sentence 1 is still the main idea, and sentence 2 still contains a major detail. However, the new information in sentence 3 is a specific piece of information that supports and explains "the highest land on the eastern seaboard" in sentence 2. Therefore, sentence 3 is a minor detail.

Authors also use combination sentences. A combination sentence includes two major details, two or more minor details, or a major detail along with its supporting minor detail(s).

EXAMPLE   Consider the relationships among the ideas in this paragraph.

¹Acadia National Park in Maine offers visitors a variety of wonderful scenery. ²For example, it includes a rugged coastal region of great natural beauty with the highest land on the eastern seaboard. ³The park's Cadillac Mountain is 1,530 feet above sea level and is largely composed of pink granite with forests of spruce and pitch pine.

Explanation   Sentence 1 is still the main idea, and sentence 2 still contains a major detail. Sentence 3 now contains three minor details—three specific pieces of information about "the highest land on the eastern seaboard."

In addition to major and minor details, some paragraphs include a **transition sentence** that connects what you have just read with what you are about to read.

EXAMPLE   Consider the relationships among the four sentences in this paragraph.

> [1]Acadia National Park in Maine offers visitors a variety of wonderful scenery. [2]For example, it includes a rugged coastal region of great natural beauty with the highest land on the eastern seaboard. [3]The inland portion of the park is forested with spruce and fir, and contains lakes and mountains carved by glacial action. [4]In addition to the wonderful scenery in Acadia, the park offers many opportunities for outdoor activities.

Explanation   Sentence 1 is still the main idea. Sentences 2 and 3 contain major details that directly support and explain the main idea. The new information in sentence 4 recaps the main idea of this paragraph and transitions to the main idea of the next paragraph—the many opportunities for outdoor activities.

Occasionally, a paragraph contains **irrelevant information**, or information that is interesting but does not support or develop the main idea.

EXAMPLE   Consider the relationships among the four sentences in this paragraph.

> [1]Acadia National Park in Maine offers visitors a variety of wonderful scenery. [2]For example, it includes a rugged coastal region of great natural beauty with the highest land on the eastern seaboard. [3]The inland portion of the park is forested with spruce and fir, and contains lakes and mountains carved by glacial action. [4]The park was known as Lafayette National Park from 1919 to 1929.

Explanation   Sentence 1 is still the main idea. Sentences 2 and 3 contain major details that directly support and explain the main idea. The new information in sentence 4 is interesting and important, but irrelevant to this main idea.

Although the relationships among the ideas and sentences may not be this obvious in all the paragraphs you read, you can use the same strategy to figure them out:

Does the idea or sentence directly support and explain the main idea?
If yes, it's a major detail. If no,
Does the idea or sentence support and explain a major detail?
If yes, it's a minor detail. If no,
Does the idea or sentence transition to the next idea or sentence?
If yes, it's a transition. If no, it's probably irrelevant to this main idea.

EXAMPLE   Look again at this paragraph on the devices people created to mark the passage of time. Earlier, you determined the main idea is stated in the last sentence. Now, decide the role of each of the other sentences: major detail, minor detail, transition, or irrelevant.

> [1]The earliest device created to measure the passage of time was the sundial. [2]It measured the sun's shadow. [3]The water clock was an improvement over the sundial, since it didn't depend on the sun. [4]Once the art of glass making was perfected, the hourglass was created to mark the passage of time with sand. [5]People created several ways of keeping track of the passage of time before the invention of the modern clock.

Sentence 1 _____   Sentence 3 _____

Sentence 2 _____   Sentence 4 _____

Sentence 5 Main idea _____

Explanation   Sentence 1 is a major detail because it directly supports and explains the main idea by giving the sundial as an example of "several ways of keeping track of the passage of time." Sentence 2 is a minor detail because it supports and explains the major detail in sentence 1 by telling how a sundial works. Sentences 3 and 4 are major details because they directly support and explain the main idea by giving additional examples of "several ways of keeping track of the passage of time."

Keep Your Purpose in Mind

Although you must understand the relationships among all the ideas and sentences in a paragraph, the number of major and minor details you need to remember depends on your purpose for reading. Even when you are reading to learn—to have a thorough understanding of the main ideas and the significant details that support and develop them—how many major and how many minor details you need to remember depends on the specific assignment.

Exercise 1   **Identifying How Ideas and Sentences in a Paragraph Relate to One Another**

The main idea is underlined in each paragraph. Determine the role of each of the other sentences: major detail, minor detail, combination of details, transition, or irrelevant.

EXAMPLE   [1]<u>Studies show that keeping a positive attitude pays off</u>. [2]Research has found that individuals with positive outlooks do better in school, their careers, and personal lives than pessimists. [3]In one study, for instance, insurance salespeople who had positive outlooks sold 56 percent more insurance than less optimistic coworkers. (Bruce and Foley, "Is It Time for an Attitude Adjustment?" *USA Today*)

Sentence 2 <u>major detail</u>

Sentence 3 <u>minor detail</u>

Explanation   Sentence 1 is the main idea. It tells us "what" the authors are writing about—keeping a positive attitude—and "what they want us to know about" keeping a positive attitude—that it pays off. Sentence 2 is a major detail because it directly supports and develops the main idea by giving an example of how keeping a positive attitude pays off: research shows people who have it do better in school, their careers, and personal lives. Sentence 3 is a minor detail because it directly supports and develops the major detail by giving an example of how they do better in their careers.

1. ¹<u>By staying on top of things from day to day, you can make housework easier and more manageable</u>. ²For example, teach the family the beauty of hanging up clothes when they take them off. ³Throwing them on the floor creates more laundry and more work. ⁴To save time, try cleaning a drawer or dusting the blinds while you talk on the phone. (Pinkham, *TIPical Mary Ellen*)

   Sentence 2 <u>major detail</u>   Sentence 4 <u>major detail</u>

   Sentence 3 <u>minor detail</u>

2. ¹<u>Shy people tend to lack social skills</u>. ²They avoid eye contact and are inclined to withdraw when spoken to. ³They show little interest or vitality, and they pause too long in conversations. ⁴Many have not learned how to meet others. ⁵For instance, they have not learned how to start a conversation and keep it going or how to end social encounters. ⁶Most shy people have social anxiety. ⁷For example, they fear being evaluated, embarrassed, ridiculed, rejected, and found inadequate. (Alexander, *Adjustment and Human Relations*)

   Sentence 2 <u>major detail</u>   Sentence 5 <u>minor detail</u>

   Sentence 3 <u>major detail</u>   Sentence 6 <u>major detail</u>

   Sentence 4 <u>major detail</u>   Sentence 7 <u>minor detail</u>

3. ¹<u>Tomorrow, a new wave of technologies will emerge that will continue to cause radical changes in our lives</u>. ²For example, if you're in the market for a new home, you will spend less time in the seat of a Realtor's car because you will be able to "visit" any home for sale in the country via computer from the comfort of your home. ³All you will need to do is select a city and enter your criteria to take advantage of the ultimate real estate multilist. ⁴The electronic Realtor will then list those houses that meet your criteria, provide you with detailed information on the house and surrounding area, then offer to take you on a tour of the house—inside and out. ⁵After the electronic tour, you will be able to "drive" through the neighborhood, looking left and right as you would in your automobile. (Long and Long, *Computers*)

   Sentence 2 <u>major detail</u>   Sentence 4 <u>minor detail</u>

   Sentence 3 <u>minor detail</u>   Sentence 5 <u>minor detail</u>

4. ¹<u>Everyone copes with stress in different ways</u>. ²For some people, drinking and taking drugs helps them to cope. ³Others choose to get help from counselors. ⁴Still others try to keep their minds off stress or to

engage in positive activities such as exercise or relaxation techniques.
(Donatelle and Davis, *Access to Health*)

Sentence 2 major detail   Sentence 4 major detail

Sentence 3 major detail

5. ¹Positive reinforcers are events or stimuli such as food, water, money,
    or praise that are presented after the target response occurs. ²For ex-
    ample, a real estate agent earns a commission for each house she sells;
    the commissions reinforce her for selling as many houses as possible.
    ³Your little brother is allowed to watch cartoons on Saturday morning
    after he has cleaned his room; as a result, he cleans his room every
    Saturday. ⁴You have been praised for receiving good grades on psychology
    tests; the praise should encourage you to study even harder. (Davis and
    Palladino, *Psychology*)

Sentence 2 major detail   Sentence 4 major detail

Sentence 3 major detail

6. ¹Every rock contains clues about the environment in which it formed.
    ²For example, some rocks are composed entirely of small shell frag-
    ments which tells Earth scientists that the particles came from a shal-
    low marine environment. ³Other rocks contain clues that indicate they
    formed from a volcanic eruption, or deep in the Earth during mountain
    building. ⁴Thus, rocks contain a wealth of information about events
    that have occurred over Earth's long history. (Lutgens and Tarbuck,
    Foundations of Earth Science)

Sentence 2 major detail   Sentence 3 major detail

Exercise 2   Identifying How Ideas and Sentences in a Paragraph Relate to One Another

Read each paragraph. Determine the main idea and write it in the space provided. Then, decide the role of each sentence. Label each sentence as main
idea (or part of the main idea), major detail, minor detail, combination of
details, transition, or irrelevant information.

1. ¹The demand for registered nurses (RNs) is on the upswing. ²Two of the
    reasons for the increase are our aging population and more hospital-
    ized patients who are older and acutely ill. ³However, as the demand is
    increasing, nursing school enrollments are declining. ⁴For example, en-
    rollments of nursing school students in entry-level bachelor's degree
    programs fell 4.6 percent in the fall of 1999. ⁵Most RNs in the United
    States are women. (Medical PressCorps News Service)

Main idea The demand for registered nurses is increasing, but the

enrollments in nursing schools is decreasing.

Sentence 1 ___part of main idea___   Sentence 4 ___major detail___

Sentence 2 ___major detail___   Sentence 5 ___irrelevant___

Sentence 3 ___part of main idea___

2. [1]Setting a specific, reasonably difficult goal improves performance. [2]A major reason is that when we guide our lives with goals, we tend to focus our efforts in a consistent direction. [3]Without goals, our efforts may become scattered in many directions. [4]We may keep trying, but without goals we will go nowhere unless we happen to receive more than our share of luck. (Adapted from DuBrin, *Human Relations*)

Main idea ___Setting specific, reasonably difficult goals improves___

___performance.___

Sentence 1 ___main idea___   Sentence 3 ___major detail___

Sentence 2 ___major detail___   Sentence 4 ___restatement of main idea___

3. [1]Many factors influence when we eat, what we eat, and how much we eat. [2]Sensory stimulation, such as smelling, seeing, and tasting foods, can entice us to eat. [3]Social pressures, including family traditions, social events that involve eating, and busy work schedules, can also influence our diets. [4]Cultural factors also play a role in how we eat. [5]People from Middle Eastern cultures tend to eat more rice, fruits, and vegetables than does the typical American. [6]The Japanese eat more fish. (Adapted from Donatelle and Davis, *Access to Health*)

Main idea ___Many factors influence when we eat, what we eat, and how___

___much we eat.___

Sentence 1 ___main idea___   Sentence 4 ___major detail___

Sentence 2 ___major detail___   Sentence 5 ___minor detail___

Sentence 3 ___major detail___   Sentence 6 ___minor detail___

4. [1]As people age, physical changes occur in the body. [2]These changes affect many body systems. [3]In addition, there are many role changes that occur in aging persons. [4]These work, family, and social changes affect many aspects of both physical and mental health. (Adapted from Badasch and Chesebro, *Health Occupations*)

Main idea ___As people age, the changes in their bodies and their roles___

___affect many aspects of their physical and mental health.___

Sentence 1 ___part of main idea___   Sentence 3 ___part of main idea___

Sentence 2 ___major detail___   Sentence 4 ___major detail___

5. [1]The key to a healthy, well-balanced diet is eating the correct amounts of a variety of essential foods. [2]These essential foods are divided into six groups on *The Food Guide Pyramid.* [3]If you eat the recommended number of portions of food from each group on the pyramid every day, your diet will be adequate for good health. [4]The number and size of portions will depend on the age, size, and activities of the individual. (Wolgin, *A Nursing Assistant*)

Main idea   The key to a healthy, well-balanced diet is eating the

correct amounts of a variety of essential foods.

Sentence 1 main idea   Sentence 3 major detail
Sentence 2 major detail   Sentence 4 major detail

6. [1]Your choice of a bank is usually determined by a variety of factors. [2]Perhaps the most important of these is convenience. [3]In addition, the range of services provided by the bank is also often considered. [4]Finally, what the bank charges to service the account and what it offers in interest on average balances must be evaluated. [5]Shop around to find a checking account that fills your needs best. (Winger and Frasca, *Personal Finance*)

Main idea   Your choice of a bank is usually determined by a variety of

factors.

Sentence 1 major detail   Sentence 4 major detail
Sentence 2 major detail   Sentence 5 irrelevant
Sentence 3 major detail

7. [1]Many people advocate controlling drug use through educational programs. [2]Designed to discourage people from trying drugs in the first place, such programs operate in the schools and target young people. [3]The most widespread drug education program is DARE (Drug Abuse Resistance Education), begun in 1983, which brings officers into schools to instruct children on the dangers of drugs. (Macionis, *Social Problems*)

Main idea   Many people advocate controlling drug use through

educational programs.

Sentence 1 main idea   Sentence 3 minor detail
Sentence 2 major detail

8. [1]Your body and the bodies of other organisms can survive only within a limited temperature range. [2]High temperatures may damage enzymes that guide the chemical reactions essential to life. [3]Low temperatures are also dangerous, because enzyme action slows as temperatures drop. [4]Subfreezing temperatures within the body are usually lethal, because spearlike ice crystals can rupture cells. (Audesirk, Audesirk, and Byers, *Biology*)

Main idea   Your body and the bodies of other organisms can survive

only within a limited temperature range.

Sentence 1 main idea   Sentence 3 major detail

Sentence 2 major detail   Sentence 4 major detail

9. [1]Wars disrupt the economy in two ways. [2]First, they interfere with ordinary processes of production and exchange. [3]Second, because wars are always expensive, they require some combination of increased taxation and deficit spending. (Boydston, Cullather, Lewis, McGerr, and Oakes, *Making A Nation*)

Main idea Wars disrupt the economy in two ways.

Sentence 1 main idea   Sentence 3 major detail

Sentence 2 major detail

10. [1]When giving an oral presentation, you may want to use a prop or model to engage your audience and help make your point. [2]Motivational speakers often use one prop as a symbol of their message. [3]For example, a speaker might use a glass of water ("your choice: half empty or half full") or a tennis ball ("it's in your court"). [4]Sales representatives often bring a model or samples of their products for the audience to touch or hold. [5]As you will see, there are also some things you can do to engage your audience and help make your point when you need to make a written presentation. (Bienvenu and Timm, *Business Communication*)

Main idea When giving an oral presentation, you may want to use a prop or model to engage your audience and help make your point.

Sentence 1 main idea   Sentence 4 major detail

Sentence 2 major detail   Sentence 5 transition

Sentence 3 minor detail

UNDERSTANDING HOW IDEAS AND SENTENCES ARE ORGANIZED

Because a paragraph can contain any number of sentences and have any number of major and minor details, authors try to organize them in a way that will best help the reader understand them. In textbooks, the ways in which authors organize information are predictable and identifiable.

Not every paragraph uses just one recognizable pattern of organization. However, when you can identify the way the author develops the details, it helps you to become a more active and successful reader.

For instance, if you determine an author has developed a paragraph using **compare** (similarities) and **contrast** (differences) you can actively look for the ways the author thinks two or more things, ideas, or people are the same and/or different. On the other hand, if you discover the author is using time order (listing details in the order in which they happened or will happen), you know to look for a sequence of times and dates.

Six common structures, or rhetorical patterns, used in expository text like textbooks are examples, comparison and/or contrast, cause and effect, process or sequence, classification, and definition. In addition, authors often combine two patterns.

Fortunately, identifying an author's pattern of organization is not a guessing game. To help you identify the structure and thus understand the relationships among the ideas and sentences, an author often uses common words, phrases, or punctuation marks as clues. Called **signal words**, directional words, and sometimes transitions, they signal a particular type of information or move you in a specific direction of thought.

There are many words, phrases, and punctuation marks that can be clues. For example, when you see phrases such as *in summary, in conclusion,* or *to sum up,* you know that the next information will be a recap or summary of the previous information. When you see words such as *central, principal, chief, major, main, key, primary,* or *significant,* you know to look for an important point.

Consider the words and phrases in these two paragraphs.

EXAMPLE 1   As you reread this paragraph by Alexander from a previous exercise, identify what kind of information the underlined phrases are signaling.

> ¹Shy people tend to lack social skills. ²They avoid eye contact and are inclined to withdraw when spoken to. ³They show little interest or vitality, and they pause too long in conversations. ⁴Many have not learned how to meet others. ⁵<u>For instance</u>, they have not learned how to start a conversation and keep it going or how to end social encounters. ⁶Most shy people have social anxiety. ⁷<u>For example</u>, they fear being evaluated, embarrassed, ridiculed, rejected, and found inadequate. (Alexander, *Adjustment and Human Relations*)

The phrase in sentence 5 signals to look for _____

The phrase in sentence 7 signals to look for _____

Explanation   The signal phrase "for instance" points out the relationship of sentence 5 to 4 (5 gives an example of 4), and "for example" points out the relationship of sentence 7 to 6 (7 gives an example of 6).

EXAMPLE 2   Identify the signal phrase Carter and Troyka use in sentence 3 and what it signals.

> ¹You make decisions every day. ²Some of them are insignificant, such as whether you wear a blue shirt or a red shirt. ³On the other hand, some decisions are crucial to your future, such as where you will attend college or what major you choose. (Carter and Troyka, *Majoring in the Rest of Your Life*)

The signal phrase in sentence 3 is _____

The phrase signals to look for _____

Explanation   The phrase "on the other hand" signals a change in direction of thought from the previous sentence. Sentence 2 is about insignificant decisions. Sentence 3 is about significant decisions.

Please remember, however, that discovering an author's organizational pattern or structure is not your reason for reading; you are just using what you can discover about the way information is organized to help you understand the relationships among the ideas and sentences.

Text Structure: Examples

Using specific, relevant examples or illustrations is one of the most common ways authors organize information to support and develop a main idea. Authors also often use examples in combination with other patterns of organization, such as definition and classification.

Words and punctuation that may signal examples include

for example
to illustrate
for instance
such as
specifically
namely
the abbreviations *i.e.* and *e.g.*
punctuation marks like the dash (—) and colon (:)

Words that signal a continuation of thought or list include

and
too
in addition
moreover
or
also
another
further
furthermore
as well as
besides
in other words
likewise

In this pattern the author may state the main idea in the first sentence and begin the second sentence with a word or phrase designed to alert you to the example:

An inability to cope with stress often causes serious problems at home and at work. For example . . .

You would read for details that give examples of the problems stress can cause at home and at work.

Or, the author may signal the examples in the topic sentence:

There are many examples of how most of our closely held beliefs are those we got while growing up.

You would read for details that give examples of beliefs we got from influential adults while growing up.

PRACTICE   Identify Manz and Neck's main idea and how they use an example to develop and support that idea.

[1]Most of our activities possess what we would consider both pleasant and unpleasant characteristics. [2]A runner, for example, can think about heat and sweat, sore muscles, exhaustion, blisters, and a score of other things most people would consider unpleasant; or, a runner can think about praise from others for his or her excellent physical condition, of a potentially longer life due to improved health, and the feeling of power and strength that accompanies a conditioned runner's stride. [3]Both types of thoughts are available to a runner, and the type the runner chooses will significantly affect his or her enjoyment of the activity. (Manz and Neck, *Mastering Self-Leadership*)

_____

_____

Explanation   The main idea is that the aspects of an activity we choose to focus on—pleasant or unpleasant—influence how much we will enjoy it. Sentences 2 and 3 give a specific example of how thinking about the pleasant or unpleasant characteristics of running will influence how much the runner enjoys running.

Text Structure: Compare and Contrast

To compare means to tell how two or more objects, places, events, people, or ideas are alike. To contrast means to tell how they are different. Authors can develop and support their main idea by giving the likenesses, the differences, or both the likenesses and differences between or among objects, places, events, people, or ideas.

By having us look at two or more objects, places, events, people, or ideas, authors help us see similarities we hadn't seen before or notice the unique features of each more clearly.

Words that may indicate comparisons or likeness include

similarly

like

the same as

compared to

in the same way
likewise
parallels
resembles
equally
just as
also
as well as
resembling

Words that may indicate a change in thought or a contrast include

but
yet
on the other hand
however
instead
nevertheless
on the contrary
unlike
in contrast to
whereas
in spite of
although
conversely
different from
rather than
just the opposite

Topic sentences such as these alert you to watch for likenesses and/or differences:

Despite the differences between a computer and WebTV, they are alike in some ways.
You would read for details that tell how a computer and WebTV are alike.
While both African and American Black music contain an absolute regularity of pulse, the character of the rhythm of the two musics shows marked differences. (Brooks, *American Black Musical Heritage*)
You would read for details that give the differences in the rhythm of the two musics.
Both oral and written communication involve the creation and sending of messages. However, they differ in a number of ways. (Barker and Barker, *Communication*)
You would read for details that give the differences between oral and written communication.

There are many similarities between watching a movie and watching a play. However, there are also startling differences.

You would read for the ways in which watching a movie and a play are the same and they ways in which they are different.

PRACTICE   Determine Stassel's main idea and what she compares and/or contrasts to develop and support that idea.

¹Since *A is for Alibi* was published in 1982, Sue Grafton has been working her way to Z, chronicling the adventures of Kinsey Millhone, a tough, unpretentious private detective. ²With 16 book completed and only ten to go, Grafton and her fictional alphabet sleuth have a lot in common. ³Both have an all-purpose long-sleeved black dress, which Millhone uses to blend in at cocktail parties, courthouse proceedings and funerals. ⁴They stay physically fit. ⁵Both are squeamish about needles, have a strong attachment to their purses and are expert at telling white lies. (Adapted from Stassel, "Grafton Keeps Mystery Alive")

_____

_____

Explanation   The main idea is that writer Sue Grafton and her fictional character Kinsey Millhone have a lot in common. Stassel supports and develops that idea in sentences 3, 4, and 5 with specific details on how they are alike. Both have an all-purpose long-sleeved black dress, stay physically fit, are squeamish about needles, have a strong attachment to their purses, and are expert at telling white lies.

PRACTICE   Determine Pirsig's main idea and what he compares and/or contrasts to develop and support that idea.

¹You see things vacationing on a motorcycle in a way that is completely different from any other. ²In a car you're always in a compartment, and because you're used to it you don't realize that through that car window everything you see is just more TV. ³You're a passive observer and it is all moving by you boringly in a frame.
⁴On a cycle the frame is gone. ⁵You're completely in contact with it all. ⁶You're *in* the scene, not just watching it anymore, and the sense of presence is overwhelming. ⁷That concrete whizzing by five inches below your foot is the real thing, the same stuff you walk on, it's right there, so blurred you can't focus on it, yet you can put your foot down and touch it anytime, and the whole thing, the whole experience, is never removed from immediate consciousness. (Pirsig, *Zen and the Art of Motorcycle Maintenance*)

_____

_____

Explanation   The main idea is "you see things vacationing on a motorcycle in a way that is completely different from any other." Pirsig's details in sentences 2 through 7 describe the differences between seeing things from a car and seeing things from a motorcycle.

Text Structure: Cause and Effect

Authors use cause and effect—reasons and results—to explain why or how something happened and the result of the action. Using a cause-and-effect structure, an author can examine the reasons for events or situations and their consequences, look at the known benefits or outcomes of a set of conditions, or predict the possible consequences of a given situation.

An author can begin with the cause and give the result, or can begin with the result and give the cause. There can be a single cause with a single effect, a single cause with multiple effects, multiple causes with a single effect, or multiple causes with multiple effects.

Furthermore, cause-effect can be a causal chain—where, like falling dominoes, an action results in an effect, which causes something else, which causes something else, and so on.

Words that signal cause include

because

for this reason

due to

cause

on account of

if [this], then [this]

Words that signal a result or effect include

as a result

since

consequently

as a consequence

so

hence

it follows that

therefore

thus

in effect

resulting

the outcome is

Topic sentences such as these alert you to look for a cause-and-effect relationship:

There are many reasons Americans are choosing to get less and less news from traditional newspapers and network television.

You would read for details that give the reasons (causes) why Americans are getting less news from newspapers and TV (effect).

Although it is difficult to predict all of the long-term effects of air pollution, a few are already known.

You would read for details that give the effects of air pollution (cause).

Three interrelated factors contributed to the demise of ragtime as a piano style (Brooks, *American Black Musical Heritage*).

You would read for the details that give the three reasons (causes) why ragtime music lost popularity (effect).

PRACTICE   Determine Nebel and Wright's main idea and how they use cause and effect to develop and support that idea.

[1]From the dawn of human history until the beginning of the 1800s, population increased slowly and variably with periodic setbacks. [2]The main reason for this slow and uncertain population growth was the often-deadly diseases, such as smallpox, diphtheria, measles, and scarlet fever. [3]These diseases hit infants and children particularly hard. [4]For example, it was not uncommon for a woman who had seven or eight live births to have only one or two children reach adulthood. [5]In addition, epidemics of diseases such as the black plague of the fourteenth century, typhus, and cholera would kill large numbers of adults. Famines, severe shortages of food, also took their toll. (Adapted from Nebel and Wright, *Environmental Science*)

_____

_____

Explanation   The main idea, "from the dawn of human history until the beginning of the 1800s, population increased slowly and variably with periodic setbacks," is the result (effect). Their details in sentences 2 through 5 give the reasons (causes) for the slow and erratic population growth: deadly diseases that killed infants and children, epidemics of diseases that killed adults, and famines.

Text Structure: Sequence or Process

Sequence and process are similar structures that use many of the same signal words. However, the kind of information presented is different.

Authors use sequence when they want you to understand the order in which something has, will, or should happen according to chronological, or time order, such as directions, instructions, or historical events. For example, authors of history texts often use sequence to help readers understand when events happened.

Authors use process when they want you to understand how a complex system works or develops. For example, authors of anatomy and physiology texts often use process to explain body functions.

Words and punctuation that may indicate a sequence or process include

previously

earlier

before

meanwhile

at the same time

simultaneously

while

during

last

later

next

after

afterward

eventually

in the past

in the future

at present

next

then

finally

eventually

following this

steps

at the start

to begin

initially

during the next hour, day, or year

specific times or dates

first, second, etc.

Topic sentences such as this can alert you to a sequence of activities:

The interview, like any research, is a time-consuming process that involves a number of steps.

> *You would read for details that give the steps.*

Topic sentences such as this can alert you to a process:

A caterpillar passes through many stages on its journey to become a butterfly.

> *You would read for the details that describe the stages.*

PRACTICE   Determine the main idea and the sequence of steps the details give to develop and support that idea.

[1]To bring out the beauty of a gem diamond, a number of processes are necessary. [2]These processes, which include cleaving, sawing, cutting, and polishing, are usually known collectively as diamond cutting and are the most exacting and difficult techniques of lapidary art. [3]The first step in cutting a diamond is the careful examination of the stone when the expert cutter determines the cleavage planes of the diamond and

decides how the stone can best be divided by cleaving and sawing. [4]The rough diamond is then marked with lines of India ink as a guide for the later operations.

[5]The stone is then firmly cemented into a wooden holder and the holder firmly mounted in a vise. [6]The cutter then holds a cleaving iron, an instrument like a heavy, blunt knife, on the line and parallel to the cleavage plane of the diamond. [7]The stone is cleft by striking the iron with a light blow of a hammer. [8]In present-day practice, diamonds are sawed more often than they are cleaved. [9]The saw is a thin metal disk, the edge of which is charged with a mixture of diamond dust and oil.

[10]The final step in the cutting of a diamond, called polishing, consists of forming the facets of the finished stone. [11]For the polishing process the gem is held firmly in a mount called a dop. [12]Diamonds are most often cut in the form of brilliants with a total of 58 facets. [13]Facets are formed on a flat, horizontally revolving cast-iron wheel that is charged with a mixture of diamond dust and oil. [14]The stone in its dop is held against the surface until the facet is formed. [15]In the course of polishing, the stone is moved many times in its dop to present new surfaces to be polished. (Adapted from *Funk & Wagnalls New Encyclopedia*)

_____

_____

_____

_____

Explanation   The main idea is "to bring out the beauty of a gem diamond, a number of processes are necessary." The steps in the process are as follows: (1) the stone is carefully examined to determine the cleavage planes; (2) the diamond is marked with lines of India ink; (3) the stone is firmly cemented into wooden holder and the holder firmly mounted in a vise; (4) the cutter cleaves (strikes) or saws along the marked cleavage plane of the diamond; (5) the gem is held firmly in a mount called a dop; (6) the stone in its dop is held against the surface of a flat, horizontally revolving cast-iron wheel until a facet is formed; (7) the stone is moved many times in its dop to present new surfaces to be polished.

Text Structure: Classification

Authors commonly use classification when they want to break a large subject into parts to examine how each part contributes to the whole. Additionally, when an author needs to bring order to a group of ideas, activities, or things, he or she often organizes information according to parts, characteristics, functions, or types. An author can also use classification to divide things into categories, or groups, with several individual units within each group.

The main idea usually identifies what will be classified and often tells how many groups will be considered.

Words that can signal that the information is divided or classified include categories

classifications

groups

classes

ways

elements

features

methods

kinds

types

parts

factors

issues

reasons

sorts

numbered elements or lists

Topic sentences such as these alert you to division or classification of information:

Before you can create a healthy menu, you must understand the three essential elements of a healthy diet.

You would read to find out the three essential elements.

Mutual funds are broadly divided into three classes according to their investment objectives.

You would read to find out the three classes of investment objectives.

PRACTICE   Determine the main idea and how details are developed to support that idea.

[1]To write an effective mystery, you must first decide what type of mystery you really want to write. [2]This is because "mystery" is only an umbrella term for a type of fiction with several subcategories. [3]A mystery can be a detective story, a police procedural, or a romantic suspense. [4]It could also be a spy story like the fast-paced, sexually charged work of Ian Fleming, who created the British secret service agent James Bond. [5]Another subcategory is the adventure novel, such as Clive Cussler's *Serpent*. [6]Still another type of mystery story is based on actual events never fully resolved by the authorities. (McGrath, *Magazine Article Writing Handbook*)

———————————————————

———————————————————

Explanation   The main idea is, "to write an effective mystery, you must first decide what type of mystery you really want to write." To develop and support that idea, the large category of "mysteries" is divided into six subcategories:

detective story, police procedural, romantic suspense, spy story, adventure novel, and unresolved actual events.

Text Structure: Definition

Authors often need to clarify a definition or explain their personal interpretation of the meaning of a term or concept. Rarely, however, do they just state a definition. To help readers fully understand a term or concept, they usually define through combinations of one or more dictionary definitions, one or more connotative meanings, the etymology, comparisons and/or contrasts with other terms, examples, and negation—telling what it doesn't mean.

Words that may signal definition include

define as

is

known

the term means

is stated as

is used to mean

Topic sentences such as these alert you to watch for definitions:

The first definition of communicate in the dictionary states that it is "to make known, impart; transmit." Now, let us look at other possible definitions. (Adapted from Bittner, *Each Other*)

You would read for details that give additional definitions for communicate.

The word *diet* has many meanings.

You would read for details that give various meanings of the word diet.

PRACTICE   Determine the main idea and how the details develop and support that idea.

[1]Sexual harassment is defined by federal regulations as "unwelcome sexual advances, requests for sexual favors, and other verbal and physical contact of a sexual nature." [2]However, there are as many different definitions of what constitutes sexual harassment in the workplace as there are workers. [3]To some, an offensive comment or joke is sexual harassment. [4]Some define it as sexually explicit pictures or written material, while others interpret sexual harassment to mean inappropriate physical contact.

_____

_____

Explanation   The main idea is that although there is an official definition, there are probably as many different definitions of what constitutes sexual harassment in the workplace as there are workers. The author provides the official definition in sentence 1 and three additional definitions in sentences 2, 3, and 4.

Combination of Text Structures

For the purpose of learning about the ways authors structure information, it's useful to practice on paragraphs that have one primary pattern of organization. However, in real reading situations authors often combine structures to develop their paragraphs. As you'll see in the next chapter, they almost always use a combination of structures to develop multiparagraph selections such as a chapter. This means that most of the paragraphs and multiparagraph selections you read will use a combination of patterns such as examples of likenesses and differences, a definition that clarifies a cause or an effect, and a time sequence that helps you understand the classification of an issue.

This is why it is important to remember that your goal in understanding the structure is to use it as a clue to understanding the ideas and details you need.

PRACTICE   Determine DuBrin's main idea and how he develops and supports that idea.

> [1]One of the major consequences of high self-esteem is good mental health. [2]People with high self-esteem feel good about themselves and have a positive outlook on life. [3]For example, a person with high self-esteem will probably shrug off a negative comment about their appearance as simply being the other person's point of view. [4]On the other hand, a person with low self-esteem might crumble if somebody insulted his or her appearance. [5]If faced with an everyday setback such as losing keys, the high self-esteem person might think, "I have so much going for me, why fall apart over this incident?" whereas the low self-esteem person would fall apart. (Adapted from DuBrin, *Human Relations for Career and Personal Success*)

Explanation   The main idea, "one of the major consequences of high self-esteem is good mental health," states a cause and effect. The cause, high self-esteem, results in good mental health. To develop and support the idea, DuBrin gives examples that compare how high self-esteem people and low self-esteem people would handle the same situation.

PRACTICE   Identify Callwood's main idea and how she develops and supports that idea.

> [1]We have many examples to support the view that the Canadians were much more law-abiding than the Americans during the Klondike gold rush. [2]For instance, the American town of Skagway in the Alaskan panhandle was run by a ruthless American gangster and miners were often robbed of their gold on main street in broad daylight. [3]Across the border in Canada, Yukon mining towns were so law-abiding that a miner could leave his gold in an unlocked cabin. (Adapted from Callwood, "Portrait of Canada")

Explanation   The main idea is "the Canadians were much more law abiding than the Americans during the Klondike gold rush." To develop and support that idea, Callwood gives an example that compares how a miner would be treated in both areas: he would be robbed of his gold by the lawless Americans; his gold would be safe with the law-abiding Canadians.

Exercise 3   **Using Signal Words, Phrases, and Punctuation**

Circle the letter of the term that best describes what the underlined word, phrase, or punctuation signals.

1. Both oral and written communication involve the creation and sending of messages. <u>However</u>, they differ in a number of ways. (Barker and Barker, *Communication*)

   a. continuation of thought   **c.** definition
   (b.) change in direction of thought   **d.** example

2. By law, a learning disability <u>is defined as</u> a significant gap between a person's intelligence and the skills the person has achieved at each age. (National Institute of Mental Health, *Learning Disabilities*)

   a. change in direction of thought   **(c.)** definition
   b. summary   **d.** effect

3. <u>In short</u>, the goal of this book is to develop a framework to help you motivate yourself to achieve your personal goals. . . . (Manz and Neck, *Mastering Self-Leadership*)

   a. cause   **c.** continuation of thought
   (b.) summary   **d.** example

4. The roots of rock and roll can be found in the basic popular forms of music in the United States<u>—folk, jazz, and pop</u>. (Brown, *Rock and Roll*)

   a. classification   **c.** process
   (b.) examples   **d.** change in direction of thought

5. <u>Like</u> Lincoln, Johnson was an ambitious self-made man from southern yeoman stock. (Unger, *These United States*)

   (a.) comparison   **c.** definition
   b. contrast   **d.** effect

6. The self-concept, or the way a person thinks about himself or herself in an overall sense, is an important part of personality development. A successful person—one who is achieving his or her goals in work or personal life—usually has a positive self-concept. <u>In contrast</u>, an unsuccessful person often has a negative self-concept. (DuBrin, *Human Relations*)

   a. comparison   **c.** cause
   (b.) contrast   **d.** process

7. [1]Many plants begin life as germinating seeds. [2]Germination <u>starts when</u> the seed absorbs water and <u>ends when</u> the primary root emerges. [3]<u>After</u> germination, the seedling goes through a period called establishment, which lasts until the seedling is independent. (Rice and Rice, *Practical Horticulture*)

    a. comparison   **c.** example
    b. contrast   **(d.)** process

8. Selecting subjects is only the first step in carrying out a survey. <u>Also</u> needed is a plan for asking questions and recording answers. (Macionis, *Sociology*)

    (a.) continuation of thought   **c.** definition
    b. change in direction of thought   **d.** effect

9. One quality that is important for a successful marriage is a couple's commitment to one another. The <u>term</u> commitment <u>means</u> the determination to develop a fulfilling relationship. (Pruitt, Crumpler, and Prothrow-Stith, *Health Skills for Wellness*)

    a. continuation of thought   **(c.)** definition
    b. change in direction of thought   **d.** example

10. Physiologist Nathaniel Kleitman spent his entire career studying sleep. <u>As a result</u> of his research, today we know that during sleep, periods of rapid eye movement (REM) alternate with periods of fewer eye movements, or non-REM, in a cycle that recurs every 90 minutes or so. (Wade and Tavris, *Invitation to Psychology*)

    a. cause   **c.** continuation of thought
    b. summary   **(d.)** effect

Exercise 4   **Using Signal Words, Phrases, and Punctuation**

Identify the signal word, phrase, or punctuation the author uses and tell what it signals.

1. [1]Congress can exercise considerable control over the states by attaching federal money to certain federal mandates. [2]States may be required to create programs that accord with federal policy goals. [3]For example, a program to increase employment might have a provision setting aside 10 percent of the grant for minority hirings, or a national health grant may place restrictions on teenage smoking. (Berman and Murphy, *Approaching Democracy*)

The signal phrase in sentence 3 is <u>for example</u>

It signals <u>examples of programs states might be required to create</u>
<u>that accord with federal policy goals.</u>

2. [1]We begin by studying a communication model and the three types of communication important to our study in this text: intrapersonal, interpersonal, and mass communication. (Bittner, *Each Other*)

    The signal punctuation is <u>colon</u>

    It signals <u>three types of communication</u>

    _____

3. [1]Watching television is an especially significant popular custom for two reasons. [2]First, it is the most popular leisure activity in developed countries throughout the world. [3]Second, television is the most important way by which knowledge of popular customs, such as professional sports, is rapidly spread across Earth's surface. (Rubenstein, *Introduction to Human Geography*)

    The signal word in sentence 2 is <u>first</u>

    It signals <u>first reason watching television is an especially significant</u>

     <u>popular custom.</u>

    The signal word in sentence 3 is <u>second</u>

    It signals <u>second reason watching television is an especially</u>

     <u>significant popular custom.</u>

4. [1]Consumers are demanding more organic-friendly building materials and "green" woods (not endangered) and leading manufacturers and retailers are responding. [2]For example, Home Depot stores sell only woods from managed forests. (Universal Press Syndicate, "Consumer Buying Habits are Changing")

    The signal phrase in sentence 2 is <u>for example</u>

    It signals <u>example of how a retailer is responding to consumer</u>

     <u>demand for more organic-friendly and green woods.</u>

5. [1]Downhill skiing and snowboarding, the flashiest winter sports, attract more than 11 million participants a year. [2]But other cold-weather activities are getting their fair share of enthusiasts, too. [3]For example, in 1998, 7.8 million Americans ice skated, and 2.6 million Americans went cross-country skiing. (Doheny, "Winter Sports," *LA Times*)

    The signal word in sentence 2 is <u>but</u>

    It signals <u>information that downhill skiing and snowboarding are not</u>

     <u>the only popular winter sports.</u>

    The signal phrase in sentence 3 is <u>for example</u>

    It signals <u>examples of other popular cold-weather activities.</u>

    _____

6. [1]The number of violent crimes reported to the police do not reflect the actual amount of violent crime in society. [2]This is because many crimes are never reported to police. (Davis and Palladino, *Psychology*)

The signal phrase in sentence 2 is __this is because_____

It signals __reason why the number of violent crimes reported to the__

__police do not reflect the actual amount of violent crime in society.__

7. [1]In what ways might a computer and the human memory be alike? [2]Like the computer, human memory has been characterized as an information-processing system that has three separate stages—an input or encoding stage, a storage stage, and a retrieval stage during which an already stored memory is called into consciousness. [3]Let's take a closer look at each of these stages. (Davis and Palladino, *Psychology*)

The signal word in sentence 2 is __like_____

It signals __how a computer and human memory are alike._____

_____

8. [1]Exercise is a significant contributor to stress management. [2]Exercise reduces stress by raising levels of endorphins, mood-elevating, pain-killing hormones, in the blood stream. [3]As a result, exercise often increases energy, reduces hostility, and improves mental alertness. (Donatelle and Davis, *Access to Health*)

The signal phrase in sentence 3 is __as a result_____

It signals __results of exercise._____

_____

9. [1]If we compare Notre-Dame Cathedral in Paris with St-Étienne Cathedral at Caen we see that they share some basic features. [2]These include the pier buttresses that reinforce the corners of the towers, the placing of the portals, and the three-story arrangement. (Janson and Janson, *A Basic History of Art*)

The signal word in sentence 1 is __compare_____

It signals __ways the two cathedrals are alike._____

_____

10. [1]In general, try to state your message without using words that might hurt or offend your audience. [2]Substitute euphemisms (mild terms) for those that have unpleasant connotations. [3]You can be honest without being harsh. [4]Gentle language won't change the facts, but will make them more acceptable. [5]On the other hand, don't carry euphemisms to extremes. (Bovée, Thill, and Schatzman, *Business Communication Today*)

The signal phrase in sentence 5 is __on the other hand_____

It signals __a contrasting thought._____

_____

Exercise 5   **Determining Relationships Among Ideas and Sentences**

Read each paragraph and answer the questions.

EXAMPLE   [1]Physical noise may interrupt the communication process. [2]For example, if a truck goes by when Sally and Jim are speaking and they do not hear each other, that would be an example of physical noise. [3]Perhaps it starts to rain and they need to interrupt the conversation to take cover. [4]That would also be physical noise. (Adapted from Bittner, *Each Other*)

Explanation

    a. Main idea: Physical noise is sound that may interfere with conversations.

    b. What are two examples of how physical noise can interfere with conversations? (1) a passing truck preventing people from hearing each other, (2) a sudden rain forcing people to stop talking and take cover

    c. Primary structure: example

  1. [1]Andrew Johnson lacked Abraham Lincoln's winning personal qualities. [2]Lincoln was confident in his own abilities. [3]Johnson suffered from severe self-doubts, a weakness that made him open to flattery. [4]Lincoln was friendly and enjoyed people. [5]Johnson was a loner with few friends or close advisers. [6]Lincoln was flexible, a natural compromiser. [7]Johnson was a rigid man who could be sweet-talked out of a position, but when defied directly, refused to budge. (Adapted from Unger, *These United States*)

    a. Main idea   <u>Andrew Johnson lacked Abraham Lincoln's winning</u>

      <u>personal qualities.</u>

    b. What are three differences between Johnson and Lincoln? _____

      <u>(1) Lincoln was confident in his own abilities; Johnson suffered from</u>

      <u>severe self-doubts, a weakness that made him open to flattery.</u>

      <u>(2) Lincoln was friendly and enjoyed people; Johnson was a loner with</u>

      <u>few friends or close advisers. (3) Lincoln was flexible, a natural</u>

      <u>compromiser; Johnson was a rigid man who could be sweet-talked out</u>

      <u>of a position, but when defied directly, refused to budge.</u>

    c. Primary structure   <u>contrast</u>

  2. [1]Before 1860 most fresh meat came from local butchers. [2]Dressed carcasses spoiled too quickly to come from distant sources and shipping live animals created large losses in weight. [3]But in the generation following the Civil War, three developments helped transform the business of supplying the public with meat. [4]First, an increasing proportion of Americans came to live in cities, remote from the farms where meat animals were fattened. [5]Second, an expanding railroad network made the products of the prairies and plains of the West more accessible to city consumers. [6]Third, in the 1870s, the railroads introduced refrigerated cars, allowing chilled fresh beef and pork to be shipped long distances without spoilage. (Unger, *These United States*)

a. Main idea Following the Civil War, three developments helped transform the business of supplying the public with meat.

b. What three developments helped transform the business of supplying the public with meat?

(1) Increasing proportion of Americans came to live in cities, remote from the farms where meat animals were fattened. (2) Expanding railroad network made the products of the prairies and plains of the West more accessible to city consumers. (3) The railroads introduced refrigerated cars, allowing chilled fresh beef and pork to be shipped long distances without spoilage.

c. Primary structure cause-effect

3. [1]America has had many "Wests." [2]The colonial West was the forested region just beyond the settled Atlantic coastal plain. [3]On the eve of the American Revolution, the West was the great river valley across the Appalachian Mountains. [4]For the generation preceding the Civil War, it was the land between the Mississippi and the Missouri. [5]The "Last West" of 1865 to 1910 was the broad expanse of territory stretching from the Missouri River to the Pacific Ocean. (Unger, *These United States*)

a. Main idea America has had many "Wests."

b. List two definitions of the "West."

Answers will vary; please see Answer Key.

c. Primary structure example and/or definition

4. [1]Vegetarians can be classified according to their dietary restrictions. [2]Strict vegetarians, or vegans, avoid all foods of animal origin, including dairy products and eggs. [3]The few people who fall into this category must work hard to ensure that they get all of the necessary nutrients. [4]Far more common are lacto-vegetarians, who eat dairy products but

avoid flesh foods. [5]Their diet can be low in fat and cholesterol, but only if they consume skim milk and other low- or nonfat products. [6]Ovo-vegetarians add eggs to their diet, while lacto-ovo-vegetarians eat both dairy products and eggs. [7]Pesco-vegetarians eat fish, dairy products, and eggs, while semivegetarians eat chicken, fish, dairy products and eggs. (Adapted from Donatelle and Davis, *Access to Health*)

a. Main idea   <u>Vegetarians can be classified according to their dietary</u>

<u>restrictions.</u>

b. List six categories of vegetarians.   _____

<u>(1) vegans, (2) lacto-vegetarians, (3) Ovo-vegetarians, (4) lacto-ovo-</u>

<u>vegetarians, (5) pesco-vegetarians, (6) semivegetarians</u>

c. Primary structure   <u>classification</u>

5. [1]The drought of 1988 was one of North America's worst droughts in this century. [2]In the United States alone, direct economic losses were estimated to be $40 billion. [3]In July, at the height of the drought, 40 percent of the country experienced either severe or extreme drought conditions. [4]By October, over 70 percent of the United States had suffered some socioeconomic losses. [5]In addition to widespread crop damage, fires raged in parts of the Northwest, and reservoirs in many areas were dry or critically low. [6]One of the most unexpected impacts of the drought was the disruption of barge traffic on the Mississippi, Missouri, and Ohio Rivers. [7]Heavy economic losses resulted because 45 percent of all grain, coal, and petroleum shipped in the central United States moves by barge. (Lutgens and Tarbuck, *The Atmosphere*)

a. Main idea   <u>The drought of 1988 was one of North America's worst</u>

<u>droughts in this century.</u>

b. What were three effects of the drought of 1988?   _____

<u>Answers will vary; please see Answer Key.</u>

_____

_____

_____

_____

_____

c. Primary structure   <u>cause-effect</u>

6. [1]If you were to search through the library for books about the atmosphere, many of the titles would contain the term *weather*, whereas oth-

ers would have the word *climate*. [2]What is the difference between these two terms? [3]Weather is a word used to denote the state of the atmosphere at a particular place for *a short period of time*. [4]Weather is constantly changing—hourly, daily, and seasonally. [5]Climate, on the other hand, might best be described as an aggregate or composite of weather. [6]Stated another way, the climate of a place or region is a generalization of the weather conditions over *a long period of time*. (Lutgens and Tarbuck, *Foundations of Earth Science*)

a. Main idea ___Weather and climate have different meanings.___

_____

b. What is one major difference between weather and climate? _____

___Weather is the state of the atmosphere at a particular place for a *short*___

___*period of time*, whereas the climate of a place or region is a___

___generalization of the weather conditions over a *long period of time*.___

c. Primary structure ___contrast___

7. [1]Instruments with keyboards have been popular for several hundred years. [2]For example, the harpsichord and clavichord were well known in the sixteenth century. [3]Another keyboard instrument, the pipe organ, reached a high point of development in the eighteenth century. [4]The piano was invented in the early eighteenth century and gradually replaced the harpsichord as the most popular keyboard instrument. (Adapted from Politoske, *Music*)

a. Main idea ___Keyboard instruments have been popular for several___

___hundred years.___

b. List four popular keyboard instruments. _____

___(1) harpsichord, (2) clavichord, (3) pipe organ, (4) piano___

_____

c. Primary structure ___examples___

8. [1]The breakup of the Beatles was undoubtedly caused by some of the following: (1) the end of group creativity, (2) a need for individual creativity, (3) a personality conflict, (4) family pressures, (5) legal complications, and (6) financial necessity. [2]We can argue for any or all of these causes. (Brown, *The Art of Rock and Roll*).

a. Main idea ___A combination of several factors probably led to the___

___breakup of the Beatles.___

b. What are three possible causes of the breakup of the Beatles? _____

Answers will vary; please see Answer Key.

_____

_____

c. Primary structure ___cause-effect___

9. [1]The differences between Los Angeles and San Francisco are striking. [2]First, the climates are totally different. [3]San Francisco has hills and fog. [4]It rains a lot and the weather is colder. [5]Also, it is, relatively speaking, a much more sophisticated town. [6]Whereas Los Angeles is a relaxed community of sun worshipers, San Francisco is artistic, cultured, and just a bit snobbish. [7]Its history is no longer than that of Los Angeles but it is substantially more cosmopolitan. [8]While Los Angeles had quick increases in population, San Francisco stayed basically the same. (Adapted from Brown, *The Art of Rock and Roll*)

a. Main idea ___The differences between Los Angeles and San Francisco are striking.___

b. What are three differences between Los Angeles and San Francisco?

(1) The climates are totally different. (2) Los Angeles is a relaxed community of sun worshipers, while San Francisco is artistic, cultured, and just a bit snobbish. (3) Los Angeles had quick increases in population, while San Francisco stayed basically the same.

c. Primary structure ___contrast___

10. [1]In 1822 a French inventor named Joseph Nicéphore Niépce (1765–1833) succeeded in making the first permanent photographic image. [2]In approximately 1825 he joined forces with a younger man, Louis-Jacques-Mandé Daguerre (1789–1851), who had devised an improved camera. [3]After ten more years of chemical and mechanical research, the daguerreotype, using positive exposures, was unveiled. [4]That announcement encouraged the Englishman William Henry Fox Talbot (1800–1877) to complete his own paper negative photograph process in about 1836. (Adapted from Janson and Janson, *A Basic History of Art*)

a. Main idea ___Although the first step in the development of photography came in 1822 when Joseph Nicéphore Niépce, a French inventor, succeeded in making the first permanent photographic image, the development of photography took many years.___

b. List the chronology of the development of photography. _____

1822: Joseph Nicéphore Niépce succeeds in making the first

permanent photographic image. 1825: Niépce joins forces with Louis-

Jacques-Mandé Daguerre, who had devised an improved camera.

1835: The daguerreotype, using positive exposures, was unveiled.

1836: Englishman William Henry Fox Talbot completed his own

paper negative photograph process.

c. Primary structure _____sequence_____

Exercise 6   Determining Relationships Among Ideas

First, identify the main idea. Then, use the author's structure to identify the relationships among ideas and sentences.

1. [1]Two types of thought patterns that a person could adopt are what might be called opportunity thinking and obstacle thinking. [2]Opportunity thinking involves a pattern of thoughts that focus on the opportunities and possibilities that situations or challenges hold. [3]Creative, innovative individuals who contribute to the major breakthroughs and advances in our world most likely possess this sort of pattern of thinking. [4]Their beliefs, their imagined future experiences, and their self-talk probably spur them on to undertake new opportunities. [5]Obstacle thinking, on the other hand, involves a focus on the roadblocks and pitfalls of undertaking new ventures. [6]Such a mental pattern fosters avoidance of challenges in favor of more secure actions, often with substantially lesser potential payoffs. (Manz and Neck, *Mastering Self-Leadership*)

   a. Main idea __Two types of thought patterns a person can adopt__

   __are opportunity thinking and obstacle thinking.__

   b. What is the relationship of sentence 5 to sentence 2?
       i. Sentence 5 continues the same thought as sentence 2.
      ⓘ ii. Sentence 5 presents a contrasting thought to sentence 2.
      iii. Sentence 5 presents an effect of sentence 2.
      iv. Sentence 5 presents examples for sentence 2.

2. [1]The United States has a higher rate of violent crime than does any other industrialized nation. [2]For example, the risk of being murdered in the United States is now 7 to 10 times that in most European countries (Lore and Schultz, 1993). [3]Comparable differences exist between the United States and Europe for rape and robbery. (Alexander, *Adjustment and Human Relations*)

a. Main idea   <u>The United States has a higher rate of violent crime</u>

<u>than any other industrialized nation.</u>

b. What is the relationship of sentence 2 to sentence 1?
   i. Sentence 2 continues the same thought as sentence 1.
   ii. Sentence 2 gives a contrasting thought to sentence 1.
   iii. Sentence 2 gives an effect of sentence 1.
   (iv.) Sentence 2 gives an example of sentence 1.

3. [1]Biotechnology has raised the prospect of making some remarkable advances in food production. [2]The revolutionary potential of genetic engineering has made it possible to crossbreed genetically different plants and to incorporate desired traits into crop lines and animals. [3]Without a doubt, this technology can help the developing world to produce more food. [4]There is a downside to biotechnology, however. (Nebel and Wright, *Environmental Science*)

a. Main idea   <u>Although there is a downside, biotechnology can make</u>

<u>some remarkable advances in food production.</u>

b. What is the relationship of sentence 4 to sentences 1, 2, and 3?
   (i.) Sentence 4 gives a contrasting thought to sentences 1, 2, and 3.
   ii. Sentence 4 gives an example of sentences 1, 2, and 3.
   iii. Sentence 4 gives a definition for sentences 1, 2, and 3.
   iv. Sentence 4 gives a cause for sentences 1, 2, and 3.

4. [1]A quiet but powerful revolution is reshaping the United States. [2]The number of elderly people—women and men aged sixty-five and over—is increasing more than twice as fast as the population as a whole. [3]Between 1970 and 1996, while the overall U.S. population rose 31 percent, the number of seniors climbed by 69 percent, and the number over age eighty-five soared by 167 percent. [4]This "graying" of the United States promises profound effects. (Macionis, *Sociology*)

a. Main idea   <u>The United States will experience significant changes as</u>

<u>the number of people over sixty-five continues to increase.</u>

b. What is the relationship of sentence 2 to sentence 1?
   i. Sentence 2 continue the same thought as sentence 1.
   ii. Sentence 2 presents a contrasting thought to sentence 1.
   iii. Sentence 2 presents an effect of sentence 1.
   (iv.) Sentence 2 presents a cause for sentence 1.

5. [1]Understanding what someone is saying often involves much more than listening and speaking. [2]It is often what is *not* actually said that may speak louder than any words. [3]Rolling your eyes, looking at the floor or ceiling when speaking rather than maintaining eye contact, body movements, hand gestures—all these nonverbal clues influence the way we interpret messages. [4]Researchers have found that only 7 percent of the meaning of a message comes from the words spoken. [5]An astounding 93 percent of the meaning comes from nonverbal cues. (Donatelle and Davis, *Access to Health*)

a. Main idea Understanding what someone is saying involves

interpreting nonverbal clues as well as listening and speaking.

b. What is the relationship of sentence 3 to sentence 2?
    i. Sentence 3 presents a contrasting thought to sentence 2.
    ii. Sentence 3 provides a definition of terms in sentence 2.
    iii. Sentence 3 presents examples of sentence 2.
    iv. Sentence 3 presents an effect for sentence 2.

6. [1]Shy people tend to lack social skills. [2]They avoid eye contact and are inclined to withdraw when spoken to. [3]They show little interest or vitality, and they pause too long in conversations. [4]Many have not learned how to meet others. [5]For instance, they have not learned how to start a conversation and keep it going or how to end social encounters. [6]Most shy people have social anxiety. [7]For example, they fear being evaluated, embarrassed, ridiculed, rejected, and found inadequate. (Alexander, *Adjustment and Human Relations*)

a. Main idea Shy people tend to lack social skills.

b. What is the relationship of sentence 5 to sentence 1?
    i. Sentence 5 continues the same thought as sentence 1.
    ii. Sentence 5 presents a contrasting thought to sentence 1.
    iii. Sentence 5 presents an example of sentence 1.
    iv. Sentence 5 presents a cause for sentence 1.

7. [1]Earth's crust is the source of a wide variety of minerals, many of which are useful and essential to people. [2]In fact, practically every manufactured product contains material obtained from minerals. [3]Most people are familiar with the common uses of basic metals, including aluminum in beverage cans, copper in electrical wiring, and gold in jewelry. [4]But fewer are aware that pencil "lead" does not contain lead metal but is really made of the soft black mineral called graphite. [5]Baby powder (talcum powder) is ground-up rock made of the mineral talc, with perfume added. [6]Drill bits impregnated with pieces of diamond (a mineral) are used by dentists to drill through tooth enamel. [7]The common mineral quartz is the main ingredient in ordinary glass and is the source of silicon for computer chips. [8]And on and on. [9]Thus, as the material demands of modern society grow, the need to locate additional supplies of useful minerals also grows and becomes more challenging as the easily mined sources become depleted. (Lutgens and Tarbuck, *Foundations of Earth Science*)

a. Main idea   <u>Earth's crust is the source of a wide variety of minerals,</u>

<u>many of which are useful and essential to people.</u>

b. What is the relationship of sentences 3 to 7 to sentence 2?
     i. Sentences 3 to 7 present definitions for sentence 2.
     ii. Sentences 3 to 7 present contrasting information to sentence 2.
     (iii.) Sentences 3 to 7 present examples of sentence 2.
     iv. Sentences 3 to 7 present causes of sentence 2.

8. [1]In recent years evidence has clearly shown that the dangers of smoking are not restricted to the smoker. [2]Tobacco smoke in the air is damaging to anyone who inhales it, not just the smoker. [3]For this reason, many states require restaurants to have smoking and nonsmoking sections. [4]And in many parts of the country, smoking in public places has been restricted, if not prohibited. (Miller and Levine, *Biology*)

a. Main idea   <u>Tobacco smoke in the air is damaging to anyone who</u>

<u>inhales it, not just to the smoker.</u>

b. What is the relationship of sentences 3 and 4 to sentences 1 and 2?
     (i.) Sentences 3 and 4 present effects of sentences 1 and 2.
     ii. Sentences 3 and 4 present contrasting thoughts to sentences 1 and 2.
     iii. Sentences 3 and 4 present examples of sentences 1 and 2.
     iv. Sentences 3 and 4 present causes for sentences 1 and 2.

9. [1]Police frequently use wiretapping and other sophisticated means of "bugging." [2]In its first wiretapping case, in 1928, the Supreme Court held that intercepting telephone conversations without a warrant was not an unreasonable search or seizure. [3]In 1967 it reversed that decision, however. (McClenaghan, *Magruder's American Government*)

a. Main idea   <u>Reversing an earlier decision, the Supreme Court now</u>

<u>requires that police have a valid warrant to intercept conversations.</u>

b. What is the relationship of sentence 3 to sentence 2?
     i. Sentence 3 continues the same thought as sentence 2.
     (ii.) Sentence 3 presents a contrasting thought to sentence 2.
     iii. Sentence 3 presents an example of sentence 2.
     iv. Sentence 3 presents a cause for sentence 2.

10. [1]The development of sophisticated computer technology has made information on almost any topic widely available. [2]Yet new problems have surfaced in the Information Age. [3]For example, many computer databases show the health, employment, or credit history of individuals. [4]The unauthorized use of such personal information has become a widespread concern. [5]Breaking into computer systems to steal, alter, or

destroy data is another problem of the Information Age. (Cayton, Perry, Reed, and Winkler, *America: Pathways to the Present*)

a. Main idea   The development of sophisticated computer technology has

made diverse information available, but it has also created new problems.

b. What is the relationship of sentence 2 to sentence 1?

  i. Sentence 2 presents a definition of sentence 1.

 ⓘⓘ Sentence 2 presents a contrasting thought to sentence 1.

 iii. Sentence 2 presents an example of sentence 1.

 iv. Sentence 2 presents a cause for sentence 1.

SUMMARY OF KEY IDEAS

■ In addition to the main idea, paragraphs have one or more specific sentences that contain details to develop and support the main idea. However, the number of sentences and the number of details vary from paragraph to paragraph. To understand a paragraph, you must understand how each of the details and sentences relate to the main idea and/or to the other details and sentences.

■ There are two general categories of details that support main ideas: major details and minor details. A major detail is a specific piece of information that directly supports and explains the main idea. A minor detail is a very specific piece of information that supports and explains a major detail.

■ In addition to major and minor details, some paragraphs include a transition sentence that connects what you have just read with what you are about to read. Occasionally, a paragraph contains irrelevant information: information that is interesting but does not support or develop the main idea.

■ Although you must understand the relationships among all the ideas and sentences in a paragraph, the number of major and minor details you need to remember depends on your purpose for reading.

■ Because a paragraph can contain any number of sentences and have any number of major and minor details, authors try to organize them to best help the reader understand them. In textbooks, the ways in which authors organize or structure information are predictable and identifiable.

■ Six common structures, or rhetorical patterns, used in expository text like textbooks are examples, comparison and/or contrast, cause and effect, process or sequence, classification, and definition. Authors often combine two patterns.

■ To help you identify the structure, and thus understand the relationships among the ideas and sentences, an author often uses common words, phrases, or punctuation marks as clues. Called signal words, directional words, and sometimes transitions, they indicate a particular type of information or move you in a specific direction of thought.

Use Your Strategies 1

Answer the questions following each paragraph.

1. [1]Americans generally agreed that their new nation should be a <u>democracy</u>, or government by the people. [2]Specifically, they favored the creation of a <u>republic</u>, a government run by the people through their elected representatives. [3]Yet people held widely differing views on how much influence ordinary citizens should have in the governing of the republic. (Clayton, Perry, Reed, and Winkler, *America: Pathways to the Present*)

    a. A democracy is <u>government by the people.</u>

    b. A republic is <u>government run by the people through their elected</u>

    <u>representatives.</u>

    c. main idea <u>Although most early Americans wanted a government</u>

    <u>run by the people, they had widely differing views on how much</u>

    <u>influence ordinary citizens should have in that government.</u>

    d. The signal word in sentence 3 is <u>yet</u>

    e. It signals
        (i.) a change in direction of thought
        ii. a continuation of the same thought
        iii. an effect

2. [1]Not everyone who is convicted of a crime and sentenced ends up in prison. [2]Some offenders are ordered to prison only to have their sentences suspended and a probationary term imposed. [3]They may also be ordered to perform community service activities as a condition of their probation. [4]During the term of probation these offenders are required to submit to supervision by a probation officer and to meet other conditions set by the court. [5]Failure to do so results in <u>revocation</u> of probation and <u>imposition</u> of the original prison sentence. [6]Other offenders, who have served a portion of their sentences, may be freed on parole. [7]They will be supervised by a parole officer and assisted in their readjustment to society. [8]As in the case of probation, failure to meet the conditions of parole may result in parole revocation and a return to prison. (Schmalleger, *Criminal Justice*)

    a. Revocation means <u>cancellation</u>

    b. Imposition means <u>reinstatement</u>

    c. main idea <u>Not everyone who is convicted of a crime and</u>

    <u>sentenced ends up in prison.</u>

   d. The relationship of sentences 2 and 6 to sentence 1 is

   (i.) Sentences 2 and 6 give major details to support sentence 1.

   ii. Sentences 2 and 6 give minor details to support sentence 1.

   iii. Sentences 2 and 6 are irrelevant to sentence 1.

3. [1]Humans use birds for many purposes. [2]People in cold climates discovered long ago that in addition to being soft and comfortable, down feathers are good <u>insulators</u>. [3]Therefore, down feathers are frequently used in making comforters and jackets. [4]Many birds are favorite foods the world over, and raising them is part of the economy in many countries. [5]With its low fat content, bird meat is a healthful source of protein in a balanced human diet. [6]Birds such as chickens and turkeys have been specially bred for their meat. [7]Because <u>domestic</u> strains of chickens and turkeys do not fly, their chest muscles are seldom used, making this part of the bird juicy and tender "white meat." [8]The leg and thigh muscles of these birds, used constantly for walking and running, are the "dark meat." (Miller and Levine, *Biology*)

   a. Insulators are <u>protection to hold in the heat</u>

   b. Domestic means <u>bred for home use</u>

   c. main idea <u>Humans use birds for many purposes.</u>

   d. The signal word in sentence 3 is <u>therefore</u>

   e. It signals

   i. continuation of thought

   ii. cause

   iii. definition

   (iv.) effect

4. [1]Drag boat racing, which has been taking place across the United States since the 1950s, was once known as a high-speed, high-thrill, but highly dangerous sport. [2]After eight driver <u>fatalities</u> in 1986, many predicted the end of organized drag boat racing. [3]But drag boat racers aren't the kind of folks to give up. [4]They analyzed the situation and, with the support of the International Hot Boat Association (IHBA), developed a variety of safety measures, including the now-<u>mandated</u> driver safety capsules for the high-danger pro classes. [5]Today, drag boat racing is back stronger and safer than ever. [6]It's kept its high speed—racers routinely eclipse numbers in the 240 mph range—and high excitement edge. [7]It's drawing ever-increasing numbers of racers and spectators, and ESPN coverage of IHBA races is now common. (McGrath and McGrath, *Performance Racing Industry*)

   a. Fatalities means <u>deaths</u>

   b. Mandated means <u>required</u>

c. main idea   Drag boat racing is back stronger and safer than ever.

_____

d. The signal word in sentence 3 is   but

e. It signals
  i. continuation of thought
  (ii.) a change in direction of thought
  iii. definition
  iv. effect

5. [1]Of the various elements of weather and climate, changes in air pressure are the least noticeable. [2]In listening to a weather report, generally, we are interested in moisture conditions (humidity and precipitation), temperature, and perhaps wind. [3]It is the rare person, however, who wonders about air pressure. [4]Although the hour-to-hour and day-to-day <u>variations</u> in air pressure are not <u>perceptible</u> to human beings, they are very important in producing changes in our weather. [5]For example, it is variations in air pressure from place to place that generate winds that in turn can bring changes in temperature and humidity. [6]Air pressure is one of the basic weather elements and a significant factor in weather forecasting. (Lutgens and Tarbuck, *The Atmosphere*)

a. Variations means   changes, differences

b. Perceptible means   detectable, apparent

c. main idea   Air pressure is one of the most basic elements of
  weather and climate and a significant factor in weather forecasting;
  however, changes in air pressure are the least noticeable.

d. How does sentence 5 relate to sentence 4?
  i. Sentence 5 gives a definition of sentence 4.
  ii. Sentence 5 gives an example of sentence 4.
  (iii.) Sentence 5 gives a contrast to sentence 4.

e. The signal phrase that points out the relationship is   for example

6. [1]When rap music first appeared on the scene, music critics said it wouldn't last, record companies felt it was too harsh and black-oriented to cross over, and parents dismissed it as the latest fad. [2]By January 1992, rappers were found as high as #3 on *Billboard*'s top 200 album list. [3]Within ten years, rap had become a powerful and <u>controversial</u> force in American popular culture. [4]Rap music grew from its <u>humble</u> street beginnings in Harlem and the South Bronx to a <u>dominant</u> media through traditional music vehicles like cassettes and CDs, as well as television coverage in videos and talk shows, rappers as actors, film themes, concerts, advertising, and other promotional components.

[5]Now, groups such as Hammer, Public Enemy, Ice Cube, Ghetto Boyz, Salt 'N Pepa, 2 Live Crew, NWA, Tone Loc, and Queen Latifah have reached mainstream popularity. (Adapted from Berry, "Redeeming the Rap Music Experience")

a. Controversial means   subject to argument and strong feelings

b. Humble means   modest, simple

c. Dominant means   important

d. main idea   Rap music overcame significant difficulties to become an important part of American media.

e. The primary structure is
   i. cause-effect
   (ii.) sequence
   iii. comparison/contrast
   iv. definition

7. [1]The presence of the ozone layer in our atmosphere is of vital importance to those of us on earth. [2]The reason lies in the capability of ozone to absorb damaging ultraviolet radiation from the sun. [3]Ultraviolet rays are the "burning" rays of the sun, those that allow some people to acquire a tan and many others to suffer a sunburn. [4]If ozone did not act to filter out a great deal of the ultraviolet radiation and these rays were allowed to reach the surface of the earth, our planet would likely be uninhabitable for most life as we know it. (Lutgens and Tarbuck, *The Atmosphere*)

a. Vital means   critical, essential

b. Uninhabitable means   unlivable, unable to support life

c. main idea   The presence of the ozone layer in our atmosphere is vitally important to those of us on earth.

d. How does sentence 2 relate to sentence 1?
   i. Sentence 2 gives an example of sentence 1.
   (ii.) Sentence 2 gives the cause of sentence 1.
   iii. Sentence 2 gives an effect of sentence 1.

8. [1]The life of a student can be stressful. [2]Among the stressors to cope with are exams in subjects you do not understand well, having to write papers on subjects unfamiliar to you, working your way through the complexities of registration, or having to deal with instructors who do not see things your way. [3]Another source of severe stress for some students is having too many competing demands on their time. [4]On most campuses you will find someone who works full-time, goes to school full-time, and has a family. (Adapted from DuBrin, *Human Relations for Career and Personal Success*)

    a. Stressors are   <u>elements that create tension and anxiety</u>

    b. Competing means <u>vying for</u>

    c. main idea   <u>The life of a student can be stressful.</u>

    d. How does DuBrin develop and support the main idea?
       (i.) with examples
       ii. with definitions
       iii. with effects

9. [1]In the 1800s Louis Pasteur and others made the major discovery that diseases were caused by infectious agents (now identified as bacteria, viruses, and parasites) and that they were <u>transmitted</u> via water and food, insects, and other vermin. [2]These discoveries caused major improvements in sanitation and <u>personal hygiene</u>. [3]Then, techniques of providing protection by means of vaccinations were discovered. [4]With the discovery of antibiotics such as penicillin in the 1930s, often-fatal diseases such as pneumonia could be cured. [5]Improvements in nutrition began to be significant as well. [6]In short, better sanitation, medicine, and nutrition brought about spectacular reductions in death rates, especially among children and infants. (Adapted from Nebel and Wright, *Environmental Science*)

    a. Transmitted means   <u>spread, carried</u>

    b. Personal hygiene means   <u>individual cleanliness</u>

    c. main idea   <u>Better sanitation, medicine, and nutrition brought</u>
    <u>about spectacular reductions in death rates, especially among</u>
    <u>children and infants.</u>

    d. How does sentence 2 related to sentence 1?
       i. Sentence 2 continues the thought with another example.
       ii. Sentence 2 changes direction of thought with a contrasting example.
       iii. Sentence 2 gives the cause.
       (iv.) Sentence 2 gives the effect.

    e. The signal phrase that points out the relationship is   <u>caused</u>

10. [1]As adults, we're often tempted to skip breakfast and start the day with a cup of coffee on the run. [2]But the old <u>adage</u> that "breakfast is the most important meal of the day" is absolutely right; and it's even more important for our kids than it is for us. [3]It has been shown that children who eat a healthy breakfast do better in school. [4]They concentrate more intently, and have more energy and <u>stamina</u>. [5]They even score higher on tests. [6]In fact, students who participated in one school breakfast

program had significantly higher math grades than those who didn't.
(Kraft Foods, *Family Roundtable*)

a. Adage means   saying, proverb

b. Stamina means   strength, endurance

c. main idea   Although eating a good breakfast is important for
everyone, it's especially important for kids.

d. How does sentence 3 relate to sentence 2?
    i. Sentence 3 gives an example of sentence 2.
    ii. Sentence 3 gives a cause of sentence 2.
    (iii.) Sentence 3 gives an effect of sentence 2.

e. How does sentence 4 relate to sentence 3?
    (i.) Sentence 4 gives an example of sentence 3.
    ii. Sentence 4 gives a cause of sentence 3.
    iii. Sentence 4 gives an effect of sentence 3.

Use Your Strategies 2

Answer the questions following each paragraph.

1. [1]The capacity of a muscle or a group of muscles to exert or resist a force is called muscular strength. [2]In contrast, muscular endurance is the ability of muscles to keep working for an extended time. [3]For example, the amount of weight you can lift is one measure of your muscular strength. [4]How long you can hold that weight—or how many times you can lift it—is a measure of your muscular endurance. (Pruitt, Crumpler, and Prothrow-Stith, *Health Skills for Wellness*)

a. To exert is to   apply

b. main idea   Muscular strength is the capacity of a muscle or a group of muscles to exert or resist a force; muscular endurance is the ability of muscles to keep working for an extended time.

c. Are muscular strength and muscular endurance the same or different?
Muscular strength and muscular endurance are different.

What was the authors' clue?   in contrast

d. What is one measure of muscular strength?   the amount of weight you can lift

2. ¹The largest population concentration in the Western Hemisphere is in the northeastern United States and southeastern Canada. ²This cluster extends along the Atlantic Coast from Boston to Newport News, Virginia, and westward along the Great Lakes to Chicago. ³About 2 percent of the world's people live in the area. ⁴Like the Europeans, most Americans are urban dwellers, less than 5 percent are farmers. (Rubenstein, *An Introduction to Human Geography*)

   a. Urban dwellers live in <u>cities</u>

   b. main idea <u>The largest population concentration in the Western</u>

   <u>Hemisphere is in the cities of the northeastern United States and</u>

   <u>southeastern Canada</u>

   c. Do most Europeans live in cities or rural areas? <u>cities</u>

   What was the author's clue? <u>like</u>

   d. Is sentence 3 a major detail or a minor detail? <u>minor detail</u>

3. ¹A convenient starting point in understanding the communication process is to look at the three major steps involved in communicating a message. ²Step 1 is when the sender encodes the message. ³Encoding is the process of organizing ideas into a series of symbols, such as words and gestures, designed to communicate with the receiver. ⁴Step 2 is when the sender transmits the message to the receiver via a communication medium, such as voice, telephone, paper, or e-mail. ⁵It is important to select a medium that fits the message. ⁶Step 3 is when the receiver decodes the message. In decoding, the receiver interprets the message and translates it into meaningful information. (Adapted from DuBrin, *Human Relations*)

   a. To decode is to <u>interpret, make sense of</u>

   b. main idea <u>A convenient starting point in understanding the</u>

   <u>communication process is to look at the three major steps involved in</u>

   <u>communicating a message.</u>

   c. What are the three major steps in communicating a message? _____

   <u>(1) When the sender encodes the message, (2) when the sender</u>

   <u>transmits the message to the receiver via a communication medium,</u>

   <u>such as voice, telephone, paper, or e-mail, (3) when the receiver</u>

   <u>decodes the message.</u>

4. ¹Formations that develop on the floor of a cavern and reach upward toward the ceiling are called stalagmites. ²The water supplying the calcite for stalagmite growth falls from the ceiling and splatters over the surface. ³As a result, stalagmites are usually more massive in appearance

and more rounded on their upper ends than stalactites. (Lutgens and Tarbuck, *Foundations of Earth Science*)

a. Stalagmites are __formations that develop on the floor of a cavern__ __and reach upward toward the ceiling.__

b. main idea __Formations that develop on the floor of a cavern and__ __reach upward toward the ceiling are called stalagmites.__

c. What causes stalagmites to form? __Water supplying the calcite for__ __stalagmite growth falls from the ceiling and splatters over the surface__ __of the cavern floor, forming stalagmites.__

d. What happens as a result of the way stalagmites are formed?_____
__As a result of the way stalagmites are formed, they are usually more__ __massive in appearance and more rounded on their upper ends than__ __stalactites.__

5. [1]AIDS is a global epidemic. [2]In the United States, deaths from AIDS dropped 47 percent between 1996 and 1997. [3]The drop was due primarily to expensive drug treatments, which are available mainly to affluent nations. [4]However, elsewhere in the world, especially in impoverished African and Asian countries, the rates of infection and death are soaring. (Adapted from Kornblum and Julian, *Social Problems*)

a. Impoverished means __poor__

b. main idea __Thanks to expensive drug treatments, deaths from AIDS__ __are down in the United States; however, the death rate from AIDS is__ __soaring in poor countries that cannot afford the drug treatments.__

c. What is the primary cause of the decline in deaths from AIDS in the U.S. between 1996 and 1997? __Expensive drug treatments.__

d. What is one cause of the increase in deaths from AIDS in poor countries between 1996 and 1997? __The unavailability of expensive__ __drug treatments in poor nations.__

6. [1]In the early fifth century, Italy and the "eternal city" of Rome suffered a series of devastating blows. [2]In 410, the Visigoths, led by Alaric, revolted and sacked Rome. [3]In 452, the Huns, led by Atilla—known to contemporaries as the "scourge of God"—invaded Italy. [4]And in 455 Rome was overrun yet again, this time by the Vandals. (Kagan, Ozment, and Turner, *The Western Heritage*)

a. Devastating is _destructive, dreadful_

b. main idea _In the early fifth century, Italy and the "eternal city" of_
Rome suffered a series of devastating blows.

c. What were the "devastating blows," and when did they occur? ____
(1) 410: The Visigoths, led by Alaric, revolted and sacked Rome. (2)
452: The Huns, led by Atilla, invaded Italy. (3) 455: Rome was overrun
yet again, this time by the Vandals.

7. [1]During the 1960s the country enjoyed the longest sustained economic boom in its history. [2]For example, the Gross National Product grew at the average rate of 4 percent annually, well above that for the preceding fifteen-year period. [3]Between 1960 and 1970 average per capita real income increased 48 percent. [4]The major American industries were unchallenged at home and enjoyed large markets abroad. [5]Moreover, compared to the 1990s, the gap between the most affluent and the other Americans was relatively modest. (Unger, *These United States*)

a. Sustained means _continued, without stopping_

b. main idea _During the 1960s the country enjoyed the longest_
sustained economic boom in its history.

c. Explain how sentences 2 through 5 relate to sentence 1. _Each gives_
an example of the economic boom.

8. [1]In Western societies, a whole pharmacopia of recreational drugs exists, and each year seems to see the introduction of new ones, both natural and synthetic. [2]Most of these drugs can be classified as stimulants, depressants, opiates, or psychedelics, depending on their effects on the central nervous system and their impact on behavior and mood. (Wade and Tavris, *Invitation to Psychology*)

a. A pharmacopia is _large assortment of pharmaceuticals_

b. main idea _Most of the recreational drugs in Western society can_
be classified as stimulants, depressants, opiates, or psychedelics,
depending on their effects on the central nervous system and their
impact on behavior and mood.

c. How are recreational drugs classified? _Recreational drugs are_
classified as stimulants, depressants, opiates, or psychedelics,

depending on their effects on the central nervous system and their impact on behavior and mood.

d. What do you predict follows this paragraph? Explanations and examples of each of the classifications.

9. [1]Because murder is such a serious crime, it consumes substantial police resources. [2]Consequently, over the years the offense has shown the highest clearance rate (solved through arrest or other means) of any index crime. [3]Sixty-nine percent of all homicides were cleared in 1998. (Schmalleger, *Criminal Justice Today*)

a. Consumes substantial resources means uses much time, people, and money

b. main idea Because murder cases receive substantial police resources, it has the highest clearance rate of any index crime.

c. Why do murder crimes have a high clearance rate? Because they consume substantial police resources.

d. Explain the relationship of sentence 2 to sentence 1. Sentence 2 gives the effect or result of sentence 1.

10. [1]Psychological tests usually generate information about people indirectly. [2]In contrast, surveys are questionnaires and interviews that gather information by asking people directly about their experiences, attitudes, or opinions. [3]Most of us are familiar with surveys in the form of national opinion polls, such as the Gallup and Roper polls. (Wade and Tavris, *Invitation to Psychology*)

a. Generate means create, produce

b. main idea Psychological tests usually generate information about people indirectly, while surveys gather information directly.

c. Explain how psychological tests and surveys are alike or different.

Tests usually generate information about people indirectly, while surveys gather information directly.

What was the authors' clue? in contrast

REFLECT AND CONNECT

A. Compare and contrast what going to school is like for you now with the last time you were in school. Some of the factors you might consider are your attitude and the attitudes of your classmates, the amount of reading and study required, and the teachers.

B. Recall a teacher who stands out in your memory. Decide what makes the teacher memorable, such as personality, teaching style, or mannerisms. Describe him or her using specific examples.

C. Being "successful" means different things to different people—writers, movie stars, professional athletes, friends, family. Find at least five definitions of success. Describe how you define success.

LOG ON TO THE WEB

Practice good reading skills as you check out what a reviewer thinks about the latest books. Log on to one of these sites, one of the online bookstores, or use your favorite search engine to locate a review of a book that sounds interesting.

http://www.cnn.com/books/reviews/
http://www.usatoday.com/life/enter/books/leb1.htm

Print out the review.
Write the name of the person who wrote the review and what you know about him or her; the main idea of the review; how the writer primarily developed and supported that main idea, such as with examples; and why you would or would not read the book.

CROSSWORD PUZZLE

Word List (not all used)

acutely	effect	obvious
adage	essential	optimistic
advocate	inclined	perceptible
cause	insignificant	pessimist
classification	interrelated	predictable
compare	irrelevant	process
consistent	lethal	reinforce
contrast	major detail	relevant
cope	mandated	revocation
disrupt	meteor	ridiculed
dominant	minor detail	sequence
drought	nonverbal	transition

Across

2 doesn't support main idea

4 interrupt

7 wise saying

9 how a complex system works or develops

11 fatal

13 find differences

15 support

18 result

19 unspoken

21 made fun of

23 manage

26 reason

27 information supporting major detail

28 required

29 noticeable

Down

1 a falling star

3 fundamental

5 interconnected

6 connects what you've just read with what you're about to read

8 leading

10 order of events

12 extremely

14 information supporting main idea

16 positive

17 apparent

20 coherent, related and purposeful

22 period without rain

24 apt to

25 significant

26 find similarities

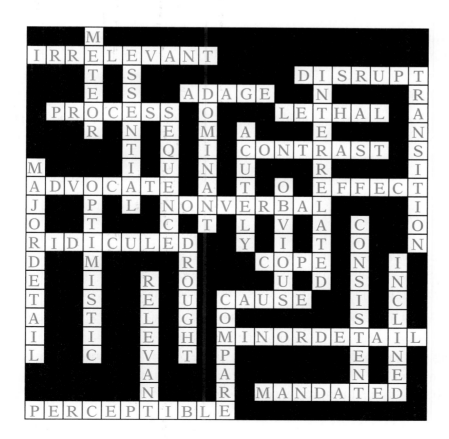

read-ing (red´in) *adj.* **1** inclined ad or study **2**
reading n. **1** the act or practic   person who r
of books **2** a public entertainm   which litera
aloud **3** the extent to which a   has read **4**
meant to be read **5** the amoun   easured as by a
thermometer **6** the form of a specified word, sent

CHAPTER

6   **Reading Multiparagraph Selections**

Think about all the reading you do during a routine day. For example, you might locate a specific piece of information in a ten-page report for your boss, catch up on the day's events in the newspaper, surf the Internet, read a text assignment for class, make a casserole from a new cookbook, and spend some time with your favorite author's latest novel.

Now, think about how each of these situations requires you to "read" a little differently than the others. Even among school assignments, you make adjustments in how you read. Consider, for instance, how you would read these two assignments:

Assignment 1 For your Introduction to Computers class, you are to read the first chapter—35 pages—in the text to prepare for tomorrow's lecture. You've used a computer at work and home for several years and know quite a bit about them. Your professor wrote the text in easy-to-read language for beginning students. It includes many illustrations to help explain the information.

Assignment 2 For your Introduction to Art History class, you are to read a three-page magazine article on Michelangelo to prepare for a small group discussion about Italian Renaissance art. You've never taken an art class before and rarely read anything about art or artists. An art historian wrote the article for people who work in museums. The article is available only on microfiche.

Among the factors you would consider as you plan to read the assignments: The computer assignment is longer, but the content will be familiar and it is written in language you are likely to understand easily. You need a general understanding of the material so you can take good notes on the concepts during lecture.

The article on Michelangelo is not very long, but it will be difficult to "see"— even if you can make a photocopy from the microfiche. It will also be difficult to understand since you are not familiar with the ideas and the article is written for museum professionals. Since you need to use the information about Michelangelo in a small group discussion about Italian Renaissance art, you may need to read additional articles to help you prepare.

In other words, based on your purpose, your knowledge of the subject, the author's writing style, and the medium, you would read the two assignments very differently.

Knowing *why you're reading* and *what you're reading* before you begin is critical to your success.

CHAPTER 6 AT A GLANCE

Chapter Focus	**Use Your Strategies 1**
Plan to Be Successful	**Use Your Strategies 2**
Set a Purpose for Reading	**Use Your Strategies 3**
Preview	**Use Your Strategies 4**
Activate Prior Knowledge	**Reflect and Connect**
Estimate Difficulty Level	**Log On to the Web**
Read Actively	**Crossword Puzzle**
Identify the Thesis	
Monitor Your Comprehension	

CHAPTER FOCUS

As you have discovered, reading individual paragraphs accurately and efficiently is critical to academic success. However, a paragraph is usually part of a longer multiparagraph work such as a chapter or article. This is because authors need more than one paragraph to fully explain and support their overall idea.

This chapter focuses on strategies you can use to increase your success with multiparagraph selections. The first four "Plan to Be Successful" strategies give you a head start on good comprehension.

The "Read Actively" strategies help keep you an active, thinking participant in the reading process.

PLAN TO BE SUCCESSFUL

Reading is an active, thoughtful process that requires you to use a variety of skills and strategies. The unique combination of skills and strategies you use for a particular assignment depends on elements such as

- your purpose for reading
- your knowledge of the subject
- the author's writing style
- the length of the reading
- the medium (the type and form of the publication)

Planning strategies, such as setting a purpose, previewing, activating your prior knowledge, and estimating the difficulty level of the material, help you become an active reader and give you a head start on good comprehension; they set you up to be successful.

Set a Purpose for Reading

As I walk through the library, I often ask students "Why are you reading that text chapter or article?" Unfortunately, their answer is usually "because it was assigned." I say unfortunately because if your only purpose for reading an assignment is "it was assigned," when you finish reading—whether or not you understand the information—you have fulfilled your purpose. Successful readers always go beyond the "it was assigned" purpose. They develop general and specific reasons for reading based on what they need to know when they finish reading.

Without a clear understanding of why you are reading a selection and what you need to know when you finish reading, you must read everything in the selection with equal emphasis and try to learn it all in complete detail. Although this total-mastery approach may be necessary in a few reading assignments each term, it usually leads to frustration and information overload. However, when you can clearly identify your reasons for reading, you can clearly focus your attention.

For example, if you were preparing to take a quiz on key vocabulary in the second chapter of your psychology text, you wouldn't need to read the chapter with the same emphasis on the **thesis** (the overall main idea) and main idea of each paragraph that you would need if you were preparing for a discussion group. On the other hand, if you were going to give an oral report on that chapter, you would read it with more attention to main ideas and major details than if you were preparing to listen to a lecture about it.

Deciding what kind of information you need to know before you begin to read will make you a more effective and efficient reader.

Preview

As you learned in Chapter 1, previewing is like looking at a completed jigsaw puzzle before you try to put individual pieces together.

Previewing a multiparagraph reading assignment—examining it in an orderly way before you begin to read—takes only a few minutes and can help you clarify your reasons for reading and improve your comprehension. When you **preview**, you read key structural organizers, like titles and subtitles, to get an overview of how the selection is organized and its core ideas. It gives you a way to make connections between what you know and what you are going to read. Although the organizing features vary among different kinds of reading material, they emphasize important content and are key to improving your comprehension.

Previewing a Text Chapter

When you preview a chapter, you read any element that helps give you a general understanding of the core ideas and their organization such as:

- titles, headings, and subheadings
- introduction or introductory paragraphs
- chapter objectives

- margin notes and annotations
- bold, underlined, and italic words
- pictures, charts, and diagrams
- summary or concluding paragraphs
- end-of-chapter questions and exercises

Once you are in the habit previewing, you should be able to preview a thirty-page text chapter with clear **structural organizers** in about ten minutes. Of course, if a selection lacks organizing features or is particularly complex, you may need to spend a little more time previewing.

Exercise 1   **Previewing a Text Chapter**

To complete Exercise 1, read the following elements from *Being a Nursing Assistant*, eighth edition, by Francie Wolgin:

- title
- introduction
- chapter objectives
- key terms

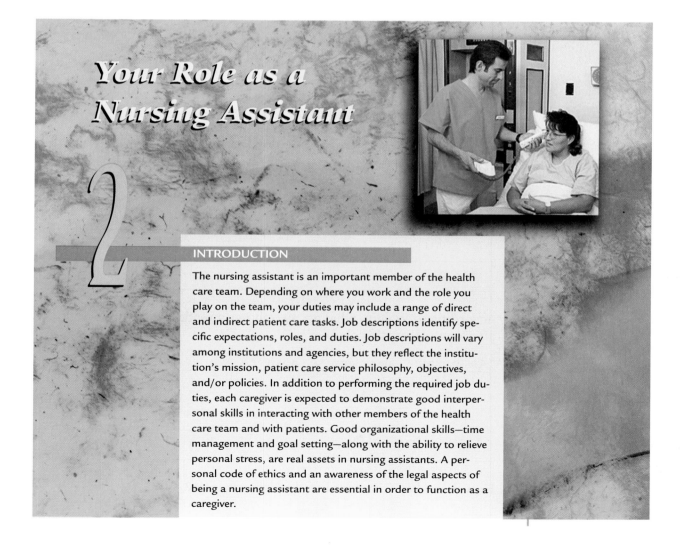

Your Role as a Nursing Assistant

INTRODUCTION

The nursing assistant is an important member of the health care team. Depending on where you work and the role you play on the team, your duties may include a range of direct and indirect patient care tasks. Job descriptions identify specific expectations, roles, and duties. Job descriptions will vary among institutions and agencies, but they reflect the institution's mission, patient care service philosophy, objectives, and/or policies. In addition to performing the required job duties, each caregiver is expected to demonstrate good interpersonal skills in interacting with other members of the health care team and with patients. Good organizational skills—time management and goal setting—along with the ability to relieve personal stress, are real assets in nursing assistants. A personal code of ethics and an awareness of the legal aspects of being a nursing assistant are essential in order to function as a caregiver.

OBJECTIVES

When you have completed this chapter, you will be able to:

- Display qualities that are desirable in a good patient/nursing assistant.
- Identify duties and role functions of nursing assistants.
- Practice good personal hygiene.
- Behave ethically.
- Keep confidences to yourself.
- Work accurately.
- Be dependable.
- Follow rules and instructions.
- Develop cooperative staff relationships.
- Show respect for patients' rights.
- Explain how laws affect you and the patients you care for.
- Report incidents.

KEY TERMS

accountable

accuracy

competency

cooperation

dependability

ethical behavior

hazard

hygiene

incident

informed consent

interpersonal skills

malpractice

negligence

stress

1. What is the title of this chapter?

    "Your Role as a Nursing Assistant"

2. What are two important ideas in the introduction?

    Answers will vary; please see Answer Key.

3. According to Wolgin, what are two things a reader will be able to do after completing this chapter?

    Answers will vary; please see Answer Key.

4. How many key terms are listed for this chapter? 14

Exercise 2 ▶ **Previewing a Text Chapter**

To complete Exercise 2, read the following elements from Wolgin's *Being a Nursing Assistant:*

- headings and subheadings
- margin notes and annotations
- bold, underlined, and italic words

THE NURSING ASSISTANT: AN IMPORTANT CAREGIVER

accountable To be answerable for one's behavior; legally or ethically responsible for the care of another

competency A demonstrable skill or ability

Being a nursing assistant is not just another job—it is a serious occupation. There are many new things to learn and so many things to do as a caregiver. The fundamental patient care tasks and procedures for which you will be **accountable** can be found on the health care institution's or agency's job description. Your instructor can review any state licensing or certification **competency** requirements that apply to you.

KEY IDEA

Remain sensitive to what you would want if you or one of your loved ones were the patient. *Empathy* and *understanding* from those caring for a patient are part of the treatment. Frequently, they are as important as medicine or therapy in helping the patient to get well.

▮Role of the Nursing Assistant

Whether you are called nursing assistant, patient care assistant, patient care associate, certified nurse assistant, or some other title to reflect these roles, you will be working under the supervision of the nurse manager or team leader. We will use the terms *nursing assistant* and *immediate supervisor* to refer to you and the person who supervises you. Your immediate supervisor usually makes your assignments, provides feedback on how well you are doing, and keeps track of your overall performance. Ask your immediate supervisor for help when you do not know how to do an assigned procedure or when you are unsure of yourself. It is better to get help than to do something wrong.

If you think you are being asked to do more than you were taught to do, remember that everything you do as a nursing assistant will be supervised by a registered professional nurse. That professional nurse can either provide any additional instruction you may need or will direct you to the proper person or department for such education. Everyone in health care is expected to be continually learning new and updated information on how to best care for patients and their loved ones.

▮Duties and Functions of the Nursing Assistant

A general summary of a job description will state that the nursing assistant works under the direct or general supervision of a registered nurse, contributing to the delivery of patient care through performance of selected day-to-day activities; maintenance of a functional and aesthetic environment conducive to patient well-being; demonstration of unit/area designated competencies; and interaction with patients considering their developmental, age-specific, cultural, and spiritual preferences. Refer to Table 2–1 to review an example of the specific duties and functions expected of three different levels of nonlicensed caregivers. Special education is provided for each level.

KEY IDEA

Caregivers are expected to have good interpersonal skills that enable them to get along well with others, approach and resolve conflicts constructively, problem solve, and maintain confidentiality of information acquired in their role as caregivers.

1. List the chapter's main heading and subheadings. (Let the different sizes and styles of type used in the headings and subheadings help you indent specific subheads under their more general head.)

    Your Role as a Nursing Assistant

    The Nursing Assistant: An Important Caregiver

    Role of the Nursing Assistant

    Duties and Functions of the Nursing Assistant

2. What do you predict the paragraphs under the subheading "Role of the Nursing Assistant" contain?

    The paragraphs under the subheading "Role of the Nursing Assistant"

    contains information on what nursing assistants do and who they

    work with and report to.

3. How does Wolgin define *accountable?*

    Wolgin defines *accountable* as "to be answerable for one's behavior;

    legally or ethically responsible for the care of another."

4. What is the purpose of the margin note *Key Idea?*

    The margin note *Key Idea* highlights an important idea.

Exercise 3   **Previewing a Text Chapter**

To complete Exercise 3, read the following elements from Wolgin's *Being a Nursing Assistant:*

■ Summary
■ End-of-chapter questions.

SUMMARY

The nursing assistant is an important member of the health care team. In your role as caregiver, you will be ensuring that patients do not suffer any extra pain and will be making a patient's stay in the health care institution easier. Good interpersonal skills and hygiene are expected in a nursing assistant. Good organizational skills can help make the many duties and responsibilities of the job more manageable and less stressful. As a member of the nursing team, a nursing assistant will be expected to subscribe to the high standard that professional nurses and health care providers set for themselves. Always remember that patients are entitled to respect for their human rights. They must be kept safe and properly cared for at all times. Laws concerning patients and workers in health care institutions protect both the patients and the workers. Be aware of the legal aspects of your job and understand the importance of reporting incidents in your institution's overall safety program.

CHAPTER REVIEW

FILL IN THE BLANK

Read each sentence and fill in the blank line with a word that completes the sentence.

1. When you are legally or ethically responsible for the care of another, you are said to be _____.

2. Working or acting together for mutual benefit is called _____.

3. Good _____ includes good personal cleanliness and appearance.

4. You demonstrate good _____ when you plan, prioritize, and organize your work in order to get it done in a given time period.

5. _____ behavior includes keeping promises, doing what you should do, and acting in accordance with the rules and standards for right conduct and practice.

MULTIPLE CHOICE

Choose the best answer for each question or statement.

1. Caregivers are expected to have good communication skills to allow them to understand their patients and to work as a team.
   a. True.
   b. False.

2. Positive traits in a nurse assistant are all of the following except
   a. being trustworthy.
   b. enjoying working with others.
   c. liking things only a certain way.
   d. liking to learn new things.

3. The code of ethics includes following all of these standards except
   a. carrying out faithfully the instructions you are given.
   b. respecting the right of all patients to beliefs that are different from yours.
   c. letting the patient know it is your pleasure to do your job.
   d. All of the above.

4. Do not discuss patient information with
   a. other patients.
   b. relatives and friends of the patient.
   c. your family.
   d. All of the above.

5. Negligence is doing something or not doing something when a reasonably prudent nursing assistant would have done it under the same conditions.
   a. True
   b. False

6. Whenever an incident happens, remember that it is an unforeseen event that occurs without intent and so does not need to be reported.
   a. True
   b. False

1. What are two important ideas in the summary that were also in the introduction?

   Answers will vary; please see Answer Key.

   _____

   _____

   _____

2. What is one important idea in the summary that was not in the introduction?

   Answers will vary; please see Answer Key.

   _____

3. What is the answer to the Chapter Review's fill-in-the-blank question 1?

   The answer to the Chapter Review's Fill-in-the-Blank Question 1 is

   "accountable."

   Where did you find the answer? _in the margin vocabulary note._

Exercise 4 **Previewing a Text Chapter**

Preview a chapter in a textbook for one of your other classes and answer these questions.

1. List the chapter's title, headings, and subheadings. (Indent appropriately.)

   Answers for the seven questions will vary.

   _____

   _____

   _____

   _____

   _____

2. What information do you predict the paragraphs under the first heading will contain?

   _____

   _____

   _____

   _____

3. List one key idea from the introduction or introductory paragraphs.

   _____

   _____

4. Are objectives listed? _____

   _____

5. Are key terms identified in any way, such as listed or set in bold type?

_____

_____

6. If there is a summary, list one key idea:

_____

_____

7. Are there end-of-chapter questions, exercises, or other elements? _____

_____

Previewing an Article

Like textbooks, magazine and journal articles use organizing structures to guide you through the content. An article typically has a title and author, and sometimes includes brief information about the author. Generally, the content is organized under headings and subheadings, particularly in a lengthy article. An article often contains an introduction and/or a summary as well as bold or italic type to emphasize important information.

Previewing an article gives you a head start on good comprehension.

Exercise 5 **Previewing an Article**

Preview the following article, "Facts about Anxiety Disorders." Answer the questions as you preview.

FACTS ABOUT ANXIETY DISORDERS

National Institute of Mental Health and National Institutes of Health

On July 3, 1946, President Truman signed the National Mental Health Act, which called for the establishment of a National Institute of Mental Health (NIMH). Today, NIMH is a part of the National Institutes of Health (NIH) under the direction of the U.S. Department of Health & Human Services. The mission of NIMH is to diminish the burden of mental illness through research.

INTRODUCTION

Fear and anxiety are a necessary part of life. Whether it's a feeling of anxiety before taking a test or a feeling of fear as you walk down a dark street, normal anxiety can be protective and stimulating. Unfortunately, more than 19 million Americans face much more than just "normal" anxiety. For those with anxiety disorders, life is filled with fear. However, research supported and conducted by the National Institute of Mental Health (NIMH) has produced many effective treatments.

1. From the title and introduction, what do you predict is the topic of the article?

   Topic: anxiety disorders

2. Who are the authors?   National Institute of Mental Health and

   National Institutes of Health

Most people experience feelings of anxiety before an important event such as a big exam, business presentation, or first date. Anxiety disorders, however, are illnesses that fill people's lives with overwhelming anxiety and fear that are chronic, unremitting, and can grow progressively worse. Tormented by panic attacks, obsessive thoughts, flashbacks, nightmares, or countless frightening physical symptoms, some people with anxiety disorders even become housebound. Fortunately, through research conducted by the NIMH, there are effective treatments that can help. NIMH is conducting a national education campaign to increase awareness of these disorders and their treatments.

HOW COMMON ARE ANXIETY DISORDERS?

- Anxiety disorders are the most common mental illness in America: More than 19 million Americans are affected by these debilitating illnesses each year.

- Anxiety disorders cost the U.S. $46.6 billion in 1990, nearly one-third of the nation's total mental health bill of $148 billion.

WHAT ARE THE FIVE PRIMARY TYPES OF ANXIETY DISORDERS?

Panic Disorder: Repeated episodes of intense fear that strike often and without warning. Physical symptoms include chest pain, heart palpitations, shortness of breath, dizziness, abdominal distress, feelings of unreality, and fear of dying.

Obsessive-Compulsive Disorder: Repeated, unwanted thoughts or compulsive behaviors that seem impossible to stop or control.

Posttraumatic Stress Disorder: Persistent symptoms that occur after experiencing a traumatic event such as rape or other criminal assault, war, child abuse, natural disasters, or crashes. Nightmares, flashbacks, numbing of emotions, depression and feeling angry, irritable, or distracted and being easily startled are common.

Phobias: Two major types of phobias are social phobia and specific phobia. People with social phobia have an overwhelming and disabling fear of scrutiny, embarrassment, or humiliation in social situations, which leads to avoidance of many potentially pleasurable and meaningful activities. People with specific phobia experience extreme, disabling, and irrational fear of something that poses little or no actual danger; the fear leads to avoidance of objects or situations and can cause people to limit their lives unnecessarily.

Generalized Anxiety Disorder: Constant, exaggerated, worrisome thoughts and tension about everyday, routine life events and activities, lasting at least six months. Almost always anticipating the worst even though there is little reason to expect it; accompanied by physical symptoms such as fatigue, trembling, muscle tension, headache, or nausea.

WHAT ARE EFFECTIVE TREATMENTS FOR ANXIETY DISORDERS?

Treatments have been largely developed through research conducted by NIMH and other research institutions. They help many people with anxiety disorders and often combine medication and specific types of psychotherapy.

More medications are available than ever before to effectively treat anxiety disorders. These include groups of drugs called antidepressants and benzodiazepines. If one medication is not effective, others can be tried. New medications are currently under development to treat anxiety symptoms.

Two clinically proven effective forms of psychotherapy used to treat anxiety disorders are behavioral therapy and cognitive-behavioral therapy. Behavioral therapy focuses on changing specific actions and uses several techniques to stop unwanted behaviors. In addition to the behavioral therapy techniques, cognitive-behavioral therapy teaches patients to understand and change their thinking patterns so they can react differently to the situations that cause them anxiety.

DO ANXIETY DISORDERS COEXIST WITH OTHER PHYSICAL OR MENTAL DISORDERS?

It is common for an anxiety disorder to accompany depression, eating disorders, substance abuse, or another anxiety disorder. Anxiety disorders can also coexist with physical disorders. In such instances, the accompanying disorders will also need to be treated before beginning any treatment. However, it is important to have a thorough medical examination to rule out other possible causes of symptoms.

3. Which section would you read if you wanted to know about the specific types of anxiety disorders?

   "What Are the Five Primary Types of Anxiety Disorders?"

   _____

   How many primary types of anxiety disorders are there? _____

   There are five primary types of anxiety disorders.

4. What is the NIMH? _The NIMH, National Institute of Mental Health;_

see Answer Key for additional information.

5. What information do you predict will be included in the section "Do Anxiety Disorders Coexist with Other Physical or Mental Disorders?"

The section will likely explain if anxiety disorders can coexist with

other physical or mental disorders.

Remember, previewing a multiparagraph selection takes only a few minutes, but it can significantly improve your comprehension, reduce your frustration, and help you clarify your purpose for reading.

Activate Prior Knowledge

Research confirms what most of us have figured out by trial and error: the more we know about the subject we're reading, the easier it is to understand. So, just as you take time to think about a subject before you begin to write about it, you should take time to think about a subject before you begin reading about it.

For example, as you preview, jot down what you already know—your **prior knowledge**—about the topics in the chapter's headings and subheadings. If you have turned the headings and subheadings into questions, try answering them based on your current knowledge. Then, you can modify and add to your answers as you read.

Estimate Difficulty Level

Based on your reading purpose and what you have learned by previewing, you can estimate how difficult an assignment will be for you. For example, if you are reading the article "Facts About Anxiety Disorders" just to be able to list the five primary types of anxiety disorders and you are already familiar with the terminology, you can predict the assignment will be relatively easy and you'll cover the material quickly. On the other hand, if you haven't read much about mental health and you are reading for details to prepare a speech on anxiety disorders, you can predict the assignment will take you some time.

By planning *before* you begin to read, you are more likely to understand the material and less likely to waste time.

READ ACTIVELY

Did you ever fall asleep while you were playing a game or watching your favorite television comedy? Probably not. Did you ever fall asleep while you were reading an assignment for class? Probably.

The difference is in how mentally and physically involved you are in the activity—whether you are an active or passive participant. For example, when you are actively involved in an activity—playing a game, laughing at a comedy—your mental and physical energy are focused on the task.

Unfortunately, students often view reading as a passive task that doesn't require attention or action. Passive readers are content to sit back and let the words pass by their eyes as their mind slips into neutral or considers what to have for lunch. They "wake up" a few pages later and wonder if they've missed anything "important." When you become passive, you rapidly lose interest and drift away.

Successful readers, like successful athletes, stay actively involved. Active mental and physical involvement keeps you interested and committed. Strategies for staying active include identifying the thesis and monitoring your comprehension.

Identify the Thesis

Multiparagraph selections like journal articles and text chapters are packed full of ideas. But you can still point to one idea—a topic and controlling thought—that is the selection's overall main idea. This overall idea is called the **thesis**.

Just as a main idea is the unifying idea that holds a paragraph together, the thesis is the unifying idea that holds the many paragraphs of the essay or chapter together. When you know the thesis of a selection, you have the idea that helps you connect, understand, and remember all the other ideas. When you read to learn, you must understand the thesis.

The thesis sentence is often stated in the first paragraph of a selection to prepare the reader for the rest of the paragraphs. However, the thesis can appear anywhere in the selection. In addition, the thesis can be implied. This means that in many selections you must put all of the author's ideas together and infer the thesis. Like other inferences, inferring the thesis requires your best reasoned conclusion based on the information you are given.

No matter where the thesis is located, your strategy for identifying and understanding the thesis is the same:

1. Identify the topic by answering the question, "Who or what is the entire selection about?" (You should have identified the topic during your preview.)
2. Clarify the controlling thought by answering, "What does the author want me to know or understand about the topic?" (Think about how each main idea helps to develop and explain the whole multiparagraph selection.)
3. Combine the topic and controlling thought to form the thesis.
4. State the thesis in your own words.

In the same way it is important to understand how the details and sentences of a paragraph relate to the main idea and the other sentences in the paragraph, it is important to understand how a paragraph relates to the thesis and to the other paragraphs.

Practice 1   **Your purpose for reading this selection is to identify the thesis.**

GETTING ORGANIZED

excerpted from **Adjustment and Human Relations**
by Tricia Alexander

[1]Sometimes we are so busy that we feel we don't have time to plan, but in fact, no matter how busy we are, we should find it worthwhile to take time to plan our activities. Perhaps we don't have time to plan *and* do absolutely everything else we would like to get done. Yet, by neglecting to plan, we will free very little time; and by failing to plan, we shall probably not discriminate among the essential and nonessential activities. If we spend only ten minutes at the beginning or end of the day planning, our efforts will be repaid many times over. The less time we feel we have to spare, the more important it is to plan our time carefully.

[2]Planning and making choices involve careful thinking and decision making. In the process, we learn to recognize what criteria we use in setting priorities. In all types of planning, we make lists and set priorities. A most useful planning strategy is to make a daily "To Do" list. Not all of the items on the list are of equal value. Once we have made a list, we need to set priorities on the basis of what is important to us on this particular day.

[3]To make this task easier, we can use an ABC Priority System. Write a capital letter *A* next to those items on the list that have a high value, a *B* for those with medium value, and a *C* for those with a low value. As we do this, we'll be using our subjective opinion as to the relative value of each item. By comparing the items with one another, we'll help ourselves come up with the ABC priority choices for each entry on the list. If it seems necessary, the activities can be broken down further so that A items become A-1, A-2, and A-3.

[4]Our ABC priorities may change over time. Today's C may become tomorrow's A. For instance, grocery shopping may be a C activity for a while, but eventually the cupboards become bare. Our priorities can be adjusted continually, according to the best use of our time right now. If we start with our A activities and always do them first, we can rest assured that we'll always be making the best use of our time. Our C activities may *never* get done if they do not become more urgent with the passage of time. That's okay! If we chronically have more activities on our list than we can manage to get done, we may eventually discard some C items, realizing that we are simply too busy to get to them.

[5]"To Do" lists are most effective when made each day, when the items are prioritized in an ABC fashion, and when items are crossed off as each task is completed. The list should be kept in sight so that we can look at it several times a day. We can make a game out of trying to plan just the right

amount of activities for each day so that we can score a "bingo" at the end of each day. The bingo means that all of the items for the day get crossed off. It's a good idea to get started on top priority items right away before any unexpected events of the day crop up and interfere with our plan. Toward the end of the day, we can initiate whatever actions are necessary to finish up our "bingo card" for a perfect score [Lakein, *How to Get Control of Your Time and Your Life*].

⁶One of the most important strategies to keep in mind is that getting panicky is never productive. It's amazing how much can be accomplished when one keeps plugging away, making little bits of progress toward the finish line. Be calm, and be relentless in your efforts.

Who or what is Alexander writing about? (the topic) _____

_____

What does Alexander want you to understand about the topic? (controlling thought)

_____

_____

Therefore, the thesis of this selection is _____

_____

Explanation   Who or what is Alexander writing about? *Planning.* What does Alexander want you to understand about planning? *It saves time and helps you be more efficient.* Therefore, the thesis is, *Taking a few minutes to plan will actually save you time and make you more efficient.*

Practice 2   **Your purpose for reading this selection is to identify the thesis.**

CAUSES OF CULTURAL CHANGE

excerpted from Sociology, by John J. Macionis

¹Cultural changes are set in motion in three ways. The first is *invention*, the process of creating new cultural elements. Invention has given us the telephone (1876), the airplane (1903), and the aerosol spray can (1941), each of which has had a tremendous impact on our way of life. Invention goes on constantly, as indicated by the thousands of applications submitted annually to the United States Patent Office.

²*Discovery*, a second cause of cultural change, involves recognizing and better understanding something already existing—from a distant star to the athletic prowess of U.S. women. Many discoveries result from scientific research. Yet discovery can also happen quite by accident, as when Marie Curie left a rock on a piece of photographic paper in 1898 and thus discovered radium.

³The third cause of cultural change is *diffusion*, the spread of cultural traits from one society to another. The technological ability to send information around the globe in seconds—by means of radio, television, facsimile (fax), and computer—means that the level of cultural diffusion has never been greater than it is today.

Who or what is Macionis writing about? (the topic) _____

_____

_____

What does Macionis want you to understand about the topic? (controlling thought)

_____

_____

Therefore, the thesis of this selection is _____

_____

_____

Explanation   Who or what is Macionis writing about? *Cultural changes.* What does Macionis want you to understand about cultural changes? *There are three causes.* Therefore, the thesis is, *Three factors can cause changes in our culture.*

Monitor Your Comprehension

Consider what would happen if you were putting a bicycle together but were missing a gear chain or handlebars. If a critical element were missing, you'd stop and try to solve the problem. If you didn't, you'd wind up investing hours of your time in a bike that didn't work. For similar reasons, active readers don't wade through twenty pages of text and then stop and say, "I missed something on page four," or "I didn't understand pages five through fifteen."

By continuously monitoring, or checking, your comprehension, you can keep track of your progress. For example, stop at the end of a sentence or paragraph and make sure you can put the idea into your own words.

When you run into problems such as words you don't understand, examples that don't make sense, or facts that are in conflict, develop the habit of stopping to solve the problem quickly.

Exercise 6 **Reading a Multiparagraph Selection**

ROBERT L. McGRATH

Mr. McGrath is a freelance writer. His work appears in numerous national publications. This selection is from Young Americans.

VOCABULARY

affecting (¶ 1): happening to, impacting
seasonal clothing (¶ 9): clothing appropriate to the season and temperature

IDEAS TO THINK ABOUT

Have you ever gotten caught out in a storm and gotten wet? Did you get cold? How did you get warm? *As you read,* find out why getting cold can be dangerous and what you can do about it.

WHEN X-COLD STRIKES

Robert L. McGrath

¹X-cold is hypothermia—body temperature lowered too rapidly by chilling from wet, wind, and cold. It brings quick collapse of mental and physical functions, affecting anyone, young or old.

²It's exception-cold, extensive-cold. X-cold happens when unexpected winter wind, rain, or snow arrives. Your clothes get wet and lose up to 90 percent of their insulating value. Water is held against your body with a chilling effect, even though outside temperatures can be as high as 50°F.

³Your body temperature, normally 98.6°F, drops to 94°F or below. If it cools further, it's a danger point—X-cold—because cooling to 80°F can produce death.

⁴If you know how to prevent it, X-cold won't spoil your outdoor fun. Watch for these signals:

Chattering teeth and shivering.

Slow, hard-to-understand speech.

Forgetfulness, confusion.

Fumbling hands.

Stumbling, difficulty in walking.

Sleepiness (the person going to sleep may never wake up).

Exhaustion (if the person can't get up after a brief rest, X-cold has taken over).

⁵X-cold reduces reasoning power and judgment because of lack of oxygen to the brain. The affected person usually denies that anything is wrong.

⁶What can you do? Find shelter. Build a fire. Get the victim out of wind, rain, snow. Strip off wet clothing and put on dry clothes or wrap up in a sleeping bag. Give warm drinks. Avoid medicines—they may slow down body processes even more.

⁷Body heat trapped by insulating clothing is the best protection against cold. Wear loose-fitting, lightweight clothing in several layers. Put on a knit cap—more than half the body's heat can be lost through the head. That extra warmth will send added blood to your feet, making them feel more comfortable.

⁸Remember, weather may pull surprises. Unexpected changes can bring sharp wind, driving rain, snow—conditions producing X-cold.

⁹Use your head. Wear seasonal clothing. Don't let X-cold—hypothermia—keep you from enjoying our great outdoors the year around.

Exercise 6 Questions

VOCABULARY

Circle the letter of the best definition for the italicized word.

1. "It brings quick *collapse* of mental and physical functions, affecting anyone, young or old." (¶ 1)

    a. rise   **c.** breakdown
    b. increase   **d.** growth

2. "Your clothes get wet and lose up to 90 percent of their *insulating* value." (¶ 2)

    a. heavy   **c.** fashionable
    b. protection   **d.** knit

COMPREHENSION

Determine whether the statements in sentences 3–5 are true or false, and circle your answer. If the statement is false, rewrite it to make it true.

T F **3.** Hypothermia can affect anyone of any age.

_____

_____

T F **4.** A person affected by hypothermia usually asks for help immediately.

False. A person affected by hypothermia usually denies that anything

is wrong.

T (F) **5.** It's important to wear gloves because more than half the body's heat can be lost through the hands.

 False. It's important to wear a knit cap because more than half the

 body's heat can be lost through the head.

6. Circle the letter of the sentence that best expresses the thesis.

    a. Insulating clothing is the best protection against cold.

    b. Hypothermia reduces reasoning power and judgment.

    (**c.**) X-cold can be deadly, so take immediate steps to reverse it, or better yet, prevent it.

    d. The weather is unpredictable.

7. What are four warning signs of hypothermia?

 Answers will vary; please see Answer Key.

8. What are four positive actions you can take to counteract hypothermia?

 Answers will vary; please see Answer Key.

9. In paragraph 5, what does the word *because* signal? Circle the letter of the correct answer.

    a. continuation of thought   (**c.**) cause

    b. change in direction of thought   **d.** effect

10. Write the main idea of paragraph 5.

 Main idea of paragraph 5: X-cold reduces reasoning power and

 judgment because of lack of oxygen to the brain.

> ### Exercise 7   Reading a Multiparagraph Selection

SELECTION: "HEALTHY AGING: A LIFELONG PROCESS"

REBECCA J. DONATELLE AND LORRAINE DAVIS

Dr. Donatelle, is an associate professor and Coordinator of Graduate Studies in the Department of Public Health at Oregon State University. Dr. Davis, is a professor of health education and Vice Provost for Academic Personnel at the University of Oregon. This selection is from chapter 21 of their text Access to Health.

VOCABULARY

prolong (¶ 1): lengthen, extend
inevitable (¶ 3): certain, cannot be avoided
chronological age (¶ 3): calendar age, number of years lived
predispositions (¶ 4): tendencies toward
vulnerabilities (¶ 4): susceptibility for, sensitivity to
ostracism (¶ 6): exclusion from, segregation

AN IDEA TO THINK ABOUT

How do you describe an "old" person? At what age do you think someone is old? Do all people act old when they reach that age? Do some people act old before they reach that age? *As you read,* find out what experts say about the aging process and if "older" always means a decline in physical and mental health.

HEALTHY AGING: A LIFELONG PROCESS

Rebecca Donatelle and Lorraine Davis

¹In a society that seems to worship youth, researchers have finally begun to offer some good—even revolutionary—news about the aging process: Growing old doesn't have to mean a slow slide to disability, loneliness, and declining physical and mental health. Health promotion, disease prevention, and wellness-oriented activities can prolong vigor and productivity, even among those who haven't always had model lifestyles or given healthful habits priority. In fact, getting older may actually mean getting better in many ways—particularly socially, psychologically, and intellectually.

GROWING OLD: LIFE PASSAGES

²Every moment of every day, we are involved in a steady aging process. Everything in the universe—animals, plants, mountain peaks, rivers, planets, even atoms— changes over time. This process is commonly referred to

as aging. Aging is something that cannot be avoided, despite the perennial human quest for a fountain of youth. Since you can't stop the process, why not resolve to have a positive aging experience by improving your understanding of the various aspects of aging, taking steps toward maximizing your potential, and learning to adapt and develop strengths you can draw upon over a lifetime?

[3]Who you are as you age and the manner in which you view aging (either as a natural part of living or as an inevitable move toward disease and death) are important factors in how successfully you will adapt to life's transitions. If you view these transitions as periods of growth, as changes that will lead to improved mental, emotional, spiritual, and physical phases in your development as a human being, your journey through even the most difficult times may be easier. No doubt you have encountered active, vigorous, positive 80-year-olds who wake up every morning looking forward to whatever challenges the day may bring. Such persons are socially active and have a zest for life. Many of them seem much younger than their chronological age, even though their physical casing may be weathered and gray. In contrast, you have probably met 50-year-olds who lack energy and enthusiasm, who seem resigned to tread water for the rest of their lives. These people often appear much older than their chronological age.

[4]From the moment of conception, we have genetic predispositions that influence our vulnerabilities to many diseases, our physical characteristics, and many other traits that make us unique. Maternal nutrition and health habits influence our health while we are in the womb and during the early months after birth. From the time we are born, we begin to take on characteristics that distinguish us from everyone else. We grow, we change, and we pass through many physical and psychological phases. Aging has traditionally been described as the patterns of life changes that occur in members of all species as they grow older. Some believe that it begins at the moment of conception. Others contend that it starts at birth. Still others believe that true aging does not begin until we reach our 40s.

[5]Typically, experts and laypersons alike have used chronological age to assign a person to a particular lifecycle stage. However, people of different chronological ages view age very differently. To the 4-year-old, a college freshman seems quite old. To the 20-year-old, parents in their 40s are over the hill. Have you ever heard your 65-year-old grandparents talking about "those old people down the street"? Views of aging are also colored by occupation. For example, a professional linebacker may find himself too old to play football in his mid-30s. Although some baseball players have continued to demonstrate high levels of skills into their 40s, most players are considering other careers by the time they reach 40. Airline pilots and policemen are often retired in their 50s, while college professors, U.S. senators, and even U.S. presidents may work well into their 70s. Perhaps our traditional definitions of aging need careful reexamination.

REDEFINING AGING

[6]Discrimination against people based on age is known as ageism. When directed against the elderly, this type of discrimination carries with it social ostracism and negative portrayals of older people. A developmental

task approach to life-span changes tends to reduce the potential for ageist or negatively biased perceptions about what occurs as a person ages chronologically.

[7]As people pass through critical periods in their lives, they are either successful or unsuccessful in their attempts to achieve specified goals. Those who are successful usually develop positive coping skills that carry over into other areas of their lives. They tend to think confidently and independently and are more prepared to "experience" life. Those who fail in these rites of passage either develop a sense of learned helplessness and lose confidence in their ability to succeed or learn to cope by compensating for their failures in productive ways.

[8]The study of individual and collective aging processes, known as gerontology, explores the reasons for aging and the ways in which people cope with and adapt to this process. Gerontologists have identified several types of age-related characteristics that should be used to determine where a person is in terms of biological, psychological, social, legal, and functional life-stage development:

- [9]*Biological age* refers to the relative age or condition of the person's organs and body systems. Does the person who is 70 years old have the level of physiological functioning that might be expected of someone in that age group? You have heard of the 70-year-old runner who has the cardiovascular system of a 40-year-old. In contrast, a 20-year-old suffering from progeria (symptoms resembling accelerated aging) may be physiologically closer to a 60-year-old. Arthritis and other chronic conditions often accelerate the aging process.

- [10]*Psychological age* refers to a person's adaptive capacities, such as coping abilities and intelligence, and to the person's awareness of his or her individual capabilities, self-efficacy, and general ability to adapt to a given situation. Although chronic illness may render someone physically handicapped, that person may possess tremendous psychological reserves and remain alert and fully capable of making decisions. Psychological age is typically assessed on the basis of everyday behavior, personal interviews, or tests.

- [11]*Social age* refers to a person's habits and roles relative to society's expectations. People in a particular life stage usually share similar tastes in music, television shows, and politics. Whereas rap music and/or heavy metal often appeal to teenagers and people in their 20s, they may repel middle-aged and older people. Cartoons and children's shows probably don't offer the same attraction for you in college that they did when you were a child.

- [12]*Legal age* is probably the most common definition of age in the United States. Legal age is based on chronological years and is used to determine such things as voting rights, driving privileges, drinking age, eligibility for Social Security payments, and a host of other rights and obligations.

- [13]*Functional age* refers to the ways in which people compare to others of a similar age. Heart rate, skin thickness, hearing, and other individual characteristics are analyzed and compared. A person's ability to perform a given job-related task is also part of this assessment. It is difficult to separate functional aging from many of the other types of aging, particularly chronological and biological aging.

WHAT IS NORMAL AGING?

[14]Contemporary gerontologists have begun to analyze the vast majority of people who continue to live full and productive lives throughout their later years. In the past, our youth-oriented society has viewed the onset of the physiological changes that occur with aging as something to be dreaded. The aging process was seen primarily from a pathological (disease) perspective, and therefore as a time of decline; the focus was not on the gains and positive aspects of normal adult development throughout the life span. Many of these positive developments occur in the areas of emotional and social life as older adults learn to cope with and adapt to the many changes and crises that life may hold in store for them.

[15]Gerontologists have devised several categories for specific age-related characteristics. For example, people who reach the age of 65 are considered to fit the general category of old age. They receive special consideration in the form of government assistance programs such as Social Security and Medicare. People aged 65 to 74 are viewed as the young-old; those aged 75 to 84 are the middle-old group; those 85 and over are classified as the old-old.

[16]You should note that chronological age is not the only component to be considered when objectively defining aging. The question is not how many years a person has lived, but how much life the person has packed into those years. This quality-of-life index, combined with the inevitable chronological process, appears to be the best indicator of the "aging gracefully" phenomenon. The eternal question then becomes "How can I age gracefully?" Most experts today agree that the best way to experience a productive, full, and satisfying old age is to take appropriate action to lead a productive, full, and satisfying life prior to old age. Essentially, older people are the product of their lifelong experiences, molded over years of happiness, heartbreak, and day-to-day existence.

Exercise 7 Questions

VOCABULARY

Match each word in the left column with the best definition in the right column.

1. perennial (¶ 2) __b__   **a.** disgust
2. quest (¶ 2) __e__   **b.** constant
3. laypersons (¶ 5) __c__   **c.** nonexperts
4. render (¶ 10) __d__   **d.** make
5. repel (¶ 11) __a__   **e.** search

COMPREHENSION

Determine whether the statements in sentences 6 and 7 are true or false, and write your answer. If the statement is false, rewrite it to make it true.

Ⓣ F **6.** Discrimination against people based on age is known as ageism.

_____

_____

T Ⓕ **7.** Chronological age is the only component that should be considered when objectively defining aging.

False. Chronological age is [not] the only component that should be

considered when objectively defining aging.

8. Circle the letter of the sentence that best expresses Donatelle and Davis's thesis.

    a. Everything in the universe ages.

    ⓑ We can and should try to lead happy and productive lives no matter what our chronological age.

    c. Gerontology explores the reasons for aging and the ways in which people cope with and adapt to this process.

    d. Some people seem much younger than their chronological age.

9. Gerontologists have identified five types of "age." List and explain them.

Answers will vary; please see Answer Key.

_____

_____

_____

_____

10. What do Donatelle and Davis say appears to be the best indicator of the "aging gracefully" phenomenon?

The quality-of-life index; see Answer Key for additional information.

11. Circle the letter of the sentence that best expresses the main idea of paragraph 3.

    a. If you have a positive outlook about getting older, your journey through even the most difficult times may be easier.

    ⓑ Who you are as you age and the manner in which you view aging are important factors in how successfully you will adapt to life's transitions.

c. Fifty-year-olds can appear much older than their chronological age, and eighty-year-olds can appear much younger than their chronological age.

d. If you have a negative outlook about getting older, your journey may be more difficult.

12. What is the relationship of paragraphs 9 through 13 to paragraph 8? Which of the following do they provide?

(a.) examples   c. causes
b. steps in a process   d. effects

Exercise 8 **Reading a Multiparagraph Selection**

B. E. (BUZZ) PRUITT, KATHY TEER CRUMPLER, AND DEBORAH PROTHROW-STITH

Dr. Pruitt is Professor of Health Education at Texas A&M University. Dr. Crumpler is Health and Safety Supervisor for the Onslow County School in Jacksonville, North Carolina. Dr. Prothrow-Stith is Associate Dean for Faculty Development at the Harvard School of Public Health. This selection is from Chapter 10, "Childhood and Adolescence" of their text Health: Skills for Wellness.

IDEAS TO THINK ABOUT

Have you ever heard stories about how old you were when you learned to walk or talk or share your toys with playmates? Do you think such stages of development are predictable? As you read, look for the various stages physical and mental development we go through as we age.

1 INFANCY THROUGH CHILDHOOD

As you grow up, you go through different stages of development. You develop both physically and mentally. For example, if you have young brothers and sisters, you have probably noticed that they do not behave, feel, or think the way older children and adults do. Babies and young children are not miniature adults. At each stage, the child's physical and mental development determines how it will interact with the other people in its life and with its environment.

Birth to Eighteen Months

Have you ever seen or held a newborn baby? A newborn is born with some physical skills. It can suckle, cry, and look right at you and see you–or direct its gaze. However, it will not learn to smile until it is about one month old. At birth, many of the baby's organs and systems are not fully developed. Its bones are still soft and flexible.

By the time it is 3 or 4 months old, the baby's brain, nerves, and muscles are ready for more coordinated movement. It recognizes its parents and siblings and can get what it needs by crying or responding to attention with obvious delight. By the time it is 18 months old, the baby has grown a great deal. It has probably learned to sit, crawl, stand, and walk and may be able to say a few words. It has "baby" teeth and can chew solid food. If you have ever lived with an

Figure 10-1 *Toddlers and babies grow and develop rapidly.*

18-month-old child, you know how active they are. Most children this age have completed a stage of growth and development that will not be equaled until they are ready to change from child to adult.

Parents of babies between birth and 18 months have one main responsibility: the physical care of their child. Babies need to be held and touched. Without hands-on, physical nurturing, the child will not survive.

Eighteen Months to Three Years

You probably learned to talk between 18 months and 3 years of age. This is also the age when children lose their babylike appearances. Appetite decreases as growth slows down. Baby fat is lost, the arms and legs get longer, and physical coordination improves.

During this time, most children are learning to assert themselves and to manipulate objects, such as toys. They may show off around family and friends but be shy around strangers. When they are with others their age, toddlers tend to play alongside, but not with, each other. They are not ready to share or to play interactively because they are busy learning how to do things for themselves. Most children between these ages learn to use the toilet.

Physical care continues to be an important parental responsibility, but it is slightly less intense. The child is no longer helpless. The main parental responsibility at this stage is to "keep an eye on" the child at all times. People who take care of toddlers have to be alert, because toddlers are too young to know when something can hurt them.

Three to Six Years

Between the ages of 3 and 6, most children lose all traces of babyhood. They become more independent and active. Muscles grow, energy is high, and the curious child is "into everything." Communication skills advance rapidly. You can understand what most 4-year-olds are saying. By the age of 5, most children begin to lose baby teeth.

During this stage, children learn to play interactively and to make friends. They begin school and learn how to behave in a group. Between 3 and 6, most children start spending less time with their parents and more time with their peers and teachers. This transition is sometimes difficult, unless they have a good sense of security and receive reassurance from their parents.

Parents of children between 3 and 6 find themselves in the role of teacher. The child still needs reassuring touches and hugs, but times of physical contact are less frequent. These tend to occur during specific activities, such as at bath time or while reading the child a story.

SHARPEN YOUR SKILLS

Working in Groups

With a group of students, find photos or illustrations of children at various stages of development, from birth to age 12. Use the pictures to make an illustrated time line of child development.

Figure 10-2 *Children between 3 and 6 are curious about everything that surrounds them.*

Exercise 8 Questions

VOCABULARY

Circle the letter of the correct answer.

1. The term *toddler* refers to a child who is

    a. birth to eighteen months   **c.** three years to six years
    (b.) eighteen months to three years

2. Between eighteen months and three years, most children are learning to assert themselves and to manipulate objects, such as toys. *Manipulate* means to

    a. enjoy   **(c.)** work, use
    b. destroy   **d.** share

COMPREHENSION

Determine whether the statements in sentences 3–5 are true or false, and circle your answer. If the statement is false, rewrite it to make it true.

T (F) **3.** Young children are miniature adults

   . False. Young children are [not] miniature adults. _____

(T) F **4.** At birth, a baby's bones are soft and flexible.

_____

(T) F **5.** Children become more independent and active between three and six years of age.

_____

6. Circle the letter of the sentence that best expresses the thesis.

    a. Newborn babies have some physical skills.
    b. Children learn to talk between eighteen months and three years.
    (c.) As you grow up, you go through different stages of physical and mental development that determine how you interact with other people and the environment.
    d. Between the ages of three and six, children become more independent.

7. What is the authors' primary structure in this portion of the chapter?

    (a.) sequence or process   **c.** comparison and contrast
    b. definition   **d.** classification

8. To help you understand each stage of development the authors use many

    a. definitions   **c.** comparisons
    (b.) examples   **d.** contrasts

9. What is the primary role of the parents in caring for children of these ages?

   a. birth to eighteen months: ___the physical care of their child___

   b. eighteen months to three years: ___to "keep an eye on" the child at all times___

   c. three to six years: ___teacher___

10. What do you predict the next section is about? _____

    ___ages six years and above.___

SUMMARY OF KEY IDEAS

- Reading is an active, thoughtful process that requires you to use a variety of skills and strategies. The unique combination of skills and strategies you use for a particular assignment depends on elements such as:

  your purpose for reading

  your knowledge of the subject

  the author's writing style

  the length of the reading

  the medium (the type and form of the publication)

- Planning strategies like setting a purpose, previewing, activating your prior knowledge, and estimating the difficulty level of the material help you become an active reader and give you a head start on good comprehension; they set you up to be successful.

- Successful readers always go beyond the "it was assigned" purpose. They develop specific reasons for reading based on what they need to know when they finish reading. Without a clear understanding of why you are reading a selection and what you need to know when you finish reading, you must read everything in the selection with equal emphasis and try to learn it all in complete detail.

- Previewing gives you an overview of how the selection is organized and its core ideas. It helps you make connections between what you know and what you are going to read. Previewing takes only a few minutes and can significantly improve your comprehension, reduce your frustration, and clarify your purpose for reading.

- The more we know about the subject we're reading, the easier it is to understand. So, just as you take time to think about a subject before you begin to write about it, you should take time to think about a subject before you begin reading about it.

- Based on your purpose and what you have learned by previewing, such as how difficult the vocabulary is and your knowledge about the topic, you should always estimate how difficult the assignment will be for you.

- Successful readers stay actively involved. Active physical and mental involvement keeps you interested and committed. Strategies for staying active include identifying the thesis and monitoring your comprehension.

- Multiparagraph selections like journal articles and text chapters are packed full of ideas. But you can still point to one idea—a topic and controlling idea—that is the selection's overall main idea, called the thesis.

- Just as a main idea is the unifying idea that holds a paragraph together, the thesis is the unifying idea that holds the many paragraphs of the essay or chapter together. When you know the thesis of a selection, you have the idea that helps you connect, understand, and remember all the other ideas.

- The thesis can appear anywhere in a chapter or essay, or it can be implied. However, no matter where the thesis is located, your strategy for identifying and understanding the thesis is the same:

  1. Identify the topic by answering the question, "Who or what is the entire selection about?" (You should have identified the topic during your preview.)
  2. Clarify the controlling thought by answering, "What does the author want me to know or understand about the topic?" (How does each main idea help to develop and explain the whole multiparagraph selection?)
  3. Combine the topic and controlling thought to form the thesis.
  4. State the thesis in your own words.

- In the same way it is important to understand how the details and sentences of a paragraph relate to the main idea and the other sentences in the paragraph, it is important to understand how a paragraph relates to the thesis and to the other paragraphs.

- By continuously monitoring, or checking, your comprehension, you can keep track of your progress. When you run into problems such as words you don't understand, examples that don't make sense, or facts that are in conflict, develop the habit of stopping to solve the problem quickly.

Use Your Strategies 1

ROBERT EPSTEIN

Dr. Epstein is a professor at United States International University in San Diego and an editor for Psychology Today. *His recent books include* Self-Help Without the Hype *and* Pure Fitness: Body Meets Mind. *This article is from* Treatment Today.

VOCABULARY

proposed (¶ 1): suggested
distinctly (¶ 2): clearly

regimens (¶ 3): regular pattern of exercise
exaggeration (¶ 6): overstatement
strides (¶ 7): steps forward, progress
gizmos (¶ 11): gadgets
spurred (¶ 13): urged

AN IDEA TO THINK ABOUT

How do you change a habit? Say, for example, you were in the habit of nibbling on junk food every evening as you watch television. If you wanted to stop snacking, how would you do it? *As you read,* find out what researchers think are the three best ways to change a habit.

CHANGE YOUR BAD HABITS TO GOOD
To Get Yourself Started in a New Direction, Try the Three M's

Robert Epstein

[1]At the University of California, my students and I surveyed more than 2000 years of self-change techniques—perhaps most of the major self-change methods that have ever been proposed by religious leaders, philosophers, psychologists, and psychiatrists. We also reviewed the scientific research literature on self-change, a topic that behavioral scientists began to explore in earnest in the 1960s.

[2]Here is what we found: of the hundreds of self-change techniques that have been suggested over the centuries, perhaps only a dozen are distinctly different. Many have now been subjected to scientific study, meaning that researchers have tried to see which ones work best.

[3]Three deserve special mention: they're powerful, simple, and easy to learn. What's more, individuals who have made successful changes in their lives—changes in eating habits, exercise regimens, career paths, coping strategies, and so on—often relied on one or more of these methods.

[4]To get yourself started in a new direction, try the Three M's:

MODIFY YOUR ENVIRONMENT

[5]People who have never tried this are astounded by the enormous effect it often has. One of my students got herself bicycling every day simply by putting her bicycle in her doorway before she left for school. When she returned home that was the first thing she saw, and that's all she needed to start pedaling away. I've known several people who have overcome nail-biting simply by buying 50 nail files and distributing them everywhere: in their pockets, their desks, and their bedrooms. With a nail file always within reach, they tended to groom rather than bite.

[6]My children have used this simple technique many times. Justin, my 17-year-old, often places small fluorescent reminder notes at eye level on the inside of the frame of his bedroom door. A recent one read "Remember to shampoo the dog on Saturday or Dad will kill you." (Here he was using exaggeration to good effect.)

⁷The power of rearranging one's space has been well demonstrated in studies since it was first reported in the 1960s. Psychologist Israel Goldiamond of the University of Chicago taught this technique to patients with a variety of personal problems. For example, a young woman who had difficulty studying made dramatic strides when she got a better desk lamp and moved her desk away from her bed.

⁸Psychologist Richard Stuart, who ultimately became a director at Weight Watchers International, showed in the 1960s that overweight women could lose pounds by modifying both their eating behavior and "stimulus environment"—for example, eating from smaller plates and confining all food to the kitchen. To change your *self*, change your world.

MONITOR YOUR BEHAVIOR

⁹I've been reading research studies on self-monitoring for 20 years, and I've conducted some myself. To be honest, I still don't fully understand why this technique works, but it does, and remarkably well for most people. The fact is, if you monitor what you do, you'll probably do better.

¹⁰Weigh yourself regularly and you may well start to lose weight. Keep a record of what you eat and you'll probably start eating more wisely.

¹¹Use gizmos. If you say "you know" too much, wear a golf counter on your wrist, and press the count button whenever you catch yourself saying "you know." I'll bet you say it less frequently in just a few days. If a wrist counter is embarrassing, then make a small tear in a piece of paper in your pocket each time you say "you know." The result is the same: you become more aware of what you're doing, and that makes you perform better.

¹²If techniques like this sound silly, keep in mind that the power of self-monitoring has been demonstrated by a variety of research conducted over the last four decades. In a study I published in 1978 with Claire Goss, for example, we taught a disruptive fifth-grade boy to rate his own classroom behavior twice a day. He simply checked off a score for himself, indicating how well-behaved he had been in the morning or afternoon. With his awareness increased, he stayed in his seat more than usual, completed more assignments, and rarely got in trouble.

¹³A similar study by Canadian researchers Thomas McKenzie and Brent Rushall showed that teenagers arrived more promptly at a swim practice when they were given an attendance sheet to record their arrival times. Working with emotionally disturbed children, Sonya Carr of Southeastern Louisiana University and Rebecca Punzo, a New Orleans teacher, reported that self-monitoring improves academic performance in reading, mathematics, and spelling. Recent research even demonstrated that students will compose better stories given a simple checklist that includes elements of good writing. Dozens of studies have similar results, all spurred by heightening our awareness of our behavior.

MAKE COMMITMENTS

¹⁴When you make a commitment to another person, you establish what psychologists call a contingency of reinforcement; you've automatically arranged for a reward if you comply and a punishment if you don't. It puts some pressure on you, and that's often just what you need.

[15]For instance, if you want to exercise more, arrange to do it with a friend. If you don't show up, your friend will get angry, and that may be just the ticket to keeping you punctual. Decades of research have demonstrated the power of this strategy. For example, in 1994 Dana Putnam and other researchers at the Virginia Polytechnic Institute and State University showed that patients who made written commitments were far more likely to take prescribed medicine than patients who hadn't. Mary Lou Kau and Joel Fischer of the University of Hawaii reported a case of a woman who got herself to jog regularly by setting up a simple arrangement with her husband: he paid her quarters and took her out on weekends whenever she met her jogging goals.

[16]There's good news here for all of us. We can meet many of the demands and overcome many of the challenges of life with simple skills—straightforward practices that anyone can master and that don't require willpower—in other words, with skill, not will.

Use Your Strategies 1 Questions

VOCABULARY

Circle the letter of the best definition for the underlined word.

1. ". . . behavioral scientists began to explore in <u>earnest</u> in the 1960s." (¶ 1)

   a. seriously   **c.** in laboratories
   b. honestly   **d.** in teams

2. "People who have never tried this are <u>astounded</u> by the enormous effect it often has." (¶ 5)

   a. angered   **c.** amazed
   b. confused   **d.** insulted

COMPREHENSION

Determine if the statements in sentences 3–5 are true or false, and write your answer. If the statement is false, rewrite it to make it true.

T F **3.** Modifying your environment often involves rearranging your living space.

_____

T F **4.** If you monitor what you do, you'll probably do better.

_____

T F **5.** Making a commitment to another person often helps us do better.

_____

6. Circle the letter of the sentence that best expresses the thesis.

  (a.) Using three simple self-change skills can help us meet and overcome many of life's demands and challenges.

  b. Of the hundreds of self-change techniques suggested over the centuries, perhaps only a dozen are distinctly different.

  c. The power of rearranging one's space has been well demonstrated in studies since it was first reported in the 1960s.

  d. If you want to exercise more, arrange to do it with a friend.

7. List the Three M's.

  Modify your environment.

  Monitor your behavior.

  Make commitments.

8. Give an example of a behavior you might want to change and one thing you could do to start to change it.

  Answers will vary.

9. What is the relationship of paragraph 10 to paragraph 9? Which of the following does it provide?

  (a.) examples   **c.** causes
  b. definitions   **d.** effects

10. What is the relationship of paragraph 15 to paragraph 14? Which of the following does it provide?

  (a.) examples   **c.** causes
  b. definitions   **d.** effects

Use Your Strategies 2

EDWARD T. THOMPSON

When Edward Thompson was Editor-in-Chief of Reader's Digest, *International Paper asked him to share some of what he had learned in his more than twenty years with the magazine famous for making complicated subjects understandable to millions of readers.*

VOCABULARY

clarity (¶ 9): clearness, precision
detract (¶ 10): take away from, lessen
ironically (¶ 14): appears to be contradictory
endeavoring (¶ 22): attempting, trying
belabor (¶ 31): to discuss for an unreasonably long period of time

AN IDEA TO THINK ABOUT

Are you one of the thousands of students who don't like to write? If so, what is it about writing that discourages you? *As you read,* find out three basic requirements that might make writing easier for you.

HOW TO WRITE CLEARLY

Edward T. Thompson

¹If you are afraid to write, don't be.

²If you think you've got to string together big fancy words and high-flying phrases, forget it.

³To write well, unless you aspire to be a professional poet or novelist, you only need to get your ideas across simply and clearly.

⁴It's not easy. But it is easier than you might imagine.

⁵There are only three basic requirements:

⁶First, you must *want* to write clearly. And I believe you really do, if you've stayed with me this far.

⁷Second, you must be willing to *work hard.* Thinking means work— and that's what it takes to do anything well.

⁸Third, you must know and follow some *basic guidelines.*

⁹If, while you're writing for clarity, some lovely, dramatic, or inspired phrases or sentences come to you, fine. Put them in.

¹⁰But then with cold, objective eyes and mind ask yourself: "Do they detract from clarity?" If they do, grit your teeth and cut the frills.

FOLLOW SOME BASIC GUIDELINES

¹¹I can't give you a complete list of "dos and don'ts" for every writing problem you'll ever face.

¹²But I can give you some fundamental guidelines that cover the most common problems.

1. Outline What You Want to Say

¹³I know that sounds grade-schoolish. But you can't write clearly until, *before you start,* you know where you will stop.

[14]Ironically, that's even a problem in writing an outline (i.e., knowing the ending before you begin).

[15]So try this method:

- On 3″ × 5″ cards, write—one point to a card—all the points you need to make.
- Divide the cards into piles—one pile for each group of points *closely related* to each other. (If you were describing an automobile, you'd put all the points about mileage in one pile, all the points about safety in another, and so on.)
- Arrange your piles of points in a sequence. Which are most important and should be given first or saved for last? Which must you present before others in order to make the others understandable?
- Now, *within* each pile, do the same thing—arrange the points in logical, understandable order.

[16]There you have your outline, needing only an introduction and conclusion.

[17]This is a practical way to outline. It's also flexible. You can add, delete, or change the location of points easily.

2. Start Where Your Readers Are

[18]How much do they know about the subject? Don't write to a level higher than your readers' knowledge of it.

[19]Caution: Forget that old—and wrong—advice about writing to a 12-year-old mentality. That's insulting. But do remember that your prime purpose is to *explain* something, not prove that you're smarter than your readers.

3. Avoid Jargon

[20]Don't use words, expressions, phrases known only to people with specific knowledge or interests.

[21]Example: A scientist, using scientific jargon, wrote, "The biota exhibited a one hundred percent mortality response." He could have written "All the fish died."

4. Use Familiar Combinations of Words

[22]A speech writer for President Franklin D. Roosevelt wrote, "We are endeavoring to construct a more inclusive society." F. D. R. changed it to, "We're going to make a country in which no one is left out."

[23]Caution: By familiar combinations of words, I do *not* mean incorrect grammar. *That* can be *un*clear. Example: John's father says he can't go out Friday. (Who can't go out? John or his father?)

5. Use "First-Degree" Words

[24]These words immediately bring an image to your mind. Other words must be "translated" through the first-degree word before you see the image. Those are second/third degree words.

First-degree words	Second/third-degree words
face	visage, countenance
stay	abide, remain, reside
book	volume, tome, publication

[25]First-degree words are usually the most precise words, too.

6. Stick to the Point

[26]Your outline—which was more work in the beginning—now saves you work. Because now you can ask about any sentence you write: "Does it relate to a point in the outline? If it doesn't, should I add it to the outline? If not, I'm getting off the track." Then, full steam ahead on the main line.

7. Be as Brief as Possible

[27]Whatever you write, shortening—*condensing*—almost always makes it tighter, straighter, easier to read and understand.

[28]Condensing, as *Reader's Digest* does it, is in large part artistry. But it involves techniques that anyone can learn and use.

- [29]*Present your points in logical ABC order:* Here again, your outline should save you work because, if you did it right, your points already stand in logical ABC order—A makes B understandable, B makes C understandable, and so on. To write in a straight line is to say something clearly in the fewest possible words.

- [30]*Don't waste words telling people what they already know:* Notice how we edited this: "Have you ever wondered how banks rate you as a credit risk? ~~You know of course, that it's some combination of facts about your income, your job, and so on But actually, m~~ Many banks have a scoring system. . . ."

- [31]*Cut out excess evidence and unnecessary anecdotes:* Usually, one fact or example (at most, two) will support a point. More just belabor it. And while writing about something may remind you of a good story, ask yourself: "Does it really help to tell the story or does it slow me down?"

  [32](Many people think *Reader's Digest* articles are filled with anecdotes. Actually, we use them sparingly and usually for one or two reasons: either the subject is so dry it needs some "humanity" to give it life; or the subject is so hard to grasp, it needs anecdotes to help readers understand. If the subject is both lively and easy to grasp, we move right along.)

- [33]*Look for the most common word wasters:* windy phrases.

Windy phrases	Cut to...
at the present time	now
in the event of	if
in the majority of instances	usually

- [34]*Look for passive verbs you can make active:* Invariably, this produces a shorter sentence. "The cherry tree *was* chopped down by

George Washington." (Passive verb and nine words.) "George Washinton chopped down the cherry tree." (Active verb and seven words.)

- [35]*Look for positive/negative sections from which you can cut the negative:* See how we did it here: "The answer ~~does not rest with carelessness or in competence. It lies largely~~ in is having enough people to do the job."

- [36]Finally, to write more clearly by saying it in fewer words: when you've finished, stop.

Use Your Strategies 2 Questions

VOCABULARY

Match each word in the left column with the best definition in the right column.

1. aspire (¶ 3) __c__   **a.** basic
2. fundamental (¶ 12) __a__   **b.** shortening
3. prime (¶ 19) __e__   **c.** desire
4. precise (¶ 25) __f__   **d.** stories
5. condensing (¶ 27) __b__   **e.** primary
6. anecdotes (¶ 31) __d__   **f.** accurate

COMPREHENSION

Determine whether the statements in sentences 7–9 are true or false, and circle your answer. If the statement is false, rewrite it to make it true.

(T) F **7.** According to Thompson, you must know where you want your writing to stop before you begin.

_____

_____

T (F) **8.** You need a large vocabulary with big fancy words to write well.

False. You [do not] need a large vocabulary with big fancy words to

write well.

(T) F **9.** Using active verbs instead of passive verbs usually makes writing shorter and clearer.

_____

_____

10. Circle the letter of the sentence that best expresses Thompson's thesis.

    a. You must want to write clearly.

    b. You can't write clearly without an outline.

    (c.) To write well, you need to get your ideas across simply and clearly.

    d. Whenever you write, be a brief as possible.

11. Thompson says there are three basic requirements for getting your ideas across simply and clearly. List them.

    a. You must want to write.

    b. You must be willing to work hard.

    c. You must know and follow some basic guidelines.

12. List the signal words Thompson used to alert you to the three basic requirements.

    Signal words: First, Second, Third

13. List Thompson's "fundamental guidelines" that cover most common writing problems.

    Outline what you want to say.

    Start where your readers are.

    Avoid jargon.

    Use familiar combinations of words.

    Use "first-degree" words.

    Stick to the point.

    Be as brief as possible.

14. What is the relationship of paragraphs 29 through 35 to paragraph 28? Which of the following do they provide?

    a. examples　　　　**c.** causes

    (b.) steps in a process　　**d.** effects

**COURTLAND BOVÉE, JOHN THILL,
AND BARBARA SCHATZMAN**

Dr. Bovée is professor of Business Communication, C. Allen Paul Distinguished Chair at Grossmont College. Dr. Thill is chief executive officer of Communication Specialists of America. Dr. Schatzman is with the Keller Graduate School of Management and president of Summit One Global Business Solutions. This selection is excerpted from Chapter 2, "Communicating in Teams and Mastering Listening and Nonverbal Communication Skills," of their text Business Communication Today, *seventh edition.*

AN IDEA TO THINK ABOUT

Do you ever communicate your feelings without saying a word? For example, do you smile to show you agree, wave your hand to say goodbye, or shrug your shoulders to say, "I don't know"? *As you read,* find out how the various types of nonverbal communication impact our lives.

IMPROVING YOUR NONVERBAL COMMUNICATION SKILLS

*Courtland Bovée, John Thill,
and Barbara Schatzman*

[1]The old maxim is true: People's actions often do speak louder than their words. In fact, most people can deceive others much more easily with words than they can with their bodies. Words are relatively easy to control; body language, facial expressions, and vocal characteristics are not. By paying attention to these nonverbal cues, you can detect deception or affirm a speaker's honesty.

[2]Because nonverbal communication is so reliable, people generally have more faith in nonverbal cues than they do in verbal messages. If a person says one thing but transmits a conflicting message nonverbally, listeners almost invariably believe the nonverbal signal.[1] Chances are, if you can read other people's nonverbal messages correctly, you can interpret their underlying attitudes and intentions and respond appropriately.

[3]Nonverbal communication is also important because it is efficient. You can transmit a nonverbal message without even thinking about it, and your audience can register the meaning unconsciously. At the same time, when you have a conscious purpose, you can often achieve it more economically with a gesture than with words. A wave of the hand, a pat on the back, a wink—all are streamlined expressions of thought. However, nonverbal communication usually blends with speech to carry part of the message—to augment, reinforce, and clarify that message.

TYPES OF NONVERBAL COMMUNICATION

[4]According to one estimate, there are more than 700,000 forms of nonverbal communication.[2] For discussion purposes, however, these forms can be grouped into the following general categories: facial expression, gesture and posture, vocal characteristics, personal appearance, touching behavior, and use of time and space.

Facial Expression

[5]Your face is the primary site for expressing your emotions; it reveals both the type and the intensity of your feelings.[3] Your eyes are especially effective for indicating attention and interest, influencing others, regulating interaction, and establishing dominance.

[6]In fact, eye contact is so important in the United States that even when your words send a positive message, averting your gaze can lead your audience to perceive a negative one.[4] Of course, people sometimes manipulate their expressions to simulate an emotion they do not feel or to mask their true feelings. Of course, the interpretation of facial expressions, and of all nonverbal signals, varies from culture to culture. . . . However, even though many nonverbal gestures and expressions are interpreted differently in different cultures, six fundamental facial expressions are understood around the globe—fear, surprise, sorrow, joy, disgust, and anger.

Gesture and Posture

[7]By moving your body, you can express both specific and general messages, some voluntary and some involuntary. Many gestures—a wave of the hand, for example—have a specific and intentional meaning, such as "hello" or "good-bye." Other types of body movement are unintentional and express a more general message. Slouching, leaning forward, fidgeting, and walking briskly are all unconscious signals that reveal whether you feel confident or nervous, friendly or hostile, assertive or passive, powerful or powerless.

Vocal Characteristics

[8]Like body language, your voice carries both intentional and unintentional messages. On a conscious level, you can use your voice to create various impressions. Consider the sentence "What have you been up to?" If you repeat that question four or five times, changing your tone of voice and stressing various words, you can convey quite different messages. However, your vocal characteristics also reveal many things of which you are unaware. The tone and volume of your voice, your accent and speaking pace, and all the little *um*'s and *ah*'s that creep into your speech say a lot about who you are, your relationship with the audience, and the emotions underlying your words.

Personal Appearance

[9]People respond to others on the basis of their physical appearance. Because you see yourself as others see you, their expectations are often a self-fulfilling prophecy; that is, when people think you're capable and attractive, you feel good about yourself, and that feeling affects your behavior, which in turn affects other people's perceptions of you. Although

an individual's body type and facial features impose limitations, most people are able to control their attractiveness to some degree. Grooming, clothing, accessories, "style"—all modify a person's appearance. If your goal is to make a good impression, adopt the style of the people you want to impress.

Touching Behavior

[10]Touch is an important way to convey warmth, comfort, and reassurance. Perhaps because it implies intimacy, touching behavior is governed by relatively strict customs that establish who can touch whom and how in various circumstances. The accepted norms vary, depending on the gender, age, relative status, and cultural background of the persons involved. In business situations, touching suggests dominance, so a higher-status person is more likely to touch a lower-status person than the other way around. Touching has become controversial, however, because it can sometimes be interpreted as sexual harassment.

Use of Time and Space

[11]Like touch, time and space can be used to assert authority. Some people demonstrate their importance by making other people wait; others show respect by being on time. People can also assert their status by occupying the best space. In U.S. companies, the chief executive usually has the corner office and the prettiest view. Apart from serving as a symbol of status, space can determine how comfortable people feel talking with each other. When others stand too close or too far away, we are likely to feel ill at ease. Again, attitudes toward punctuality and comfort zones vary from culture to culture. . . .

TIPS FOR MAXIMIZING YOUR NONVERBAL COMMUNICATION SKILLS

[12]When communicating orally, pay attention to your nonverbal cues. Avoid giving others conflicting signals. For instance, if you tell an employee that you are free to talk to her about her raise but your nonverbal signals suggest that this is not the best time to discuss the subject, she will be confused. So try to be as honest as possible in communicating your emotions. Here are some additional tips for honing your nonverbal skills:[5]

- [13]Smile genuinely. A fake smile is obvious because the timing isn't right and the wrinkles don't follow.
- [14]Be aware that people may give false nonverbal cues.
- [15]Keep an appropriate distance between you and others, and use touch only when appropriate.
- [16]Respect status with your eye contact.
- [17]Adopt a handshake that matches your personality and intention.

[18]Few gestures convey meaning in and of themselves; they have to be interpreted in clusters, and they should reinforce your words. To improve your nonverbal skills, pay more attention to the kinds of signals discussed in this chapter.

REFERENCES

1. David Lewis, *The Secret Language of Success* (New York: Carroll & Graf, 1989), 67, 170.

2. Nido Qubein, *Communicate Like a Pro* (New York: Berkeley Books, 1986), 97.

3. Dale G. Leathers, *Successful Nonverbal Communication: Principles and Applications* (New York: Macmillan, 1986), 19.

4. Gerald H. Graham, Jeanne Unrue, and Paul Jennings, "The Impact of Nonverbal Communication in Organizations: A Survey of Perceptions,"*Journal of Business Communications*, 28, no. 1 (Winter 1991): 45–62.

5. Gerald H. Graham, Jeanne Unrue, and Paul Jennings, "The Impact of Nonverbal Communication in Organizations: A Survey of Perceptions,"*Journal of Business Communications*, 28, no. 1 (Winter 1991): 45–62.

Use Your Strategies 3 Questions

VOCABULARY

Circle the letter of the best definition for the underlined word.

1. ". . . most people can <u>deceive</u> others much more easily with words than they can with their bodies." (¶ 1)

   (a.) mislead   **c.** reinforce

   b. anger   **d.** hurt

2. "However, nonverbal communication usually blends with speech to carry part of the message—to <u>augment</u>, reinforce, and clarify that message." (¶ 3)

   a. diminish   **c.** detract from

   (b.) add to   **d.** lessen

COMPREHENSION

Determine whether the statements in sentences 3–5 are true or false, and circle your answer. If the statement is false, rewrite it to make it true.

T (F) **3.** It's easier to mislead someone with body language than it is with verbal language.

   False. It's [harder] to mislead someone with body language than it is

   with verbal language.

(T) F **4.** Your face is the primary site for expressing your emotions.

(T) F **5.** Many nonverbal gestures and expressions are interpreted differently in different cultures.

_____

_____

6. Circle the letter of the sentence that best expresses the thesis.

   a. There are more than 700,000 forms of nonverbal communication.
   b. Physical appearance and style contribute to one's identity.
   c. Actions speak louder than words.
   (**d.**) Improving your understanding and use of nonverbal communication skills is important to personal and business success.

7. The authors group the many forms of nonverbal behavior into six general categories. List them.

   facial expressions

   gesture and posture

   vocal characteristics

   personal appearance

   touching behavior

   use of time and space

8. Give an example, mentioned in the reading or from personal experience, of a nonverbal gesture or expression that means different things in different cultures or circumstances.

   Examples of nonverbal gestures or expressions that mean different

   things in different cultures or circumstances will vary.

9. The authors advise us to "avoid giving others conflicting signals." Explain what they mean.

   Don't say one thing verbally and another nonverbally.

10. Give a personal example to explain and support the maxim "Actions speak louder than words."

   Personal examples to explain and support the maxim, "Actions speak

   louder than words" will vary.

_____

_____

_____

Use Your Strategies 4

ANDREW CAYTON, ELISABETH ISRAELS PERRY, LINDA REED, AND ALLAN M. WINKLER

Dr. Cayton is Professor of History at Miami University in Oxford, Ohio. Dr. Perry is Research Professor of History at Vanderbilt University in Nashville, Tennessee. Dr. Reed directs the African American Studies Program at the University of Houston. Dr. Winkler is Professor of History at Miami University in Oxford, Ohio. This selection is excerpted from Chapter 28, "The Kennedy and Johnson Years: 1960–1968," of their text America: Pathways to the Present.

AN IDEA TO THINK ABOUT

From what you've read and heard about President John F. Kennedy, how would you describe him, his 1960 election, and his time in office? *As you read,* find out about the programs he proposed to improve the economy, to address the issues of poverty and civil rights, and to expand the space program.

	1961	1962			
1960	**Alan Shepard**	**John Glenn**	**1962**		
John F. Kennedy	becomes first	becomes first	**Michael Harrington**	**1963**	
elected President	American to	American to	publishes The	**President Kennedy**	
	travel in space	orbit Earth	Other America	assassinated	

1960	**1962**	**1964**

1 The New Frontier

SECTION PREVIEW

Objectives

1 Describe the election of 1960 and its outcome.
2 Summarize Kennedy's domestic programs.
3 Explain Americans' reaction to President Kennedy's assassination.
4 *Key Terms* Define: mandate; New Frontier; Warren Commission.

Main Idea

Before his assassination in 1963, President John F. Kennedy proposed a number of domestic programs to improve the economy and to address issues of inequality, including poverty and civil rights. Most of Kennedy's proposals were defeated in Congress.

Reading Strategy

Reinforcing Main Ideas As you read the section, create a list of the programs that Kennedy proposed.

On September 26, 1960, millions of Americans turned on their televisions to watch as two presidential candidates squared off in the country's first televised debate. The two candidates were Republican Richard Nixon (Eisenhower's Vice President) and Democrat John F. Kennedy. With studio lights glaring, Nixon appeared tired and hot. Kennedy, in contrast, looked polished and relaxed. He had hired consultants to help him with makeup and clothes. This debate and the three that followed had a major impact on the outcome of the election. The debates also changed forever the role that television would play in American politics.

The Election of 1960

Kennedy, a Massachusetts Democrat who had served in the United States House of Representatives and Senate, faced serious obstacles in his quest for the presidency. He was only forty-three years old, and many questioned whether he had the experience needed for the nation's highest office. In addition, Kennedy was a Roman Catholic, and no Catholic had ever been elected President. Kennedy put an end to the

religion issue when he won the primary in the largely Protestant state of West Virginia. With that hurdle behind him, he campaigned hard, with promises to spur the sluggish economy.

During the last years of the Eisenhower administration, the Gross National Product (GNP) had grown very slowly. In addition, the economy had suffered several recessions. During the campaign, Kennedy proclaimed that it was time to "get America moving again."

In the election, Kennedy won by an extraordinarily close margin.[†] Though the electoral vote was 303 to 219, Kennedy won by only 120,000 popular votes out of more than 34 million cast. If but a few thousand voters in Illinois or Texas had cast ballots for Nixon, the Republicans would have won. As a result of

Presidential candidates Richard Nixon and John F. Kennedy squared off in a series of televised debates in 1960.

[†] Although the youngest person ever to be elected President, Kennedy was not the youngest ever to hold the office. Theodore Roosevelt, who became President when McKinley was assassinated, was the youngest to hold the office.

Jacqueline and John F. Kennedy dazzled the nation with their beauty, youth, and glamour. *Government Why was Kennedy's administration later nicknamed Camelot?*

this razor-thin victory, Kennedy entered office without a strong **mandate**. A mandate is a set of wishes expressed to a candidate by his or her voters. Without such a mandate, Kennedy would have difficulty pushing his more controversial measures through Congress.

No matter how slim his margin of victory, Kennedy was now President. In ringing phrases he declared in his Inaugural Address:

> **KEY DOCUMENTS** ❝Let the word go forth from this time and place, to friend and foe alike, that the torch has been passed to a new generation of Americans, born in this century, tempered by war, disciplined by a hard and bitter peace. . . . And so, my fellow Americans, ask not what your country can do for you; ask what you can do for your country.❞
>
> —*John F. Kennedy*, Inaugural Address

The new administration was buoyant, energetic, and full of optimism. Jacqueline Kennedy, the President's wife, charmed the country with her grace. Nobel Prize winners visited the White House. The Kennedys and their friends loved to play touch football on the lawn or take long hikes.

The administration, which seemed full of idealism and youth, later earned the nickname

"Camelot" after a 1960 Broadway musical. The musical portrayed the legendary kingdom of the British King Arthur. Arthur dreamed of transforming medieval Britain from a country in which "might makes right," or the strong always get their way, into one where power would be used to achieve right.

Kennedy's Domestic Programs

In a speech early in his administration, Kennedy said that the nation was poised at the edge of a **New Frontier.** The name stuck and was used to describe Kennedy's proposals to improve the economy, give aid to the poor, and breathe new life into the space program.

The Economy Concerned about the continuing recession, Kennedy hoped to work with the business community to restore prosperity to the nation. Often, however, he faced resistance from executives who were suspicious of his plans. The worst fears of business leaders were realized in the spring of 1962. When the U.S. Steel Company announced that it was raising the price of steel by $6 a ton, other firms did the same. Worried about inflation, Kennedy called the price increase unjustifiable and charged that it showed "utter contempt for the public interest." He ordered a federal investigation into the possibility of price-fixing. Under that pressure, U.S. Steel and the other companies backed down. Business leaders remained angry, and the stock market fell in the steepest drop since the Great Crash of 1929.

On the larger issue of ending the economic slump, Kennedy proposed cutting taxes. In 1963 the President called for a $13.5 billion cut in taxes over three years. The measure would reduce government income and create a budget deficit at first. Kennedy believed, however, that the extra cash in taxpayers' wallets would stimulate the economy and bring added tax revenues in the end. The tax-cut proposal was soon bottled up in a congressional committee and stood little chance of passage.

Combating Poverty and Inequality Kennedy also was eager to take action against poverty and inequality. In his first two years in office, Kennedy hoped that he could help the poor simply by stimulating the economy. In 1962 author Michael Harrington described the situation of the poor in his book, *The Other America.* Harrington's book revealed that while many Americans were enjoying the prosperity of the

1950s, a shocking one fifth of the population was living below the poverty line. Kennedy began to believe that direct aid to the poor was necessary.

Despite his concern, Kennedy rarely succeeded in pushing legislation through Congress. Kennedy's ambitious plans for federal aid for education and medical care for the aged both failed. Kennedy did succeed, however, in raising the minimum wage and passing the Housing Act of 1961. This act provided $4.9 billion for urban renewal. Congress also approved the Twenty-Fourth Amendment to go to the states for ratification. This amendment outlawed the poll tax, which was still being used in five southern states to keep poor African Americans from voting.

The Space Program Kennedy was more successful in his effort to breathe life into the space program. Following the Soviet Union's launch of *Sputnik* in 1957, numerous government agencies and industries had been working furiously with NASA, the National Aeronautics and Space Agency, to place a manned spacecraft in orbit around Earth. As part of the Mercury program, seven test pilots were chosen to train as astronauts in 1959. Government spending and the future of NASA seemed uncertain, however, when a task force appointed by Kennedy recommended that NASA concentrate on exploratory space missions without human crews.

All of this changed in April 1961. The Soviet Union announced that Yuri Gagarin had become the first human to travel in space and had circled Earth on board the Soviet spacecraft *Vostok*. Gagarin's flight rekindled Americans' fears that the United States was falling behind the Soviet Union.

Twenty-three days later, on May 5, 1961, the United States made its own first attempt to send a person into space. Astronaut Alan Shepard made a 15-minute suborbital flight that reached an altitude of 115 miles. Though this flight did not match the orbital flight of the Soviets, its success did convince Kennedy to move forward. On May 25, Kennedy issued a bold challenge to the nation. He said the United States "should commit itself to achieving the goal, before this decade is out, of landing a man on the moon."[†]

Both the nation and the government accepted the challenge, and funding for NASA

[†] For the remainder of the decade, succeeding NASA flights brought the country closer and closer to its goal. On July 20, 1969, United States astronaut Neil Armstrong became the first person to set foot on the moon.

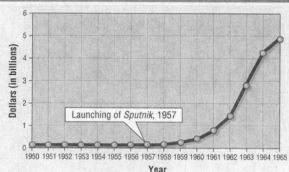

Federal Funding of NASA, 1950–1965

y-axis: Dollars (in billions), *x*-axis: Year

Launching of *Sputnik*, 1957

*National Aeronautics and Space Administration
Source: *Historical Statistics of the United States, Colonial Times to 1970*

Interpreting Graphs NASA grew out of the National Advisory Committee for Aeronautics, which was established in 1915. Alarmed by the launching of *Sputnik*, in 1958 Congress authorized the new federal agency to promote the research and development of air and space. *Economics How does the graph illustrate the influence of the Soviet Union's* Sputnik *on United States policy?*

was increased. Less than a year later, on February 20, 1962, John Glenn successfully completed three orbits around Earth and landed in the Atlantic Ocean near the Bahamas. Later that year Kennedy spoke at Rice University in Houston, Texas:

AMERICAN VOICES ❝We set sail on this new sea because there is new knowledge to be gained, and new rights to be won, and they must be won and used for the progress of all people. . . . [O]nly if the United States occupies a position of preeminence can we help decide whether this new ocean will be a sea of peace or a new, terrifying theater of war.❞

—*John F. Kennedy*

Main Idea CONNECTIONS

Why did Kennedy's space program succeed while most of his other domestic programs did not?

Kennedy Is Assassinated

On November 22, 1963, as Kennedy looked ahead to reelection the following year, he traveled to Texas to mobilize support. Texas Governor John Connally and his wife Nelly met Kennedy and his wife at the airport in Dallas. Together they rode through the streets of Dallas in an open limousine. Thousands of supporters lined the route of the motorcade. Suddenly shots rang and bullets struck both Connally and the President. While Connally

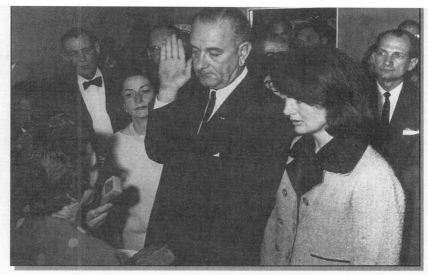

A sad and solemn-looking Lyndon Johnson is sworn in as President aboard Air Force One shortly after President Kennedy's assassination. A grief-stricken Jacqueline Kennedy (right) looks on. *Culture What was the nation's reaction to Kennedy's death?*

was only wounded, President Kennedy was pronounced dead soon after his arrival at a nearby hospital. The country was shattered. Millions of Americans remained glued to their television sets for the next four days as the impact of the tragedy sank in.

Shortly after Kennedy's death, a commission headed by Chief Justice Earl Warren was formed to investigate the crime. The prime suspect in Kennedy's assassination was Lee Harvey Oswald, a former marine and supporter of Cuba's Fidel Castro. Two days after Kennedy's assassination, Oswald was transferred from one jail to another. While the nation watched on television, Dallas nightclub owner Jack Ruby stepped through the crowd of reporters and

fatally shot Oswald. After months of investigation, the **Warren Commission** declared that Oswald had worked alone in shooting the President. Since then, however, some people have argued that Oswald was involved in a larger conspiracy, and that he was killed in order to protect others who had helped plan Kennedy's murder.

Lyndon Johnson, who had also traveled to Dallas with Kennedy, took the presidential oath of office on board Air Force One just ninety minutes after Kennedy's death. Johnson went on to make good use of the spirit of hope and the desire for change that Kennedy had inspired. He saw enacted much of the legislation that his predecessor had tried to push through Congress.

SECTION 1 REVIEW

Comprehension

1. *Key Terms* Define: (a) mandate; (b) New Frontier; (c) Warren Commission.

2. *Summarizing the Main Idea* What were some of the successes and failures of Kennedy's domestic policies?

3. *Organizing Information* Create a time line of the major events in the space program between 1959 and 1962.

Critical Thinking

4. *Analyzing Time Lines* Review the time line at the start of the section. How did President Kennedy respond to Michael Harrington's book, *The Other America*?

5. *Drawing Inferences* Why was the Kennedy administration nicknamed "Camelot"? How did the dream of Camelot end?

Writing Activity

6. *Writing an Expository Essay* Write an essay describing the role of television in the election of 1960 and its role today.

Use Your Strategies 4 Questions

VOCABULARY

Circle the letter of the best definition for the underlined word.

1. Kennedy faced serious <u>obstacles</u> in his quest for the presidency.

   a. opposition candidates   c. Republicans
   (b.) problems   d. debates

2. "Only if the United States occupies a position of <u>preeminence</u> can we help decide whether this new ocean will be a sea of peace or a new, terrifying theater of war.

   a. inferiority   c. weakness
   b. inadequacy   **(d.)** superiority

COMPREHENSION

Determine whether the statements in sentences 3–5 are true or false, and circle your answer. If the statement is false, rewrite it to make it true.

T **(F)** **3.** The televised Kennedy–Nixon debates had very little impact on the election.

   False. The televised Kennedy–Nixon debates had [great] impact on the

   election.

(T) F **4.** The first manned U.S. space flight took place when Kennedy was president.

   _____

   _____

(T) F **5.** Kennedy rarely succeeded in pushing legislation through Congress.

   _____

   _____

6. Write the main idea (thesis) of this section.

   Thesis (from first page of excerpt): Before his assassination in 1963,

   President John F. Kennedy proposed a number of domestic programs

   to improve the economy and to address issues of inequality, including

   poverty and civil rights. Most of Kennedy's proposals were defeated in

   Congress.

7. The text says, "Kennedy entered office without a strong mandate." Explain what that means and what effect it had on his work with Congress.

"A mandate is a set of wishes expressed to a candidate by his or her

voters." Without a mandate, Kennedy had difficulty getting legislation

through Congress.

8. Early in his administration, Kennedy said that the nation was poised at the edge of a *New Frontier*. The name stuck and was used to describe proposals Kennedy made in three important areas. List the proposal areas:

the economy

combating poverty and inequality

the space program.

9. Explain why the Kennedy administration earned the nickname Camelot.

The Kennedy administration earned the nickname Camelot after the

1960 Broadway musical that portrayed the legendary kingdom of the

British King Arthur. Kennedy, like Arthur, dreamed of transforming

his nation into one where power would be used to achieve "right."

10. Describe how a timeline is useful in helping to understand historical information.

A timeline is useful in understanding historical information because it

shows the sequence.

REFLECT AND CONNECT

A. It is estimated that people entering the workforce today will change careers about six times during their lives. Visit your college's career center and gather information on three potential careers for yourself. Compare and contrast the skills and attitudes needed among the three careers.

B. Each time you read, your purpose for reading, your knowledge of the subject, the author's writing style, the length of the reading, and the medium (the type and form of the publication) are different. Which of these factors make reading most difficult for you? What positive actions do you take to reduce the problems? What advice would you give to other readers on how to improve their comprehension?

C. Today you can choose to take many of your college courses in classrooms at your college or over the Internet. What do you see as some of the positive effects and some of the negative effects of each alternative?

LOG ON TO THE WEB

The Web offers a wealth of information on almost any topic you can imagine. Log on to one of these sites or use a search engine to locate a site with information that interests you.

> The Food and Drug Administration: *http://www.fda.gov/*
> Classic Crime Stories: *http://va.crimelibrary.com/classicstories.htm*
> The Great Outdoor Recreation Pages: *http://www.gorp.com*
> CBS's SportsLine: *http://www.sportsline.com/*
> Time magazine's top 100 people: *http://www.time.com/time100*

Read a selection with the specific purpose of understanding the thesis.
Print out the selection you read and write down (1) the complete Web address, (2) the name of the person or company who sponsors and maintains the site, (3) the name of the person who wrote the information you read, (4) what you know about the writer, and (5) the thesis of the selection.

CROSSWORD PUZZLE

Across

1 rejection or exclusion

6 shorten

10 extend

13 overstatement

16 change

19 regulated systems

20 correct

21 in a contradictory way

23 protecting from cold

25 make active

26 unify

27 intelligibility

28 use

Down

2 main idea of multi-
paragraph selection

3 breakdown

4 watch over

5 discuss for an unreasonably
long time

7 steps forward

8 take away from

9 make an educated guess

11 gadgets

12 certain

13 attempting

14 impacting

15 search

17 look over in advance

18 clearly

22 inactive

24 involved

Word List (not all used)

accurate

activate

active

affecting

astounded

belabor

chronological age

clarity

collapse

condense

detract

distinctly

endeavoring

estimate

exaggeration

gizmos

inevitable

insulating

integrate

ironically

manipulate

modify

monitor

ostracism

passive

predispositions

preview

prolong

quest

regimens

strides

thesis

vulnerabilities

read-ing (rēd´in) *adj.* **1** inclined to read or study **2** reading n. **1** the act or practice of person who r of books **2** a public entertainment which litera aloud **3** the extent to which a person has read **4** meant to be read **5** the amount measured as by a thermometer **6** the form of a specified word, sent

THEME

1 It's All About Attitude

Some people are always grumbling because roses have thorns;
I am thankful that thorns have roses.

Alphonse Karr

When you look at this glass, do you see it as half full or half empty?

How you answer may tell a lot about your view of the world and your chances for happiness and success.

This is because people who are optimistic—those who see the glass as half full—expect great things, work hard for those things, and are likely to achieve them. People with a positive attitude look for the "can do" side of every situation. On the other hand, pessimists—those who see the glass as half empty—seem to search for the "cannot do" side of a situation.

According to Dr. Norman Vincent Peale, author of the phenomenal multimillion-copy best-seller, *The Power of Positive Thinking,* "Attitudes are more important than facts." Certainly, you can't ignore a fact, he said, "but the attitude with which you approach it is all-important. The secret of life isn't what happens to you but what you do with what happens to you."

Now, psychologists, neurologists, sociologists, and even economists are joining together in the fast-growing field of "happiness studies" to investigate how we can improve our attitude and use it to make the most of what happens to us. Martin E. P. Seligman, Ph.D., former head of the American Psychological Association and author of the best-selling book *Learned Optimism,* is a leader in "positive psychology," the basic idea of which is that "you can train yourself to spin the events in your life from an optimistic point of view." For example, if you're fired from your job, you see it as an opportunity for a new beginning.

Putting a positive spin on events does appear to have real benefits. For example, studies on the link between happiness and healthiness show that you may stay healthier if you think the glass is half full. Research also shows that your attitude is contagious: you can "give" your attitude to others or "catch" their attitude. For example, when your attitude is upbeat and sincere, people around you are likely to relate to you and your activities with an energy and positive attitude that creates a winning, successful environment.

But a positive attitude does not necessarily pop into your mind by itself. How you feel and react are decisions you make every day. The authors in this theme provide insight and advice for making those decisions.

Dr. Charles Swindoll opens the theme with "Attitudes," a short essay on why he believes a person's attitude is important. Next, Dr. Barbara K. Bruce and Ms. Denise Foley ask, "Is It Time for an Attitude Adjustment?"

In "Why Aren't We Happier?" Neil Rosenthal urges us to "stop focusing on what is terrible and begin focusing on what is wonderful." Then Ziggy, Tom Wilson's cartoon philosopher, ponders the same dilemma. "How to Be an Optimist," by Lise Funderburg, discusses current research that suggests optimism is a scientifically proven way to get happier and healthier.

In an excerpt from their classic text *Your Attitude Is Showing: A Primer of Human Relations,* professors Elwood N. Chapman and Sharon Lund O'Neil discuss how to "Hold on to Your Positive Attitude." And finally, Ana Veciana-Suarez reminds us how the "'Little Engine' Holds a Valuable Life Lesson."

Selection 1 "Attitudes"

CHARLES SWINDOLL

Dr. Swindoll is president of Dallas Theological Seminary, senior pastor of the Stonebriar Community Church in Frisco, Texas, and the main speaker on the worldwide radio broadcast Insight for Living.

VOCABULARY

> *convey* (¶ 1): communicate, tell
> *incredible* (¶ 1): unbelievable

AN IDEA TO THINK ABOUT

What do you think is the most important decision you make every day? *As you read,* find out what Dr. Swindoll thinks is his most important decision.

ATTITUDES

Charles Swindoll

[1a]Words can never adequately convey the incredible impact of our attitude toward life. [1b]The longer I live, the more convinced I become that life is 10 percent what happens to us and 90 percent how we respond to it.

²ᵃI believe the single most significant decision I can make on a day-to-day basis is my choice of attitude. ²ᵇIt is more important than my past, my education, my bankroll, my successes or failures, fame or pain, what other people think of me or say about me, my circumstances, or my position. ²ᶜAttitude keeps me going or cripples my progress. ²ᵈIt alone fuels my fire or assaults my hope. ²ᵉWhen my attitudes are right, there's no barrier too high, no valley too deep, no dream too extreme, no challenge too great for me.

Selection 1 Questions

VOCABULARY

Circle the letter of the best definition for the italicized word.

1. "The longer I live, the more convinced I become that life is 10 percent what happens to us and 90 percent how we *respond* to it." (¶ 1)

   a. question   **c.** disagree
   (b.) react   **d.** agree

2. "I believe the single most *significant* decision I can make on a day-to-day basis is my choice of attitude." (¶ 2)

   (a.) important   **c.** minor
   b. unimportant   **d.** timely

COMPREHENSION

3. Circle the letter of the sentence that best expresses the thesis.

   a. Attitude keeps us going.
   b. Words can't describe the impact of our attitude.
   (c.) Choosing to have a positive attitude every day makes our life better.
   d. Our happiness depends on how much education, money, fame, and success we achieve.

4. What does Swindoll think is the most important decision he can make every day?

   Most important decision: "my choice of attitude."

   _____

5. According to Swindoll, "life is __10 percent__ what happens to us and

   __90 percent__ how we respond to it."

6. What does Swindoll think can happen when his "attitudes are right?"

   When his "attitudes are right," there's "no barrier too high, no valley

   too deep, no dream too extreme, no challenge too great for me."

7. What is the relationship of sentences 2c and 2d to sentence 2b?

   (**a.**) They continue the same thought.
   b. They define terms.
   c. They tell the cause.
   d. They change the direction of thought.

8. What does the word *it* refer to in sentences 2b and 2d?

   a. I
   b. amount of money
   c. day-to-day living
   (**d.**) choice of attitude

Selection 2 "Is It Time for an Attitude Adjustment?"

BARBARA K. BRUCE AND DENISE FOLEY

Dr. Bruce, a psychologist at the Mayo Clinic, Rochester, Minnesota, is on the editorial board of Mayo Clinic Women's HealthSource. Ms. Foley, a contributing writer for Mayo Clinic Women's HealthSource, is co-author of The Women's Encyclopedia of Health. *This article is from* USA Today Magazine, *September 1998.*

VOCABULARY

inherit (¶ 1): to receive certain characteristics from ancestors
provocatively suggests (¶ 2): implies information that excites
stature (¶ 3): height, build
susceptibility for (¶ 3): capacity or sensitivity for
chronic (¶ 4): constant, continuous
invariably (¶ 5): always, without fail
Pollyanna-like attitude (¶ 7): excessively and persistently optimistic
Chicken Little [attitude] (¶ 8): excessively and persistently pessimistic
berate (¶ 15): yell at, belittle
plausible (¶ 16): possible, probable
salvage (¶ 17): recover, retrieve

AN IDEA TO THINK ABOUT

Is your general attitude—optimistic or pessimistic—the same today as it was when you were in elementary school? How about when you were in high school? *As you read,* find out if Bruce and Foley think people can change their attitude.

IS IT TIME FOR AN ATTITUDE ADJUSTMENT?

Barbara K. Bruce
and Denise Foley

[1]You got your blue eyes from Dad and your strawberry blond hair from Mom. The tiny bump on the bridge of your nose definitely is from Grandpa William. However, did you also inherit your pessimistic attitude or your sunny outlook? Are you genetically programmed to see the glass as half empty or half full?

[2]Recent research suggests that some personality traits and attitudes indeed may be part of your genetic blueprint. In 1996, scientists announced they had located genes linked to anxiety, addiction, happiness, and pessimism. Their studies provocatively suggest that you may have been born to be grumpy, hostile, a worrier, outgoing, or cheerful. You even may be one of those people who is born to be wild because you carry a thrill-seeking gene.

[3a]If you have struggled all your life with chronic worry, dark moods, or a short fuse, does this research mean you are a born loser in a biological game of chance? [3b]The answer is "no." [3c]Biology is not destiny, nor is your attitude entirely a matter of luck. [3d]Part of your personality is inherited, but, at most, only half is. [3e]That leaves a lot of room for self-improvement. [3f]Even more encouraging, the genes for personality aren't like those for eye color and height. [3g]Your blue eyes and short stature are determined by your DNA. [3h]You merely inherit a susceptibility for doom and gloom—and, conversely, cheerfulness. [3i]Whether you see the glass as half empty or half full is largely up to you.

[4]Chronic worrying, flying into a rage at the slightest provocation, or always expecting the worst are traits worth changing, but there are other reasons to adjust your attitude. Studies show that being positive pays off. Research has found that individuals with positive outlooks do better in school, their careers, and personal lives than pessimists. In one study, for instance, insurance salespeople who had positive outlooks sold 56 percent more insurance than less-optimistic co-workers. That result convinced one of the nation's largest insurance companies to start hiring people based on their optimism, not just their salesmanship.

[5]Optimists invariably are physically and mentally healthier. Studies have found that they rarely get depressed and anxious. Optimists are more likely to take better care of themselves by eating right, exercising, and getting checkups. One study found that young women who considered themselves "positive" knew more about cancer and did more to prevent it than those who were more pessimistic.

[6]When optimists do get sick, they recover quicker. Heart bypass patients who were more upbeat recovered faster from surgery and felt better at a five-year follow-up than pessimists who had the same operation. In another study, pregnant women who were upbeat during their third trimester were less likely to have postpartum depression.

[7]Being positive isn't a Pollyanna-like attitude that somehow things will work out for the best. Optimists believe they can make things succeed. They look at setbacks as temporary and failures as learning experiences. Like the "Little Engine That Could," they think they can, which gives them the energy and motivation to make it happen. Their positive attitude buffers them against stress because they react to adversity by planning and taking action. That makes them feel in control. When things do go wrong, they make the best of it. They face life's slings and arrows with a sense of hope.

[8]On the other hand, if you have a gloomy outlook on life, are hostile, or, like Chicken Little, are fretting constantly that the sky is falling, studies show you are at high risk for developing depression and anxiety. That's because, when you predict the future—and you do—it always looks bleak. You are more likely to do poorly in school and work largely because you have so little confidence in your abilities. Even your health may suffer. Research has found that pessimism can shorten your life, and hostility—specifically having an aggressive and cynical view of people and the world around you—predisposes you to heart disease. You are more likely to feel helpless, not hopeful, when adversity strikes.

[9]In small doses, some of these negative attitudes can be constructive. There are times when anger is appropriate—if you are snubbed by a good friend or feel you have been passed over for a promotion, for example. If you are worried that your marketing presentation won't go over or that you haven't prepared well enough for your meeting, anxiety can prod you to work even harder. Even a little caution is healthy—ask any safety engineer, CEO, or mother.

[10]If you are consumed by worry, though, you won't have the energy to put into your preparation. If you are too cautious, you may not take calculated risks that could be beneficial to you. If you don't believe anything you can do will make a difference, you are likely to quit too soon, perhaps within reach of your goal.

[11]There is no way to know whether your personality traits are the result of nature or nurture. Nevertheless, whether your negativity is inborn or just an entrenched habit, you can learn to be more upbeat.

[12]Your first obstacle will be your automatic thoughts. You may not even be aware of what you are thinking when, for instance, someone cuts you off in traffic or your best friend doesn't return your call. You may know that you react with anger when the car swerves in front of you or automatically assume that your friend either hates you or is deathly ill, but you may not know why. Recognizing your automatic thoughts will be the first step toward changing them.

[13]*Keep a daily log.* Carry a notebook and pen with you and jot down what you are thinking and feeling when faced with a problem. Look for patterns, especially of blame, guilt, anger, and despair. Note how often you use the words "always" and "never," as in "I always mess up" and "My friends never come through for me." Note all-or-nothing statements such as "If I don't get this promotion, I'm no good." Rate the intensity of your thoughts and feelings, from mild to extreme.

[14]*Challenge your thoughts.* Put your automatic thoughts to the test. Ask yourself these questions:

- How true and reasonable are my thoughts?
- What proof do I have to support my thinking?

- Is there another possible explanation or conclusion I can draw? If so, what?
- Do I think worrying about something is necessary to my success?
- Is there someone else I can ask to test the reality of my thinking?
- Does it help—or hurt—me to think this way?
- Even if I am right, is it something I can deal with?

[15]*Be nice to yourself.* Don't beat yourself up when things go wrong. Don't call yourself names. If your best friend was having a bad day, you wouldn't berate her for everything she did wrong. You would treat her like a friend—which is how you should treat yourself.

[16]*Look for the silver lining.* Psychologists call this "reframing." You need to learn a new way to look at things. Instead of being discouraged by criticism or a setback, consider these things feedback that will help you find new and better ways to accomplish what you want. For example, if your boss suggests that you may have missed an important market in your report, use the information to make the report better. Look for other plausible explanations for events that make you angry or upset. Maybe your best friend hasn't returned your phone call because he's busy or his answering machine is broken, not because he is angry with you, inconsiderate, or dead. Moreover, the driver who cut you off could be rushing to the hospital.

[17]*Use bad experiences to your advantage.* Researchers at the University of California at Davis asked 2,000 people about the worst times in their lives—ranging from divorce to job loss to combat. They were surprised to find that most individuals were able to salvage something positive from their most traumatic experiences. Some learned how strong they were; others, what wonderful friends and resources they had. Some found a renewed faith in God. Most thought their experiences made them better able to cope with other problems that came along.

[18]*Distract yourself.* To calm angry feelings or lift a bad mood, do something positive and engrossing. Rent a funny movie. Do a 3-D puzzle. Plan a dream vacation. Plant some flower bulbs. Take a brisk walk outdoors. Count your blessings. One of the best coping skills optimists have is their ability to remember all the good things in their lives when bad times come along. Make a list of your blessings. Pick something from every realm of your life—family, work, and community. When things go wrong, pull out your list and remind yourself of what is going right.

[19]*Create a success.* When you feel down, tackle a moderately challenging chore you have been putting off, like inserting family photos in an album or painting your bathroom. Afterwards, you'll feel a sense of accomplishment.

[20]*Try a dose of good humor.* The act of laughing, even if it is forced, tends to improve your mood and enhance your ability to come up with creative solutions to your problems. One way to get a quick laugh—especially when there is nothing funny about what is happening to you—is to do the "tee-hee" exercise developed by psychotherapist Annette Goodheart. Simply add the words "tee-hee" to the end of a sentence describing your gloom, as in "I'm going to be downsized, tee-hee" or "I just burned a $40 standing rib roast and my in-laws are coming, tee-hee." It sounds so silly, you just have to laugh.

What Words Do You Live By?

Many of us share automatic thoughts—platitudes we heard from our parents when we were growing up. Unconsciously, these may be the words we live by. Take the following test to learn if you face life with a positive or negative outlook. Put a check mark next to the phrases that best describe your feelings.

1. Every dark cloud has a silver lining.
2. It's better to be safe than sorry.
3. Seize the day.
4. Look before you leap.
5. Treat everyone the way you would like to be treated.
6. When it rains, it pours.
7. The best things in life are free.
8. There's no such thing as a free lunch.
9. Love is the answer.
10. Every person for himself/herself.

Scoring: Count up the odd-numbered and even-numbered phrases you picked. The more odd-numbered platitudes you chose are an indication that you do indeed look for the silver lining in every dark cloud. If you chose more even-numbered phrases, you are more focused on the dark cloud.

Selection 2 Questions

VOCABULARY

Match each word in the left column with the best definition in the right column.

1. chronic (¶ 3) __b__   **a.** makes susceptible
2. destiny (¶ 3) __e__   **b.** constant, habitual
3. provocation (¶ 4) __f__   **c.** credible, believable
4. buffers (¶ 7) __g__   **d.** securely established
5. predisposes (¶ 8) __a__   **e.** fate, inevitable future
6. entrenched (¶ 11) __d__   **f.** reason, cause
7. plausible (¶ 16) __c__   **g.** shields, protects

Complete sentences 8–11 below with the most appropriate form of the following words:

pessimist (n) pessimistic (adj)
optimist (n) optimistic (adj)

8. People with a positive outlook on life are more likely to succeed than

   those with a __pessimistic (adj)__ attitude.

9. A __pessimist (n)__ is often depressed and anxious.

10. A person with a positive outlook on life is called an ___optimist (n)___ .

11. ___Optimistic (adj)___ people believe they can succeed.

COMPREHENSION

Determine whether the statements in sentences 12–14 are true or false, and circle your answer. If the statement is false, rewrite it to make it true.

(T) F **12.** Whether you see the glass as half empty or half full is largely up to you.

_____

_____

T (F) **13.** People with a gloomy outlook are just as healthy as optimists.

___Answers will vary; please see Answer Key.___

_____

T (F) **14.** All of our personality traits and attitudes are inherited.

___False. Some of our personality traits and attitudes are inherited.___

_____

15. Circle the letter of the sentence that best expresses the thesis.

    a. Research suggests our personality is inherited.

    (**b.**) Even though we may inherit a susceptibility for some personality traits, we can choose and control our attitude.

    c. Most individuals are able to salvage something positive from even their most frightening experiences.

    d. Pessimists are not as healthy as optimists.

16. According to Bruce and Foley, being an optimist pays off. List two examples of the payoff.

___Answers will vary; please see Answer Key.___

_____

17. Why are pessimists more likely to do poorly in school and work?

___Pessimists are more likely to do poorly in school and work because___

___they have so little confidence in their abilities.___

18. In paragraph 3, sentence h, what does the word *conversely* signal?

    a. continuation of thought   **c.** definition

    (**b.**) change in direction of thought   **d.** effect

19. Circle the letter of the sentence that best expresses the main idea of paragraphs 5 and 6.

   a. Optimists get more exercise than pessimists.
   b. Pessimists don't recover from surgery as fast as optimists.
   c. Women who have a positive outlook know more about cancer and do more to prevent it.
   (d.) Optimists are physically and mentally healthier than pessimists.

20. What signal/transition phrase do Bruce and Foley use to begin paragraph 8?

   On the other hand

That phrase signals:

   a. a continuation of the same thought
   (b.) a change in direction of thought (contrast)
   c. an effect

21. In paragraph 16, Bruce and Foley say people should "look for the silver lining." What does that mean? Why is it a good thing to do?

   A "silver lining" is the positive aspect of an event. Looking for the positive helps keep us optimistic and reduces the time we spend dwelling on negatives.

22. What is the relationship of paragraphs 13–20 to paragraph 12? Which of the following do they provide?

   (a.) examples   c. causes
   b. definitions   d. effects

REFLECT AND CONNECT

23. What advice would you give a friend who wants to "adjust" his or her attitude?

   Answers will vary.

   _____

   _____

Selection 3 "Why Aren't We Happier?"

NEIL ROSENTHAL

Dr. Rosenthal is a licensed marriage and family therapist in Colorado. His weekly column "Relationships" appears in the Daily Camera *(Boulder, Colorado), and he maintains a Web site at <www.heartrelationships.com>.*

VOCABULARY

> *exuberance* (¶ 1): enthusiasm
> *immersed* (¶ 6): submerged, drowned
> *embodies* (¶ 12): expresses, combines
> *revel* (¶ 13): enjoy, rejoice, delight

AN IDEA TO THINK ABOUT

What do you need to do to live well and enjoy life? *As you read,* find out how Rosenthal answers that question.

WHY AREN'T WE HAPPIER?

Neil Rosenthal

[1]When was the last time you can remember walking around with a smile on your face, a laugh in your belly, a lightness in your heart, and a sense of exuberance at the sheer wonder of being alive?

[2]There is so much that seems to be weighing us down that lightness and fun are missing elements in many people's lives. Just look around. Business is serious. Sports are serious. Relationships are serious. Parenting is serious. Even food has become serious.

[3]We worry about the preparations for our outdoor party as we concern ourselves with the weather. We don't enjoy the miracle of our children's growth as we worry about how they will turn out. We don't enjoy the abundance we have in our lives as we worry about the future—of our health, careers, relationships, and our retirement accounts. We diminish the present as we worry about the future. In essence, we lose the freedom to soar that comes from enjoying the vast riches that life has to offer in the here and now.

[4]What if you knew your life would work beautifully even if it rained the day of the party? Even if your children didn't turn out the way you hoped, even if you lost money in your investments.

[5]Susan Jeffers, in the book *End the Struggle and Dance With Life* (St. Martins Griffin), talks about taking off on an airplane on a very cloudy day. The plane climbed through the fog and dense cloud cover. It was dark and gloomy and, to some, frightening. At one point, the clouds began to lighten, and all of a sudden the plane burst into the glorious light of the sun. She described that it was hard to believe that reaching a place of intense clarity and light was simply a matter of rising above the clouds.

[6]Rising above the clouds is a metaphor for how many of us live—our refusal to live our lives. Most of the time, we are immersed in fog and heaviness, not understanding that all we have to do is learn how to fly above the various clouds we inevitably encounter in our lives.

[7a]Jeffers suggests that most of us have an immense capacity for taking things for granted. [7b]But when we take things for granted, we never get to see the magnitude of the gifts that are constantly being placed before us.

[7c]As a result, we feel only scarcity—instead of feeling abundance. Taking things for granted is one of the greatest assaults on the quality of our lives. Yes, the world is a mess. Your life might be a mess. And despite those facts, there is so much to be grateful for that it staggers the imagination.

[8]The riches of the world envelop us, yet we cannot see. Why? We are in the habit of focusing on what is terrible about life and ignoring what is wonderful. Our task, then, seems very simple—to stop focusing on what is terrible and begin focusing on what is wonderful.

[9]We all know that becoming older is supposed to be our time for harvesting, for reaping the rewards of our lives. But for many of us who have plowed and sown seed, we are not very good at the harvesting part. We have to get past our conditioning that has taught us that enjoyment is supposed to come only after all the work has been done, which seems to be never. Harvesting is a learned skill. Many people retire hoping to finally reap the rewards of all their hard work. But they simply have never learned how to harvest their lives, and therefore a fair number find their retirement disappointing or depressing.

[10]Here are some secrets about how to gather the riches every day of our lives; about how to live well and enjoy life:

[11]What are you grateful for? Where is your life abundant? It's so easy to ignore what we have or what's good in our lives, and to focus on what we don't have, or what has disappointed us. Look mindfully and deeply at the blessings in your life. As we start looking for the good, our focus is automatically taken off the bad.

[12]Train yourself to be appreciative of your life every day. Each night before you go to sleep, create a word or two that embodies a sense of appreciation of all that has been given to you during the day. And as you close your eyes to go off to sleep, fall asleep to the words "thank you." This simple ritual will keep you from dwelling on annoying and petty daily events that might ordinarily keep you awake. Any of the following words might also work for you: embrace, breathe, trust, heal, open, lighten, enjoy, delight, appreciate, care, share, enough, savor, receive, let go, touch, flow, I am at peace, I trust, I am blessed.

[13]So much would be added to our lives if we could just learn how to revel in the incredible gifts inherent in our ordinary lives and ordinary experiences.

[14]Learn the art of jumping for joy. Many of us have not jumped for joy (literally or figuratively) in a very long time. We must remember to celebrate every inner or outer "win" in our lives. Learn how to wisely whoop-di-do your successes and accomplishments. Astarius Reiki-Om reminds us "It does not matter how much or how little we achieve. If we don't jump for joy about it, we don't feel the emotional mileage."

[15]Don't hang on so tightly to the way it's "supposed" to be. Trust that whatever happens—good or bad—will still provide you with ample opportunities to learn and grow, to better yourself, and to realize your highest potential. The ebb and flow of life can be faced from a place of harmony rather than from struggle.

[16]Focus your attention on your senses. On seeing the beauty around you. On hearing the rich collection of sounds most of us simply take for granted.

[17]"Give every day the chance to be the best day of your life." Margaret Mitchell

Selection 3 Questions

VOCABULARY

Circle the letter of the best definition for the italicized word.

1. "...learn how to fly above the various clouds we *inevitably encounter* in our lives." (¶ 6)

   a. are certain to experience   c. are unlikely to experience
   b. may be able to avoid   d. could not understand

2. "...for *reaping* the rewards of our life." (¶ 7)

   a. sacrificing   c. gathering
   b. letting go   d. distributing

3. "...dwelling on annoying and *petty* daily events...." (¶ 12)

   a. happen over and over   c. large and important
   b. essential to well-being   d. little and unimportant

COMPREHENSION

4. Circle the letter of the sentence that best expresses the thesis.

   a. Rising above the clouds is a metaphor for the way many of us live.
   b. We need to stop focusing on what is terrible and begin focusing on what is wonderful.
   c. Business and sports and relationships are serious.
   d. Focus your attention on your senses.

5. In paragraph 3, Rosenthal says, "We diminish the present as we worry about the future." What does he mean? Does he think this helps us to be happy or keeps us from being happy?

   It means that we're so busy worrying about what might happen in the

   future that we forget to enjoy the present. Rosenthal thinks this keeps

   us from being happy.

6. In paragraph 7, what is the relationship of sentence c to sentence b?

   a. Sentence 7c gives an effect of sentence 7b.
   b. Sentence 7c defines terms used in sentence 7b.
   c. Sentence 7c presents a contrasting thought to sentence 7b.

   What signal/transition phrase does Rosenthal use in sentence c to signal the relationship?

   As a result

7. According to Rosenthal, many people find retirement "disappointing or depressing." Why does he think this happens? What can you infer he thinks would help people enjoy retirement more?

   Rosenthal believes many people find retirement "disappointing or de-

   pressing" because we are conditioned to believe we can't enjoy any-

   thing until "all the work has been done"—which we've never

   experienced and thus don't know how to do. We can infer that Rosen-

   thal thinks we should all enjoy (harvest) more every day, not waiting

   until "everything" is done.

8. Rosenthal lists several "secrets" for gathering riches in our daily life. List three of them.

   Answers will vary; please see Answer Key.

   _____

   _____

9. What is the relationship of paragraphs 11–16 to paragraph 10?

   a. They give examples of ways to "gather riches every day."
   b. They define key terms about "how to be happy."
   c. They tell the causes of happiness.

REFLECT AND CONNECT

10. What advice would you give a friend about how to live well and enjoy life?

    Answers will vary.

    _____

    _____

    _____

Selection 4 Ziggy

TOM WILSON

Prepare to Read

Tom Wilson's cartoon creation Ziggy first appeared in 1971 on the comic pages of 15 American newspapers. Through the years he's encouraged us to take things less seriously, have a little laugh at ourselves, and focus on the "rainbow instead of the storm." Today, in addition to appearing in 600 newspapers, he pops up in numerous books, calendars, animated specials, and greeting cards. Tom II has been drawing Ziggy with his father since 1987.

AN IDEA TO THINK ABOUT

How do you typically react when your plans don't work out the way you thought they would? *As you read,* try to answer Ziggy's "what if" question.

(ZIGGY ©ZIGGY AND FRIENDS, INC. Reprinted with permission of UNIVERSAL PRESS SYNDICATE. All rights reserved.)

Selection 4 Questions

1. What does Ziggy want us to think about?

   Ziggy wants us to think about how often we miss the real lessons of

   life because we are too busy being frustrated and impatient that

   things aren't going the way they are supposed to go.

2. Compare Ziggy's message to Rosenthal's message in paragraph 15 of "Why Aren't We Happier?" Are the messages the same or different? Please explain.

   Both Rosenthal and Ziggy want us to quit hanging on so tightly to the

   way things are "supposed" to be and to trust that whatever happens—

   good or bad—will provide us with ample opportunities to learn and

   grow, to better ourselves, and to realize our highest potential.

Selection 5 How to Be an Optimist

LISE FUNDERBURG

Ms. Funderburg is an essayist, feature writer, and book critic based in Philadelphia. She graduated from Reed College and earned her masters at the Columbia University School of Journalism. Her first book is a collection of oral histories called Black, White, Other: Biracial Americans Talk about Race and Identity, *and she has contributed to numerous anthologies. She is a senior writer for* Time *and has written for numerous other magazines, including* The Nation, New York Times Magazine, Oprah Magazine, *and* Life.

VOCABULARY

sunny Pollyannas (¶ 1): a person who is excessively and persistently optimistic
blithely (¶ 1): cheerfully, in high spirits
resilient (¶ 4): able to bounce back
panacea (¶ 10): cure-all

AN IDEA TO THINK ABOUT

When you experience a setback such as having trouble getting a new computer program to work, how do you react? What do you typically say to yourself? *As you read,* find out why your reaction to a setback is important.

HOW TO BE AN OPTIMIST

Lise Funderburg

[1]Many of us have a hunch—though it hasn't been proven beyond the shadow of doubt—that the only category of humanity more annoying than street mimes is relentless optimists. You know them: endlessly, unbearably sunny Pollyannas, clearly in denial about the world's harsh realities, skipping along blithely, head in the clouds, and no doubt (everyone else can't help hoping) about to step in something very, very unpleasant.

[2]But optimism is much more than a reckless chirping through life. According to experts in the field, optimism is a high-voltage power tool in the life-skills toolbox. Researchers have characterized it as everything from a coping mechanism to a physical patterning of neurobiological pathways established in the earliest years of life. Susan C. Vaughan, MD, author of *Half Empty Half Full: How to Take Control and Live Life as an Optimist,* describes it as a psychological righting reflex. "It's like cats," she says. "When you throw them out the window, they land on their feet."

[3a]Optimists, in other words, know how to bounce back. [3b]Martin Seligman, professor of psychology at the University of Pennsylvania and author of *Learned Optimism: How to Change Your Mind and Your Life,* explains it this way: "If a setback is thought about as temporary, changeable, and local, that's optimism. [3c]If it's thought about as permanent, unchangeable, and pervasive, that's pessimism." [3d]Victories are just the reverse: Optimists think of them as permanent and far-reaching; pessimists think of them as fleeting and situation-specific. [3e]For instance, if an optimist encounters a recipe she can't make work, she's likely to perceive the failure as external and temporary ("I'm just having an off day"), while the pessimist makes it internal and indelible ("I'll never learn to cook"). [3f]As

Seligman explains, optimism serves as a crucial framework for relating to experiences. [3g]"It's the skeleton of hope," he says.

[4]If you approach life with a sense of possibility and the expectation of positive results, you're more likely to have a life in which possibilities are realized and results are positive. You'll have a better chance of being promoted, fighting off the cold that's been going around, and attracting people to you—platonically and (hubba-hubba) otherwise. According to Seligman, pessimistic people are two to eight times more at risk of depression, a significant statistic in a country that seems a half step away from putting Prozac in its drinking water. Optimists are more productive at certain jobs—one company made sales-force hiring decisions based partially on the outcome of psychological tests. (People who tend to see themselves as responsible for positive situations are more resilient and more likely to bear up under repeated rejection.) And researchers have found that optimists are less likely to develop cancer or to die from heart disease.

[5]Where are all these sunny-side uppers? Jeffrey E. Garten, dean of the Yale School of Management, interviewed 40 of the world's most successful business executives for his book *The Mind of the CEO*. Garten found every last one of them to be extremely optimistic. "I didn't find a lot of other common traits," he says. "For example, there's a conventional wisdom that these are all alpha people who exude aggressiveness and do nothing in life besides work. I didn't find that. But the one thing they had in common was how they all talked about the mountains they had to climb every single day." His subjects kept a perspective on the tasks at hand by placing them within a larger, long-term vision. "Their view was, I know I have succeeded in the past, and I'm quite confident that if I can look beyond today's problems to a point on the horizon, I know I'm going to get there."

[6]How do people turn out this way? Lifelong optimism can be explained in one of three ways, says Seligman. About 50 percent is due to inheritable conditions, he says. Seligman circulated a questionnaire at an annual twins convention (in Twinsburg, Ohio) and found identical twins more similar than fraternals in levels of optimism and pessimism. "You might think that means there is an optimism gene," Seligman says. "But I don't think so. Identical twins are also similar in terms of physical traits: how they look, what talents they have—the things that can attract people to you and make you successful in life. And we know success tends to produce optimism and failure tends to produce pessimism.

[7]Another source, Seligman says, is a person's mother: "There's a markedly high correlation between your level of optimism and your mother's, but not your father's." Although no one knows why this is, one hypothesis is that mothers still tend to be primary caretakers and therefore have a greater influence on their offspring. Another theory is that women have evolved to be more cerebral and expressive, so they're more likely to communicate their outlook, positive or negative.

[8]"The third source is the reality of the bad events that happen to you," says Seligman. "If you want to be an athlete but you're born clumsy, you're likely to expect one setback after another. A sequence of failures naturally leads to the expectation of failure."

[9]According to Seligman, almost everyone can learn how to be more optimistic, except, perhaps, those who are severely depressed and may

benefit only from professional counseling or medication. A key component of optimism seems to be a willingness to look for the bright side, even if that means distorting reality. You can also begin to recognize and catalog the negative messages you tell yourself, then dispute those thoughts as if debating an external foe. Gradually, the new responses become automatic.

[10]Even though he teaches techniques for learning optimism, Seligman warns that no one should think of it as a panacea. "It doesn't give you wisdom, compassion, or a direct line to the truth," he says. Seligman advocates a "flexible optimism," which factors in risk, rather than a blind faith in positive outcomes. You don't want an overly optimistic pilot to look out the cockpit and say, "Oh, the weather doesn't look so bad from here. Let's not bother deicing the plane."

[11]Pessimism and optimism aren't mutually exclusive, agrees Edward C. Chang, assistant professor of psychology at the University of Michigan. He believes that the two can in some circumstances coexist and argues that pessimism shows up in the attitudes of certain groups, the result of life-shaping forces such as world events, socioeconomic circumstances, and culture. "I see myself as a pessimist," says Chang, whose family emigrated from South Korea to Brooklyn when he was 5 years old. Chang says his outlook is rooted in the Confucian emphasis on striking a balance in life—not being overly positive or negative. Chang also believes that his parents' experience as immigrants in a new, unknown land made them particularly cautious and inclined to prepare for the worst at all times.

[12]Chang sees pessimism as a sensibility, not a biological trait or an automatic marker for depression. He believes it can serve as a viable strategy for a positive outcome. In his study of Asian-American college students, participants had above-average levels of pessimism but, notably, no less optimism than European-Americans. Their version of pessimism was more elevated but not debilitating.

[13]"I have a 1-year-old daughter," he says. "In some ways, I'm a naive optimist. I believe everything in her life will be wonderful and that she's going to be a beautiful, intelligent woman. But I can assure you that when the time comes for her to marry, I will use a pessimistic strategy to make sure the caterers show up, the musicians are on time, and that the outcome is positive. Say it's an outdoor wedding; even if an unexpected storm came through, I'd have plans B, C, and D ready."

[14]Outcome is the point here: Beefing up your optimism isn't the ultimate goal, proponents argue, happiness is. According to research psychologist David T. Lykken, each of us has a happiness "set point." We've each been dealt a happiness hand, some of us with higher cards than others. But as Lykken points out in his book *Happiness: What Studies About Twins Show Us About Nature, Nurture, and the Happiness Set Point,* we can increase our potential for joy by taking steps to get involved with people, causes, and ideas. According to Seligman, one of the hallmarks of depression is self-absorption. And so optimism, with its emphasis on seeking and seeing what's good outside of ourselves and in the world, helps us take those steps.

VOCABULARY

Match each word in the left column with the best definition in the right column.

1. relentless (¶ 1) __b__
2. pervasive (¶ 3) __e__
3. indelible (¶ 3) __g__
4. platonically (¶ 4) __c__
5. hypothesis (¶ 7) __a__
6. foe (¶ 9) __d__
7. debilitating (¶ 12) __f__

a. assumption, unproved theory
b. determined, won't give up
c. friendly, unsexual
d. enemy, opponent
e. everywhere
f. crippling, keep from action
g. permanent

COMPREHENSION

Determine whether the statements in sentences 8–11 are true or false, and circle your answer. If the statement is false, rewrite it to make it true.

(T) F **8.** Optimists are more likely than pessimists to bounce back from a disappointment.

_____

_____

T (F) **9.** Very few people can learn to be more optimistic.

_False. Most people can learn to be more optimistic._____

_____

T (F)**10.** A person cannot be both optimistic and pessimistic; they are mutually exclusive traits.

False. A person can be both optimistic and pessimistic; they are not

_mutually exclusive traits._____

(T) F **11.** Many people who are depressed are self-absorbed.

_____

_____

12. Circle the letter of the sentence that best expresses the thesis.

a. Optimism is more than a reckless chirping through life.
(b.) If you approach life with optimism, you're more likely to enjoy a life in which possibilities are realized and results are positive.
c. Optimism is the skeleton of hope.
d. No one should think of optimism as a panacea.

13. Garten found only one common characteristic among the world's successful business executives. What was it?

The world's successful business executives were all optimistic

14. In paragraph 3, what is the relationship of sentence 3e to sentences 3a–3d?

    a. It defines a term.

    (b.) It gives an example.

    c. It tells a cause.

    d. It presents a contrast.

What signal/transition phrase does Funderburg use in sentence 3e to signal the relationship?

For instance

15. According to Seligman, lifelong optimism can be explained in one of three ways. List them.

Three ways lifelong optimism can be explained: (1) inheritable condi-

tions, (2) optimism level of a person's mother, (3) the reality of the

bad events that happen to you.

REFLECT AND CONNECT

16. If you're working on adopting a more optimistic attitude, what should you do and say the next time your plans don't go as you hoped they would?

Answers will vary, but in general, people working on adopting a more

optimistic attitude, should remain hopeful and look for the positive

aspects of the situation when something doesn't go as they hoped it

would.

Selection 6 "Hold on to Your Positive Attitude"

ELWOOD N. CHAPMAN AND SHARON LUND O'NEIL

Dr. Chapman was a professor at Chaffey College and a nationally known speaker and consultant until his death in 1995. Dr. O'Neil is a professor and associate vice provost at the University of Houston. She has received many teaching awards and is widely published in human relations. This is Chapter 3 from their text Your Attitude Is Showing: A Primer of Human Relations, *tenth edition.*

VOCABULARY

attribute (¶ 1): characteristic
subtle : (¶ 4): indirect
stimulus : (¶ 6): anything that causes action
preceding : (¶ 22): coming before, previous
complement : (¶ 26): add to, completes
complimentary : (¶ 27): making a positive, flattering statement
passive : (¶ 29): submissive, offering no opposition
insolvency : (¶ 31): cannot pay debts, bankrupt
clique : (¶ 34): small, often snobbish group of people
frivolous : (¶ 43): silly, not serious

AN IDEA TO THINK ABOUT

Think about your job—the work you do for a business or at home. What are the first five words that pop into your mind? Are the words mostly positive or mostly negative? *As you read,* look for how much influence Chapman and O'Neil think those words—your attitude—have on your success.

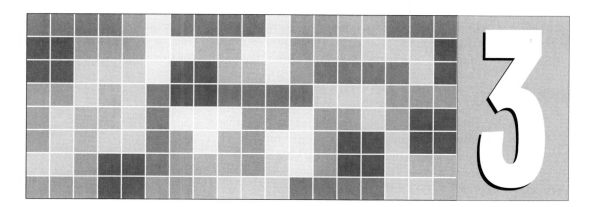

3

Hold On to Your Positive Attitude

"It's hard to stay positive under pressure."

Thought for the Day: If your attitude has thorns, you cannot expect others to want to get close to you.

Attitude is a common word. You hear it almost every day. Professors use it on campus. Managers discuss it at work. Employment counselors look for it among applicants. You hear people say: "He's got an attitude" (indicating a possible problem), while others say "I wish I had her consistently positive attitude." No other attribute will have more influence upon your future. A positive attitude can be your most priceless possession.

If you can create and keep a positive attitude toward your job, your company, and life in general, you should not only move up the ladder of success quickly and gracefully, you should also be a happier person. If you are unable to be positive, you may find many career mobility doors closed to you, and your personal life less than exciting.

Three Faces of Communication

There are three forms of communication between people. One is the written form—letters, memos, faxes, e-mails, etc. The second is the verbal form—face-to-face conversations, telephone conversations, voice mail, intercom discussions, video conferencing, etc. The third involves the transmission of attitudes.

The first two forms of communication are so important to the profitable operation of an organization that we tend to think they are the only ones. We forget that we also communicate our attitudes through facial expressions, hand gestures, and other more subtle forms of body language. Sometimes people will greet others with a positive voice, but their body language (negative facial expression) sends a contrasting signal. As the expression claims, sometimes your attitude speaks so loudly that others cannot hear what you say.

Your Attitude Is Showing

Every time you report for work, every time you attend a staff meeting, every time you go through a formal appraisal, every time you take a coffee break, and every time you go out socially, be aware that *your attitude is showing.*

Because attitude can play such an important role in your future, let's take a closer look at the meaning of the word itself. *Attitude* is defined by most psychologists as a mental set that causes a person to respond in a characteristic manner to a given stimulus. You have many attitudes, or mental sets. You have attitudes toward certain makes of automobiles, toward certain social institutions (schools, churches, and the like), toward certain careers, lifestyles, and people.

You also have a wide variety of job attitudes. You build attitudes toward your supervisor and the people with whom you work, toward the job you do, toward company policies, toward the amount of money you are being paid. In addition to these specific attitudes, you have a basic, or total, attitude toward your job and toward life itself. Strictly speaking, then, attitude is the *way you look at your whole environment.*

You can look at your job in any way you wish. On the one hand, you can focus your attention on all its negative aspects (odd hours, close supervision, poor location). On the other hand, you can focus your attention on the more positive factors of the job (harmonious work environment, good learning opportunities, good benefits). All jobs have both positive and negative factors. How you choose to perceive yours is an important decision.

Attitude is the way you view and interpret your environment. Some people can push unpleasant things out of sight and dwell largely on positive factors. Others seem to enjoy the unpleasant and dwell on these negative factors.

What You See in Life Influences Your Attitude

If you go around looking for what is wrong with things, wondering why things are not better, and complaining about them, then you will be a negative person in the minds of most people. If you do the opposite—look for what is good and focus on pleasant things—you will be a positive person in the minds of most people.

Some people (through imaging) keep their positive attitudes by viewing life as a circle with both positive and negative factors competing to gain as much "mind time" as possible. Negative factors constantly try to command attention, pushing positive factors to the side.

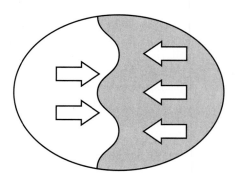

To offset a negative drift, positive people discipline their minds to concentrate primarily upon positive factors, thus pushing the negative to the outer perimeter of their thinking.

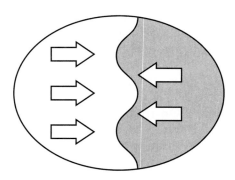

There is no perfect job or position. One job may have more favorable aspects than another, but all jobs have some unpleasant ones. The employee who dwells on the unfavorable factors has a negative attitude. The employee who is determined to look for factors that are favorable will slowly become a more positive person.

Therefore, even if you start a new job or assignment with a positive attitude, you must make sure that it remains positive. It is possible that you will meet a few people with negative attitudes who will attempt to persuade you to think as they do. These factors could influence you and destroy what otherwise would have been an excellent start.

To be a positive person, you need not think your world or company is perfect. That would be foolish. You would eventually become disillusioned. On the other hand, unless you feel that the majority of factors are favorable, you will eventually become negative, and you will show it.

The Moment You Can No Longer Be Positive about Your Career with Your Company, Your Chances for Success Diminish

No one can be positive all the time. You will naturally have periods of doubt. These temporary periods will not hurt you seriously. But a consistently negative attitude that persists for weeks or months will destroy your future with the organization. If you find your negative attitude cannot be improved in your present setting, and you honestly feel such an attitude is justified, you should resign.

A positive attitude is essential to career success for many reasons:

1. When you are positive you are usually more energetic, motivated, productive, and alert. Thinking about negative things too much has a way of draining your energy. Put another way, a positive attitude opens a gate and lets your inner enthusiasm spill out. A negative attitude, on the other hand, will keep the gate closed.

2. First impressions are important on the job because they often have a lasting effect. Co-workers you meet for the first time appear to have little radar sets tuned in to your attitude. If your attitude is positive, they receive a friendly, warm signal, and they are attracted to you. If your attitude is negative, they receive an unfriendly signal, and they try to avoid you.

3. A positive employee contributes to the productivity of others. A negative employee does not. Attitudes are caught more than they are taught. Both negative and positive attitudes are transmitted on the job. They are picked up by others. A persistently negative attitude, like the rotten apple in the barrel, can spoil the positive attitudes of others. It is very difficult to maintain a high level of productivity while working next to a person with a negative attitude.

4. Co-workers like you when you are positive. They like to be around you because you are fun. Your job is more interesting and exciting because you are in the middle of things and not on the outside complaining. When you are negative, people prefer to stay clear of you. A negative person may build good relationships with a few other people (who are perhaps negative themselves), but such a person cannot build good relationships with the majority of employees.

5. The kind of attitude you transmit to management will have a considerable influence on your future success. Management constantly reads your mental attitude, even though you may feel you are successful in covering it up. Supervisors can determine your attitude by how you approach your job, react to directives, handle problems, and work with others. If you are positive, you will be given greater consideration when special assignments and promotion opportunities arise.

If your job involves customer, client, or patient contacts, you should place additional emphasis on everything stated in the preceding list. Your attitude is significant in all relationships, but it is crucial when you are in a service position.

It is important to realize that a positive attitude involves far more than a smile. A smile, of course, is helpful in transmitting a positive attitude. However, some people transmit a positive attitude even when they seldom smile. They convey positiveness by the way they treat others, the way they look at their responsibilities, and the perspective they take when faced with a problem.

Attitude is a highly personal thing. It is closely tied to your self-concept, or the way you look at yourself. Because attitude is so personal, talking about it is not easy. People often freeze when the word is mentioned. As a result, management may never talk to you about your attitude. They may never say, for example, "Let's be honest. Your attitude is negative. What are you going to do about it?" *But everyone will know when your attitude is showing.*

How, then, do you make sure you keep your positive attitude when things get tough? How do you keep a good grip on it when you are discouraged? How do you keep it in good repair on a day-to-day basis over the years? Here are a few simple suggestions.

Build a More Positive Attitude in One Environment and You Will Be More Successful in Another

Your positive or negative attitude is not something that you can hang on a hook. It follows you wherever you go. It is reasonable to assume, then, that if you make a greater effort to be a more positive person in your social and personal lives, your effort will automatically spill over and help you on the job. By the same token, if you make a greater effort to develop a more positive attitude at work, your effort will make a contribution to your social and personal lives. One effort will complement the other.

Talk about Positive Things

Negative comments are seldom welcomed by fellow workers on the job; nor are they welcomed by those you meet in the social scene. The best way to be positive is to be complimentary. Constant gripers and complainers seldom build healthy and exciting relationships with others.

Look For the Good Things in the People with Whom You Work, Especially Your Supervisors

Nobody is perfect, but almost everybody has a few worthwhile qualities. If you dwell on people's good features, it will be easier for you to like them and easier for them to like you. Make no mistake about one thing: People usually know how you react to them even if you don't communicate verbally.

Look For the Good Things in Your Organization

What are the factors that make it a good place to work? Do you like the hours, the physical environment, the people, the actual work you are doing? What about opportunities for promotion? Do you have chances for self-improvement? What about your wage and benefit package? Do you have the freedom you seek? No job is perfect, but, if you concentrate on the good things, the negative factors may seem less important. Seeing the positive side of things does not mean that you should ignore negative elements that should be changed. Far from it! A positive person is not a weak person. A positive person is usually confident, assertive (within limits), and an agent of change within an organization. Management is not seeking passive people who meekly conform. They want spirited, positive people who will make constructive and thoughtful improvements.

If you decide to stay with an organization for a long time, you would be wise to concentrate on its good features. Staying positive may take a considerable amount of personal fortitude, but it is the best way to keep your career on an upward track. If you think positively, you will act positively and you will succeed.

Avoid Financial Problems through Planning and Discipline

On-campus surveys indicate that students frequently fail academically and drop out because of financial problems. It also appears that career employees troubled with financial worries often turn negative and lose the promotions that would provide the extra money that could help them pay off their bills. Unfortunately, few of these individuals realize that their positive attitudes are being sacrificed along with their credit ratings. Instead of seeking and accepting family or professional financial counseling, they permit their insolvency to lead them into attitudinal bankruptcy. When attitudinal bankruptcy happens, they pay a double penalty.

Don't Permit a Fellow Worker—Even a Supervisor—Who Has a Negative Attitude to Trap You into His (or Her) Way of Thinking

You may not be able to change a negative person's attitude, but at least you can protect your own positive attitude from becoming negative. The story of Sandy will emphasize this point.

> **Sandy.** Sandy was a little uneasy about her new job. It was a fine opportunity, and she knew the standards were very high. Would she have the skills needed? Could she learn fast enough to please her supervisor? Would the older employees like her? Although Sandy's concern was understandable, it was not justified. In addition to being highly qualified for the job, she had a happy, positive attitude that wouldn't stop. She was seldom depressed.
>
> Everything went very well for Sandy for a while. Her positive attitude was appreciated by all. Slowly, however, her fellow workers and supervisor noticed a change. Sandy became more critical of her colleagues, her job, and the company. Her usual friendly greetings and helpful ideas were gradually replaced by complaints. What had happened? Without realizing it, Sandy was showing the effects of the friendships she had made on the job. Needing acceptance in a strange environment, she had welcomed the attention of a clique of employees who had a negative attitude—a group that management already viewed critically.

Sandy was not able to confine her negative attitude to her job. Soon, again without realizing it, she let her negative attitude spill over into her social life. In fact, it troubled her boyfriend so much that he had it out with her one night. His words were a little rough. "Look, Sandy. When you are happy, you are very attractive and fun to be around. But frankly, when you are negative you are a real bore, and I never have a good time with you. I think those so-called friends you hang round with on the job are killing what was once a beautiful personality."

It wasn't a happy evening, but Sandy got the message. She made a vow to recapture and hang on to the positive attitude she had previously enjoyed. Not only was she successful in recapturing her positive attitude, but she also converted a few of her previously negative friends to her way of thinking. Her action saved her career.

Make Frequent Self-Assessments

When friends casually ask me "How are you doing?" I often jokingly reply: "I'm not sure but I intend to sit under a tree tomorrow and ask myself some questions to find out." Most employees make the mistake of waiting around for their organizations to complete an annual formal appraisal instead of frequently sitting under a shady tree somewhere and asking themselves questions similar to these.

Am I currently transmitting a positive or negative attitude?

Is my attitude influencing the quality and quantity of my personal productivity in a positive way?

Am I sufficiently positive to be considered a fun and comfortable co-worker?

Am I communicating to superiors through my attitude that I seek career advancements?

Are my customers, clients, or co-workers responding to my attitude in an upbeat manner?

Whatever form your self-assessment takes (attitude is a most personal matter), *use it frequently.* Check your attitude as you would the amount of gasoline in your car. Talk to yourself about the progress you are making. Don't sit around expecting someone else to do it for you.

John. John's boss is a believer in formal appraisal programs. Instead of annual evaluations, he would prefer going through the process twice each year. In discussing the good showing John made on his current appraisal, his boss said: "John, I have noticed that your attitude and productivity always improves shortly before appraisal time and then settles back a few weeks afterward. I think it would be smart for you to appraise yourself every few weeks during the year. By periodic appraisal checks you would keep a more positive attitude and deserve a higher rating than I can give you now. Consistency is a big factor and I recommend frequent self-appraisals."

Serendipity

Holding on to your positive attitude will never be easy. There are many techniques, however, that can help. Some will be discussed later in this book. One that will help you get started, especially when an irritating problem surfaces, is saying the word *serendipity.*

The word *serendipity* was coined by Horace Walpole in 1754 when he put the fairy tale *The Three Princes of Serendip* to paper. A modern version by Elizabeth Jamison Hodges was published in 1964. It is a delightful story of three princes who travel from kingdom to kingdom in a lighthearted, compassionate manner. In helping others solve their problems, they are led to the solution of a problem in their own kingdom.

Serendipity lends itself to many interpretations. To some, it is a gift to help them find agreeable things not sought. To everyone it is a "happiness" word. The magic comes into play when we realize that a "lighter approach" can often not only solve a problem but cause something good to happen in our lives.

In short, serendipity is an attitude—an apparently frivolous mental set that can help us view our work environment in a more humorous and forgiving manner. It is an attitude that temporarily moves responsibility aside and encourages one to rise above any negative situation. A serendipitous attitude is within the reach of everyone and, when achieved, fortuitous things may happen. For example, when you have a lighthearted, mischievous, festive way of looking at things, others are intrigued and may invite you to share beautiful experiences with them that, in turn, can enhance your life. Serendipity is a state of mind. It is a wonderful attitude to take to a party. There are also times when it can be a lifesaver in the workplace.

> *Like plants, your attitude needs nurturing in order to grow.*

Case 3

"Financial solvency helps keep my attitude positive."

Credit Blues

Manuel, a graphics artist with multi-media skills, was constantly praised by his college professors for his creative works. He was also rewarded by winning a number of prizes in campus art shows. Upon graduating, Manuel made many attempts to find a job in commercial art. No luck. After many disappointments, he reluctantly accepted a position with a large retail chain that would have only limited use for his talent in the area of merchandising display.

Manuel decided to make the most of his situation and began his career with a positive attitude. He quickly demonstrated that he had both talent and managerial ability. His future looked bright. He was happy. Some time later, however, his supervisor noticed that Manuel's enthusiasm had started to dwindle. He began giving excuses for not getting things done on time. Manuel's merchandise displays were not up to previous standards. His relationships with other workers started to deteriorate.

In a heart-to-heart talk with his sensitive and supportive manager, Manuel revealed that he was having serious financial problems. Manuel's quest for finding satisfying challenges had led him to obsessive and impulsive Internet shopping and stock trading. As it took more and more stimuli to satisfy his "needs," Manuel's acquisitions and debts grew too. Through the purchase of a new sports car and other consumer items, Manuel was behind on his credit payments, and the high interest rates were keeping him in the hole. Manuel's manager told him he was suffering from a severe case of "plastic blues" and sent him to a company counselor with expertise in financial planning.

Would you agree that financial problems can damage a positive attitude and derail one's career? What suggestions would you give to Manuel to help him stay positive while he digs himself out of his financial hole? (For a suggested answer, see page 225.)

Selection 6 Questions

VOCABULARY

Circle the letter of the best definition for the underlined word.

1. "If your job involves customer, client, or patient contacts, you should place additional <u>emphasis</u> on everything. . . ."

   a. work   **c.** importance
   b. people, workers   **d.** time

2. "Management is not seeking passive people who <u>meekly</u> conform."

   a. mildly   **c.** happily
   b. boldly   **d.** impatiently

3. "Am I currently <u>transmitting</u> a positive or negative attitude?"

   a. writing   **c.** keeping
   b. communicating   **d.** holding

Rephrase the underlined passages using your own words.

4. "If you are unable to be positive, <u>you may find many career mobility doors closed to you</u>. . . ."

   You won't be promoted; you won't be able to change jobs easily.

5. "Staying positive may take a considerable amount of <u>personal fortitude</u>. . . ."

   courage; guts

6. "Instead of seeking . . . financial counseling, they permit their insolvency to lead them into <u>attitudinal bankruptcy</u>."

   a depressed state of mind; unhappy, irritable, and angry

7. "John's boss is a believer in formal <u>appraisal programs</u>."

   performance review; job evaluation

8. "A serendipitous attitude is within the reach of everyone and, when achieved, <u>fortuitous things may happen</u>."

good, lucky, fortunate things may happen

COMPREHENSION

Determine whether the statements in sentences 9 and 10 are true or false, and circle your answer. If the statement is false, rewrite it to make it true.

(T) F **9.** All jobs have both positive and negative factors.

T (F) **10.** A positive attitude isn't really essential to career success.

False. A positive attitude is really essential to career success.

11. Circle the letter of the sentence that best expresses the thesis.

(a.) Keeping a positive attitude about your job, the company you work for, and life in general will help you be a happier and more successful person.

b. There are three forms of communication between people.

c. Attitude is the way you view and interpret your surroundings.

d. If you spend your time looking for what is wrong with things and complaining about them, you will be viewed as a negative person.

12. Complete this outline map of paragraph 3. Label each entry as a main idea, major detail, or minor detail.

three forms of communication between people (_main idea_)

  written forms (**major detail**)

    letter (_minor detail_)

    memo (_minor detail_)

    fax (_minor detail_)

    e-mail (_minor detail_)

  verbal forms (_major detail_)

    face-to-face conversations (_minor detail_)

    telephone conversations (_minor detail_)

    voice mail (_minor detail_)

    intercom discussions (_minor detail_)

    video conferencing (_minor detail_)

  transmitting attitudes (_major detail_)

13. How do Chapman and O'Neil define *attitude*?

Chapman and O'Neil define attitude as: "the way you look at your

whole environment."

14. Chapman and O'Neil quote the expression, "sometimes your attitude speaks so loudly that others cannot hear what you say." List two specific examples of body language that we use to communicate our attitudes.

Answers will vary; please see Answer Key.

15. Chapman and O'Neil list several reasons that a positive attitude is essential to career success. List three.

Answers will vary; please see Answer Key.

REFLECT AND CONNECT

16. Give three specific suggestions you might make to a friend who is having trouble holding on to her or his positive attitude at work.

Answers will vary.

| Selection 7 "'Little Engine' Holds a Valuable Life Lesson" |

ANA VECIANA-SUAREZ

Ms. Veciana-Suarez, an award winning syndicated columnist for The Miami Herald, *explores the human experience, touching on family and personal issues as well as events that are shaping our country. Her work also includes the best-selling novel* The Chin Kiss King, *the story of three generations of Cuban women in Miami;* Birthday Parties in Heaven: Thoughts on Love, Life, Grief, and Other Matters of the Heart, *a collection of essays; and the anthology* Father.

VOCABULARY

embodies (¶ 1): incorporates, brings together
mantra (¶ 2): personal inspirational chant
classic morality tale (¶ 2): traditional story with a moral
stymied (¶3): frustrated, unable to explain
analogy (¶3): comparison
traits (¶4): characteristics
laments (¶6): whining, complaints
shroud ourselves (¶9): wrap ourselves
catastrophic (¶12): disastrous, terribly harmful
laud (¶17): praise

AN IDEA TO THINK ABOUT

When you are faced with a difficult task, do you most often tell yourself "I think I can" or "I don't think I can"? How often are you right? *As you read,* find out why Veciana-Suarez believes such self-talk is important.

'LITTLE ENGINE' HOLDS A VALUABLE LIFE LESSON

Ana Veciana-Suarez

[1]"The Little Engine That Could" is one of my favorite children's stories. Chugging, struggling, forcing itself to do what it fears most, the little engine embodies much of what I try to teach my children.

[2]I think I can . . . I think I can . . . I think I can. Consider it a personal mantra. To be able to do anything, you must first "believe" you can. And to believe you can, you must possess a certain sense of confidence and hope. "The Little Engine That Could" is the classic morality tale of someone who chooses to see the glass half-full.

[3]I thought of this long-forgotten story during a conversation with a friend the other day when, stymied for an explanation about a mutual acquaintance's behavior, I cited the little engine. It struck her as incredibly funny, but she agreed the analogy fit.

[4]Our mutual acquaintance shares few traits with the little engine, which is really too bad. Her glass is always half-empty. Maybe too many of us see it that way, and then wonder why we're so unhappy and frustrated.

[5a]Our acquaintance has managed, in small ways and by large acts, to isolate herself. [5b]Ask her to break routine, to try something new, to give a stranger a chance, to open her heart, and she won't because she believes she can't. [5c]The world she sees is a threatening, conspiring one.

[6a]Her laments are legendary. [6b]They have become a joke among those who know her. [6c]Nothing escapes the pallor of her unfounded gloom. [6d]Not the weather—which is always too cold or too hot. [6e]Not a party—too

many people or not enough of the right ones. [6f]Not even an unexpected windfall—it could have come sooner or could have been better.

[7]She is defeated before she begins. There's never any "I think I can . . . I think I can . . ." only "I won't . . . I won't . . . I won't."

[8]"She's so negative," my friend said.

[9]All of us shroud ourselves in that negativism at one time or another. And we should—occasionally. We need to wallow in misery every once in a while. It's only when we stay too long in the mire or make it a lifelong personal statement that it repels.

[10]Pessimism is like a bad smell. You can't get away from it fast enough; you want to flush it out of your life.

[11]I would much rather spend my time with someone who will remark about the spectacular spring morning instead of worry about the predicted afternoon thunderstorm.

[12]What always has fascinated me are stories of people who overcome great odds to recover from tragedies: the woman with a terrible childhood who becomes an exemplary mother; the rich man who, after losing it all, wins it back and devotes his life to the poor; the athlete who comes back from a catastrophic injury. They are the real-life examples of little engines that could.

[13]About five years ago, I interviewed a teen-age boy, a defensive lineman on his football team, who had been hit by an 18-wheeler while riding his bike down a rural road in Palm Beach County, Florida. The impact crushed not only his body but also his dreams of playing college football.

[14]But the kid refused to wallow in what unquestionably was a miserable situation. He got over his initial despair and put all his efforts first into moving his toes, then his feet, then his legs. He worked so hard at rehabilitating himself that he sobbed while relearning to walk. He finally did, more than two years later. He never played college ball—that happens only in movies—but he could play tag in his back yard.

[15]"I could have been dead," he said.

[16]Thousands of interviews later, I still remember his words.

[17]There's a lot to be said about the philosophy of "it could be worse." There's plenty more to laud about "making the best of a bad situation." I have told my children just that so, so many times.

[18]I truly believe you can teach optimism, nourish hopefulness, bestow enthusiasm. It all starts with the belief: I think I can . . . I think I can . . . I think I can.

Selection 7 Questions

VOCABULARY

Circle the letter of the best definition for the underlined word.

1. "And to believe you can, you must <u>possess</u> a certain sense of confidence and hope." (¶2)

   a. forfeit   c. have
   b. give up   d. pretend

2. "... I <u>cited</u> the little engine." (¶3)

    a. ignored   **c.** explained

    (b.) referred to   **d.** neglected

3. "... becomes an <u>exemplary</u> mother. ..." (¶12)

    a. well-known   **c.** poor

    b. popular   **(d.)** excellent

Rephrase these sentences using your own words.

4. "Her glass is always half-empty." (¶4)

    She always sees the negative side of things.

5. "Our acquaintance has managed, in small ways and by large acts, to isolate herself." (¶5)

    Because of the way she acts, no one wants to be around her.

6. "Nothing escapes the pallor of her unfounded gloom." (¶6)

    No matter how good something might be, she finds a negative way to look at it.

COMPREHENSION

Determine whether the statements in sentences 7–9 are true or false, and circle your answer. If the statement is false, rewrite it to make it true.

    (T) F **7.** To be able to do anything, you must first "believe" you can.

    (T) F **8.** "The Little Engine That Could" is a children's story.

    T (F) **9.** Most of us prefer to spend time with people who are pessimistic rather than optimistic.

    False. Most of us prefer to spend time with people who are optimistic rather than pessimistic.

10. Circle the letter of the sentence that best expresses the thesis.

    a. You should read classic stories with a moral to children.

    b. The world is a threatening and conspiring place.

    c. You'll have a better chance of accomplishing what you want if you think you can.

    d. People can recover from devastating accidents.

11. What is the relationship of sentence 5b to sentence 5a? Which of the following does it provide?

    a. examples

    b. a change in direction of thought (contrast)

    c. a definition

12. What is the relationship of sentences 6d, 6e, and 6f to sentence 6c? Which of the following do they provide?

    a. examples   c. definitions of terms

    b. causes

13. In paragraph 14, Veciana-Suarez says ". . . that happens only in movies. . . ." Explain what she means.

    Unbelievable or miraculous endings are unlikely in real life.

    _____

REFLECT AND CONNECT

14. Veciana-Suarez mentions several people she believes are real-life examples of "little engines that could." Describe one person you know or have read about who you believe is an example of a "little engine that could."

    Answers will vary.

    _____

    _____

    _____

LOG ON TO THE WEB

You can find dozens of sites on the Web that have information about how to keep a positive attitude. For example,

<http://www.saywhynot.com/> has articles and stories "dedicated to inspiring you to reach your goals and overcome obstacles by saying, 'Why Not!'"

<http://www.utexas.edu/student/utlc/handouts/1318.html>, from The Learning Center at the University of Texas at Austin, is about "How to Build a Positive Attitude About Yourself as a Writer."

<http://www.uihealthcare.com/topics/stressandcope/stre5136.html> is part of the University of Iowa Healthcare site with information about the "Power of a Positive Attitude."

Log on to one of these sites or use a search engine to locate a site that gives you information about how to keep a positive attitude.

Read one article or story. Write down (1) the complete Web address, (2) the name of the person or company who sponsors and maintains the site, (3) the name of the person who wrote the information, (4) what you know about the writer, and (5) one idea or suggestion about how to keep a positive attitude that you learned from the information.

REFLECT AND CONNECT

A. The authors in this theme share a common viewpoint about the importance of our attitude. Explain their viewpoint.

B. Describe a person you know who is almost always upbeat. What does he or she say and do to communicate his or her positive attitude? How do you think he or she maintains a positive attitude?

C. We all know negative individuals—those who see every glass as half empty. Which of their words and actions are most annoying or troublesome? What techniques can you use to counteract their negative influence?

THEME

2 A Healthy Environment

There are no passengers on spaceship earth. We are all crew.

Marshall McLuhan

Air. Water. Food. Basic necessities of everyday life we assume are available to us in clean, affordable, unlimited quantities. But are they?

According to the President's Task Force on Environmental Health Risks and Safety Risks to Children, as many as 25 percent of children in America live in areas that regularly exceed the U.S. Environmental Protection Agency's (EPA) limits for ozone—more than 25 percent of which comes from auto emissions. In fact, residents in many parts of the country increasingly hear the warning "Young children, the elderly, and people with breathing problems should remain inside today" because the air quality index (AQI) is in the unhealthy range. (The AQI is an index for reporting daily air quality prepared by the EPA to tell us how clean or polluted our air is.)

A 2002 report by United Nations (UN) agencies estimated that nearly one third of the global disease burden is the result of environmental factors. Such factors include exposure to toxic chemicals, such as lead (especially from leaded gasoline) and pesticides. The report "Children in the New Millennium: Environmental Impact on Health" also indicates that pollution-related diseases kill millions of children a year.

In 2000, a survey of 2,251 ocean and lake beaches showed the nation had at least 11,270 combined days of beach closings and advisories against swimming. The leading cause of U.S. beach closings is mismanagement of sewage-handling systems and urban storm-water runoff according to the Natural Resources Defense Council (NRDC).

A 2003 newspaper article warned that in addition to industrial pollution, "household products increasingly contaminate U.S. waterways." The article reported that hydrologists with the U.S. Geological Survey have found in our waterways contaminants known as pharmaceutical and personal care pollutants—painkillers, insect repellents, perfumes, nicotine—and that the long-term effects of exposure to these pollutants are unclear.

The authors in this theme provide ideas, information, and personal accounts about how we affect the environment and how the environment affects us.

238

"A Healthy Environment," Chapter 25 in Health Skills for Wellness by B. E. Pruitt, Kathy Teer Crumpler, and Deborah Prothrow-Stith, opens the theme. They provide a context for the topic with a discussion of what we mean by "the environment," and specific air, water, ground, and noise pollution issues.

Essayist Kimi Eisele considers one effect of air pollution in "With Every Breath You Take," and then Pulitzer Prize–winning editorial cartoonist Clay Bennett gives us his opinion on where to get some "fresh air." However, because indoor air pollution is one of the top five risks to public health in the United States, according to John Manuel of the National Institutes of Health, we consider the article "NASA Study Shows Common Plants Help Reduce Indoor Air Pollution."

In "The Oil Was Everywhere," Bruce Gray takes us to Prince William Sound, Alaska, for the ten-year anniversary of the Exxon Valdez oil spill and a look at the long-lasting effects of man-made pollution. Next, Dorothy Lockhart Lawrence provides information on noise pollution and warns us "It's Everywhere and It's Worse Than You Think!"

Environmental writer Kim Todd closes the theme by asking "Are You Big Foot?"—her plea for us to think about how much of the planet we use.

Selection 1 "A Healthy Environment"

B. E. (BUZZ) PRUITT, KATHY TEER CRUMPLER, AND DEBORAH PROTHROW-STITH

Dr. Pruitt is Professor of Health Education at Texas A&M University. Dr. Crumpler is Health and Safety Supervisor for the Onslow County School in Jacksonville, North Carolina. Dr. Prothrow-Stith is associate dean for Faculty Development at the Harvard School of Public Health. This is Chapter 25 in their introductory text Health Skills for Wellness.

VOCABULARY

AN IDEA TO THINK ABOUT

Key vocabulary appears in bold face type and is defined in context.
How healthy is your environment—at home, at work, at school, and in your community? *As you read,* look for the various ways you affect the environment and the various ways the environment affects you.

A HEALTHY ENVIRONMENT

Every day, people depend on the environment for their food, water, air, and other material needs. More and more, people are realizing how important the environment is and why it should be protected. In this chapter, you will learn what harms the environment, how the health of the environment affects your health, and what you can do to keep the environment healthy.

CHAPTER PREVIEW

25-1 The Environment— Your Home

- Explain how the environment affects people and how people affect the environment.

25-2 Air Pollution and Health

- Name some sources of air pollution and tell what can be done to prevent it.

25-3 Water Pollution and Health

- Describe the sources of water pollution and the methods of controlling it.

25-4 Ground Pollution and Health

- Discuss the problems resulting from land disposal of solid and hazardous wastes.

25-5 Radiation and Noise Pollution

- Tell what you can do to minimize your exposure to radiation and noise pollution.

BUILDING HEALTH SKILLS

- Practice ways to be assertive.

CHECK YOUR WELLNESS

Are you doing all you can to protect the environment? See if you can answer *yes* to the questions below.

- Do you walk, bicycle, or carpool whenever possible?

- Do you turn off lights and appliances when they are not in use?

- Do you recycle newspapers, cans, bottles, and plastic containers?

- Do you support local groups or other organizations that work to keep the environment clean?

- Do you listen to radio, TV, or stereo at a moderate volume level?

KEEPING A JOURNAL

In your journal, write what you think about the current state of the environment where you live. Then explain how you think you affect the environment and how it affects you.

Take it to **the Net**

www.phschool.com

THE ENVIRONMENT— YOUR HOME

GUIDE FOR READING

Focus on these questions as you read this lesson.

• How does the health of people depend on the health of the environment?

• How is the health of the environment affected by the activities of people?

SKILLS

• Finding the Facts

ave you ever thought about how dependent you are on the environment? The **environment** (en VY run munt) is everything that makes up your surroundings—air, water, soil, rocks, plants, animals, and microorganisms. All living things are part of the environment and depend on it for all their needs. The air you breathe, the water you drink, and the food you eat come from the environment.

You, in turn, contribute to the environment in many ways. For example, as shown in Figure 25-1, as you breathe in oxygen, eat and use food, and drink water, you produce carbon dioxide and other body wastes, which enter the environment. Bacteria and other microorganisms use the wastes as food, breaking them down and releasing minerals and more carbon dioxide. Plants use the minerals and carbon dioxide to make their own food, and, in the process, release oxygen. You and other organisms use the plants as food and also use the oxygen they produce. Thus, materials in the environment are continually being used and reused in a never-ending cycle.

The Balance of Nature

The cycling of materials helps to keep conditions relatively constant in the environment. This steady state, known as **homeostasis** (hoh mee oh STAY sis), is maintained as long as all the parts of the environment are healthy. When any part of the environment is harmed or destroyed, the environment's homeostasis, or the "balance of nature," is changed.

Environmental Damage

The environment is constantly being disturbed—by natural events and by human activities. Natural events such as volcanoes, earthquakes, and floods can be devastating, but the environment eventually recovers from them. In fact, these events are part of cycles of renewal in the environment, as, for example, when ash from a volcano creates new soil. In contrast, many human activities such as clearing rain forests or polluting a lake cause harm that may permanently damage the balance of nature.

HABITAT DESTRUCTION   Humans have been altering the environment for thousands of years—for farming, settlement, and harvesting resources such as lumber. In modern times, however, the demand for land—on which to grow crops and live and for water and other resources—is accelerating as the human population rapidly expands.

Figure 25-1 *Raw materials such as carbon dioxide and oxygen are continuously being cycled in the environment.*

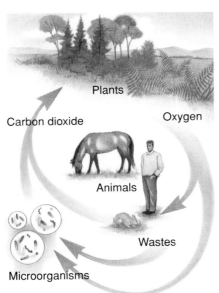

Plants

Carbon dioxide

Oxygen

Animals

Wastes

Microorganisms

Increasingly, more natural areas are being destroyed. When this happens, the survival of many types of organisms is threatened. As a result, the environment as a whole becomes less stable.

POLLUTION All living things depend on the environment. **Pollution**—the accumulation of harmful wastes or other harmful substances in the environment—harms you and all other living things. **When the environment becomes polluted, the air you breathe, the water you drink, and the food you eat become polluted.** Substances that cause pollution are known as **pollutants.**

As part of the normal processes of life, all organisms produce wastes. These wastes usually do not cause pollution. Why? Because, as you see in Figure 25-1, they are broken down by microorganisms and reused by other living things. Wastes that can be broken down by microorganisms are called **biodegradable wastes**. Pollution from biodegradable wastes occurs only if the wastes are released into the environment more rapidly than they can be decomposed. This happens, for example, when raw, or untreated, sewage is released into a river.

In addition to biodegradable body wastes, humans create wastes that are not, or are only partially, biodegradable. Wastes of this type include motor oil, pesticides, solvents, mercury, arsenic, and lead. Many of these wastes are poisonous or cause cancer. Such wastes are serious pollutants because they accumulate in the environment and contaminate organisms.

The environmental damage resulting from human activities is serious, but there are solutions. Land use can be controlled, and many forms of pollution can be eliminated through new technologies. Even simple actions can bring about enormous improvements. People are beginning to recycle materials, for example. **Recycling,** the use over and over again of materials such as metal and glass, is one practical way to help keep the environment healthy.

SHARPEN YOUR SKILLS

Finding the Facts

The single greatest source of air pollution from human activities is the burning of fossil fuels. Alternative sources of energy include solar, wind, water, and nuclear power. Choose one of these energy sources and research its advantages and disadvantages.

LESSON 1 REVIEW

1. What is the environment?
2. What is pollution?
3. How does the environment's health affect your health?
4. How is the balance of nature affected by pollution?

What Do You Think?

5. What could you do to help reduce pollution in your immediate environment?

2 AIR POLLUTION AND HEALTH

GUIDE FOR READING

Focus on these questions as you read this lesson.

• What is the major source of air pollution?

• What can be done to reduce air pollution?

SKILLS

• Recognizing Misleading Claims

You breathe in air and any pollutants that are present in the air. Some of these pollutants may damage the delicate tissues of your respiratory system. Others may enter your bloodstream and harm other parts of your body. The same air pollutants that are harmful to you also harm plants and animals in the environment.

Gases That Pollute

Air is a mixture of gases and small particles. The one gas you need—oxygen—makes up about 20 percent of the air. The remaining 80 percent of the air consists mainly of nitrogen plus small amounts of other naturally occurring gases, including carbon dioxide and argon.

When harmful gases and particles enter the air, the air becomes polluted. **Burning is the greatest source of air pollution.** Whenever substances such as coal, oil, natural gas, gasoline, wood, paper, and trash are burned, particles and harmful waste gases are produced. Harmful gases also are released into the air when liquids such as gasoline or paint thinner evaporate or when gases are released from natural sources such as volcanoes.

CARBON DIOXIDE   The primary waste given off during burning is the nonpoisonous gas **carbon dioxide**. Carbon dioxide is normally present in the atmosphere, and, as you know from Figure 25-1, is essential for living things. Why do some people consider it a pollutant? The answer is that the widespread burning of coal, petroleum, and other fossil fuels has caused a substantial increase in the level of carbon dioxide in the atmosphere. Carbon dioxide absorbs heat. When Earth is warmed by the sun, the heat that would normally escape into outer space is absorbed by the carbon dioxide in the atmosphere. As a result, the atmosphere is warmed more than it would be if carbon dioxide levels were lower. Many scientists think that this warming effect, called the **greenhouse effect,** will lead to harmful changes in global weather patterns.

CARBON MONOXIDE   A poisonous waste produced when most substances are burned is **carbon monoxide**, a colorless, odorless gas. Carbon monoxide is dangerous because it combines with **hemoglobin** (HEE muh gloh bin), the substance in your red blood cells that carries oxygen to all the cells of your body. Carbon

Figure 25-2 *Motor vehicles are the major source of air pollution in most cities.*

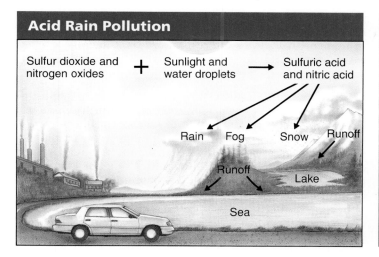

Acid Rain Pollution

Sulfur dioxide and nitrogen oxides + Sunlight and water droplets → Sulfuric acid and nitric acid

Rain Fog Snow Runoff

Runoff

Lake

Sea

Figure 25-3 *Acid rain, which results from the burning of fossil fuels, is damaging forests in many parts of the world.*

monoxide binds to hemoglobin, preventing it from carrying oxygen. As a result, your body does not receive enough oxygen. Tobacco smoke and the exhaust gases from motor vehicles are sources of carbon monoxide.

OXIDES OF NITROGEN AND SULFUR   Other gases that form when fossil fuels are burned include nitrogen oxides and sulfur oxides. These gases may cause your eyes to burn and tear. They also can damage lung tissues and worsen existing respiratory problems. As you can see in Figure 25-3, when these gases mix with water in the air, **nitric acid** (NY trik) and **sulfuric acid** (sul FYOOR ik) are formed. Rain that contains one or both of these acids is called **acid rain**. Snow, sleet, and fog also can contain these acids, which dissolve stone, corrode metals, and damage plants. Acid rain and snow increase the acidity of lakes, ponds, and streams, preventing the growth of many water-dwelling organisms. When acid rain enters the soil, it releases certain toxic minerals, which are then taken up by plants. In many parts of the world, acid rain has caused severe damage to trees, as you can see in Figure 25-3.

HYDROCARBONS   Liquid fuels and solvents that evaporate, natural gas that escapes into the air, and incompletely burned fossil fuels are sources of airborne hydrocarbons. **Hydrocarbons** (hy druh KAHR bunz) are substances made up of hydrogen and carbon. Many hydrocarbons are poisonous, and some can cause cancers. Motor vehicles are a major source of hydrocarbons. When hydrocarbons react with nitric oxide in the presence of sunlight, a brownish haze called **smog** forms. Substances in smog are harmful to plants as well as animals.

OZONE   In the presence of sunlight, nitrogen oxides and hydrocarbons from sources such as motor vehicles react to produce ozone. **Ozone** is a form of oxygen that chemically reacts with many things. It causes severe damage to plants. In humans, it irritates the respiratory tract and aggravates respiratory conditions such as asthma, bronchitis, and emphysema.

CHLOROFLUOROCARBONS   Chemicals containing chlorine, fluorine, and carbon are called **chlorofluorocarbons** (klawr oh floor oh KAHR bunz), or CFCs. These chemicals have been widely used as the cooling fluids in air conditioners and refrigeration units, as propellants in aerosol spray cans, and in foam insulating materials. CFCs are serious air pollutants because they destroy the **ozone layer**, a region of the atmosphere with a high concentration of ozone.

In contrast to its role as a pollutant near Earth's surface, the ozone in the ozone layer has a protective role. Most of the ultraviolet light from the sun is absorbed by Earth's ozone layer. Ultraviolet light is a form of radiation that is harmful to all living things. In humans, it causes skin cancer and cataracts (cloudiness of the eye's lens) and may damage the immune system. Scientists are concerned that increasing levels of ultraviolet radiation will damage plants, reducing food supplies on land and in oceans as well. Since CFCs are destroying the ozone layer, more ultraviolet light than ever before is reaching Earth's surface.

Particle Forms of Air Pollution

Particles in the air—such as dust, soot, and mold spores—are another type of air pollution. You see evidence of this if you wipe a windowsill with a clean, white cloth. The dirt on the cloth is mostly particles, or **particulates** (pahr TIK yuh lits), that settled out of the air. Particle pollution enters your breathing system with the air you breathe. The tiny hairlike structures, or **cilia** (SIL ee uh), that line your breathing passages trap many of these particles before they reach your lungs, but they can still damage your body.

Figure 25-4 *The use of unleaded gasoline in the United States has reduced lead air pollution.*

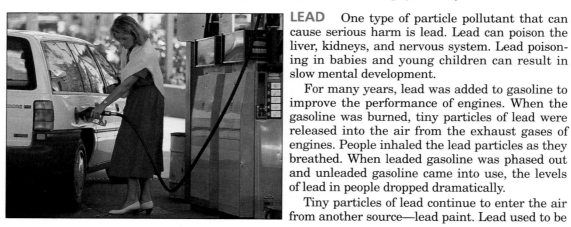

LEAD   One type of particle pollutant that can cause serious harm is lead. Lead can poison the liver, kidneys, and nervous system. Lead poisoning in babies and young children can result in slow mental development.

For many years, lead was added to gasoline to improve the performance of engines. When the gasoline was burned, tiny particles of lead were released into the air from the exhaust gases of engines. People inhaled the lead particles as they breathed. When leaded gasoline was phased out and unleaded gasoline came into use, the levels of lead in people dropped dramatically.

Tiny particles of lead continue to enter the air from another source—lead paint. Lead used to be an ingredient in most paints. As old lead paint flakes off or is removed, particles of paint are released into the air. People in areas where lead paint is being removed should wear breathing filters to avoid inhaling paint dust. Most serious cases of lead poisoning occur in children who eat bits of lead paint.

ASBESTOS   Another particle-type air pollutant is asbestos. **Asbestos** (as BES tus) is a mineral that occurs in the form of fibers. Because it does not burn, asbestos was widely used in shingles, floor coverings, ceiling materials, insulation, and brake linings. Unfortunately, bits of asbestos flake off easily. When asbestos fibers are inhaled into the lungs, they damage the cells of the lungs, causing a disease called **asbestosis** (as bes TOH sis). Asbestos also may cause lung cancer, especially in people who also smoke.

Weather and Air Pollution

Although the weather does not cause air pollution, it can affect it. When the air close to Earth's surface is warmer than air at higher elevations, which is usually the case, the warm air rises, carrying air pollutants upward. This prevents pollutant levels from building up near the ground. When a **temperature inversion** occurs, however, a layer of cool air near the ground is trapped under a layer of warm air, as shown in Figure 25-5. As a result, pollutants are not carried away and may accumulate to dangerously high levels.

Weather reports for cities and other areas with air pollution problems often include government air quality ratings. The ratings, which are based on air quality standards, range from "good" to "unhealthy" to "very hazardous." People who have respiratory problems should stay indoors and avoid physical activity during periods of severe air pollution.

GEOGRAPHY CONNECTION

Depending on wind and rainfall patterns, air pollutants can settle to Earth in regions far from where they were released. For example, some radioactive material released from the nuclear reactor at Chernobyl in the former Soviet Union was carried north to Norway, Sweden, and Finland.

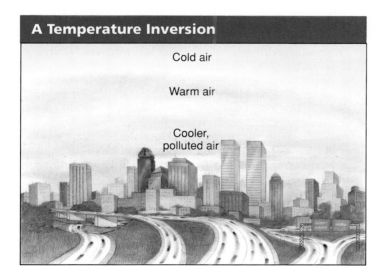

A Temperature Inversion

Cold air

Warm air

Cooler, polluted air

Figure 25-5 *A temperature inversion results in a buildup of air pollutants in a cool layer of air near Earth's surface.*

Figure 25-6 *A variety of sources may contribute to indoor air pollution.*

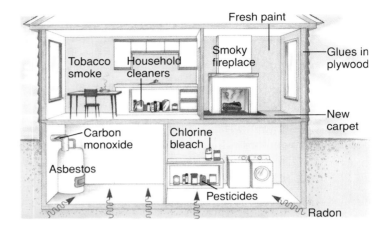

Indoor Air Pollution

Most people think that air pollution occurs only outdoors. Yet studies have shown that levels of air pollutants indoors can be higher than those outdoors. Indoor air pollution is most severe in homes and other buildings that have been sealed against air leaks, usually as a way to prevent energy loss. A building with few air leaks uses less energy for heating and cooling. Unfortunately, inside such energy-efficient buildings, pollutants can build up to high levels.

Indoor air pollutants include such things as asbestos and the gases, vapors, or particles given off by carpets, paints, pesticides, glues in plywood, foam insulation, gas stoves, fuel-burning indoor heaters, air fresheners, and burning tobacco. Another indoor air pollutant, to be discussed later in this chapter, is the naturally occurring radioactive gas radon.

What Can Be Done?

Progress in reducing air pollution has occurred because new laws were passed when people became aware of the dangers of air pollution. The Clean Air Act of 1970, for example, identified major air pollutants and set standards for air quality. Since 1970, Congress has made changes and additions to the Clean Air Act every few years. To comply with federal laws, some factories and power plants use scrubbers, or filters, on smokestacks to remove some pollutants. More efficient ways of burning oil, coal, and gas also have helped reduce the amount of pollution from these sources.

Congress has also passed separate laws to regulate pollution from automobiles. Catalytic converters on automobiles have dramatically reduced hydrocarbons and carbon monoxide in automobile exhausts. Also, many states now require that motor vehicles pass annual inspections that include a check of exhaust pollutants.

Other measures to reduce air pollution include the development of cleaner-burning fuels and alternative energy sources. Fuels such as natural gas, methanol, and hydrogen burn more cleanly than gasoline. Adapting automobile engines to burn these fuels will reduce air pollution. Electric-powered automobiles also are being developed. In addition, progress is being made to improve the efficiencies of nonpolluting energy sources such as wind and solar power.

Other sources of air pollution are also being addressed. Some countries, including the United States, have banned CFCs in aerosol cans. Scientists have already developed alternatives to CFCs that will not damage the ozone layer. The use of asbestos now is severely limited and banned entirely in construction. Asbestos removal programs for buildings such as schools have helped reduce exposure to this pollutant. Reducing indoor air pollution even extends to the design of buildings. Now, some houses are being designed to allow for adequate year-round ventilation.

Reducing air pollution depends on the actions of individuals as well as government and industry. You can help reduce air pollution by practicing some of the following:

- Whenever you can, walk or ride a bicycle instead of using a motor vehicle.
- Use public transportation instead of an automobile.
- Recycle materials such as glass, metal, plastic, and paper. Making goods from recycled materials requires less energy (fuel) than making them from raw materials.
- If you drive, avoid unnecessary trips. Also, be sure the vehicle is well-tuned so it produces the least pollution.
- Turn off lights and appliances that are not being used. Saving energy saves fuel, which reduces air pollution.
- Clean the cooling fans or coils on refrigerators and air conditioners so they will work more efficiently.
- In winter, set the thermostat lower and wear extra clothes indoors. In the summer, if you have an air conditioner, set it at the highest comfortable temperature.

SHARPEN YOUR *SKILLS*

Recognizing Misleading Claims

An advertisement for a new household air filter claims that it "…will remove all forms of air pollution from a house or apartment." Would you believe the advertisement? Why or why not? How would you go about finding out if the claim is true?

LESSON *2* REVIEW

1. What is the source of most air pollution?
2. How do chlorofluorocarbons harm the environment?
3. How does asbestos endanger human health?
4. How do temperature inversions affect air pollution?

What Do You Think?

5. Would you favor increasing taxes on gasoline? Why or why not?

3 WATER POLLUTION AND HEALTH

GUIDE FOR READING

Focus on these questions as you read this lesson.

- What are sources of water pollution?
- What are ways of reducing water pollution?

SKILLS

- Activity: Nontoxic House-cleaning

Clean, available, fresh water is something most of us take for granted until there is a crisis—for example, pollution of water supplies by toxic chemicals. More and more people are becoming concerned about our water resources. **In the United States and all over the world, wastes from household, industrial, and agricultural sources cause pollution of water resources.** Laws now help prevent some kinds of water pollution that occurred in the past. However, individuals also need to be aware of how their actions can help protect water resources.

Sources of Water Pollution

Bodies of water such as lakes, rivers, and oceans have always been used to dispose of wastes. If the wastes are biodegradable and in small enough volumes, microorganisms can break down the wastes. However, as both the volume and types of wastes increase, pollution of water becomes more and more of a problem. To understand the scope and nature of water pollution, you need to understand its sources.

SEWAGE   The waste material carried from toilets and drains is referred to as **sewage.** Most wastes in sewage are human body wastes. If released into the environment too rapidly, sewage can make water foul-smelling and unable to support life. Sewage also can contain bacteria and viruses that cause disease. For example, in coastal areas, shellfish such as clams or oysters may become contaminated with the hepatitis A virus from human sewage. People who eat the shellfish raw may develop hepatitis A.

As recently as the 1970s, many communities in the United States discharged raw, or untreated, sewage directly into rivers or the ocean. In 1972, the Clean Water Act required communities to treat their raw sewage before releasing it into the environment.

Sewage treatment makes use of microorganisms to break down the wastes in the water. Septic tanks, cesspools, and municipal sewage treatment plants are all forms of sewage treatment facilities. Each provides conditions that allow microorganisms to break down wastes before they are released into the environment.

INDUSTRIAL WASTES   Wastes produced from industrial operations, such as mining and manufacturing, can produce some of the most dangerous types of water pollution. Many industrial wastes are extremely toxic or not biodegradable, or both. Industrial wastes include such things as dyes, acids,

Figure 25-7 *Clean, unpolluted water is something no one should take for granted.*

ACTIVITY

NONTOXIC HOUSECLEANING

In this activity, you will demonstrate the effectiveness of cleaners made from nontoxic materials.

Materials

bucket	cornstarch
water	white vinegar
baking soda	stirrer
soap flakes	sponge
	rags or paper towels

Procedure

1. In a bucket, make a nontoxic, all-purpose cleaner by adding 1/2 tablespoon of baking soda and 1/8 cup of soap flakes to 1/2 gallon of hot water. Stir until all ingredients are completely dissolved.

2. With a sponge, use the cleaning solution to clean your desktop or another surface that your teacher selects. Note how easily and effectively the cleaner works.

3. Make a nontoxic glass cleaner by adding 1 tablespoon of cornstarch and 1/4 cup of white vinegar to 1/2 gallon of warm water. Stir well.

4. Moisten a rag or paper towel with the glass cleaner. According to your teacher's instructions, try cleaning a window or mirror.

Discussion

1. How well did the cleaners work? How do they compare with commercially prepared products you have used?

2. How do you think most people dispose of cleaning products? What effect do you think disposing of cleaning products would have on the environment?

3. What are the benefits and drawbacks of making your own nontoxic cleaners?

---

solvents, and heavy metals such as mercury, lead, and cadmium. In the past, it was common for industrial wastes to be discharged into ground and surface waters, contaminating organisms that lived in or drank the water.

RUNOFF   The water that drains from land into streams is called **runoff.** Runoff can carry with it many kinds of substances that pollute water supplies. Runoff from agricultural land, for example, often contains pesticides, herbicides, and fertilizers. **Pesticides** are chemicals that kill crop pests. **Herbicides** are chemicals that kill weeds. Many pesticides and herbicides are toxic and do not decompose, or decompose slowly. People who drink water contaminated with these chemicals can suffer harm. Even if the water is not used by humans, fish in the water pass the contamination on to people who eat the fish.

   Fertilizers are chemicals that contain minerals needed by plants. Some of the minerals, such as nitrates and phosphates, are carried by runoff into streams, rivers, and lakes. There these minerals cause small water plants, or **algae** (AL jee), to grow rapidly. When the algae die, they serve as food for huge populations of microorganisms. The microorganisms, which require oxygen to live, grow so rapidly that they

Figure 25-8 *Pesticides in agricultural runoff can pollute water resources.*

Figure 25-9 *Oil spills are devastating to animal and plant life.*

use up all the oxygen in the water. Without oxygen, most of the water-dwelling organisms die, and the water becomes foul-smelling and unfit for use. This process of excessive algae growth followed by decay and lack of oxygen is called **eutrophication** (yoo troh fih KAY shun).

OIL SPILLS   Oil spills are major sources of water pollution, especially in the world's oceans. The dependence of the world on petroleum means that millions of gallons of oil and petroleum products are being transported every day throughout the world. This level of activity makes it likely that oil spills will occur, and, in fact, they do. Most oil spills are not large. No matter what their size, however, the pollution that results is very damaging to the environment. The 11-million-gallon oil spill in 1989 from the *Exxon Valdez* in Alaska was but one of many oil spills that have seriously polluted large areas.

HOUSEHOLD CLEANERS   Household cleaners can be a source of pollution if they contain harsh chemicals such as chlorine, or plant nutrients such as phosphates. Chlorine is toxic to all forms of life. Chlorine also can react with certain substances dissolved in water, forming cancer-causing substances. Phosphates, which are plant nutrients, may cause excessive algae growth, leading to eutrophication.

What Can Be Done?

As you know, federal laws require communities to treat their sewage. However, sewage treatment can do nothing to decompose many kinds of pollutants that are poured into drains. Everyone can help prevent water pollution by not dumping toxic materials such as oil, solvents, paints, or pesticides into a drain. Most communities have waste collection centers to which these chemicals can be taken for safe disposal. If you have a question about how to dispose of chemicals safely, call your local health department or state agency for environmental protection.

LESSON 3 REVIEW

1. What pollutants are present in agricultural runoff?
2. How are microorganisms involved in sewage treatment?
3. Why are industrial wastes usually so damaging to the environment?
4. How have laws helped to prevent water pollution?

What Do You Think?

5. What would you suggest to reduce the chances of oil spills?

DIFFERENT VOICES SPEAKING

New Jersey native Chris Allieri is pursuing a career as an environmentalist at the University of Colorado. He has received numerous awards for his work in helping to protect the environment.

Q. Chris, how did you first become interested in protecting the environment?
A. My parents motivated me initially by their own example. They have long been nature enthusiasts, and they always taught my brothers, sisters, and me never to take what we have for granted. My big involvement as an environmental activist, however, came on the twentieth anniversary of Earth Day. I was in Central Park in New York as a volunteer, and there were speakers. I was moved by the experience and by the magnitude of the problem facing the planet. I felt that the time had come for me to spread my awareness. It was soon afterward that I founded SAFE.

Chris Allieri

Q. What is SAFE?
A. It's an environmental club that I started at my high school. The name SAFE is an acronym for Student Activists for the Environment. Initially people I discussed the idea with were skeptical, but I was persistent. Luckily, I won the support of a biology teacher I really admire. The club started with 15 members. Today the enrollment is around 80, and another chapter has formed at a junior high school in my home community.

Q. What are some of the activities SAFE has carried out?
A. One of our major tasks was storm drain stenciling. We stenciled a blue fish on storm drains all over town and then followed up with a community-wide educational program. We called it "the fish connection." We were trying to make people aware that what they put down the drain ends up in the ocean. The response from the community was great. We also initiated cleanups around the high school, the community, and area beaches. In our efforts to educate the public, we also arranged for guest speakers on recycling and set up an alumni forum for those interested in environmental careers.

Q. What do you hope to accomplish in your life goals as an environmentalist?
A. I hope to get people to embrace environmental awareness on a global scale—to wake up to the dangers that face us. We need to do that if the planet is to survive. A first step in that direction is education, so I guess you might say I plan to be an educator.

Journal Activity

Chris stresses the importance of education in saving the planet. In your health journal, write an open letter to the citizens of Planet Earth. In your letter, mention at least six steps that you feel must be taken to clean up Earth and keep it safe for future generations.

4 GROUND POLLUTION AND HEALTH

The amount of waste material produced in the United States every year is staggering—over 300 million tons. Much of the waste material is buried in landfills. A **landfill** is an area where trash, garbage, and other wastes are deposited and covered with soil. **Many of the wastes buried in landfills are toxic or cancer-causing and are potential sources of air and water pollution.**

Land Disposal of Wastes

Landfills have been widely used around the world for disposal of solid and liquid wastes. One problem with landfills is that space for them is running out. Many landfills across the country are at or near full capacity.

Another more serious problem is that many landfills contain hazardous wastes that may be leaking into water supplies. The Environmental Protection Agency (EPA), the federal agency in charge of enforcing environmental laws, calls substances **hazardous wastes** if they are flammable, explosive, corrosive, or toxic to human or other life. Each year, millions of tons of hazardous wastes are produced in the United States alone. According to the federal government, many of these wastes have been disposed of in landfills in unsafe ways. At thousands of landfills across the country, hazardous wastes are threatening to pollute underground and surface water supplies.

Fortunately, newer landfills, like the secure landfill illustrated in Figure 25-10, are designed to prevent leakage of liquid wastes into the surrounding soil. Many experts agree, however, that even these landfills may not be 100 percent

Figure 25-10 *Landfills can be designed to prevent pollution.*

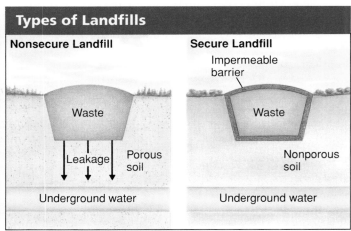

Types of Landfills

Nonsecure Landfill

Waste

Leakage | Porous soil

Underground water

Secure Landfill

Impermeable barrier

Waste

Nonporous soil

Underground water

safe and that alternative waste disposal methods need to be developed.

Most hazardous wastes that are dumped in landfills or elsewhere are produced by industries. Many of the wastes were dumped before their dangers were known. One instance of this took place between 1946 and 1958 when one chemical company dumped toxic chemical wastes into the ground around the Love Canal in upstate New York. Later, many homes and a school were constructed in the area. The chemical wastes received national attention in 1978, when heavy rains flooded basements in the Love Canal area. Oily liquids entered the basements with the rainwater. These oily liquids were leaking out of the dump site. Studies in the area showed an increase of disease, which was linked to the chemicals underneath the homes and school. Because of this evidence, the state government evacuated people from their homes. Today, the area is unpopulated because of the toxic materials in the soil.

The chemicals dumped in landfills or other hazardous waste sites may be extremely harmful. People who clean up these sites are never sure what they may encounter. They wear protective gear that prevents them from coming into direct contact with any of the waste materials. Some of the wastes are poisons that damage parts of the body such as the nervous system, lungs, liver, or kidneys. Other wastes may be cancer-causing substances, called **carcinogens** (kahr SIN uh junz). Still others may be **mutagens** (MYOO tuh junz)—chemicals that cause changes in a cell's hereditary material. The children of people exposed to mutagens have an increased risk of birth defects.

What Can Be Done?

Many sites where hazardous wastes have been dumped legally or illegally have been identified and are scheduled for cleanup. The EPA has identified over 20,000 dumps in the

SHARPEN YOUR *SKILLS*

Analyzing Risks and Benefits

A company wants to build a hazardous waste treatment facility in your community. They claim the operation will be safe and create many new jobs. Some residents claim that any benefits will be outweighed by the risks of noise and pollution. How would you analyze the risks and benefits?

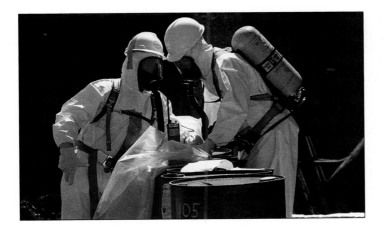

Figure 25-11 *The cleanup of hazardous waste sites requires strict safety precautions.*

E X P L O R I N G

CAREERS

Medical Writer and Biological Photographer

Issues involving health and the environment are complex. **Medical writers** help make these issues easy to understand. They may prepare articles for newspapers and magazines, or write books or scripts for radio and TV. Many medical writers are self-employed, while others work on the staffs of newspapers, magazines, research institutions, and hospitals.

Medical writers must have a knack for writing plainly about technical subjects. This career requires a bachelor's degree and a background in journalism, English, or science.

Biological photographers communicate information through visual images. They photograph things as varied as surgical procedures, bacteria under a microscope, or the effects of acid rain on a lake. Some 2- and 4-year colleges offer training in biological photography.

United States that contain hazardous substances. Many dump sites have been identified only after citizens have notified authorities. Other sites have not been identified. If you suspect hazardous chemicals have been dumped at a site, you should notify your local health department or state agency for environmental protection.

Legislation now makes it difficult for industries to dump wastes illegally. Legal dump sites for hazardous chemicals are designed to prevent the escape of wastes into the environment. Many companies are taking measures to reduce the amount of wastes they generate or to recycle their wastes. New technologies for destroying hazardous chemicals, such as high-temperature incineration, may provide a way of destroying large amounts of hazardous wastes. Many communities have special collection centers where residents can turn in hazardous wastes for proper disposal. Also, many states and communities now require residents to recycle materials such as newspapers, metals, plastics, and glass.

You can help reduce the problems associated with land disposal of wastes by doing the following:

- Recycle as much material as you can. Glass, metal, plastics, newspaper, and car batteries can be recycled.
- Avoid using disposable, nonbiodegradable products such as plastic razors and styrofoam cups.
- Use cloth bags or reuse paper bags for grocery shopping.
- Purchase products in recycled or recyclable packages.
- Buy products that are biodegradable or that are made from recycled material.
- Use only as much of a product or material as you need.
- Do not put hazardous wastes such as pesticides, oil, and batteries into your trash. Save these for hazardous waste collection centers. If you have questions about hazardous wastes, check with your local health department or state agency for environmental protection.

LESSON **4** REVIEW

1. What is a landfill?
2. What are hazardous wastes?
3. Why are landfills potential sources of water pollution?
4. What is a way you can reduce the volume of solid waste?

What Do You Think?

5. Suppose you had to develop new packaging for a fast-food restaurant. What type of packaging would you use to protect the food yet not harm the environment?

5 RADIATION AND NOISE POLLUTION

H igh-energy radiation and noise are two types of pollution that seem to be getting worse rather than better. **High-energy radiation** is a form of energy that damages living things. High-energy radiation includes ultraviolet light, X-rays, cosmic rays, and the energy that is given off by certain substances, such as uranium. Substances that give off radiation are said to be **radioactive**.

Sounds tell you something about your surroundings, but loud sound, or **noise**, is a nuisance that can harm your health. Airplanes, trains, motor vehicles, appliances, television, radio, stereo equipment, and machinery are some of the sources of noise to which you are exposed.

Radiation and Health

There are many natural sources of high-energy radiation, such as ultraviolet light from the sun, cosmic rays from space, and radiation from naturally occurring radioactive substances in the air, water, and soil. These natural sources of radiation make up what is called **background radiation**. Background radiation, along with routine exposure to X-rays for medical and dental care, are the normal sources of radiation exposure for most people.

EFFECTS OF RADIATION Under certain conditions, people may be exposed to radiation above background levels. For example, people who receive radiation therapy for cancer, who mine radioactive materials such as uranium, or who work in the nuclear weapons or nuclear power industries are exposed to doses of radiation higher than those of the average population.

Exposure to radiation may cause cancer. The greater the exposure, the greater is the risk of developing cancer. In some cases, however, even a small amount of radiation may be all that is necessary to cause cancer. To prevent radiation injury, people who work with radiation wear protective clothing and undergo periodic tests to monitor their exposure levels. Exposure to large doses of radiation results in **radiation sickness.** The symptoms of radiation sickness are nausea, diarrhea, fatigue, and hair loss. Severe radiation sickness can lead to death.

SOURCES OF RADIATION POLLUTION In the past, radioactive substances were released into the atmosphere when nuclear weapons were tested above ground. Winds carried this airborne radioactivity

GUIDE FOR READING

Focus on these questions as you read this lesson.

- What are some natural sources of high-energy radiation?
- What is the danger of exposure to loud noise?

SKILLS

- Supporting a Friend

Figure 25-12 *Nuclear wastes are a serious environmental hazard.*

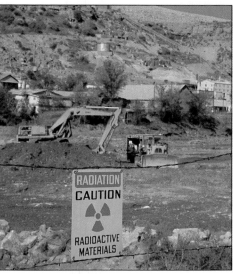

throughout the atmosphere. Eventually, the radioactive material settled to the ground in rain or snow or as dust particles. Radioactivity that falls to the ground in this manner is called **fallout.**

Nuclear power plants use radioactive materials to generate power. Because of their potential danger, nuclear power plants are highly regulated and have many safety systems built into their operation. Nonetheless, it is possible for a nuclear power plant to malfunction and release radioactive material. In 1986, tons of radioactive materials were released from a nuclear reactor at Chernobyl in the former Soviet Union. Radioactivity from this accident was spread by winds, contaminating areas in many countries of Europe. This was the worst accident to date of this type.

Other radioactive materials in the environment are the result of wastes produced by the medical uses of radioactive materials, nuclear weapons manufacturing and testing, nuclear power plants, and the mining of radioactive minerals. Since these wastes will give off radiation for thousands and even hundreds of thousands of years, they present a long-term danger to people.

The radioactive gas **radon** is estimated to cause 5,000 to 20,000 deaths from lung cancer each year. Radon is produced by radium, a radioactive substance found naturally in certain rocks. Radon becomes a serious indoor air pollutant when it leaks from the ground into the foundations of buildings and builds up to dangerous levels.

Noise and Health

Prolonged exposure to loud noise causes permanent hearing loss. The louder the noise and the longer the period of exposure, the greater the risk of hearing loss. Hearing loss in teens who listen to loud music is a growing problem.

Figure 25-13 *Noise from many sources can be harmful.*

The loudness of sound is measured in units known as **decibels.** Leaves rustling create a sound of about 10 decibels. Fifty decibels of sound can interfere with sleep. Normal conversation is about 60 decibels. Hearing loss begins to occur around 80 decibels, which is approximately the loudness of a vacuum cleaner.

Except for hearing loss, a firm connection between noise and disease has not been established. However, many experts believe that noise contributes to stress.

What Can Be Done?

Radiation and noise pollution cannot be avoided completely. They are part of our daily lives. However, you can take some preventive measures. Remember, the effects of exposure to all forms of radiation add up. Physicians recommend that you limit your exposure to the sun. If you are in the sun, wear protective clothing and sunglasses and use sunscreen. Physicians also suggest that you limit your exposure to X-rays. The risk involved in a single X-ray exposure is small, and the medical benefits of a correct diagnosis are great, but you should limit X-rays to those that are medically neccessary.

In some parts of the country, experts recommend that people test their living quarters for radon. Testing kits can be purchased at hardware and other stores. Some state environmental agencies provide these tests. If a radon problem exists, improving ventilation and sealing cracks in foundation walls and floors are recommended as corrrective actions.

Limit your exposure to loud noises. Loud music, especially when using headphones, is a major cause of permanent hearing loss in teenagers. Avoid areas where noise levels are high. If you cannot avoid loud noises, wear ear covers or plugs when you are in a noisy environment.

>> BREAKTHROUGH >>

Bioremediation

Cleaning up sites contaminated with radioactive uranium is not a simple task. If recent research is successful, however, the job may be made much easier with a process that uses bacteria that normally live more than 650 feet below Earth's surface.

In the process of bioremediation, water contaminated with dissolved uranium is pumped into a reaction tank containing the bacteria. When they are supplied with a food source, the bacteria convert the uranium from its water-soluble form to a water-insoluble form. The water-insoluble uranium settles to the bottom of the tank. It is still radioactive, of course, but because it is insoluble, it is much easier to separate and remove.

If the process works as well as expected, the bacteria may be used to help clean up uranium-contaminated sites.

LESSON **5** REVIEW

1. How is radiation a danger to human health?
2. What are some natural sources of radiation?
3. What is the natural source of radon, and how can exposure to radon be reduced?
4. What are sources of noise in your life? How do these noises affect your health?

What Do You Think?

5. What would you suggest to reduce the amount of noise in people's lives?

BUILDING HEALTH *SKILLS*

Being Assertive

While Joe and some of his friends were eating lunch in the no-smoking section of a local restaurant, cigarette smoke began drifting over from the next booth. At first Joe tried to ignore the smoke, but he soon decided that the "No Smoking" sign entitled him to a smoke-free meal. Joe politely asked the person to observe the no-smoking rule.

Joe behaved assertively when he stood up for his rights as a nonsmoker. Could you be assertive in a similar situation? If not, you are not alone. Assertiveness is a skill that many people find difficult to master, but one that is very necessary in order to function well in society.

Being assertive means expressing your feelings honestly in a way that respects your rights and the rights of others. Acting assertively can help you feel more self-confident and more in control of factors that affect your life. You will feel good that you can express your needs and stand up for yourself without hurting others.

The step-by-step process that follows will help you master the skill of assertiveness. The process is especially helpful in situations where you would like to act assertively but find it difficult to do so.

1. Evaluate your current behavior

To understand what kept you from acting assertively in a particular situation, ask yourself these questions:

- What outcome did I desire?
- What outcome did I get?
- What negative thoughts kept me from acting assertively in this situation?
- What was I afraid might have happened if I had acted assertively?

2. Observe a role model in action

Identify a person who is able to act assertively in difficult situations. Observe the person as he or she handles a situation in an assertive manner. Pay attention to the words, tone of voice, and body language the person uses. Afterwards, think about other ways in which you could act assertively in the same situation. What else could you say? How else could you say it?

3. Conduct a mental rehearsal

Conducting a mental rehearsal is like running a movie in your mind. Try to imagine yourself being assertive in a situation

you expect to be involved in. Mental rehearsal helps you think in detail about how you will look, act, and feel in the actual situation. It also helps you plan for any difficulties you might encounter.

4. Take action

Now you are ready to act assertively. When the situation you have rehearsed actually presents itself, put your plan into action. Keep the following pointers in mind:

Verbal Behavior

● Ask for what you want by using "I" messages. For example, begin statements by saying "I feel" or "I want." Do not try to blame or demand things of others by saying "You should …" or "You did…."

● Be specific about what you want to say. Try not to speak in terms that are too general.

● Be direct and unapologetic when speaking to the other person. For example, say "I believe I was ahead of you." Do not assume that the other person did something on purpose; it may have been accidental.

● Talk calmly and clearly. Take time to think things through. When listening, pay full attention to the other person.

Nonverbal Behavior

● Pay attention to your body language. Be sure to use gestures and facial expressions that match what you are saying.

● Look directly at the other person when speaking. Make direct eye contact.

● Stand a comfortable distance from the person to whom you are speaking. Standing too close may seem uncomfortable or threatening to some people.

5. Evaluate yourself

After the encounter, ask yourself these questions:

● Did I say what I intended to say?

● Was I direct and unapologetic, yet considerate?

● Did I stand up for myself without becoming defensive or infringing on the other person's rights?

● Was my body language assertive?

● Did I feel good about myself after the encounter?

● Do I think the other person felt comfortable with my interaction?

Questions to which you answered *no* indicate areas you should work to improve for future encounters.

Apply the Skill

1. Think of a situation in which you need to be assertive. Some examples are saying *no* to a friend who asks for a favor, or returning a defective product to a store. How would you handle the situation? Would you have trouble acting assertively?

2. Think of a person you know who acts assertively. Describe how he or she might handle the situation above.

3. Visualize yourself acting assertively in the situation chosen above. Write out what you would do and say. Anticipate the other person's response and your reaction.

4. Imagine returning a defective pair of sneakers. While saying "I bought these last week, and they have a defect," demonstrate how your nonverbal behavior can influence your message.

CHAPTER 25 REVIEW

KEY IDEAS

LESSON 1

- When the environment becomes polluted, the air you breathe, the water you drink, and the food you eat become polluted.

- Wastes broken down by microorganisms are called biodegradable wastes.

LESSON 2

- The burning of materials is the single greatest source of air pollution.

- Major air pollutants include carbon dioxide, carbon monoxide, oxides of nitrogen and sulfur, ozone, hydrocarbons, chlorofluorocarbons, lead, and asbestos.

LESSON 3

- Water pollution is caused by household and industrial wastes and agricultural chemicals.

- The Clean Water Act requires communities to treat their raw sewage before releasing it into the environment.

LESSON 4

- Many of the wastes in landfills are potential sources of air and water pollution.

- Some hazardous chemicals are poisonous; others act as carcinogens or mutagens.

- Individuals can help reduce land pollution by recycling wastes and by properly disposing of hazardous chemicals.

LESSON 5

- Ultraviolet light from the sun, cosmic rays from space, and radioactive substances are sources of high-energy radiation.

- Prolonged exposure to loud noise causes permanent hearing loss.

KEY TERMS

LESSON 1
biodegradable wastes
environment
pollutant
pollution
recycling

LESSON 2
acid rain
asbestos
carbon dioxide

carbon monoxide
chlorofluorocarbons
greenhouse effect
hydrocarbon
ozone
ozone layer
smog
sulfuric acid
temperature inversion

LESSON 3
eutrophication
fertilizer
herbicide
pesticides
runoff

LESSON 4
carcinogen
hazardous waste
landfill

LESSON 5
background radiation
decibels
fallout
high-energy radiation
noise
radioactive
radon

Listed above are some of the important terms in this chapter. Choose the term from the list that best matches each phrase below.

1. a site where wastes are covered with soil

2. a part of the atmosphere that absorbs ultraviolet light

3. formed when sulfur oxides react with water

4. the physical world and the living things that inhabit it

5. chemicals that destroy the ozone layer

6. a substance that causes pollution

7. when cold air is trapped below warm air

8. a gas that causes the greenhouse effect

9. a radioactive gas

10. a pollutant that binds to hemoglobin

WHAT HAVE YOU LEARNED?

On a separate sheet of paper, write the word or words that best complete each statement.

11. Water that drains from land into streams is called _____.

12. _____ results when fertilizers drain into ponds, lakes, or streams.

13. Reactions of nitric acid and hydrocarbons in the presence of light produce _____.

14. X-rays, ultraviolet light, and cosmic rays are forms of _____.

15. _____ is a form of oxygen that absorbs ultraviolet light.

16. _____ is the process by which materials are used over and over again.

17. A substance known to cause cancer is a _____.

18. A substance formerly used in building materials that is an air pollutant is _____.

Answer each of the following with complete sentences.

19. How are living things dependent on the physical environment?

20. What happens to natural wastes in the environment?

21. Why is the level of carbon dioxide in the atmosphere increasing?

22. Why are chlorofluorocarbons considered a problem in the environment?

23. What are two common particle forms of air pollution?

24. Name three sources of water pollution.

25. How can a landfill cause water pollution?

26. When is a substance considered to be hazardous to life?

27. Name an artificial source of radiation.

28. Why is loud noise harmful?

WHAT DO YOU THINK?

29. How do toxic substances dumped into the oceans affect people?

30. How do you think technology has helped to make people aware of pollution?

31. Some people say that nuclear power plants are a clean source of energy. What do you think they mean by this, and why might other people disagree with this view? What is your opinion?

32. What do you think are the advantages and disadvantages of burning trash?

33. What has caused people to be more concerned about pollution now than they were 50 years ago?

WHAT WOULD YOU DO?

34. Suppose you are offered two jobs after graduation. One job pays well, but the office you will work in is noisy and unattractive. The other job pays less, but the office is attractive and quiet. Which job would you choose? Why?

35. You recently learned that a friend has been changing her own oil and dumping the used engine oil into the town sewer system. What would you do to discourage her from this activity?

36. A friend of yours suggests that the actions of one person have little effect on the environment. What arguments could you use that might change his or her view?

Getting Involved

37. Find out what kinds of treatment facilities are available to deal with wastes in your town or city. You might be able to arrange a visit to a waste treatment facility near you. If you can, write a report that includes pictures of your visit.

38. Organize and develop support for a community volunteer clean-up project. Select a lake, stream, road, park, or other area in your community to clean up. Make a report to your class about the experience.

Selection 1 Questions

Chapter questions are on pages 262–263

Selection 2 "With Every Breath You Take"

KIMI EISELE

Essays by Ms. Eisele appear in various national publications including Orion *and* Orion Afield. *This is excerpted from her Winter 2003 essay in* OnEarth, *a publication of the National Resources Defense Council. She lives in Tucson, Arizona, where "smog increasingly threatens our blue desert skies."*

VOCABULARY

> *consensus* (¶ 6): agreement
> *virulent* (¶ 7): strong, powerful
> *caustic* (¶ 13): corrosive, dangerous substance

AN IDEA TO THINK ABOUT

Have you ever had trouble taking a breath? Do you know anyone who suffers from a breathing-related health problem such as asthma? *As you read*, find out how common respiratory problems have become and what experts believe are some of the causes.

WITH EVERY BREATH YOU TAKE

Kimi Eisele

¹When I was eight years old, I bit into a red apple and my throat closed. It was an autumn morning, and I was sitting in the back seat of the car. My mouth began to itch and I felt like I had to burp, but I couldn't. I could barely speak. Outside, dry leaves were scuttling across the sidewalk. I couldn't get enough air. My parents, twisting around in alarm to look at me from the front seat, started inhaling and exhaling deeply and slowly, as if modeling breathing would remind me how to do it. But I hadn't forgotten how to breathe. I simply couldn't.

²Soon afterward, I was diagnosed with atopic asthma—asthma caused by allergies, which is a chronic condition with no known cure. The word asthma comes from the Greek word for "panting," which is what we asthmatics do when we're trying to get air. My own panting is induced by any number of factors: dust mite dung, dry wind, cat dander, cold air, rabbits, wood smoke, pollen, guinea pigs, cigarettes, grass, horses, and some species of trees, among other things. Any of these will make my eyes itch,

my nose run, and my skin break out in a rash. Or they will shut my airways.

³Because I have asthma, for most of my life I've had to pay attention to my surroundings. I've had to be aware of hovering dust, the direction of a spring breeze, the presence of a cat. Luckily, my asthma is mild. My attacks aren't life-threatening, and as long as I have my inhaler along, they're easily relieved. And I can usually get myself out of the path of the allergens, away from the cats and rabbits, in from the pollens, and into a "clean" air space.

⁴But for the 17 million other people with asthma in the United States, controlling the air space is not always so simple, especially because some of the most common triggers of asthma—smog and soot from tailpipe exhaust and power plants—are in the air we breathe every day.

⁵It's possible that air pollution is doing more than just triggering asthma attacks. It may also be an element in the development of the disease—a criminal accomplice, not just an accessory after the fact. In industrialized countries, asthma is becoming more common and more severe. Five thousand people die of it every year in the United States. Currently it's the sixth most common chronic condition in the nation. Three times as many people have it now as in 1980. Some 6 million of them are children. For children, asthma is the most common chronic disorder, the leading cause of missed school, and the leading cause of hospitalization.

⁶Is polluted air helping to drive this epidemic? As yet, there's no scientific consensus. But the evidence pointing to air pollution as one major culprit is getting harder and harder to ignore.

⁷A seventeenth-century Belgian physician and asthmatic named Jean Baptista van Helmont called asthma the "falling sickness of the lungs." I know what he meant. As an allergic asthmatic, I am hypersensitive to substances that may have no effect at all on someone standing next to me. All it takes is a speck, a drop, a few molecules, and my immune system responds as if I were being attacked by something virulent. T cells, macrophages, eosinophils, and other immune system cells flood into the tissues of my airways, setting off an immunological train wreck. As my airways become inflamed and swollen and start producing mucus, I cough, drip, and wheeze. The immune system cells also prompt the most frightening response—constriction of the smooth muscle of my bronchial tubes. This is van Helmont's "falling" effect. It feels as if my airways were collapsing.

⁸What makes the asthmatic's airways so hypersensitive? Genetics plays a part; I probably inherited my asthma from my asthmatic father. But DNA isn't the whole story. "Genetic changes haven't occurred rapidly enough to account for the global increase in asthma," says Anne Wright of the Arizona Respiratory Center at the University of Arizona in Tucson. "It pretty clearly has something to do with our interaction with the environment."

⁹One theory suggests that modern society may be too antiseptic for our bodies. Over the last hundred years, humans' relationship to microorganisms has changed dramatically. When people were born in homes, didn't bathe as regularly, and didn't use antibiotics, they encountered more germs. Children got more sick more often. But exposure to microbes may have forced children's immune systems into maturity and strengthened them against exposure to allergens. In one study following 1,200 people

for more than two decades, Wright and her colleagues found that those who attended day care as children, or whose family owned a dog when they were growing up, tended to have less asthma than others. What do dogs and day care have in common? Bacteria—mostly from feces, Wright explains. "We all know poop's not good for you," she says. "You can get sick from it. But what also happens is that your immune system is developing antibodies and being activated by those organisms."

[10]Although Wright subscribes to the hygiene hypothesis, she and other researchers agree that asthma, like cancer, has no single cause. "We won't find treatments and cures and preventive measures if we don't address the disease from different points of view—environmental, genetic, molecular, biological," says Fernando Martinez, director of the Arizona Respiratory Center. Children and adults who have been frequently exposed to tobacco smoke and to indoor allergens from cats, cockroaches, and household dust mites have more asthma than those who haven't. The disease is more prevalent and more severe among poor people. It's more common in inner cities. Stress may cause asthma. Sedentary lifestyles and unhealthy diets have also been associated with asthma.

[11]No wonder asthma has seemed exhaustingly complicated all my life. Even the suggested remedies are overwhelming—everything from smoking marijuana to giving up dairy products to inhaling steroids to refraining from sex. And the mystery of asthma's causes has always left me asking, "Why me?" Why does standing near a horse throw my lungs into a wheezing fit, and not the next guy's?

[12]On pollution, scientists are making progress. Several long-term, multimillion-dollar studies are now underway to track children from the womb onward, measuring precisely what contaminants they're exposed to and recording who develops asthma and who doesn't. One study will investigate effects of the mix of air pollutants and pesticides that descends on children in central California. In the next few years, this research should start to shape concrete answers.

[13]And last February, researchers from the University of Southern California published the most persuasive evidence yet linking asthma and air pollution. The study followed more than 3,500 children from twelve Southern California communities, six of which endured the kind of smog for which the Los Angeles region is notorious, and six of which had fairly clean air. Smog's primary ingredient is ozone, a caustic gas formed when sunlight and heat act on certain air pollutants—namely, nitrogen oxides and hydrocarbons. In Southern California, by far the largest source of these pollutants is tailpipes.

[14]None of the children had asthma when the study began. After five years, 265 were diagnosed with it. But the critical finding was that children who lived in high-ozone areas and were involved in several team sports were three times more likely to develop asthma than couch potatoes living in less polluted communities. "Kids playing three or more sports are likely to be outdoors ventilating at high rates, and are therefore being exposed to higher levels of air pollution," explains James Gauderman, one of the study's authors.

[15]But it's only a beginning. Martinez is one researcher who says the findings are important but not conclusive. High rates of asthma in cities may be related to factors such as stress, he argues. And he points out that asthma comes in different varieties. In the days when East Germany was

highly polluted, its population had higher rates of asthma—but fewer allergies—than West Germans. It's possible, Martinez says, that pollution is not a risk factor for the allergic form of the disease, but may be a factor for another form of the disease.

[16]Phoenix, Arizona, a fast-growing, sprawling desert city, is one of the most ozone-polluted cities in the country. In mid-September, not long after dawn, I drive there to visit the Breathmobile, a mobile asthma clinic of the Phoenix Children's Hospital. Though the desert air feels crisp at this hour, from the highway I can see the thick green-gray stripe of smog that has already spread across the horizon. On especially polluted days, flashing signs on the road are turned on to warn drivers that the air is bad. . . .

[17]This morning the Breathmobile is at William T. Machan Elementary School. To get there, I drive through a residential neighborhood with tree-lined streets, single-story homes, and semi-green lawns. Though it doesn't fit the stereotype, this is an inner-city school. Downtown Phoenix and its heavy automobile traffic are only blocks away. Students here face the same challenges that children in most inner cities in America face: low family incomes, poor access to health care, and abnormally high rates of asthma. . . .

[18]Fifth-grader Elizabeth Vargas, back for a checkup, is the first patient of the day. Her lungs don't look good. Each time she exhales into a tube connected to the computer, its screen shows a picture of a balloon being blown up. A healthy child would be able to pop the balloon. But until Elizabeth inhales the bronchiodilator medication albuterol, she can pop only two out of five balloons. After her appointment, Elizabeth will take home a supply of Advair, a steroid-based preventive daily medication. Unless her asthma becomes less severe as she grows up, as sometimes happens, she may have to take it for the rest of her life.

[19]Elizabeth is a typical Breathmobile patient. Like her, 75 percent of the Breathmobile's patients are Hispanic. Also like her, many of them get their first real medical help here. Elizabeth has suffered from tight lungs all her life, so much so that when Harris asks in Spanish what happens when she runs, she answers, "My lungs get agitated, and it hurts here"—putting a hand to the center of her chest. She missed thirty days of school last winter because of asthma. Yet her condition went undiagnosed until her first visit to the clinic several months ago.

[20]When asthma gripped my own lungs, I had the middle-class advantages of good air—we lived on a quiet street in a small college town—and good health care. My parents even bought a special vacuum cleaner that sucked dust into a vat of water so it wouldn't blow back into the house. But today, those who lack such socioeconomic cushions suffer disproportionately from asthma. This fact infuriates many environmental justice advocates, who believe the link between asthma and air pollution is as obvious as the sooty air in inner-city neighborhoods.

[21]"It's certainly no accident that the neighborhoods with the highest rates of asthma also have a high incidence of polluting facilities, and that they're also low-income communities of color," says Omar Freilla. Freilla works at Sustainable South Bronx, a New York City group that seeks to reduce pollution and promote parks in one of the city's most environmentally blighted areas. The South Bronx, he points out, is the site of twenty-six waste facilities and the largest food distribution center in the world. The number of trucks passing through the food distribution center's

neighborhood has been estimated at 11,000 daily. And Freilla believes that the asthma hospitalization rate in the South Bronx—six times higher than the national average—is directly related to all those tailpipes. . . .

[22]To breathe is to live. But for us asthmatics, when the air is full of pollens and particulates, what we need most becomes our worst enemy. When I was young, asthma meant only my personal affliction and the chores it demanded: regulating my breath, paying attention to allergens, and medicating. But as an adult, I'm implicated. If air pollution causes asthma, what does that mean about the energy I use and the car I drive? What does it mean that 6 million children in the United States have trouble breathing? I know I'm supposed to stay calm. But the evidence and the reality of it make me want to hyperventilate. . . .

Selection 2 Questions

VOCABULARY

Circle the letter of the best definition for the underlined word.

1. ". . . a <u>chronic</u> condition with no known cure." (¶ 2)

   a. recurring   **c.** one-time
   b. acute   **d.** brief

2. "Kids playing three or more sports are likely to be outdoors <u>ventilating</u> at high rates. . . ." (¶ 14)

   a. running   **c.** breathing
   b. perspiring   **d.** yelling

Rephrase the passage using your own words.

3. ". . . those who lack such socioeconomic cushions suffer disproportionately from asthma." (¶ 20)

   The poor and disadvantaged have a higher incidence of untreated

   breathing problems.

4. ". . . in one of the city's most environmentally blighted areas." (¶ 21)

   In one of the city's poor/slum areas.

COMPREHENSION

Determine whether the statements in sentences 5 and 6 are true or false, and circle your answer. If the statement is false, rewrite it to make it true.

(T) F **5.** Asthma is the leading cause of children missing school.

_____

_____

T (F) **6.** There is no reason to believe the increase in asthma has anything to do with our interaction with the environment.

   False. There is good reason to believe the increase in asthma has to

   do with our interaction with the environment.

7. Circle the letter of the sentence that best expresses the thesis.

   a. It's possible that air pollution is doing more than just triggering
   asthma attacks.

   b. Kids who play three or more sports will likely become asthmatic.

   (**c.**) Although there is no single cause for asthma, it often has something to do with our interaction with the environment.

   d. Stress may cause asthma.

8. Explain the theory that "modern society may be too antiseptic for our
bodies."

   Because we attempt to keep everyone and everything "antibacterial-

   ized," we have no opportunity to build any immunity.

9. In the last paragraph Eisele says, "But as an adult, I'm implicated."
What does she mean?

   As an adult, she (and we) may be contributing to the causes of/

   triggers for asthma.

REFLECT AND CONNECT

10. What advice would you give to Eisele and others who want to reduce
air pollution?

   Advice for how to reduce air pollution will vary, but typically includes

   driving less, using less energy at home and encouraging factories to

   reduce pollution.

Selection 3 Bennett Editorial Cartoon

CLAY BENNETT

Pulitzer Prize-winning editorial cartoonist Clay Bennett has been with The Christian Science Monitor *since 1998. In addition to producing five full-color cartoons each week for* The Christian Science Monitor, *he produces fully animated editorial cartoons for the Internet and draws cartoons for distribution through King Features Syndicate.*

AN IDEA TO THINK ABOUT

Has anyone ever told you to go outside and get some fresh air? Have you ever wondered if the air outside was really "fresh"? *As you read,* decide what Bennett thinks of our outside air.

'You two need to go inside and get some fresh air.'

(Clay Bennett © The Christian Science Monitor.)

Selection 3 Questions

1. What does Bennett want us to think about?

Bennett wants us to think about how clean the air we breath really

is—or isn't.

2. Review the University of Southern California study described in Eisele's "With Every Breath You Take," paragraphs 13–14 on page 266. Is Bennett's message similar or contradictory? Please explain.

The University of Southern California study described in Eisele's "With Every Breath You Take" found that children who lived in high-ozone areas and were involved in several team sports were three times more likely to develop asthma than couch potatoes living in less polluted communities. Bennett's message is quite similar.

Selection 4 "NASA Study Shows Common Plants Help Reduce Indoor Air Pollution"

ZONE 10 AND PLANTS FOR CLEAN AIR COUNCIL

Zone 10 is a group of nurseries and plant specialists in the Florida region. This article is posted on their Web site, <http://www.zone10.com/wsdocs/tech/NASA/fyh.htm>. Additional information is available from the Plants for Clean Air Council in Davidsonville, Maryland.

AN IDEA TO THINK ABOUT

Have you ever used an electric air filter to help remove smoke, odors, or allergens from the air? Was it effective? *As you read,* find out which plants make the best natural "air filters."

NASA STUDY SHOWS COMMON PLANTS HELP REDUCE INDOOR AIR POLLUTION

Zone 10 and Plants for Clean Air Council

[1]NASA and the Associated Landscape Contractors of America (ALCA) have announced the findings of a 2-year study that suggests a sophisticated pollution-absorbing device—the common indoor plant—may provide a natural way of helping combat "Sick Building Syndrome."

[2](The Sick Building Syndrome: Numerous studies conducted by the EPA over the last 25 years have shown measurable levels of over 107 known carcinogens in modern offices and homes. The presence of these VOCs [volatile organic compounds] is due to the switch from open windows to energy efficient living and working environments combined with modern building methods and products. In some extreme cases, buildings

have such high levels of contaminants that exposure to them results in multiple symptoms by the inhabitants.)

[3]Research into the use of biological processes as a means of solving environmental problems, both on Earth and in space habitats, has been carried out for many years by Dr. Bill Wolverton, formerly a senior research scientist at NASA's John C. Stennis Space Center, Bay St. Louis, Missouri.

[4]Based on preliminary evaluations of the use of common indoor plants for indoor air purification and revitalization, ALCA joined NASA to fund a study using about a dozen popular varieties of ornamental plants to determine their effectiveness in removing several key pollutants associated with indoor air pollution. NASA research on indoor plants has found that living plants are so efficient at absorbing contaminants in the air that some will be launched into space as part of the biological life support system aboard future orbiting space stations.

[5]While more research is needed, Wolverton says the study has shown that common indoor landscaping plants can remove certain pollutants from the indoor environment. "We feel that future results will provide an even stronger argument that common indoor landscaping plants can be a very effective part of a system used to provide pollution-free homes and work places," he concludes.

[6]Each plant type was placed in sealed, Plexiglas chambers in which chemicals were injected. Philodendron, spider plant, and the golden pothos were labeled the most effective in removing formaldehyde molecules. Flowering plants such as gerbera daisy and chrysanthemums were rated superior in removing benzene from the chamber atmosphere. Other good performers are dracaena massangeana, spathiphyllum, and golden pothos.

[7]"Plants take substances out of the air through the tiny openings in their leaves," Wolverton said. "But research in our laboratories has determined that plant leaves, roots, and soil bacteria are all important in removing trace levels of toxic vapors."

[8]"Combining nature with technology can increase the effectiveness of plants in removing air pollutants," he said. "A living air cleaner is created by combining activated carbon and a fan with a potted plant. The roots of the plant grow right in the carbon and slowly degrade the chemicals absorbed there," Wolverton explains.

[9]NASA research has consistently shown that living, green, and flowering plants can remove several toxic chemicals from the air in building interiors. You can use plants in your home or office to improve the quality of the air and make it a more pleasant place to live and work—where people feel better, perform better, and enjoy life more.

TOP 10 PLANTS MOST EFFECTIVE IN REMOVING FORMALDEHYDE, BENZENE, AND CARBON MONOXIDE FROM THE AIR

COMMON NAME	SCIENTIFIC NAME
Bamboo Palm	Chamaedorea Seifritzii
Chinese Evergreen	Aglaonema Modestum
English Ivy	Hedera Helix

COMMON NAME	SCIENTIFIC NAME
Gerbera Daisy	Gerbera Jamesonii
Janet Craig	Dracaena "Janet Craig"
Marginata	Dracaena Marginata
Mass Cane/Corn Plant	Dracaena Massangeana
Mother-in-Law's Tongue	Sansevieria Laurentii
Pot Mum	Chrysantheium morifolium
Peace Lily	Spathiphyllum "Mauna Loa"
Warneckii	Dracaena "Warneckii"

CHEMICALS USED

[10]**Benzene** is a very commonly used solvent and is also present in many common items including gasoline, inks, oils, paints, plastics, and rubber. In addition it is used in the manufacture of detergents, explosives, pharmaceuticals, and dyes. . . .

[11]**Formaldehyde** is a ubiquitous chemical found in virtually all indoor environments. The major sources which have been reported and publicized include urea-formaldehyde foam insulation (UFFI) and particle board or pressed wood products used in manufacturing of the office furniture bought today. It is used in consumer paper products which have been treated with UF resins, including grocery bags, waxed papers, facial tissues, and paper towels. Many common household cleaning agents contain formaldehyde. UF resins are used as stiffeners, wrinkle resisters, water repellents, fire retardants, and adhesive binders in floor coverings, carpet backings, and permanent-press clothes. Other sources of formaldehyde include heating and cooking fuels like natural gas, kerosene, and cigarette smoke. . . .

Selection 4 Questions

VOCABULARY

Write the definition for the underlined word.

1. ". . . results in multiple symptoms by the <u>inhabitants</u>." (¶ 2)

   the people who live and/or work in a particular place

2. ". . . slowly <u>degrade</u> the chemicals absorbed there." (¶ 7)

   break down

3. "Formaldehyde is a <u>ubiquitous</u> chemical found in virtually all indoor environments." (¶ 11)

   prevalent

COMPREHENSION

Determine whether the statements in sentences 4–5 are true or false, and write your answer. If the statement is false, rewrite it to make it true.

T (F) **4.** Plants only take substances out of the air through their leaves.

False. Plants take substances out of the air through their leaves, roots and soil bacteria.

(T) F **5.** You can use plants in your home or office to improve the quality of the air and make it a more pleasant place to live and work.

_____

_____

6. Circle the letter of the sentence that best expresses the thesis.

(a.) Common ornamental plants can remove certain pollutants from the indoor environment and improve the quality of the air.

b. Future orbiting space stations will have plants.

c. Flowering plants such as gerbera daisy and chrysanthemums are best for removing benzene.

d. Formaldehyde is a ubiquitous chemical found in almost all indoor environments.

7. Why do you think the ALCA joined NASA to fund the study?

The ALCA probably joined NASA to fund the study because it is to the ALCA's advantage to show the beneficial effects of buying/having plants. (This is not intended to imply there is anything wrong or deceitful about this practice.)

8. How does paragraph 6 help to develop and support the thesis?

Paragraph 6 describes the process (how the study was conducted) and gives specific examples of plants that remove pollutants.

REFLECT AND CONNECT

9. Pruitt, Crumpler, and Prothrow-Stith state, "Studies have shown that levels of air pollutants indoors can be higher than those outdoors." Combine their examples of potential sources of indoor pollutants and the examples in the article of where benzene and formaldehyde are found to create a list of potential sources of indoor pollutants in your home or office.

Answers will vary.

_____

_____

_____

Selection 5 "The Oil Was Everywhere"

BRUCE GRAY

Mr. Gray is an NBC News producer based in Los Angeles. He was a camera-man on the NBC team that covered the Exxon Valdez *oil spill in 1989 and returned to cover the ten-year anniversary of the spill.*

AN IDEA TO THINK ABOUT

While you are watching a friend change the oil in his car, a stream of oil spurts onto the garage floor or into the dirt. How could you clean it up? How long would any residue last? *As you read,* compare the effects of that small stream of oil to the 11,000,000 gallons that spurted into Prince William Sound, Alaska, in March 1989.

THE OIL WAS EVERYWHERE

Bruce Gray

[1]We first heard of the *Exxon Valdez* grounding from a friend who was first mate on another tanker in Valdez at the time. Word was getting around the port that there was a problem, and he called us up. This gave us a 12-hour jump on everyone, and we got there late that afternoon ready to start work. But we weren't prepared for what we were to witness over the next few months.

[2]It was not an easy story to cover. Prince William Sound was—and still is—a very isolated place. Bligh Reef, where the *Exxon Valdez* ran aground, is really in the middle of nowhere, so the only way to get out there was a helicopter. A boat trip in good weather is a long journey, 25 miles each way in potentially nasty waters. And if the wind gets blowing, it can be brutal and go for 24 hours straight. So not many people made the mistake of saying, "Oh, we'll go shoot it from a boat." I was a cameraman at the time, and shooting a story in such a remote locale proved to be quite a challenge. We covered the story the best we could, however we could, and basically stayed around right through the summer.

[3]I had been to Alaska many times before. I had done North Slope stories and Alaska Pipeline stories, but I had not been out to Prince William Sound. When I stepped off the plane, I was overwhelmed by the beauty of

the area. It was one of the most beautiful spots in the world—and it still is. But then, in the middle of this pristine place, a tanker was spilling millions of gallons of oil into the water.

⁴And the oil was everywhere. It was unimaginable how bad it was. The boats were covered with oil. Anybody who was near it was covered with oil. The hotels had a horrible problem because all the carpeting, all the bedding, everything had oil on it and they could not get it off. You could not escape the stuff.

⁵Although I have returned to Prince William Sound several times since the spill, the ten-year anniversary was a milestone for me. The memory of the spill is hard to shake. When I arrived in Alaska in early March to cover this story, I was struck again by the beauty of the place.

⁶But what really amazed me, what I was not prepared for, was to go back on the beach and see oil. The thought had not entered my mind; I had not imagined that ten years later there could still be oil on the beach.

⁷I don't know why. I had thought about it and read about it, but being on the beach and seeing the oil really brought it home—especially for someone who remembers what it was like in 1989. The oil looks exactly like it did, only in smaller amounts. It is just as disgusting-looking and it still has that toxic smell. That shocked me. And it was a very sad thing to see the oil still there.

MAJOR U.S. OIL SPILLS SINCE 1975

DATE	LOCATION	GALLONS RELEASED
Mar 1989	Prince William Sound, Alaska	11,000,000
Dec 1976	Nantucket, Mass.	7,600,000
Sep 1984	Lake Charles, La.	1,800,000
Aug 1990	Galveston Bay, Texas	700,000
Jan 1988	Monongahela and Ohio Rivers, Pa.	700,000
Jan 1987	Southeastern coast, Alaska	600,000
Nov 2000	Port Sulphur, La.	554,000
Dec 1986	Savannah River, Ga.	500,000
Sep 1985	Chester, Pa. to Delaware City, Del.	435,000
Jun 1989	Newport, R.I.	420,000
Dec 1990	Huntington Beach, Calif.	400,000
Jun 1989	Delaware River, Del.	306,000
Jun 1989	Houston Ship Channel, Texas	250,000
Feb 1999	Coos Bay, Ore.	75,000
Nov 1987	Brookline, Mass.	4,500

SOURCES: U.S. Coast Guard, EarthBase, Inc., MSNBC research

⁸When we reported the story in 1989, there was a group of people who very quickly declared that this was an unprecedented environmental disaster. "This is a terrible thing," they said. "We won't recover for decades and decades."

⁹At the time I thought, "Well, that might be going a little too far. This is a horrible thing, but don't make it out to be worse than it is." I was not alone in that opinion. Much had yet to be learned about the effect of oil pollution on the environment.

¹⁰But they were right: Prince William Sound has not recovered. It is quite obvious, even today, that there was a major oil spill there. Sadly, I am sure that if I come back to do the 20th anniversary, there will still be oil to find on the beach.

¹¹Is there a lesson to all this? The most universal comment we heard from everyone involved with the spill—scientists, fishermen, people who live there—every single one of them said the same thing: What we learned from *Exxon Valdez* is once the oil is out of the boat there is nothing you can do.

¹²The lesson, then, is don't let that happen.

Selection 5 Questions

VOCABULARY

Circle the letter of the best definition for the underlined word.

1. ". . . in the middle of this <u>pristine</u> place. . . ." (¶ 3)

   a. remote   **c.** soiled
   (b.) perfect, pure   **d.** inaccessible

2. ". . . an <u>unprecedented</u> environmental disaster." (¶ 8)

   (a.) unequaled   **c.** ordinary
   b. horrible   **d.** messy

COMPREHENSION

3. Gray says the *Exxon Valdez* grounding was "not an easy story to cover." Please explain what he means.

   The *Exxon Valdez* grounding was not an easy story to cover because

   the site was so inaccessible.

4. How does Gray compare/contrast the beach he saw in 1999 to the beach he saw in 1989?

   Gray says the beach he saw in 1999 looked just like the beach he saw

   in 1989—with just a little less oil.

5. In 1989 many people predicted, "We won't recover [from the oil spill] for decades and decades." How did Gray feel about their predictions at the time? How did Gray feel about the predictions in 1999?

   In 1989 Gray thought the prediction, "We won't recover [from the oil

   spill] for decades and decades" was an exaggeration. In 1999, he felt

   the prediction was very true.

6. What lesson does Gray want us to learn from the *Exxon Valdez* grounding?

   Gray want us to understand that we can never let another disaster of

   this magnitude happen again—the damage is too severe; we can't re-

   cover from it.

REFLECT AND CONNECT

7. One of the "What would you do?" questions at the end of Pruitt, Crumpler, and Prothrow-Stith's *A Healthy Environment* Chapter asks, "What would you do to discourage a friend from dumping used engine oil into the town sewer system?" How would you answer that question now?

   What students would do to discourage a friend from dumping used

   engine oil into the town sewer system will vary. My hope is that they

   understand how one individual dumping oil can affect the environ-

   ment for all of us.

Selection 6 "Noise Pollution: It's Everywhere and It's Worse Than You Think!"

DOROTHY LOCKHART LAWRENCE

Ms. Lawrence is a staff writer and editor for an online newsletter about the Sound Health Series and the Listening Program by Advanced Brain Technologies (ABT). ABT created the Sound Health Series to mask irritating environmental noises and provide a therapeutic sound environment for children and adults. Lawrence has worked in various aspects of the publishing industry for the past 25 years.

VOCABULARY

   appease (¶ 1): satisfy the needs of another
   compelled (¶ 7): forced, required

IDEAS TO THINK ABOUT

How much environmental noise do you hear every day? For example, what sounds did you hear as you came to class today? Do you think there were any sounds that you "tuned out"? How about when you are studying? *As you read,* find out how that noise could be affecting you.

NOISE POLLUTION: IT'S EVERYWHERE AND IT'S WORSE THAN YOU THINK!

Dorothy Lockhart Lawrence

[1]A couple of years ago I was drawn to an article called "The Muffled Epidemic," which was in the July/August issue of *Health* magazine. The subheading said, "Noise is stealing the hearing of millions of Americans. Are you one of them?" The author told the story of a young woman who took a hearing test to appease her husband, who was concerned about her constant requests to repeat what he was saying. The disturbing result showed that at age 34, she needed hearing aids. When she looked at the possible causes of her hearing loss, the likeliest answer was something she had never imagined would harm her—aerobics classes. She had attended classes 5 days a week, an hour a day, for 15 years to music amplified to produce an adrenaline rush that keeps club members going. According to this article, aerobics classes can hit 105 decibels (dB), which would be like standing on the running board of a fire engine with the siren going.

[2]But that's not the only place where the decibel levels are high enough to damage the delicate hairs in your ears. I recently found an online article from Reuters called "There's a Fly in Your What?" about the noise level in many restaurants. Researchers took sound readings Thursday through Saturday at dinnertime for several one-hour periods. Then they calculated the average noise exposure a waiter or other worker might get in an 8-hour shift.

[3]In at least two cases, the continuous exposure topped the 85-decibel level. According to the National Institute of Occupational Safety and Health, this level threatens hearing loss. Noise problems were worst in restaurants with big bars, hard surfaces, high ceilings, open kitchens, and large crowds, all standard in today's newest and trendiest restaurants.

NOISE AND NATURE

[4]Loud noise is also affecting nature. ABC Science News reports that all the noise from supertankers, oil exploration, and new military sonar equipment scrambles the communications systems of sea life. A new report warns that this underwater noise pollution has forced changes in migration routes and breeding grounds. An article called "Sound and Fury" in the March 2001 issue of *Harper's* reports that certain species of birds fail to learn their mating songs and therefore to reproduce in noisy environments.

[5]As early as 1975, one researcher found that children on the train-track side of a New York public school were lagging a year behind their classmates on the other side of the building in learning to read. Numerous studies have been done about the effects of airport noise and families who live nearby, and the same results have been found. The sound of toys can range up to 100 dB. Two hours of a power drill but only 30 minutes of continuous sound in a video arcade can cause permanent hearing loss. Even a baby's rattle can be as high as 110 dB. The *Cornell Chronicle* reported a new study shows that children don't tune out sound per se when in a chronically noisy environment; rather, they have difficulty acquiring speech recognition skills.

OTHER EFFECTS OF LOUD NOISE

[6a]The effects of noise pollution are more far-reaching than just hearing loss. [6b]Persistent loud sounds have been linked to headaches, stomachaches, tinnitus, irritability, loss of sleep, learning difficulties, even heart disease and high blood pressure. One writer reports that anti-stress medications are actually tested by exposing subjects to loud sounds.

[7]Perhaps the most disturbing story I found was in the July 1998 issue of *Time* magazine entitled "Mad About Noise." It began with the opening sentences, "Ever felt like murdering your neighbor for blasting music too loud? That's exactly what 78-year-old retired farmer Lambrinos Lykouresis did two years ago in Lithakia, on the Greek island of Zabynthos." Apparently Lambrinos had complained to the neighbor for months about the noise. One evening during the evening news which he continuously had trouble hearing, he suddenly snapped. He took his hunting rifle from the shelf and rang the bell to the neighbor's apartment. When the housewife answered the door, he fired three times at point-blank range, killing her instantly and wounding her 24-year-old son. Lambrinos is now in a quieter place, a Greek maximum-security prison. This is an extreme example of what someone felt compelled to do to have a little peace and quiet. But I think all of us have felt the irritation of unwanted sound.

[8]It's pretty sad to read that an 80-year-old Sudanese villager hears better than a 30-year-old American. It's sad to read that noise may affect us morally as well as aurally. According to the March 2001 *Harper's* article "Sound and Fury" by Garret Keizer, people subjected to high levels of noise are less likely to assist strangers in difficulty, less likely to recommend raises for workers, more likely to administer electric shocks to other human subjects.

[9]The issue of environmental noise and its effect on children has long been an issue of great importance to the National Academy for Child Development (NACD). For over 20 years, NACD researched and experimented with ways to create the optimal sound environment, especially for children.

[10]If you've visited the NACD website, you know that they describe the common environment of today's student. While little Max is trying to do his homework, he can hear his older brother listening to rock music upstairs, a car going down the street, the fluorescent lights, the hum of the computer, the sound of a jet flying overhead, and his mother talking on the phone. If Max is also hypersensitive to certain sounds and already has difficulty concentrating, he's in big trouble.

EXAMPLES OF ENVIRONMENT NOISE

[11]Even relatively low levels of noise (55 to 60 dB) can interfere with conversation. The danger zone for hearing loss begins at about 85 dB. To give you an idea of noise levels in most of our environments, here are some decibel guidelines:

Hair Dryer: 75–90 dB
Lawn Mower: 90–100 dB
Leaf Blower: 95–115 dB
Rock Concert: 110–120 dB
Portable Stereo (full volume): 115 dB
City Traffic: 80–100 dB
Jet Engines: 140 dB
Subway Trains: 100 dB
Fireworks: 130–190 dB
Handgun/Rifle: 160–170 dB

[12]Become aware of the noise pollution in your life and learn to make your sound environment work for you!

Selection 6 Questions

VOCABULARY

1. In paragraph 5, Lawrence says, "children don't tune out sound per se when in a chronically noisy environment." Give two examples of chronically noisy environments.

   Answers will vary; please see Answer Key.

2. If someone is "hypersensitive to certain sounds," what does that mean?

   He or she is more bothered by the sounds and/or less able to ignore

   the sounds. The sounds would be a greater source of stress.

COMPREHENSION

3. Circle the letter of the sentence that best expresses the thesis.

   a. The issue of environmental noise and its effect on children is very important.
   b. Too much noise makes people violent.
   c. Loud noise affects nature.
   d. We should become aware of the noise pollution in our life and strive to minimize it.

4. What is one likely reason "an 80-year-old Sudanese villager hears better than a 30-year-old American"?

    The villager has lived in a more quiet environment and thus less ear

    damage has occurred.

5. List the two loudest sounds you hear on a regular basis and how long you hear them. Based on the decibel guidelines in the article, estimate how many decibels you are exposed to.

    The two loudest sounds and their decibel estimate will vary depending

    on where the person lives and works.

6. What is the relationship of sentence 6b to sentence 6a?

    (a.) Sentence 6b gives examples of the effects.
    b.   Sentence 6b gives examples of the causes.
    c.   Sentence 6b defines terms.
    d.   Sentence 6b changes the direction of thought.

7. Lawrence says that "noise may affect us morally as well as aurally." Explain what she means.

    "Noise may affect us morally as well as aurally" means noise may af-

    fect what we do and how we behave in addition to how effectively we

    hear.

REFLECT AND CONNECT

8. Reread Lawrence's description of the common environment of today's student—what "little Max" hears while he is trying to do his homework. For the next two days, keep a log of all the sounds you hear while you are trying to study. What are some steps you can take to reduce your environmental noise?

    Hopefully the "noise log" will alert students to how much ambient

    noise they contend with on a daily basis, and they will be anxious to

    find ways to reduce their environmental noise.

Selection 7 "Are You Big Foot?"

KIM TODD

Kim Todd is an environmental writer and author of Tinkering With Eden: A Natural History of Exotics in America, *which won the 2002 Sigurd F. Olson Nature Writing Award. This article is from* Sierra Magazine, *Jan/Feb 2003.*

VOCABULARY

rigorous (¶ 7): thorough and careful
lapsed (¶ 18): slipped, went back to

AN IDEA TO THINK ABOUT

How much of the planet do you think you use? Do you think you use more than your share, or perhaps less than your share? *As you read,* find out how much of the planet Kim Todd uses. If you want to check the size of your "ecological footprint," take the quiz at *<http://www.MyFootprint.org/>*.

ARE YOU BIG FOOT?

Kim Todd

¹The first few blocks of pavement are steep enough that apartments look like they'd slide off their foundations with the slightest nudge and drivers reach for the emergency brake at each stop sign. Trudging up the hill with a book-laden backpack is a strain, but the payoff at the top is the view east to San Francisco Bay. It's a flat plane of blue today, barely brighter than the gray sky over the industrial cranes at water's edge.

²Sweat pricks at the back of my neck and my muscles ache, but I'm not trying to drop a dress size or strengthen my calves on this urban hike. I'm reducing my ecological footprint.

³The Ecological Footprint Quiz, designed by the Oakland-based group Redefining Progress, shows individuals how large a share of the earth's resources they absorb. Questions on gas mileage, house size, and dining habits pinpoint consumption patterns. Driving long distances requires miles of roads and land devoted to energy production. Living in a large house means developing ground for a foundation and yard. Eating meat translates into the need for pastures where cattle can graze. Quiz results are computed in the number of productive acres—fishing grounds, forests, or agricultural fields—needed to maintain a given lifestyle. Compared with residents of other countries, U.S. citizens require far more

than their share of land—an average of 24 acres per person. This, on a planet that provides 4.5 productive acres for every individual. Canadians use 17 acres; Italians, 9; Pakistanis, 2.

[4]The quiz is meant to be sobering. "We want people to get a sense of how far past our planet's capacity we're living," says Michel Gelobter, the executive director of Redefining Progress. More than 150,000 people have taken the quiz since Earth Day last year.

[5]Curious about my own impact, I sat down to take the test. As I scanned the page, the first line of Mary Oliver's poem "Wild Geese" came to mind. *"You do not have to be good,"* she writes. My shoulders relaxed. Such comforting words when guilt creeps in about the paper plates tossed out at the last party and the bag of pink Styrofoam peanuts that sat in my kitchen for months waiting to be reused until I finally threw them away. But Mary, be real. I do have to be good. Otherwise, the world is going to hell in a hand-basket.

[6] She continues:

You do not have to walk on your knees
for a hundred miles through the desert, repenting.
You only have to let the soft animal of your body
love what it loves.

[7]If only that were true. The quiz looks like a tax form. In a way it is, tallying up the excesses and economies of the past year, all my environmental virtues and flaws. Clumped into sections covering food, shelter, and mobility, the questions promise rigorous accounting of my weight on the world. A small glimmer of hope flickered, though. I'm a recycling, composting, non-red-meat eater who doesn't drive much. How bad could it be?

[8]Here's how judgment day went:

[9]Food. Red meat is resource-intensive, so that should help. Well, apparently not that much, as I usually eat chicken or fish once a day. Since I live in agriculture-rich California, it's easy to buy good vegetables that haven't traveled far, but even claiming that they make up 25 percent of my diet is a stretch. I'm far too fond of burritos and potato chips. Total acres needed to keep me nourished: 5.5

[10]Shelter. I don't have a lot of control over this one. I'm a renter, so I can't install solar panels or buy an energy-efficient refrigerator. An apartment takes up less space than a house, but it's a roomy unit for just two. Not that great, but about what I expected. Total acres for housing: 4.8

[11]Mobility. Bring it on. I take the bus or the train almost everywhere and hardly ever drive, except for the weekends. When I do drive, my car gets decent mileage. I'm practically an angel. Wait, I can't believe I'm getting dinged a sixth of an acre for taking the subway rather than walking. And airplane trips. I hadn't even thought to count those. My transportation footprint is disappointingly high. Total acres: 3.4

[12]Run through the accounting blender, my grand total was 21. All that effort and I'm just slightly better than average for an American. If everyone in the world lived as I do, we'd need four and a half additional planets.

[13]Many of the things I worried about most—whether to take paper or plastic bags at the grocery store, if the windows on envelopes are recycla-

ble or should be torn out—didn't even factor into the calculations. The footprint focuses on the decisions with the biggest impact, not necessarily those looming largest in the popular imagination. "A recycled can is about 80 percent more efficient than a non-recycled can, but compared to all the other energy use in your life, the can doesn't make that much difference," says Gelobter. In the quiz, an avid recycler gets only a slight acreage reduction for all that aluminum and glass, while a vegan who grows her own food, never travels by plane or car, and lives in a 500-square-foot green-design home with her sweetheart enjoys a laudable ecological footprint of 3.

[14]This same discrepancy between actions perceived as important and those that really matter spurred Michael Brower and Warren Leon to write *The Consumer's Guide to Effective Environmental Choices*, a book that aims to put green decision-making in perspective. "Everyone felt a little bad if they didn't recycle, but they saw nothing wrong with having three cars," Brower says.

[15]After the quiz, I resolved to lose a shoe size or two, but how? Plane trips are my biggest environmental crime—I spent at least 50 hours flying last year—but I can't skip visiting my sister and her new baby. The apartment's going to stay the same size for the time being. The months I spent as a vegetarian were the hungriest I've ever been. Vegan? Forget it.

[16]Luckily, the quiz lets you bargain. Driving in the city is a recipe for frustration and the train is packed in the mornings—I can walk the three miles to work more often with little sacrifice. And maybe I'll pick up some compact fluorescent bulbs on the way. Making sure at least 50 percent of my food is locally grown and unprocessed shouldn't be too difficult. With all that though, I save only three-fourths of an acre. It's far from sustainable.

[17]But there are other ways to work toward a healthy planet. "Choices people make are very important, but there are also institutions that dictate the kind of house we live in, how far we drive to work, how far our food has to travel to get to us," says Gelobter. City and regional governments choose whether to revitalize their downtowns or sprawl into the countryside, whether to fund public transportation or more roads. Car manufacturers decide which models to put on the market. Demanding good laws and technological advances can be as important as weatherizing the house. "We want people to take action both at the individual level and collectively," he adds. In this light, I add up my job as an environmental writer, include weekends spent as a volunteer harbor-seal monitor, and throw in the letter I wrote my senator last week. I feel a little better.

[18]Still, my individual footprint needs reducing; three-fourths of an acre is a nice piece of land, and someone's going to need it. As I pull on my sneakers, I remember that when I first moved to San Francisco I walked because I wanted to see how the topography played out, how one neighborhood connected to the next. I walked because I loved it; then I lapsed into hopping the train to save 15 minutes.

[19]Sloping downward now, the street skirts the park where the professional dog walker exercises different pets each morning. Today, he pulls the leashes of a Border collie and a yellow Lab, both overweight and panting hard. The sidewalk curves above the elementary school, letting passersby take inventory of the red kickballs on the top of the bungalow

(three). The crossing guard who greets everyone with a smile and reaps his reward in cupcakes saved from classroom birthday parties has already left the corner. The owners of the vegetable market are out, though, hanging sacks of oranges in the tree outside their front door. The fruit looks festive next to the holiday lights.

[20]On Market Street with its smells of sweet-and-sour pork and exhaust, a man with his belongings in a shopping cart feeds half a slice of bread to the pigeons. Whole flocks circle above the Safeway, wings clattering. Traffic thickens and buses groan to life. As I near downtown, the clouds pull apart, letting the sun shine on tourists, shopping teenagers, men and women in suits bound for the financial district. Gossip and business deals in English, Spanish, Mandarin, and Hindi drift down every block.

[21]Footsore but exhilarated, I enter the office building, reach my desk, and throw down my backpack.

[22]I don't feel virtuous, but I feel good.

Selection 7 Questions

VOCABULARY

1. In paragraph 4, Todd says, ". . . the quiz is meant to be sobering." What does she mean?

   The quiz is meant to get our attention and impress on us the importance of the situation.

2. Explain what a "discrepancy between actions perceived as important and those that really matter" means. (¶ 14)

   There is a difference between what we think is important and what is really important.

COMPREHENSION

3. Explain the concept of an "ecological footprint."

   Our "ecological footprint" is how large a share of the earth's resources we use.

4. How many productive acres does our planet provide for every individual? How many productive acres does the average U.S. citizen require?

   Our planet provides 4.5 productive acres for every individual.

   The average U.S. citizen requires 24 productive acres.

5. Compare the average ecological footprint of U.S. citizens, Canadians, Italians, and Pakistanis. Were you surprised by the variations? Please explain your reactions.

Many students are surprised by the wide variations. Their explana-

tions are always enlightening.

6. In paragraph 13, Todd says, "The footprint focuses on the decisions with the biggest impact, not necessarily those looming largest in the popular imagination." Give two examples of "decisions with the biggest impact":

Answers will vary; please see Answer Key.

Give two examples of decisions that "loom large in the popular imagination":

Answers will vary; please see Answer Key.

7. Circle the letter of the sentence that best expresses the thesis.

a. U.S. citizens require far more than their share of land.

(b.) People must take action both at the individual level and collectively to reduce our ecological footprint.

c. We should eat less meat, drive fewer miles, and recycle more.

d. Whether to take paper or plastic bags at the grocery store is not an important decision in the big picture.

8. What do you think Todd hopes to accomplish—for herself and others— with the descriptions in paragraphs 19 and 20? (Remember to look at the idea they support in the last sentence of paragraph 18.)

Todd uses the descriptions in paragraphs 19 and 20 to remind herself

why she loved walking and that the enjoyment is worth as much or

more than the 15 minutes she saves by hopping the train.

9. Do Todd and Gelobter believe it is important to reduce our individual "footprints"? Do they believe reducing our individual footprints is enough to make a significant difference? Please explain.

Todd and Gelobter believe it is important to reduce our individual

"footprints." However, they believe that institutions, organizations, and governments must make changes for real progress to be

accomplished.

REFLECT AND CONNECT

10. What are three specific ways you can reduce your ecological footprint? What advice would you give to friends and family who want to reduce their footprint?

Answers will vary; please see Answer Key.

LOG ON TO THE WEB

There are hundreds of Web sites with information related to environmental topics. For example,

A variety of information about indoor and outdoor air pollution: *<http://www.lbl.gov/Education/ELSI/pollution-main.html>*

Air quality updates for many cities: *<http:www.epa.gov/airnow/where>*

An article on *Water Pollution and Society* by David Krantz and Brad Kifferstein: *<http://www.umich.edu/~gs265/society/waterpollution.htm>*

The Noise Pollution Clearinghouse, a national nonprofit organization, providing a variety of online noise-related resources: *<http://www.nonoise.org/>*

Log on to one of these sites or use a search tool to locate a site that gives you information about some aspect of the environment.

Read one article. Write down (1) the complete Web address, (2) the name of the person or company who sponsors and maintains the site, (3) the name of the person who wrote the information, (4) what you know about the writer, and (5) one idea or suggestion for creating a healthier environment that you learned from the information.

REFLECT AND CONNECT

A. Making changes in our individual behavior can help reduce almost every form of pollution. Describe one positive step you can take to reduce each of these forms of pollution: air, water, ground, and noise. We must also demand good laws and technological advances. Describe one positive step you can take to influence an organization, institution, or government to create a healthier environment.

B. Describe what you see as the major hazard to your community's healthy environment. Discuss how and why the hazard exists, who (people and organizations) could be effective in helping to reduce the hazard, and what you could do to raise public awareness of the problem and potential solutions.

C. As suggested in Pruitt, Crumpler, and Prothrow-Stith's "A Healthy Environment," write an open letter to the citizens of planet Earth. In your letter, mention at least six steps that you feel must be taken to clean up Earth and keep it safe for future generations.

Speaking with Confidence

If, when you are asked to update a team of executives at work, persuade a group of parents at a school meeting, or share your point of view during class and your stomach does a couple of flip-flops, your palms start to sweat, and you frantically search for any excuse to say "No!" you are not alone.

Everyone gets nervous when asked to speak in front of other people: According to a recent Gallup poll, public speaking ranks second—just behind snakes—as our greatest fear, and a survey reported in *The Book of Lists* says our fear of public speaking outranks our fear of death by a two-to-one margin.

But knowing how to speak with confidence and credibility is important to success in school, at work, and in everyday life. For example, according to a research study of what skills matter most in the twenty-first century by American Express Small Business Services, *verbal communications* topped the list at 86 percent.

Even so, rather than improve our skills, we go through life hoping to avoid talking in front of others. Realistically, this is hard to do. Unless we become hermits, sooner or later we will need to speak in public—to two or twenty—to accomplish an important task.

The authors in this theme provide a variety of tips, techniques, and recommendations for how we can learn to speak with confidence.

Edwin Powell opens the theme with suggestions for how to reduce our stress and get our "Butterflies in Formation" and thus increase our confidence. In "Making a Winning Presentation, or How to Think Like a Listener," John Graham proposes that truly successful speakers think of their audience first.

In "Deliver Your Message with Effective Oral Presentations," Chapter 9 of their introductory text *Business Communications Discovering Strategy, Developing Skill*, Sherron Bienvenu and Paul R. Timm describe and explain five keys to improving our ability to deliver effective oral messages. Then, syndicated cartoonist Randy Glasbergen gives us a look at how people who don't have much to say probably prepare their speech.

Kare Anderson points out "What You Can Say Without Speaking" and gives tips for improving our nonverbal communication skills. Lisa Murphy closes the theme with "Viva Voice"—a selection of strategies for making the most of your voice.

Selection 1 "Butterflies in Formation"

EDWIN POWELL III

Mr. Powell is managing editor of OfficeSOLUTIONS *and* OfficeDEALER *magazines. He holds a master's degree in technical communication from N.C. State University and was a member of Toastmasters International for many years. This article first appeared in* OfficeSOLUTIONS, *July–August 2002.*

VOCABULARY

> *extemporaneous* (¶ 13): informal, giving the feeling of off-the-cuff comments
> *honing* (¶ 22): polish, sharpen, improve

AN IDEA TO THINK ABOUT

When you are asked to make a presentation to a group at work, do you look for excuses to avoid the situation even though it would help your career? *As you read,* identify three keys to minimizing your discomfort.

BUTTERFLIES IN FORMATION

Edwin Powell III

[1]For many people, it's their number one fear, yet it has nothing to do with violence, disease, destruction, or anything else that one normally associates with threats to one's well-being. The fear in question is public speaking.

[2]While some people enjoy the limelight, even thrive on it, many others, a significant number in fact, face with absolute dread the prospect of standing in front of even a small group of peers to give a brief presentation. Stepping up to the podium, the palms sweat, the knees feel weak, breath becomes short, thoughts become jumbled, and the voice shrivels up to scarcely more than a whisper.

[3]The good news is it doesn't have to be that way. The even better news is that by developing strong oral communication skills, you can convey a sense of confidence and credibility that can be parlayed into greater success in your chosen career.

[4]So how do you go about improving your speaking skills to gain this new confidence and make the proverbial butterflies in your stomach fly in

formation? It really comes down to three things: preparation, presentation, and education.

PREPARATION

[5]There's no greater confidence builder than coming into a situation well-prepared. If a speaker knows his or her subject matter, the purpose of the talk, the aspects of the subject that are to be addressed, and the audience's needs and expectations, the speaker has the necessary components to address the topic authoritatively.

[6]Although there maybe the temptation to just wing it with little or no preparation, the end result is almost always incomplete, disjointed, and dissatisfying to the audience. It's vitally important to *know* what you're talking about and also to know *what* you're talking about. The distinction here is between what you know and how you plan to use that knowledge. Are you planning to inform or inspire, persuade or entertain?

[7]Speakers sometimes find themselves doing a little of all four. They may, for instance, use an entertaining approach to inform and inspire an audience in order to persuade them to accept their idea or product. On the other hand, you would never want to bore an audience by attempting to inform or persuade them without entertaining or inspiring them.

[8]To put it another way, a speaker should tell the audience what he or she needs them to know about the topic at hand, but without telling them everything they know about it. Knowing more than you tell can come in especially handy during the question-and-answer period.

[9]Another important consideration is how much your audience knows about the subject. If, for instance, a speaker is discussing the finer points of carburetor repair and maintenance with a group of mechanics, there's no need to explain the basic principles on which a carburetor functions, or related terminology, the way one would when speaking to a group of average motorists who may not know much more about automotive repair and maintenance than how to put gas in the tank and clean the windshield.

[10]In addition to being familiar with the subject matter and the audience, it's also helpful for a speaker to be familiar with the room, its layout, and its acoustical characteristics as well as know whether a PA system is to be used. Every room sounds different, and it's different empty or filled with people.

DELIVERY

[11]How you write a speech, that is, the type of notes you use, will have a significant impact on the way the speech is delivered. The idea of writing the text out and reading it verbatim may seem attractive, but it can result in a dry, monotone recitation with little eye contact. The audience may feel the speaker is distant and disengaged.

[12]Committing a speech to memory and reciting it may free up the speaker to maintain eye contact, but it can make for some awkward stumbles if you are momentarily distracted, much like losing your place in written text.

[13]A preferable solution is to use a brief outline on a single sheet of paper or a couple of index cards. By using an outline, the speaker relies on his or her knowledge of the material but still has a set of visual prompts to

help ensure none of the salient points are missed. The result is a more extemporaneous or natural delivery in which the speaker is able to maintain almost constant eye contact with the audience.

[14]Other aspects of delivery to be aware of include:

- [15]Volume—Speak louder than in normal conversation, but don't yell.

- [16]Rate—Nervousness can cause you to speak more rapidly than you would otherwise. To compensate, make a point of slowing down slightly and pronouncing words carefully.

- [17]Tone—It's good to vary vocal tone to keep the audience's interest. A monotone voice can put them right to sleep. Remember Ben Stein as the deadpan economics teacher in *Ferris Bueller's Day Off*?

- [18]Gestures—Appropriate body movements, hand gestures, and facial expressions can help liven things up and keep a speaker from seeming like a "talking head." Be careful not to move around too much. It could be distracting, and it's better not to give the audience whiplash.

- [19]Audible pauses—The ubiquitous *ums, ahs,* and *you knows* that often punctuate our conversational speech can make a speaker appear unprepared or uncertain. When searching for a word, try using a silent pause, but don't leave the audience hanging too long. An occasional silent pause for emphasis can be very effective.

- [20]Notes—Keep your note cards or outline flat on the lectern so as not to draw attention to them. Use only one side of the card or page. Slide pages or cards to the side when moving to the next one. Don't flip them over.

- [21]Duration—Keep the talk concise. Be aware of the allotted time for the talk and use it appropriately, making points strongly without belaboring them.

EDUCATION

[22]Learning what to do to improve one's speaking ability is all well and good, but the more pressing question for many prospective speakers is how to go about acquiring and honing these skills.

[23]Books and training materials for improving speaking and communication skills abound in bookstores and libraries. Courses are frequently offered through local community colleges, and organizations such as Dale Carnegie and Toastmasters International offer opportunities for improvement as well.

[24]Toastmasters differs from other speaking courses and seminars in that it's structured as an open-ended learning opportunity through which members can refine their speaking skills to fit their needs over time. The Toastmasters program offers members opportunities for prepared and impromptu speaking. Prepared speeches follow a manual of assignments that focus on particular speaking skills such as gestures, vocabulary, speaking to inform, or speaking to persuade. Advanced manuals allow speakers to focus on specific types of speaking, ranging from sales to storytelling. The Toastmasters program also features an evaluation component in which members help each other improve their skills through supportive and constructive critiques.

[25]As valuable as classes and self-help materials can be for learning on a theoretical level, there's no substitute for practice, practice, practice. Just as rehearsing prior to giving a presentation before an audience allows one to work the kinks out of the speech, each time in front of an audience instills greater confidence as the lectern becomes familiar territory. By doing it again and again, speaking becomes less of something to be feared and more of a means to an end.

Selection 1 Questions

VOCABULARY

1. Powell says, ". . . you can convey a sense of confidence and credibility that can be parlayed into greater success in your chosen career." (¶ 3) Please explain what *parlayed* means.

   Parlayed means turned in something of greater value

2. In the title and in paragraph 4, Powell says you can make your "butterflies fly in formation." Please explain what he means.

   Reducing the anxiety.

   See Answer Key for additional information.

COMPREHENSION

Determine whether sentences 3–4 are true or false, and circle your answer. If the statement is false, rewrite it to make it true.

(T) F **3.** There's no greater confidence builder than coming into a situation well prepared.

T (F) **4.** You should always memorize your speech and deliver it just from memory.

   False. You should not usually try to memorize your speech and deliver

   it just from memory.

5. Powell says gaining a "sense of confidence and credibility" about speaking comes down to three things. List them.

   Gaining a "sense of confidence and credibility" about speaking comes

   down to preparation, presentation, and education.

_____

_____

6. Although the idea of writing out your speech and reading it verbatim may seem attractive, why isn't it a good idea? What's a better way?

  Although committing a speech to memory and reciting it may free up

  the speaker to maintain eye contact, it can make for awkward stumbles

  if he or she is momentarily distracted. A preferable solution is to use a

  brief outline on a single sheet of paper or a couple of index cards.

7. List four things you should be aware of as you deliver your speech.

  Answers will vary; please see Answer Key.

  _____

  _____

  _____

8. In paragraph 12, what does the word *but* signal?

  a. continuation of thought   **c.** definition
  (b.) change in direction of thought   **d.** effect

9. Circle the letter of the sentence that best expresses the thesis.

  a. A speaker should tell the audience what he or she needs them to know about the topic, but not everything he or she knows.

  b. Toastmasters is a good program because it offers members opportunities to give prepared and impromptu speeches.

  (c.) Good oral communication skills are important to job success, and you can strengthen your confidence and credibility by improving three things: preparation, presentation, and education.

  d. Good verbal communications skills are necessary if you want to move up in your job.

REFLECT AND CONNECT

10. List what you think are the two best ways for you to improve your speaking ability and explain why they are "best."

  Answers will vary.

  _____

  _____

  _____

> ## Selection 2 "Making a Winning Presentation, or How to Think Like a Listener"

JOHN R. GRAHAM

Mr. Graham is president of Graham Communications, a marketing services and sales consulting firm founded in 1976. Mr. Graham writes for a variety of publications and speaks on business, marketing, and sales topics for company and association meetings. He wrote this article for American Salesman *magazine.*

VOCABULARY

> *disparage* (¶ 9): criticize, ridicule
> *disparity* (¶ 24): difference
> *bevy* (¶ 36): large number

AN IDEA TO THINK ABOUT

When you have to speak in front of others, how much thought do you give to what your audience needs? *As you read,* find out how thinking like a listener can make you a more effective speaker.

MAKING A WINNING PRESENTATION, OR HOW TO THINK LIKE A LISTENER

John R. Graham

¹The difference between closing a sale and losing it rests with the way the presentation is made. Whether it's selling a product or an idea, the ability to present effectively can make the difference between acceptance and rejection.

²Yet, most Americans would rather die than give a speech. At least this is the popular view. Whatever the facts, the idea of standing in front of an audience ranks far below going to the dentist for most people.

³Even though the fear of public speaking runs deep, the ability to get an audience's attention, hold it for a period of time, persuade the listeners to your viewpoint, and then move them to action is a skill that can be learned by just about anyone who is willing to develop it.

⁴Speaking—like writing—is valuable in business because it points to an ability to think, analyze ideas, make judgments, develop arguments that command attention, and organize information in a way that moves people to action. Just as good writers are in demand, the ability to speak can open doors of opportunity.

⁵If speaking is so rewarding and highly regarded, then why will we do almost anything to avoid doing it? While it's relatively easy to cover up

most mistakes, giving a presentation to two or 200 people is an opportunity for out-in-the-open personal failure and embarrassment. How many times a day do we hear coworkers make excuses when they are asked to explain why something did or did not happen: "I didn't know about it." "I didn't have time to get it done." "I didn't realize you needed it." "I thought someone else was taking care of that." The list is endless. However, when making a presentation, there's no room for excuses because the exposure is total. You're there by yourself; you're the one being put to the test. The emperor has no clothes.

[6]Because the fear of failing is so strong, we run for cover. We hide when it's time to get on our feet. Anyone who has taken a class in public speaking knows the feeling. When the moment comes for the next presentation, everyone slides down in their chairs, hoping not to be called on. The key to becoming an effective speaker depends on overcoming the paralyzing fear of failure.

[7]Making successful presentations is the direct result of focusing attention on the audience rather than the speaker. We overcome fear by learning to think like a listener. By following these suggestions, speaking can be an enjoyable and rewarding experience for you and your audience.

1. [8]Get yourself prepared for the critics. Even experienced, professional speakers have critics. Because speaking means exposure, there are those who delight in challenging what has been said.

[9]They enjoy poking holes in arguments and bringing up exceptions in an effort to diminish the speaker. No matter how excellent a presentation, there will be those who want to disparage what has been said and dismiss the person who said it. It's easier to maintain your mental equilibrium if you know what can happen.

2. [10]Recognize stress minimizes mental agility. "I knew exactly what I wanted to say and the minute I got on my feet, I forgot everything." Of course. It's to be expected. Because speaking is always stressful, we all forget what we planned to say. Walter Cronkite, the retired dean of TV news anchors, reports he never ended an interview with a world leader without forgetting to ask a question.

[11]The key to overcoming stress is thorough speech preparation. This doesn't mean a speech should be memorized. The task is to either write it out word-for-word or prepare a detailed outline. If speakers are haunted by worry about what they are going to say next, there's no energy left for relating to the audience.

3. [12]Set the stage for success. The overall setting includes the room and the way it's arranged, the introduction of the speaker, and how the speaker begins. It's the speaker's responsibility to control all these elements because they determine how the audience receives the presentation.

[13]There are few ideal rooms or room arrangements. Hotels are generally known for long narrow rooms with center aisles and poor lighting. This creates a "no win situation" for a speaker. The distance between the speaker and the last row creates a gulf difficult to bridge. Many times the back half of an audience is so far away, it's impossible for a speaker to establish rapport.

[14]Because the setting plays such an important role in the effect of a presentation, experienced speakers expect proper seating arrangements, lighting, and sound.

[15]Every speaker deserves a proper introduction because this establishes an atmosphere in which a speaker can be successful. More often than not, the introducer is so nervous (or unprepared) the introduction fizzles. There are two solutions to this problem: First, provide a written introduction. Second, assume the introduction will be inadequate. Be prepared to introduce yourself. This isn't self-serving. A speaker has a right to be viewed by the audience as a competent individual with a message worth communicating.

[16]The final element in setting the stage is never apologizing. "I only wish I would have had more time to prepare." "I'm not a public speaker." Many speakers seem compelled to begin their comments with self-deprecation. Apologizing only serves one useful purpose: destroying the speaker's credibility with the audience. To paraphrase Sir Winston Churchill, never, never, never, never, never, never, never apologize.

4. [17]Build the presentation on a solid structure. One outline works well for most presentations because it gives a sense of completion. It has three elements: problem, analysis, and solution.

- [18]Problem. This is the issue that brings you to your feet. It may be the reason why a new product should be introduced, a customer should buy your product or service, a branch office should be closed, or a new vision statement should be adopted. In this part of the presentation the audience must come to feel the problem is real and deserves attention.

- [19]Analysis. The analysis showcases your reasons why the problem exists. To impact the audience, actual experiences are helpful, particularly when they are supported with facts, expert opinion, and statistics. A simple guide is to tell stories and document them with objective information.

- [20]Solution. Once the problem is analyzed, it is time to spring the trap by presenting your solution.

[21]Although there are emotional elements in any effective speech, the audience will be with you to the degree that you present a reasonable case. In other words, for the solution to be accepted, the audience must view it as a sensible approach, one that does not stretch credibility.

5. [22]Understand the audience. Many speakers are so concerned with what they want to say they forget the goal is to have their ideas accepted by the audience. You must demonstrate to an audience you know who they are, why they are there, and what issues confront them. If it's a hostile audience, let them know you understand their viewpoint. Unless a speaker establishes common ground with an audience, the speech will fail.

6. [23]Speak slowly and move quickly. While a speech should seem conversational, the actual delivery is quite different. First, the listener must get the message the first time because there's no chance to go back and replay it. Therefore, speaking slowly and distinctly is essential. "Word point," or pausing between words, is a useful technique for maintaining the audience's attention.

[24]Second, the mind moves faster than the mouth, about four times as fast. We think at the rate of about 500 words a minute, while we speak at about 125 words a minute. This disparity causes the listeners' minds to wander. Therefore, a properly-paced speech is essential in order to maintain listener interest.

7. ²⁵Let the audience know where you're going. "The speech didn't seem to go anywhere" is the one audience complaint to avoid. It is the killer. A presentation may have excellent content and address critical issues, but all is lost if the audience feels the speaker is rambling.

²⁶A speaker's top priority should be to set out guideposts so the listener can follow easily. One- and two-sentence summaries along the way are helpful: this is where we have been, this is where we are, and this is where we are going. Listeners need road signs to know where they are and where they are headed.

8. ²⁷Interact with your listeners. Almost everyone agrees the worst speakers are those who go to the podium, take out notes or text, and then deliver their remarks almost as if they are speaking to an empty room. Asking questions and requesting comments at certain points changes the dynamics of the situation. Speaker and audience are both participants.

²⁸Even though speakers today often interact with audiences, any type of interaction transfers some control from the speaker to the audience. Although discussion within a presentation can be an effective method for increasing acceptance for the speaker's views, it takes experience to do it successfully.

9. ²⁹Make the presentation motivating, not motivational. If a group needs firing up, it will take far more than a speech or seminar to do it! The problem with so-called "motivational speeches" is they don't do the job. While they may give an audience a temporary emotional jolt, they don't change behavior. An effective presentation should give the audience the ideas, techniques, and tools so they can move themselves to action.

10. ³⁰You're not competing with a celebrity speaker. Audiences are often disappointed when a so-called celebrity speaker leaves the podium. Listeners come with high expectations, but what they get is a "canned talk." The "big names" don't take time to customize a presentation for a particular audience, so the message fades faster than the applause.

³¹Audiences appreciate speakers who make a genuine effort to understand the group and prepare a presentation that will be helpful to them. Besides, big names are not always great speakers.

11. ³²Make it visually interesting. Up until 100 years ago, listening to speeches was our nation's primary form of entertainment. This was the age of the orators, speakers who could hold audiences for hours. The arrival of the motion picture began a change in audience expectations that television has only enhanced.

³³Any successful presentation will include compelling visual elements, either on a screen or with props. For example, one speaker describes changes in the business environment as "dog bone demographics." Along with computer-generated visuals, he brings along a huge dog bone as a prop that immediately grabs the audience's attention. When he talks about the need for long-term marketing strategies, he holds up a six-inch fir tree and suggests the lumber industry is an example of businesses that think long-term.

³⁴While visual interest is essential, visuals should not be allowed to dominate or control a presentation. They should enhance, not overshadow, the message.

12. ³⁵You are your message. While some speakers believe what they say is all that counts, it's not true. Credibility is based in a creative and thoughtful mind that holds the listener in high regard. Good speakers are willing to share themselves as well as their ideas. A presentation is validated when this happens.

[36]In other words, effective speaking isn't contrived. The words aren't copied from a bevy of books and the text isn't sprinkled with quotations that are meant to impress but don't quite fit. When a presentation springs from experience and a desire to communicate, the audience finds itself on the side of the speaker.

13. [37]The goal is action. The only reason to speak is action. Even speeches that are designed to inform rather than persuade are action-oriented. Information in itself influences how the listener thinks about a subject. Any presenter asks one question: What do I want the audience to do? Perhaps it's just to stay the course, or maybe it's to change their minds. It may be to motivate the listeners to some overt act. Unless action is the goal, there is no presentation.

[38]Whether it's preparing a one-on-one presentation, a seminar for 100 salespeople, or a speech to an entire convention, those with the skill to speak to groups play a key role in business.

[39]The key to good speaking is thinking like a listener. These guidelines are a checklist for evaluating presentations before they are given.

Selection 2 Questions

VOCABULARY

Rephrase these excerpts in 1–3 using your own words.

1. maintain your mental equilibrium (¶ 9)

   Keep our wits about us—maintain our ability to think clearly.

   _____

2. stress minimizes mental agility (¶ 10)

   When we are stressed, we cannot think clearly or quickly.

   _____

3. [speakers] begin their comments with self-deprecation (¶ 16)

   Speakers begin with comments about how "bad" they are,

   condemning or criticizing themselves.

4. Explain what the phrase "the emperor has no clothes" means in this context. (¶ 5)

   In this context, "the emperor has no clothes" means everyone can see

   all your flaws; there is no way to hide anything.

COMPREHENSION

5. Graham says, "Speaking—like writing—is valuable in business." Please explain why he believes both of these skills are valuable.

    Speaking and writing are valuable because they point to an ability

    to think, analyze ideas, make judgments, develop arguments that

    command attention, and organize information in a way that moves

    people to action.

6. If speaking is such an important skill, why does Graham believe most of us hesitate to do it?

    Graham believes we hesitate to speak in public because of our fear

    of failing.

7. Graham says one outline structure works well for most presentations. List the structure.

    The outline structure that works well for most presentations is

    problem, analysis, and solution.

8. Graham says there is only one goal or reason to speak. What is it?

    The goal or reason to speak is action.

9. Circle the letter of the sentence that best expresses the thesis.

    a. The key to overcoming stress is thorough speech preparation.
    b. Visuals should enhance, not overshadow, the message.
    c. We think at the rate of about 500 words a minute, while we speak at about 125 words a minute.
    d. The key to good speaking is thinking like a listener.

REFLECT AND CONNECT

10. Graham says an effective presentation springs from experience and a desire to communicate, not from words and quotes copied from books. Describe what he means and how you could use that advice the next time you prepare a speech.

    Hopefully students will interpret Graham's advice that "an effective

    presentation springs from experience and a desire to communicate,

    not words and quotes copied from books" to mean they should use their own experiences, information, ideas, and words in their

presentations.

> ### Selection 3 "Deliver Your Message with Effective Oral Presentations: Speaking with Confidence and Impact"

SHERRON BIENVENU AND PAUL R. TIMM

Dr. Bienvenu is associate professor in the Practice of Management Communication at the Goizueta Business School of Emory University. She also teaches in the International MBA Program at the Helsinki School of Economics and Business Administration in Finland. Dr. Timm is a professor in the Marriott School of Management at Brigham Young University. An active author, he has written more than 30 books dealing with various management and business communication topics. This selection is Chapter 9 in their introductory text Business Communication: Discovering Strategies, Developing Skills.

AN IDEA TO THINK ABOUT

What do you think would make you more a more effective speaker? *As you read,* find out what Bienvenu and Timm believe are the five keys to improving your ability to deliver effective oral messages.

Step 2. Consider
Your Media and
Timing Options

Step 1. Define
the Context

Step 3. Select
and Organize
Your Information

Step 5. Evaluate
Feedback for
Continued Success

Step 4.
Deliver
Your
Message

SKILL OBJECTIVES

After you have studied this chapter, you should be able to:

- Maximize the skills necessary to give oral presentations for business.
- Describe several types of oral presentations frequently used in business.
- Polish your delivery using appropriate verbal, nonverbal, and platform management skills.
- Speak clearly and expressively, pay attention to timing, avoid distracting vocal patterns, and minimize verbalized pauses.
- Manage notes and visual aids comfortably and handle audience questions succinctly.
- Maintain eye contact, dress professionally, exhibit physical control, and project enthusiasm.
- Control speaker anxiety by reducing the number of unknowns you face.
- Express confidence through an understanding of your material and your audience's needs.
- Appreciate the importance of being yourself and continuing to improve your delivery skills.

Deliver Your Message with Effective Oral Presentations: Speaking with Confidence and Impact

CHAPTER 9
SKILL
FOCUS:

Building on the Foundation

Skills to Develop

Professionalism in Business Speaking

There are four things people you communicate with won't forgive you for: not being prepared, comfortable, committed, and interesting.

—Roger Ailes

(You Are the Message)

COMMUNICATING WITHOUT A STRATEGY

Uncertainty in a New Job

Brenda Flores was excited about her new internship with a high-tech company that recently moved into town. She smiled to herself as she thought of the interview last week. She scored near the top on the aptitude test, and the interview went just fine. After years of preparation, Brenda was now launching a career in a field she enjoyed. Only one thing worried her a bit.

Ms. Cheney, the woman who hired Brenda, kept talking about the importance of communication skills on the job. She said that she expected Brenda to participate in group decisions, greet visitors to the company, network with other corporate employees, and even lead tours of the company. One of Brenda's first jobs, she said, would be to teach other employees how to use the latest version of the WordGood idea-processing software.

"I've never done those kind of things," thought Brenda with some concern. In fact, Brenda saw herself as a fairly quiet person. She generally avoided getting in front of people and seldom took the lead in introducing people. She had served as a tutor for grade-school kids who had trouble reading, but other than that, she'd never really taught anything. The thought of teaching adults or, even worse, of "giving a speech" terrified her. The more she thought about this idea of communicating on the job, the more nervous she became. The more she thought about standing in front of people and speaking, the more she entertained the idea of quitting before she started the new job. "Maybe I'll stay in school a few more years," she said to herself.

Everybody worries a bit about communicating in front of others. Many people are concerned because they want others to think well of them; they care about how effective they are and sincerely want others to get their messages. They want to effectively participate in group decisions and offer suggestions and ideas. And employers want people who do exactly those kinds of things. A company's most valuable people are those who communicate well.

This chapter will provide some useful guidelines on giving successful presentations. Armed with the Strategic Communication Model, you have already defined the context for your message and have considered your media and timing options. You have decided that an oral presentation makes sense and have selected and organized the information you want to convey. You now have a well-organized outline of audience-focused information. This chapter discusses the fourth step in the Strategic Communication Model: delivering your message. Specifically in this chapter, we will build on the material presented in Chapter 3 by concentrating on five key factors necessary to deliver effective oral messages:

- Polishing your verbal delivery skills
- Polishing your platform management skills
- Polishing your nonverbal delivery skills
- Expressing confidence
- Being yourself and becoming your better self

The Widespread Use of Oral Presentations in Business

This chapter focuses on Step 4 of the Strategic Communication Model: deliver your message. Here we concentrate on oral presentations.

Oral communication in business often takes the form of *presentations*. These are not speeches, although a speech can be one form of presentation. Whenever you plan, prepare, and create a message to deliver to others, you make a presentation. Presentations vary in their degree of formality, but all are purposeful communication aimed at achieving a specific result. The following are some examples of presentations common in businesses:

- Alan Harris explains service department bills to his auto repair customers. He communicates what work was done, why it was done, and how much it cost. Alan makes presentations.
- Marilyn Pickard works as a receptionist at Frugal Farr's corporate headquarters where she greets visitors, invites them to wait in the reception area, offers them coffee, and introduces them to Farr's executives. Marilyn makes presentations.
- Heidi Ast sells clothing at the Sunshine Boutique. She greets customers, asks how she can help, suggests matching clothing, and rings up sales. Heidi makes presentations.
- Michelle Harker serves on a quality committee for her company. The committee needs her advice on purchasing cleaning supplies. As a custodial crew member, Michelle shares her expertise and recommends the best supplies for the company's needs. Michelle makes presentations.

Performance appraisals can be seen as a form of business presentation.

- Carol Tanaka is searching for a new job. She has interviews almost every day and works hard to sell her talents and skills to prospective employers. Carol makes presentations.
- Carl Steinburg is having a performance appraisal with his boss today. He feels good about his work accomplishments and hopes to be considered for a promotion. Carl will make a presentation.
- Eric Jessop represents his company in community service efforts that teach young people how to avoid drugs, alcohol, and relationship problems. Eric makes presentations.

"Hold it a second," you may be saying. "It's beginning to sound like *everything* people do is some form of presentation." Well, that's about right. We all spend a large portion of our lives making presentations—offering information and ideas to others. That is a reality of the business world.

Performance Appraisals

Performance appraisals are personal evaluations that measure the work effectiveness of employees. These take the form of one-to-one interviews between employee and manager and are used to review job expectations, productivity, work behaviors, and goals. Both the manager and the employee have opportunities to present information to each other.

FAST FACTS

Polish Your Verbal Delivery Skills

Your specific audiences and the culture of your business will help shape the decisions you make about your communication style over the course of your career. As you speak and observe the reactions to your speaking, you will learn appropriate responses and make adjustments that become your personalized style. Some generic guidelines for success—some tricks and some common mistakes to avoid—can also be helpful in polishing your delivery skills.

Your verbal delivery skills go beyond the words you choose. They also include the way you use your voice—pronunciation, articulation, volume, and pitch—and the dramatic aspects of emphasis, pace, and timing. In other words, verbal delivery skills include how you use words to speak clearly and expressively. In the following sections we will look at ways in which you can improve your message delivery.

Verbal skills go beyond the words of a message to include *how* you say those words.

Speak Clearly

Good articulation means saying words clearly and correctly.

Concentrate on improving your pronunciation, articulation, volume, and pitch so that your audience can easily and comfortably hear and understand your words.

Pronounce words correctly. Replace just one "pitcher" for "picture," and you will lose credibility with your audience. Articulate your words. Say all the letters in all the syllables of every word. Don't relax into "lemme" for "let me" or "gonna" for "going to."

Adjust the volume of your voice to your audience. Don't speak so loudly that you sound like an orator—like an old-fashioned pitchman on a soapbox. But don't speak so softly that you sound insecure or lacking in enthusiasm either. One myth is that if you speak quietly, an audience will lean in to hear you. The truth is that if you speak too softly, your audience is likely to go to sleep. Instead, simply direct your talk toward the people farthest from you. This focus will help you increase your volume.

Vary voice volume, pitch, and rate to hold your audience's attention and interest.

Use variation in volume as well as in other vocal qualities. Sameness becomes monotonous; variation attracts and holds people's attention and interest. Psychologists say that no one can pay attention to an unchanging stimulus for very long. We can't watch grass grow or paint dry. It's just too boring. Unfortunately, speakers who insist on using never-changing vocal patterns sound just about as boring.

FOCUS ON

Speaking at a Lower Pitch

In many cultures, adults sound more credible when they speak using a lower pitch. To find the lowest pitch that is comfortable for you, try this: Lie flat on your back and relax. Breath from your diaphragm without moving your shoulders (this is easier to learn while lying down than while standing up).

Then read out loud. The pitch you hear is your natural pitch. Try to maintain the same sound when you are standing up by simply relaxing and breathing from your diaphragm. Do not, however, maintain this pitch monotonously. The idea is to speak naturally, just a little lower, and with more resonance.

Speak Expressively

Different emphasis changes a sentence's implications and meaning, so be sensitive to your inflections.

Work to perfect your emphasis and pace so that your audience can easily understand the meaning of your words. When you outline your presentations and practice your delivery, determine which words are the most important and then underline or highlight those words in your notes. The words you emphasize can change the meaning of your sentences. Think of the different inflections you could give the question "What do you mean by that?"

- *What* do you mean by that?
- What *do* you mean by that?
- What do *you* mean by that?
- What do you *mean* by that?
- What do you mean by *that?*

You can hear how different emphasis changes the sentence's implications and meaning. Be sensitive to implications of various inflections. The preceding examples can sound inquisitive or accusatory, depending on the emphasis.

Many speakers get feedback that indicates that they talk too fast. But trying to slow down may seem awkward. A better alternative is to identify material that is new, difficult, unusual, or particularly important for the audience and focus on presenting that information at a slower pace. Then return to your comfortable, normal, faster pace. Again, you may want to highlight this important information on your outline.

Adjust the pace of your remarks; slow down a bit when you deliver new or complex information.

Pay Attention to Timing

One of the most dramatic effects a speaker can learn to use is timing. The pause can be a powerful emphasis tool. There are many places a pause can enhance your presentation:

Pauses help refocus the audience's attention, so learn to use them wisely.

- After you walk to the front of the room but before you begin speaking
- Before you make an important point ("This is the bottom line:" . . . pause. . .)
- After you make an important point ("Our profits would be in the millions. . ." . . .pause. . . "if we. . .")
- When you ask a question (Pausing may feel awkward; however, most speakers don't wait long enough.)
- As a transition between main points ("That sums up the problem." . . .pause. . . "We are looking at several solutions.")
- After your final statement and before "thank you."

Avoid Distracting Vocal Patterns

Some speakers get into voice patterns that undermine their professionalism. Speakers who let the end of sentences trail off into a soft mumble are one such example. Another distracting vocal pattern is what is called "up-speak." Here the speaker raises intonation at the end of a statement to make it sound like a question. Say the following sentences aloud using up-speak—raising intonation on the italicized word—and you'll hear how this can undermine a message.

Up-speak can be annoying and makes assertions sound like questions.

- She's very good at everything she *does*. (The listener will ask: Is she?)
- The management is concerned about the *costs*. (The listener will ask: Are they?)
- My name is John *Mansfield*. (The listener will ask: Are you sure?)

Notice how up-speak creates a note of uncertainty. Unfortunately, some people habitually use up-speak without noticing how it can undermine their assertiveness and make them consistently sound tentative.

Minimize Verbalized Pauses

Few things can drive an audience crazy like the liberal use of verbalized fillers, such as *ah, um, uh,* and (the popular favorite) *ya know.* Some intelligent and apparently rational men and women salt their every utterance with these expressions until their listeners want to scream at them, *ya know?*

Try to eliminate your own filler words.

The human talker abhors a vacuum. When the detested monster, silence, raises its ugly head, some beat it to death with *ah, uh, um,* or *ya know.* Do yourself a favor: Ask someone you trust to point out when you are drifting into this habit. Commit yourself to listening for and eliminating your own filler words. Rid yourself of the fear of silence.

FOCUS ON

Filler Word Use[1]

Why do some people fill the air with nonwords and sounds? For some it is a sign of nervousness; they fear silence and experience speaker anxiety. Recent research at Columbia University suggests another reason. Columbia psychologists speculated that speakers fill pauses when searching for the next word. To investigate this idea, they counted the use of filler words used by lecturers in biology, chemistry, and mathematics, where the subject matter uses scientific definitions that limit the variety of word choices available to the speaker. They then compared the number of filler words used by teachers in English, art history, and philosophy, in which the subject matter is less well defined and more open to word choices.

Twenty science lecturers used an average of 1.39 *uh*'s a minute, compared with 4.85 *uh*'s a minute by 13 humanities teachers. Their conclusion: Subject matter and breadth of vocabulary may determine the use of filler words more than habit or anxiety.

Whatever the reason, the cure for filler words is preparation. You reduce nervousness and preselect the right ways to say ideas through preparation and practice.

Polish Your Platform Management Skills

As a speaker, one of your tasks is to manage the communication process. Two aspects of platform management include the careful use of notes and visual aids and the handling of audience interaction, especially question-and-answer (Q&A) opportunities. Work to achieve professionalism in these tasks, which we will discuss in the following sections.

Use Your Notes Carefully

Be familiar enough with your topic to rely almost entirely on the outline on your slides.

If possible, avoid using notes altogether during your presentation and just use your visuals. Well-prepared visual aids provide a useful set of notes for your presentation. You should be familiar enough with your topic to rely almost entirely on the outline on your visual aids. However, you may need notes when:

- Your material is new or too complex to show using just visual aids.
- Visual aids are not appropriate, such as a speaker introduction or a less formal presentation.
- You need to emphasize certain, specific words or concepts, and precise wording is imperative.

If you use note cards, write only key words in large letters.

In such cases, we suggest writing key words or phrases on note cards that you can carry easily and unobtrusively. If you use note cards, be sure to write only key words (the fewer the better!) in large letters on the cards. Also use cards that are at least 5" × 8"; don't try to hide them from your audience.

As we have said, a big preparation mistake speakers make is to write a presentation word for word. If you write it, chances are you will read it. Reading a manuscript, no matter how well written, will negate the positive effects of all your other work on your presentation. You will appear unprepared and unprofessional, and you will greatly diminish your chances for success. The only exceptions to this may be in high-level negotiations or when presenting a carefully worded public announcement in which a misstatement could create legal difficulties.

If you choose to use handouts, determine if you want the audience to follow along with you as you speak, or if your handouts are for later reference. If the handouts cover additional material or follow a different order than your presentation, distribute them afterward.

Manage Your Visual Aids

When using visual aids, convince your audience that you are the one in control. Your visual aids should not appear to be managing you (like the dog who "walks" the owner). First, learn to work your equipment. Know, for example, how to return to your previous slide. Be prepared to use either a keyboard or a mouse. Check that bulbs are bright enough in your overhead projector and that markers are fresh for your flip chart.

When you are presenting, focus on your audience, not on your visual aids. Avoid facing the screen, either reading the slides or talking to them. You may turn and gesture toward the screen to draw your audience's attention to a bullet point or illustration, but immediately turn your face and body back toward your audience.

Almost every culture reads from left to right, and after we blink or look down, we automatically look to the left first. Therefore, you should stand to the audience's left of your visual aids so their focus is first on you and then on your visual aids. Remember, you are most important; your visual aids are just that—aids to support you and your message.

Always practice using audiovisual equipment before making a presentation.

Stand to the audience's left of your visual aids so their focus is first on you and then on your visual aids.

Handle Questions Constructively

You should consider two platform management issues regarding questions: when to take them and how to answer them. Planning the "when" part makes the "how" part easier. We will discuss these issues in the following sections.

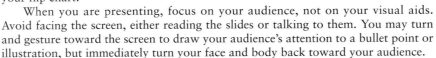

Know how to manage your visual aids.

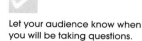

Let your audience know when you will be taking questions.

Know When to Answer Questions Some speakers feel that they lose control of the situation when the Q&A section starts, so they avoid it as long as possible in hopes that time will run out. We advise a different strategy. First, tell your audience when you are going to take questions during your presentation. If you are comfortable with interruptions, encourage them, but be aware that you are likely to be interrupted with a question about something that you are planning to cover later in the presentation. When that happens, you either have to jump ahead in your organization (not the best solution) or tell the questioner that you will address the material soon. Most speakers are better off announcing that they will take questions at the end of each section or at the end of their presentation. This avoids the problem of having the presentation organization thrown off and gives you the opportunity to answer most of the questions that would have come up.

Always have the last word. Don't end your presentation with an awkward answer to a difficult question.

Second, decide exactly when you will ask for questions at the end. You have two choices: before your summary or after your summary. Either time is fine, based on your personal preference and style. However, do not wait until after your final statement to ask for questions. If you do, you run the risk that the last question asked will be the one that is awkward for you to answer, and that will leave a lingering impression on your audience. Instead, tell your audience something such as this: "I'll take one last question, and then I have a final thought to leave with you."

If you take questions after your summary, you might want to briefly summarize again, perhaps enhancing that summary with issues you addressed in your Q&A. But always leave the audience with a strong, carefully rehearsed final word.

Know How to Answer Questions Entire books have been written on strategies for answering questions. The basic format, however, is comprised of three simple steps:

1. Answer the question directly.
2. Offer one piece of support or elaboration.
3. Stop.

Talking too much is the most common mistake speakers make when answering audience questions.

You don't need to go on and on, which is the most common mistake that speakers make when answering questions. Make your point and *stop* talking.

Don't try to bluff if you are asked a question to which you don't know the answer. It's perfectly fine—actually, it's preferred—to just say, "I don't know." Then follow up with a comment about finding the answer and getting back to the person who asked the question, if you really intend to do so.

Polish Your Nonverbal Delivery Skills

Your nonverbal skills include how you look and how you move. Obviously, you should take your cues from your target audience and your organization, but some fundamental nonverbal abilities are essential. Among these are eye contact, professional appearance, physical control, and enthusiasm, which we will discuss in the following sections.

Establish and Maintain Eye Contact

In business situations in western cultures, we expect speakers to look at us when delivering a message. Speakers who do not look us in the eyes are regarded as insecure or untrustworthy. When addressing groups, the best way to maintain eye contact is to look at one individual for a few seconds and then move on to another person. Don't just scan over the audience—really *look* at individuals. Try to get to everyone in the room, and be aware of tendencies to look too much at some people and not enough at others. (Some speakers tend to look to one side of a room more than another. Avoid this tendency.)

Don't just scan over the audience—*look* at individuals.

Dress and Groom Yourself Professionally

Appearance, dress, and grooming communicate powerful messages. Your audience will make some assumptions about you and your message based on how you look. If you aren't sure how to dress for a particular presentation, you are better off being dressed too formally than too informally. Success experts encourage people to dress like the kind of person they want to be. If you want to be an executive, dress like executives do. If you want to be perceived as having credibility, dress appropriately.

Dress like the person you aspire to become.

Most importantly, don't wear anything that is distracting. In business contexts, men should not wear ties with odd patterns or belt buckles with unusual designs. If they are short, stout, or gesture broadly, they should not wear a double-breasted jacket that makes them look wider and constricts arm movement. Women should not wear anything that moves or makes noise (such as dangling earrings or charm bracelets). They should not select bright nail polish or unusual makeup colors that distract their audience. If you ever find yourself tugging at anything, then you know what to fix next time. (For example, if your hair falls in your face, either cut it or fasten it back.) Many excellent books and magazine articles can provide dress and grooming tips. Stay current with what is acceptable for the business environment in which you work.

Generally avoid dress styles that draw attention to your clothing rather than to you as a speaker.

Exhibit Physical Control

Your sense of personal dynamism or self-confidence comes across via such body language as gestures, posture, and mannerisms. Gestures can be useful to punctuate what is being said. Your body movements should be spontaneous and natural, yet purposeful.

Dress appropriately when you give a presentation, avoiding any loud or distracting clothing.

206   Part 3: Delivering Powerful Messages and Evaluating Feedback

Contrived movements can look silly; inappropriate hand placements create distractions.

Gesture Spontaneously and Naturally   Everyone has different tendencies to use or avoid gestures. For some, it feels uncomfortable to point or raise hands in exclamation. For others, it may be said that if you tied their hands, they'd be speechless. Common mistakes people make with gestures include:

- Failing to use gestures when they can help emphasize.
- Repeating the same gesture to the point that it becomes monotonous, distracting, or annoying.
- Using contrived hand movements that look artificial or overly dramatic.
- Choosing gestures that cannot be seen clearly (a hand motion hidden from audience view by a podium is of no value).
- Leaving their hands in the wrong place for too long.

Your audience should believe that everything you are doing with your face, your hands, your feet, and the space around you is purposeful, yet not forced.

The rules for where you should put your hands have relaxed somewhat. Speech teachers used to have clear lists of "do" and "don't" positions. Now, for example, it may be acceptable to put a hand in your pocket in some speaking environments— but not at the moment when you are making your most serious point. The following are some hand movements you should still avoid:

- Crossing your arms (this may convey defensiveness) or putting your hands on your hips (this can look angry or aggressive).
- Placing your hands in front of you in the "fig leaf" position (especially for male speakers).
- Hooking your fingers together at your rib cage in the "opera singer" pose.
- Gripping the podium (the "white knuckle" syndrome) or clasping your hands behind your back (for more than a moment or two).

Make body movement purposeful, not just random.

Use Appropriate Body Movement   Body movement is another important way to bring life to a presentation. Pausing between key points and physically moving to another place in the room helps your listeners know that you have completed one point and are now ready to address another. This pause and motion helps your listeners follow your logical development. If you cannot freely move around, you may still use the pause with a shift in position or a change in the direction you're looking to indicate the same things. Whenever possible, avoid the speaker-behind-the-podium format. If you need a microphone, a cordless, clip-on mike is best for freedom of movement.

A smile communicates warmth and sincerity and relaxes your audience.

Smile   Start your presentation with a smile. It relaxes both you and your audience. Look for other places in your speech when a smile would be appropriate as well. The rest of the time use facial expressions to enhance the emotions you are communicating with your message.

We once worked with a young man who was building his career as a platform salesperson. He regularly stood before large audiences and sold business opportunities. To develop his skills, he videotaped his performance. Upon watching the video with us, he was shocked at how stern and intense he looked. He learned to lighten up and smile, and it made a dramatic difference in his sales success.

Keep your weight evenly on the balls of both feet.

Keep Your Weight on Both Feet   Speakers tend to forget that the audience can see their feet. They will cross them, bounce, and rock back and forth, all of which can be terribly distracting. To avoid this, concentrate on keeping the weight on the balls of your feet and you will be balanced and ready to move when you want to.

Smile when you begin your presentation.

Use Physical Space Wisely   In many speaking situations the space at the front of your room is yours, so use it to enhance your presentation. The rule about moving around is: Either walk or stand still. When you are standing still, stand *completely* still. Do not dance with your feet, your knees, or your shoulders. When you walk, do it for a reason. As we mentioned earlier, changing your position in the room can show a natural break or emphasize a point in the content of your talk. It can also refocus the audience's attention, allow them to adjust their own physical positions, and give them a chance to think about what you are saying.

Either walk or stand still. Don't sway, dance, or bob.

Be Enthusiastic

Remember one overriding delivery skill that will enable you to be effective with your target audiences: enthusiasm. Your audience may forgive you if you walk too much or not enough, if you sometimes talk too fast, if you look down more than you should, or if you forget to smile. They will be much less likely to forgive you— and to agree to your objectives—if you are not enthusiastic. You must project sincere enthusiasm for them, for their needs, and for your objectives.

Project sincere enthusiasm for your audience, their needs, and your objectives.

Conveying enthusiasm does not mean you need to be loud or fast-talking. A quiet enthusiasm is conveyed by careful word choices, good eye contact, and vocal variation. The obnoxious used-car commercial model is not what you normally want to emulate. If you have done your homework and have really sought to understand your communication context, you will know how to deliver an enthusiastic, sincere presentation with impact.

Express Confidence

Some degree of speaking anxiety is useful in keeping you mentally alert.

Brenda, in our opening story, is worried about giving a speech, and that is perfectly normal behavior. Do you feel that flush of nervousness when asked to introduce yourself to your class or committee members? Do you have nightmares about being forced to give a speech in front of a crowd? Have you bottled up a good idea rather than risk speaking up in a meeting?

If you answered yes to any of these questions, you are not unusual. Everyone feels some degree of these emotions. Fortunately, you can apply some proven ways to reduce discomfort—but don't expect it to go away totally. That really isn't even desirable. Anxiety plays an important role in keeping you mentally alert. Yes, nervousness can be your friend.

By reducing the number of unknowns you face, you will become a more confident speaker.

You can best cope with anxiety and improve confidence by reducing the number of unknowns you face. Fear is almost always rooted in uncertainty. As you become more certain about some facts, you reduce the worry about standing up and talking loud enough (you learned how to do that as a child), about remembering your co-workers' names (you learned them), or about organizing your thoughts (you learned some tips for this in Chapter 6). The following sections discuss ways in which you can further build your confidence in giving presentations.

Prepare Thoroughly

Nothing reduces anxiety like being well prepared, even to the point of being over-prepared—totally confident of your grasp of the subject matter. And nothing improves the likelihood of speaking success like thorough preparation of the content and delivery of the presentation as well as practice in handling anticipated questions that may arise.

Don't write a presentation word for word. If you do, it will sound like you are reading or reciting, not giving a presentation.

When preparing, put special emphasis on the opening remarks and the conclusion. If the opener goes well (because you've practiced it repeatedly), you'll gain confidence for the rest of the presentation. The best way to practice is to work on one section at a time, such as the introduction or the transition from your introduction to your first main point. As we mentioned earlier, don't write your talk word for word. If you memorize it, you will sound like you are reciting to the audience rather than having a conversation with them. Instead, practice each section until you are comfortable and fluent. Even if it comes out a little different during the actual presentation, it will still sound natural and spontaneous.

You should also time the presentation to make sure it fits the time allotment or is simply not too long. Audiences are almost always pleasantly surprised when a speech is shorter than expected; they are almost always disappointed when it runs longer than anticipated.

Videotape your practice if possible. If not, watch yourself in a mirror.

Ideally, you should have someone videotape you practicing. We highly recommend this for important, formal presentations, especially if you are inexperienced. If video is not possible, the second best place to work is in front of a large mirror so you can see your nonverbal behavior while you are going over the words. In either case, you can see and hear what works and what you want to improve. Do not practice with *only* an audio tape recorder. A flat verbal recording without the enhancement of your nonverbal skills is not sufficient feedback.

Watching yourself on video *can* be difficult, but it will help you improve your presentation skills.

For Better or Worse © UFS

Be Idea Conscious, Not Self-Conscious

Keeping your specific purpose at the top of your mind helps reduce overconcern for irrelevant details. Let your "unconscious success mechanism" work for you. This mechanism is the part of your brain that focuses on the desired goal and allows the unconscious mind to get you there. It works best when you don't think of each step needed to complete a task but instead focus on the desired result and *let* your mind get you there.

Focus on your goals and let your unconscious success mechanism get you there.

For example, baseball outfielders going after a high fly ball don't consciously think, "I'll take six steps to my left, two steps forward, raise my glove with my left hand, and shield my eyes from the sun with my right hand." Instead they fix their eyes on the ball and visualize the desired result of catching it. Their unconscious success mechanism handles the details so they don't need to think about the little things such as tripping over a shoelace, taking the wrong size steps, or raising their glove too late. They let success happen.

The same principle applies in any planned oral communication. Overconcern with mechanics once you've reached the point of giving the presentation can only distract and create anxiety. The following is some good advice we have paraphrased from speech experts:[2]

> Self-consciousness tends to be self-destructive. If you are overly worried about the way you look, you often overcompensate, and this draws attention to yourself that would not ordinarily be centered on you. It's when you are trying to walk nonchalantly that you walk stiffly or affectedly. It is when you are trying to smile naturally (say "cheese") that your smile tends to look artificial. If you are caught up in conversation or telling a story and the conversation or the story causes you to smile, you are usually unaware of the smile itself, and it is at that point that the smile is, and appears, most natural. So, when you are speaking and get caught up in the message—when you are interested in communicating the ideas to the listeners—you are not usually uncomfortable or noticeably concerned with how you look or how you sound. It's the idea that is at center stage, not the self. Simple remedies: Be listener centered; be message centered; do not be self-centered.

Relax

Relaxing is easier said than done, you may say. However, if you are well prepared and idea conscious instead of self-conscious, you should be able to relax to a degree where anxiety should not be a problem. You may still feel that flush of nervousness just as you are being introduced or beginning your talk, but it will soon leave because you are prepared. Such nervousness is perfectly natural and is seldom visible to your listeners.

Remember that "stage fright" is normal; it's your body's adrenaline kicking in, which provides extra energy. In fact, speakers who say that they are not nervous at all may face a greater challenge because an audience might perceive their relaxed attitude as apathy or a lack of enthusiasm.

Speaking anxiety (stage fright) is perfectly normal and can be useful.

Overcome Anxiety Symptoms

Everyone's nerves show in a different place. Here are some tricks for common complaints:

Try exercises to reduce symptoms of anxiety.

- **Racing heart.** If you have time before your presentation, plan a workout or a run. If your time is limited, find some way to get your heart rate up with some form of exercise such as sit-ups, push-ups, squats, or a quick walk to burn off excess energy and take advantage of the extra oxygen.
- **Dry mouth.** Chew your tongue. We know this sounds disgusting, but chewing your tongue creates saliva and helps dry mouth. Don't do it where people can see you; you'll look like a cow.
- **High or weak voice.** If you would like your voice to sound stronger or lower, try exercises to improve your voice.
- **Shaky hands.** While you are waiting to speak (and while no one is looking), make hard fists and then stretch out your hands several times to increase blood flow and control. However, if you still have the shakes, don't show the audience! Avoid holding up your hands. In most cases, your hands will stop shaking when you get involved with your presentation.

FOCUS ON

Exercises for Voice Improvement

Try the following simple exercises to build better vocal tone and a stronger-sounding voice:

1. As you are waiting to speak, concentrate on deep breathing. Your lowest natural pitch is supported by good breath control from your diaphragm.
2. Concentrate on moving your belt buckle in and out when you inhale and exhale. Don't move your shoulders when you breathe deeply. This heaving motion tightens the muscles around the throat and makes a tight voice problem worse.

3. Borrow a relaxation strategy from yoga: Inhale on two counts, hold for two counts, then exhale for four counts.
4. If you have a table in front of you, lean forward and put your elbows on the table and breathe deeply, counting your breaths. This will help you relax because you are concentrating on counting your breathing rather than stressing about your speech. Your pitch will drop because you have relaxed the muscles in your neck and chest and you are supporting your voice from your diaphragm.

■ **General insecurity.** This is our best all-purpose solution: Stand up straight. Nothing conveys personal confidence better than good posture. The extra benefits are that you look more attractive and you can breathe better. Lift your chest, pull your shoulders back and down, and raise your head. Face your audience squarely with your body and look them in the eyes. Smile. You're ready to go.

Stand up straight and you will convey personal confidence.

Know That Your Audience Wants You to Succeed

Your audience doesn't want your presentation to fail. When people have taken the time to hear what you have to say, they don't want to feel their time has been wasted. Even listeners who strongly disagree with you—what we call "hostile listeners"—want you to explain yourself clearly if for no other reason than that they can then attempt to shoot down your ideas.

Your listeners want you to succeed.

A poor presentation can be just as embarrassing and uncomfortable for the audience as it is for the speaker. Think of times that you've seen people do a poor job of expressing an idea. What has your reaction been? You probably felt some embarrassment for those persons and may have found yourself trying to rephrase their ideas for them. Remember that no one is out to get you. Just as you want speakers to succeed, your listeners want you to succeed.

Know That You and Your Audience Need Each Other

Every presentation begins with the listener needing something. By coming to your presentation or inviting you to talk, listeners are expressing a need for information, friendship, help, approval, clarification—maybe even inspiration. They hope that something you say will improve their lives.

You as a presenter have needs, too. Probably the strongest need is for approval. Only your listeners can give you this, but they can give you this in many forms from a simple vote (a raising of hands) to a signature on a document (a sales agreement) to an outburst of applause or a hearty thank you. Ron Hoff teaches that "without some indication of approval, response, endorsement, confirmation—*something*!— the presenter is lost at sea, adrift, seeking a signal. This can be tough on the ego. (*No* response is in many ways worse than outright rejection.)"[3]

Your audience can give you much need satisfaction via positive reactions and feedback.

Because listeners need what you have to offer—information, suggestions, instructions, a welcome, or even a little entertainment—and you need what they offer—approval, appreciation, or applause—work together to create a circle of rapport. A good presenter is like a duck—calm and serene on the surface and paddling like crazy underneath. Remember these pointers, and you can look and sound confident about your message content, your organization, yourself, and about handling unforeseen objections or other surprises.

A good presenter is like a duck—calm and serene on the surface and paddling like crazy underneath.

Have Confidence in Your Ideas

If you have completed your homework, including thoroughly analyzing your audience and selecting material based on the needs of that audience, you should have confidence in your point of view. The time you invest in the first four steps of the Strategic Communication Model always pays off. Avoid the temptation to skip a step. Develop the habit of being thorough and professional in developing your messages. A little extra effort and thought can pay huge dividends in your professionalism.

Be Yourself and Become Your Better Self

Let your personality shine in all your communication.

Some people who are perfectly comfortable communicating one-on-one believe that they must become someone different when they address a group. They may have seen effective speakers and try to mimic their excellent platform skills. Such emulation can be valuable as you learn delivery techniques from other people, but you should not try to become someone else. Allow your personality to be reflected in all your communication. In brief, be comfortable as yourself. You are as good as anyone, and, because you have prepared your topic, you are likely to be perceived by your audience as the expert on that topic.

Adapt your style for the corporate or social culture of your audience.

Being yourself does not mean that you should disregard the corporate culture of the organization where you are speaking or the social cultures of your audience. You may need to adapt your style. If in doubt, for example, about your casual, energetic style with an unfamiliar audience—particularly an international audience or one made up of individuals considerably older or higher in status than you are—don't try to change your style. Instead, temper your exuberance and try to be a bit more formal in your delivery. As your audience becomes comfortable with you and you build credibility with your excellent material, you can share your personality with them.

Remember Feedback and Constant Improvement

In Chapter 12, we will talk more about specific guidelines for giving, soliciting, and receiving feedback. This is a critical part of the Strategic Communication Model and is the key to becoming your better self. For now, keep in mind that improvement of delivery skills is a lifelong project, and the guidelines we have discussed in this chapter are just ways to get you moving toward improvement.

Continue to polish your verbal and nonverbal skills to develop a style that meets your audience's expectations.

It is important that you continue to polish your verbal and nonverbal skills to develop a style that meets your audience's expectations and is comfortable in their corporate culture. Speak clearly and expressively. Dress professionally. Exhibit control with appropriate facial expressions, hand gestures, and body movement. Prove that you know your material by thoroughly rehearsing in advance. Be comfortable with your notes and your visual aids. Be prepared to answer questions. Express confidence in your material based on your preparation. Display confidence in yourself through your professionalism and enthusiasm. Most of all, be yourself. That's who the audience came to see. You are the most important part of your message, and your unique personality is your most valuable platform skill.

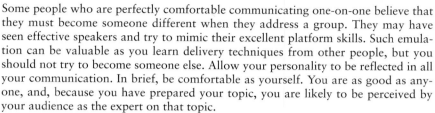

APPLYING THE STRATEGIC COMMUNICATION MODEL

As Brenda in our opening story discovered, oral communication skills are very much at the core of many jobs. She did fine in her interview for the job but suddenly found herself outside her comfort zone when required to make presentations. As she shifted to a different media option (from interview to presentation), her confidence initially left her. This need not be the case.

The major difference between interviews and presentations lies in message delivery. On the positive side, delivering a message in an oral presentation allows communicators some real advantages over a typical interview. Once you gain control over your anxiety, you, like Brenda, have the opportunity to dazzle your audience with good platform skills, visuals, and a projection of confidence that is the hallmark of professionalism. By applying each step of the Strategic Communication Model, you can achieve considerable success in that all-important part of almost any job: delivering oral presentations.

Summary of Key Ideas

- Oral presentations of many types are frequently used in business. Effective employees learn the skills necessary to maximize this medium.
- Thorough preparation for an effective business presentation includes complete context analysis and the selection and organization of material based on your analysis.
- Delivering effective oral messages depends on your ability to polish your verbal and nonverbal delivery skills, develop your platform management skills, express confidence, and be yourself.
- Polishing your verbal delivery skills includes speaking clearly and expressively, paying attention to timing, avoiding distracting vocal patterns, and minimizing verbalized pauses.
- Polishing your platform management skills includes using notes and visuals effectively and handling audience questions constructively.
- Polishing your nonverbal delivery skills includes maintaining eye contact, dressing professionally, exhibiting physical control, and projecting enthusiasm.
- Expressing confidence is accomplished by practicing your material, being idea conscious, and knowing that you and your audience meet needs for each other.
- Being yourself and becoming your better self are functions of your sensitivity to the speaking context (especially the culture) and of feedback you receive.

Application Activities

Activity 9-1 Evaluating a Successful Speaker

Attend a live presentation or view one on TV or a video. (The speaker may be someone you know personally, a business or political leader, a sales person, a television show host, or anyone who makes a living doing oral presentations.) Take notes during the presentation. Look for applications (or misapplications) of the ideas in this chapter. Then write a brief description of the speaker, commenting on this person's delivery style. Suggest ways he or she could improve.

Activity 9-2 Preparing a Team Presentation

1. As a class, select a company that is internationally known and that is currently managing multiple issues. (For example: In 2000, Coca-Cola was managing issues such as contaminated product in Europe, discrimination suits from employees, executive personnel changes, and erratic stock prices.)
2. Working in teams of three or four, select a target audience—any person or group inside or outside the company.
3. Determine a specific purpose for your presentation: You want to persuade your target audience to do something specific. Your team will have 10 minutes to present and 2 minutes to answer questions from your audience.
4. Complete the Context Worksheet found in Chapter 4.
5. Complete the Outline Worksheet found in Chapter 6.

6. Prepare computer-generated visual aids for your presentation.
7. Practice your presentation based on the information in this chapter.
8. Double-check your preparation using the Presentation Evaluation Worksheet in Figure 9-1. Your class and your instructor may use the same evaluation sheet to give you feedback on your presentation.
9. Before you present, be prepared to tell the class about your target audience so they can role-play and ask you questions as if they were that audience.

Figure 9-1
Presentation Evaluation Worksheet

PRESENTATION EVALUATION WORKSHEET

SPEAKER: _____

TOPIC: _____

SPEAKER'S TARGET AUDIENCE: _____

EVALUATOR: _____

Directions for speaker: Evaluate yourself on each point before you present.
Directions for evaluator: Evaluate the speaker on each point.

	Good!	Needs work
CONTENT		
Uses relevant material for audience's knowledge level		
Acknowledges audience's wants and concerns		
Has sufficient depth in support material		
Uses interesting examples for audience and situation		
Uses appropriate visual aids		
ORGANIZATION		
Grabs audience's attention		
States clear agenda		
Includes benefit in introduction		
Follows clear organizational plan		
Summarizes essence of main points		
Asks for clear action in conclusion		
Closes with strong final statement		
DELIVERY		
Moves comfortably and gestures naturally		
Looks at each member of the audience		
Speaks conversationally and enthusiastically		
Handles visual aids effectively		

Overall comments: _____
_____

Finally, would you hire this person, buy this product, or support this proposal? _____
Why or why not? _____

Activity 9-3 Preparing a "How-To" Presentation

Prepare a 4- to 6-minute "how-to" presentation to deliver to your class. To get double benefit from this presentation, select a topic that teaches how to improve speaking effectiveness. Some examples are:

- How to use gestures for greater communication effectiveness
- How to use vocal variation
- How to reduce speaker anxiety
- How to dress for a business presentation
- How to create and use humor in a presentation
- How to create an effective introduction (or conclusion)
- How to handle questions and answers after a presentation

You are not limited to these topics, but your presentation must be communication related. Apply the ideas discussed in this chapter. Practice in front of a mirror.

Activity 9-4 Selling a Product

Develop and deliver an effective 7- to 8-minute sales pitch. Select a product or service that would be appropriate to sell to a person who is just completing college and beginning a business career. This should be a real product (or service) and should sell for not more than $300.

Apply a persuasive pattern of arrangement and be prepared to explain why you structured the presentation as you did. If possible, videotape your delivery and review it with your instructor or a fellow student or colleague. Ask for concrete feedback.

Career Activity

Career Activity 9-1 Taking a Self-Inventory

a. Oral communication skills and attitudes improve through evaluation—by others and by you. This self-inventory identifies your starting point. It will be useful to you only to the degree to which you are totally honest in your answers. You need not show this to others. Use it as an honest look within yourself. You may want to retake it after you have finished this course or have developed your communication skills further.

Interactive CD-ROM Exercises

The following checklist shows how you see yourself as an oral communicator. Read each statement and circle yes or no. After answering yes or no, review each answer and circle the (+) or (−) to indicate how you feel about your answer. A plus means you are satisfied; a minus means you wish you could have answered otherwise.

Answer honestly based on how you actually feel or act, not how you wish you would.

1. Before I enter into an important communication event, I often consider what I can do to ensure a positive outcome.

         YES   **NO**   (+)   (−)

2. I often have great ideas I'd like to share with other people.

         YES   **NO**   (+)   (−)

3. I enjoy trying to explain my ideas to others.

         YES   **NO**   (+)   (−)

216   Part 3: Delivering Powerful Messages and Evaluating Feedback

4. I often get the conversation going among my friends and even with people I don't know.

      YES   NO   (+)   (−)

5. When I stand up to speak in any group, I feel a great deal of stage fright.

      YES   NO   (+)   (−)

6. Before trying to influence others, I make it a point to be certain that I know as much as possible about my audience(s).

      YES   NO   (+)   (−)

7. When I disagree with others, I often become too heated and afterward regret what I've said.

      YES   NO   (+)   (−)

8. I usually keep calm and poised even in discussions when I disagree.

      YES   NO   (+)   (−)

9. I am good at persuading others to my views.

      YES   NO   (+)   (−)

10. I am comfortable and efficient in preparing visual aids (PowerPoint slides, etc.).

      YES   NO   (+)   (−)

11. I would have more influence in my job and in social settings if I could better communicate my feelings and ideas.

      YES   NO   (+)   (−)

12. I like to teach groups of people new things.

      YES   NO   (+)   (−)

13. I regularly clip and save ideas from articles I read.

      YES   NO   (+)   (−)

14. When I know something that could be helpful to others, I like to tell them this information and encourage them to change.

      YES   NO   (+)   (−)

15. I enjoy planning ways to simplify and present ideas so others will understand them.

      YES   NO   (+)   (−)

16. While listening to others, I try to identify and organize the main ideas being spoken.

      YES   NO   (+)   (−)

17. When communicating, I consider audience feelings and attitudes to be at least as important as facts and ideas.

      YES   NO   (+)   (−)

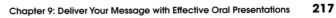

18. In comparison with my friends, I think I speak more clearly and carefully than they do.

        YES   NO   **(+)   (−)**

19. In comparison to my peers, I think I persuade better than they do.

        YES   NO   **(+)   (−)**

20. I have a good vocabulary.

        YES   NO   **(+)   (−)**

21. My physical delivery (use of hands, posture, expressiveness) is one of my strongest communication skills.

        YES   NO   **(+)   (−)**

22. My voice is pleasant and conveys enthusiasm well.

        YES   NO   **(+)   (−)**

23. I am eager to hear helpful criticism from others after I speak up.

        YES   NO   **(+)   (−)**

24. Improving my oral communication skills is one of my highest priorities.

        YES   NO   **(+)   (−)**

25. I have the basic qualities needed to be an excellent oral communicator.

        YES   NO   **(+)   (−)**

26. I speak clearly and pronounce words correctly.

        YES   NO   **(+)   (−)**

27. People seem to enjoy what I say; I hold their interest.

        YES   NO   **(+)   (−)**

28. I use humor effectively.

        YES   NO   **(+)   (−)**

29. I am a good storyteller.

        YES   NO   **(+)   (−)**

30. I handle audience questions very well.

        YES   NO   **(+)   (−)**

31. I feel that I am getting better and better in my communication skills.

        YES   NO   **(+)   (−)**

32. After a communication experience, I often think of what I should have done differently to create a positive outcome.

        YES   NO   **(+)   (−)**

b. Now review your self-inventory. For each item in which you circled a minus sign (indicating that you don't feel good about your answer), write a goal for personal improvement. Your goal should be specific and clear. For example, if you write a goal for statement 4, you might say, "I will start conversations with one person I don't know each day this week." For statement 18, you might say, "I will learn to listen more carefully." For statement 26 you might say, "I will make a list and learn the pronunciation of one difficult word each day."

Write your goals in the spaces that follow. If you have more than five areas to work on, put them in order of importance. Then write your top five goals here:

Goal 1:

Goal 2:

Goal 3:

Goal 4:

Goal 5:

c. For each goal you have set, sketch out an action plan and time line for its accomplishment. Be specific about the activities needed to achieve the goal. Where will you get the knowledge you need? How will you gain the experiences needed for growth? Be specific about what you will do.

myPHLIP Companion Web Site

Learning Interactively

Visit the myPHLIP Web site at www.prenhall.com/timm. For Chapter 9, take advantage of the interactive "Study Guide" to test your chapter knowledge. Get instant feedback on whether you need additional studying. Read the "Current Events" articles to get the latest on chapter topics, and complete the exercises as specified by your instructor. Expand your learning with a visit to the "Research Area." There you will find a wealth of information you can use to complete your course assignments.

Notes

1. Michael Waldhold, "Here's One Reason, Uh, Smart People Say 'Uh', " *Wall Street Journal*, March 19, 1991, p. B1.
2. This discussion was adapted from Harold P. Zelko and Frank E. X. Dance, *Business and Professional Speech Communication*, 2nd ed. (New York: Holt, Rhinehart and Winston, 1978), pp. 77–79.
3. Adapted from Ron Hoff, *I Can See You Naked, A Fearless Guide to Making Great Presentations* (New York: Andrew and McMeel, 1988), p. 10.

Selection 3 Questions

VOCABULARY

1. Bienvenu and Timm say oral communication in business often takes the form of presentations. How do they define a presentation?

    Whenever you plan, prepare, and create a message to deliver to

    others.

2. Bienvenu and Timm indicate they are offering generic guidelines. What are generic guidelines?

    Those that apply to most people rather than guidelines for a specific

    person or personality.

COMPREHENSION

3. Because it is not the first chapter in this text about giving oral presentations, it assumes you have already

    defined   the context for your message

    considered   your media and timing options

    decided   that an oral presentation makes sense

    selected and organized   the information you want to convey

    have a well-organized   outline of audience-focused information

4. What is the purpose of the checkmarked margin notes throughout the chapter?

    The checkmarked margin notes summarize key points.

5. According to Bienvenu and Timm, to deliver effective oral messages you must concentrate on five key factors. Please list them.

    polishing your verbal delivery skills

    polishing your platform management skills

    polishing your nonverbal delivery skills

    expressing confidence

    being yourself and becoming your better self

6. According to Bienvenu and Timm, polishing your verbal delivery skills includes

   speaking clearly

   speaking expressively

   paying attention to timing

   avoiding distracting vocal patterns

   minimizing verbalized pauses

7. What are "filler words"? Give an example of a filler word.

   Filler words are words, nonwords, and sounds we use to "fill" the

   air; they are signs of nervousness. Examples include uh, ah, so, you

   know.

8. What do nonverbal skills include? Give two examples of nonverbal skills.

   Nonverbal skills include how you look and how you move. Examples

   of nonverbal skills include establishing and maintaining eye contact,

   your dress and grooming, gestures, postures, and mannerisms.

9. Since fear and anxiety are almost always rooted in uncertainty, what are three things you can do to reduce your fear and anxiety?

   Answers will vary; please see Answer Key.

REFLECT AND CONNECT

10. Complete the Career Activity 9–1, Taking a Self-Inventory, on pages 322–325. Be sure to develop a goal, action plan, and timeline for five areas you marked with a minus that you want to improve.

   Answers to the Career Activity 9–1, Taking a Self-Inventory, will vary.

> ### Selection 4 Glasbergen Cartoon

RANDY GLASBERGEN

Mr. Glasbergen began his cartooning career while he was in high school. Aside from one year as a staff humor writer for Hallmark Cards, he has been a full-time freelance cartoonist since 1976. His cartoons regularly appear in magazines, newspapers, and newsletters around the world, and his syndicated comic panel The Better Half *appears seven days a week in newspapers around the world.*

AN IDEA TO THINK ABOUT

How important do you think graphics and props are to an effective speech? Do you sometimes spend more time creating your visual aids than you do your outline? *As you read,* decide what Glasbergen thinks sometimes happens.

"What software would you recommend to give my presentation so much flash and sizzle that nobody notices that I have nothing to say?"

(Copyright 2002 by Randy Glasbergen. www.glasbergen.com)

Selection 4 Questions

1. What does Glasbergen want us to think about?

    Glasbergen wants us to think about how we sometimes spend more

    time creating our visuals than we do our message. Also, perhaps he

    means to remind us that the message is really the important element.

2. Think back to what Graham said about the role of visuals in his article and what Bienvenu and Timm said in their text chapter. Do you think they would agree or disagree with what this presenter wants to do? Please explain.

    Graham said, "While visual interest is essential, visuals should not be

    allowed to dominate or control a presentation. They should enhance, not overshadow, the message." Bienvenu and Timm said, "Remember, you are most important, your visual aids are just that—aids to support you and your message." I think they would *disagree* with what this presenter wants to do and advise him to work on his message.

Selection 5 "What You Can Say Without Speaking"

KARE ANDERSON

Ms. Anderson is a "Say It Better" speaker and columnist. She is an Emmy-winning TV commentator, former Wall Street Journal *reporter, and author of five books, including* Walk Your Talk *and* Resolving Conflict Sooner: The Powerfully Simple 4-Step Method for Reaching Better Agreements More Easily in Everyday Life. *She prepared this article for the National Association of Realtors'* Journal of Property Management.

AN IDEA TO THINK ABOUT

How good are you at "reading" other people? For example, do you always know when someone is lying to you or brushing you off or anxious to hear your point of view? *As you read,* find out how you can read body language more accurately.

WHAT YOU CAN SAY WITHOUT SPEAKING

Kare Anderson

[1]Body language. It can often tell you much about the people with whom you are speaking. Are they open to your ideas? Are they listening to what you have to say? And perhaps most importantly, are they interested in and receptive to what you are talking about? The ability to discern and determine what a person is saying nonverbally can often be as important as the dialogue that takes place between the two parties. And though many people are "sure" that the person they're talking to is intently listening to what is going on, their body language and mannerisms may be saying something else entirely.

[2]Some of the most familiar advice you've heard about body language, for instance, was based on folklore, not research. Consider, for example, "open" and "closed" body stances. People with crossed arms are often not

any more closed to your thoughts, while people with open arms are not necessarily open to you and your ideas.

To test your knowledge of body language basics, take this quick nine-question quiz. Some of the answers may surprise you. By remembering these insights, you can go a long way toward cultivating genuine, enduring professional and personal relationships you can savor.

1. Do people get along better when talking to each other if they are facing each other or if they are standing side by side?

2. Who (men or women) tends to face the person with whom they are speaking and who (women or men) tends to stand side by side, facing more or less the same way?

3. If you want to increase the chance of knowing if someone is lying to you, what is one helpful factor to notice about that person's face when he or she is talking to you?

4. If you want to keep someone's attention, is it better to wear a patterned shirt or blouse or a plain blouse or shirt?

5. What is the most directly emotional of all the senses, [the one that] bypasses the thinking facilities and causes a quicker, more intense reaction in the limbic (emotions) system than any other sense?

6. Are you more likely to get someone to support you or buy something if you give them something up front, unasked, before you ask for the favor?

7. Who tends to maintain wider peripheral vision when entering a new place—men or women?

8. Who tends to be more specific in their descriptions—adults or children?

9. Of the previous eight questions, which is the one question people are most likely to ask for the answer to first, and if reading the questions in a group, are they most likely to comment on first?

BODY LANGUAGE BASICS QUIZ ANSWERS

1. People get along better when they "sidle" stand or sit side by side rather than when they "face off," stand or sit facing each other.

2. Men are more likely to "sidle" than women.

3. Note the timing and duration of the first "reactive" expression on someone's face when you think that person is not telling you the truth. When lying, most people can put an innocent expression on their faces, yet few (except pathological liars) will have the right timing or duration of that expression. If you ignore the expression itself and, instead, consider whether the timing and duration of the expression seem natural, you'll greatly increase your chances of knowing if that person is lying.

4. Wearing a plain, unpatterned shirt or blouse will increase the chances that the listener will hear you longer. A patterned top or ornate jewelry or loud tie will break up the listener's attention span sooner, and that person is more likely to take "mental vacations" sooner.

5. Smell is the most directly emotional of the senses. The right natural scent can refresh or relax you and others in your home or work site. Vanilla, apple, and chocolate are the scents Americans most prefer.

6. Yes, up to 14 times more likely to get their support or a purchase. This gut instinct is often called "reciprocity reflex."

7. Women. That is why storeowners who serve men will increase their sales if they have prominent, eye-level signage over large displays where men will see the signage soon after entering the store.

8. Children are more vividly specific, hitting their prime around fourth grade and then beginning to speak in generalities, more like adults. Yet the specific detail proves the general conclusion. Specifics are more memorable and more credible.

9. Question number 3. It seems that we have an inordinate interest in lying.

⁴So how did you do? Surprisingly, many people either do not realize or do not understand the importance of body language when it comes to speaking and relationships. Here are some tips that will help you not only improve your ability to communicate with others, but also indirectly aid their acceptance of your thoughts and ideas.

TIP: MAKE MORE MOMENTS MEANINGFUL AND MEMORABLE

⁵Move to motivate, because motion is emotional. It increases the emotional intensity of whatever is happening. Motion attracts attention and causes people to remember more of what's happening and feel more strongly about it, for better or for worse.

⁶Imagine the bizarre picture of someone swinging his whole body around, sweeping down low before you, and then reaching out to shake hands. While moving in many dimensions will surely make you more memorable, it won't necessarily make you more credible. Get others involved in motions with you that create good will: walking, sharing a meal, handing or receiving a gift, shaking hands, turning to face a new scene. You are more likely to literally get "in sync" (vital signs become more similar: eye pupil dilation, skin temperature, heartbeat) and to then get along.

TIP: TRUE TIMING CAN BE VITAL TO IMPRESSING A POINT TO YOUR LISTENER

⁷If a person likes the way he acts when he is around you, he sees the qualities in you that he most admires. The opposite is also true. Two universal truths: people like people who are like them, and people like people who like them.

⁸Pick the moments when someone feels most at ease and happy to move the relationship forward. Don't make suggestions or requests when they are acting in an unbecoming way. Your efforts will only backfire. Praise the behavior you want to flourish. Don't ask for more from someone until they have invested more time, money, other resources, or emotional "chits" in the relationship.

HERE ARE FIVE MORE TIPS FOR GETTING ALONG BETTER

1. If you embarrass someone, you will probably never have his or her full attention again.

2. Even, and especially, when you have the upper hand, do not make a victim of the underdog.

3. Offering something free and valued up front, unasked, often instills the desire to reciprocate, even beyond the value of the offer.

4. Problems seldom exist at the level at which they are discussed. Until you get some notion of the underlying conflict, you will not be able to find a solution.

5. If you want more from another person, wait to ask for it until after they have invested time, money, or other resources.

[9]By incorporating these techniques into your everyday speaking and presenting, not only will you find that people will listen to what you have to say, but they will be interested in how you say it. By getting people excited about your ideas, you have already cleared a huge hurdle in developing relationships and communicating new concepts.

Selection 5 Questions

VOCABULARY

Match each word in the left column with the best definition in the right column.

1. discern (¶ 1) __c.__   **a.** lasting
2. enduring (¶ 3) __a.__   **b.** thrive, grow
3. savor (¶ 3) __d.__   **c.** understand
4. bizarre (¶ 6) __e.__   **d.** enjoy
5. flourish (¶ 8) __b.__   **e.** weird

COMPREHENSION

6. Explain what Anderson means when she says most of the familiar advice we've heard about body language is based on folklore, not research. In most cases, do you think folklore or research is more convincing?

   Anderson means that advice about body language is based on anec-

   dote and personal stories rather than on proven information. In most

   cases research is more convincing.

   _____

   _____

7. Explain how you could use the "reciprocity reflex" to your advantage.

   Examples of how to use the "reciprocity reflex" vary—but students

   rarely have trouble finding an example.

8. Circle the letter of the sentence that best expresses the thesis.

   a. Most of the advice we've heard about body language is based on folklore, not research.

   b. People get along better when they stand or sit side by side than when they stand or sit facing each other.

   c. People like people who are like them, and people like people who like them.

   (d.) Our ability to effectively send and receive messages nonverbally is often as important as our ability to communicate verbally.

9. Describe in your own words what it means to be "in sync." Why do you think people who are in sync communicate more effectively?

   To be in sync means to be attuned to one another, compatible. People

   who are in sync communicate more effectively because they are well

   matched and typically share many characteristics.

REFLECT AND CONNECT

10. Look back over Anderson's "Body Language Basics" and her various tips for improving communications. Which one idea surprised you the most? Why? Which idea do you think will be most useful to you in your daily communications?

    Within a class I rarely have consensus on the "most surprising" or

    "most useful" idea.

Selection 6 Viva Voice

LISA MURPHY

Ms. Murphy's articles and essays appear in a variety of national magazines, including Chatelaine, *where this essay first appeared in 2002.*

VOCABULARY

quotidian (¶ 18): daily
strident (¶ 18): shrill, unpleasant

AN IDEA TO THINK ABOUT

Do you have a distinctive voice that is recognizable in any crowd? Have you ever wished your voice were different—lower, higher, deeper? *As you read,* find out some strategies for making the most of the voice you have.

VIVA VOICE

Lisa Murphy

[1]In the dusty-peach gloom of a Toronto conference room, we braced our-selves for the ultimate act of bravery: listening to our voices on tape. Larry Green, or "Uncle Larry," as he jokingly called himself, shuffled through cassettes for what seemed like an eternity before popping one in the tape recorder. Green, a former voice agent, veteran broadcaster, and the in-structor for this class called How to Put Your Voice to Work, had already pooh-poohed any whining about hating our voices. "I don't care if it's good or bad," he boomed. "My MO is to make you the best you can be in four weeks."

[2]It wasn't boot camp, but a course offered by the Learning Annex, one of the few North American institutions that can teach you how to be-come both a computer whiz and psychic medium. While its brochure's de-scriptions of "dreaming your dharma" and "how to make $100,000 as a private eye" seemed intriguing, the voice-work class jumped out at me: "Has anyone ever said your interesting, unusual, or seductive voice should be on commercials?"

[3]Why, yes. People often ask whether I've ever considered working in radio. (I choose to believe that's due to my unique throaty sound rather than my looks.) I still remember the Halloween party when I met my fu-ture husband's friends for the first time, one of whom happened to be an old classmate I hadn't seen in eight years. Before I even entered the room—fully costumed, I might add—she called out, "That's gotta be the Lisa Murphy I know. I'd recognize that voice anywhere!"

[4]Woody Woodpecker has a distinctive voice, too. Was I a sultry vocal superstar or a grating mouthpiece? I've certainly wondered more than once whether my sound and delivery could be improved—such as the time my voice broke, betraying my desperation at a coveted job interview, or when a liberal sprinkling of *likes, ums,* and *ahs* exposed my verbal and mental incompetence in front of a long-admired fellow writer.

[5]Green's voice-work class promised to solve those problems and maybe even earn me some money. Suddenly, the idea of supplementing my meager income with work as a radio host or phone-sex operator seemed entirely plausible. By Green's second session, however, two things were clear: his course covered only the legitimate business of radio and

television voice-overs, and giving good voice required a lot more effort than I had ever imagined.

[6]Listening to our taped commercials one after the other, we critiqued one another's attempts at broadcast fame. "Was she reading or telling?" Green would gleefully roar after a tape finished. "Who's your audience? Pump up the energy! Try it again and this time, use your hands!" Taking a deep breath, we read again and again until we nailed it. In the process, I discovered that the voice God gave us is less important than what we do with it. Adding inflection, controlling our pitch and tone, and even—gasp—thinking before we speak can go a long way to making our voices heard.

THE AUDIENCE IS LISTENING

[7]Now, before you dismiss this as an exercise for the vocal peacocks among us, think about the hours you've clocked doing business on the phone, delivering presentations, or recording and rerecording your voice-mail message to achieve that perfect breezy tone. Consider also the times when monotone droning or high-pitched Valley-girl speak distracted you from what others were saying. Your voice conveys more about you than anything else, confirms Susan Stackhouse, a voice expert, speech specialist, and associate professor of theatre at Dalhousie University in Nova Scotia. "We're judged on how we sound."

[8]One gent in my workshop, for instance, seemed fairly nondescript until he revealed a nuanced buttery voice that could sell me anything, any time. But many of us lack the technique to express ourselves, Stackhouse says, even when we feel passionate about the subject. This can profoundly affect the way people perceive you, particularly in business. As Stackhouse points out, "You want to know that you're enhancing your career, not sabotaging it." Acknowledging the effect of your voice is key to improving your sound. Then the real work begins. Read on—preferably, out loud.

THE VOICE–BODY CONNECTION

[9]Women complain most about voice fatigue or weakness, says Stackhouse, and with good reason. First, we have smaller voice boxes than men. Second, we talk a lot, whether we're in the classroom or courtroom, yelling over our·kids, or gabbing with friends. Finally, we forget that our vocal cords need the same TLC as the rest of our body. For starters, that means drinking plenty of water, never whispering to keep your voice from becoming hoarse, and avoiding cigarette smoke and excessive drinking. (That scared me more than listening to myself on tape, I admit. I guess the gals and I will have to meet for tea from now on.)

[10]Stackhouse and Green also invoked that four-letter word: exercise. To sound our best, we need to work the right muscles and keep them limber. Most of us force sound from our throats and strain our vocal cords because we don't know any better. Strong voices are powered using the diaphragm (the muscle below your lungs) to push air into your windpipe and through your voice box. To get a sense of the size of your larynx, look at your thumbnail, says Dr. Brian Hands, an ear, nose, and throat specialist known as the "voice doctor to the stars" in Toronto. "That's the size of your voice box. The white of the nail is the size of each vocal cord."

[11]Practice breathing from the diaphragm by placing your hands on your stomach, feeling the air fill your abdomen as you deeply inhale, and pulling your tummy in as you exhale and speak. This exercise works for one of Canada's best-known broadcasters. "I think of it as warming up my voice before it comes out of my mouth," says Shelagh Rogers, host of CBC Radio's *This Morning.* "It also connects you more to what you're saying."

[12]Other star secrets can help you to sound your best. Mark Dailey, the news anchor whose bass-baritone voice has become synonymous with Toronto's *Citytv,* told me he sings in his car on the way to work to loosen his vocal cords. Stretching your mouth, reading aloud, and reciting tongue twisters improves articulation, adds Green. Smiling and using your hands will also enliven your tone. These days, I prepare for tough business calls by practicing my questions aloud and breathing deeply. Then I make the calls standing up with my hands free.

[13]Once in front of your audience—your boss or a dashing next-door neighbor, let's say—try to stay relaxed, adding color and inflection in your voice when appropriate. "Like an instrument, you're actually hitting notes, even though you're just speaking," says Dailey of his approach. Don't be afraid to pause for emphasis, urges Green. "Let them wait! The silence will entice them to focus harder and pick up on what you're trying to say." Thanks to his advice, I'm no longer known in my circle as "the conversation hijacker" (I think).

THE HAPPY HOOKER (NOT)

[14]Giving up my sultry-voice reflex has been a harder habit to kick. Heck, I thought it was a compliment when people described my voice as sexy. I'm not alone. One friend proudly describes her sound as a "gravelly purr," but if talking with you makes people feel as though they've stumbled onto a porno shoot, experts say you're probably sending the wrong message, not to mention hurting your voice. "It's called the Bogart-Bacall syndrome," says Dr. Hands. "People talk in what they think is a lower sensual mode, which creates significant strain on their vocal cords."

[15]Other women may speak at an extremely high pitch. My friend Lynda, for instance, complains that callers always ask for her mother. If that sounds familiar, you probably fall into this camp. Your optimal speaking pitch is the fullest, richest, most effortless note that comes out of your body, explains Stackhouse. (That's usually two notes below your centre singing note on a piano.) Although you can expand your range through exercises, Dr. Hands recommends the pitch that's least painful and most comfortable for everyday use. Once you've got your sound down, it's time to say something interesting.

CONTENT IS STILL KING

[16]Carefully chosen language not only makes your speech more effective, it can offset the impression of your voice alone. In tough interviews, for example, Rogers consciously uses powerful words to play down her warm plummy sound. Thinking about what you're saying will also help you avoid the *ahs, ums,* and other overworked words such as *cool* or *great.*

[17]"These take the concentration away from the person you're addressing," Green said after I produced another embarrassingly adolescent

stream of slang in class. To identify those distracting vocal tics, as well as other no-nos such as poor posture or knee slapping, Stackhouse suggests watching a videotape of yourself speaking. Or ask a friend—a really good friend—for an honest critique. Taking a voice workshop or consulting a speech pathologist can also be valuable.

[18]By Green's fourth and final session, I had abandoned my radio dreams for the quotidian (but far worthier) goal of "making every word count." Although I didn't jump-start a new career, empowering my voice, thinking before I speak, and being natural has helped me enormously. I now listen between the words—both mine and others. While my own self-conscious and jargon-peppered speech spoke volumes about my need for reassurance, today the rapid-fire strident voices of others cue me to their insecurities or lack of preparation. Best of all, I've learned not to crow about—or cringe at—my voice on tape, but to learn from it.

Selection 6 Questions

VOCABULARY

1. In paragraph 7, Murphy compares people to peacocks. Describe people who are "vocal peacocks."

   People who are "vocal peacocks" are showoffs.

   _____

   _____

2. In paragraph 8, Murphy describes a man as having "a nuanced buttery voice." Was that a positive or negative description? What clue(s) did Murphy provide to help you understand?

   "A nuanced buttery voice" was a positive description. Clue: he "could

   sell me anything, any time."

   _____

3. Murphy says that Stackhouse and Green "invoked that four-letter word: exercise." (¶ 10) Obviously, the word *exercise* has more than four letters, so what does she mean?

   We use the "four-letter word" descriptor to represent something

   obscene or unpleasant—exercise is often thought of as obscene and

   unpleasant.

4. Murphy says she's no longer known as "the conversation hijacker." (¶ 13) What does a conversation hijacker do? If she's no longer a conversation hijacker, what does she do now?

A conversation hijacker is someone who takes over a conversation and moves it in the direction he or she wants. If Murphy is no longer a conversation hijacker, she now listens more than she talks.

5. In paragraph 17, Murphy says she produced another "adolescent stream of slang." Give an example of what she might have said. Was she pleased with her language?

Murphy was not pleased with her "adolescent stream of slang." Examples might include "That's cool." "Wow, how sweet."

6. Explain the meaning of the heading "Content Is Still King."

The heading "Content Is Still King" means no matter how wonderful your voice, you must have something worthwhile to say.

COMPREHENSION

7. What are three techniques that can go a long way to "making our voices heard"?

Three techniques that can go a long way to making our voices heard: adding inflection, controlling our pitch, and thinking before we speak.

8. Describe three strategies you can use to help you sound your best.

Answers will vary; please see Answer Key.

9. Circle the letter of the sentence that best expresses the thesis.

a. How we sound and what we say affects the way people perceive us, so it is worth the work to make our voice and our words sound their best.

b. Women have smaller voice boxes than men.

c. Stretching your mouth, reading aloud, and reciting tongue twisters improves articulation.

d. Our voice is important, and we should take care of it.

REFLECT AND CONNECT

10. The experts say we're all judged on how we sound. For the next two days, keep a log of every instance when using your voice to its best advantage is helpful—speaking with a professor or your boss, asking your children to do something, trying to convince a salesclerk to help you, leaving a voice-mail message. When you complete your log, develop a strategy for one way to improve your voice.

See the Answer Key for additional information.

LOG ON TO THE WEB

There are several resources for better speaking strategies on the Web. For example,

How to Conquer Public Speaking Fear, by Martin C. Orman, M.D.: <*http://www.stresscure.com*>

Speech Tips: <*http://www.speechtips.com*>

Patricia C. Fripp: <*http://www.fripp.com*>

Toastmasters International: <*http://www.toastmasters.com*>

Log on to one of these sites or use a search tool to locate a site that gives you information about some aspect of public speaking.

Read one article. Write down (1) the complete Web address, (2) the name of the person or company who sponsors and maintains the site, (3) the name of the person who wrote the information, (4) what you know about the writer, and (5) one idea or suggestion you learned about how to speak with more confidence.

REFLECT AND CONNECT

A. Presentations are more successful when they have
  1. structure (a beginning, middle, and end)
  2. a clearly defined message (with "guideposts" for your listeners)
  3. creativity (personal stories, visuals)
  4. good delivery (appropriate nonverbal language, color, and inflection in your voice).
      Select one of these four major areas—structure, message, creativity, delivery—and describe techniques you can use to improve that area of your presentation.

B. Although public speaking is stressful for most people, there are ways you can reduce the stress. First, list two or three common reasons for our fear of public speaking. Then, describe ways to reduce the fear and stress of speaking in front of others.

C. Compile a list of local resources—classes, Toastmasters' groups, books, and videos—you could use to improve your speaking abilities. Describe the resource, including contact information, costs, and what aspects of speaking would be covered.

Appendices

Facts, Opinions, and Reasoned Judgments

Tips for Preparing for and Taking Standardized Reading Tests

Using Textbook Design Clues

FACTS, OPINIONS, AND REASONED JUDGMENTS

Not everything that is written is factual, nor does it need to be. The problem is that authors don't usually say which of their statements are factual and which are their opinions. Therefore, part of your job as a reader is to distinguish among the facts, opinions, and reasoned judgments.

FACTS

A fact is an objective statement that can be proved true or false. A fact can be verified. That is, you can check the accuracy of the information, and no matter where you look or whom you ask, the information is the same. Examples of facts include the following:

■ Five candidates are running for the school board in next week's election.
■ As people age, physical changes occur in the body.

Facts, when proven to be true, are reliable support for main ideas and good sources of information.

OPINIONS

An opinion is a subjective statement that cannot be proved true or false. Opinions express the author's thoughts, feelings, beliefs, and attitudes. Opinions cannot be verified; the information can change depending on where you look or whom you ask. Examples of opinions include the following:

■ The candidates in next week's school board election are the best we've ever had running for the office.
■ Loss of hearing is the most difficult effect of aging.

Judgmental words like these often signal an opinion:

bad	pretty
dangerous	safe
dumb	smart
good	the best
important	the worst
insignificant	ugly
nice	wonderful

Conditional words like these often signal an opinion:

apparently	perhaps
likely	possibly
maybe	probably
often	seemingly

Phrases like these usually signal an opinion:

I believe	it is believed
I feel	it is likely that
I suspect	it is usually the case that
in all likelihood	one explanation is
in my view	this suggests

REASONED JUDGMENTS

An opinion is not right or wrong, or good or bad. However, depending on the amount and type of information the author considered before forming the opinion, it can be valid or invalid.

Valid opinions can be very helpful. Thoughtful, coherent evaluations (opinions) that informed individuals make from the available evidence are *reasoned judgments*. An author's reasoned judgments can often help you understand ideas better than can a simple list of facts. However, you should be skeptical of opinions that are formed on the basis of emotion, peer pressure, politics, and other unpredictable passions.

Exercise 1

Read each sentence. Decide if it is a statement of fact or an opinion. Remember, a fact is an objective statement that can be verified, and an opinion is a subjective statement that cannot be verified. Mark it *F* if it is a fact or *O* if it is an opinion.

EXAMPLE

__O__ The typical kitchen in 2010 will probably be more like a living room with comfortable seating, furniture-like cabinets, and lavish entertainment centers.

Explanation   Even though many predictions are based on reliable information and made by informed individuals, they are still opinions about what might happen in the future. Since they cannot be proved true or false at this time, statements like this one should be marked *O* for opinion.

__O__ **1.** There's no question that word-processing programs streamline the writing process.

__F__ **2.** Phoenix is the sixth-largest rental car market in the nation.

F   **3.** A typical 20-year-old house with adequate attic insulation loses more energy to air leaks than from any other source.

F   **4.** The book *Basic Woodworking* includes complete step-by-step instructions for seven patterns for beginning woodworkers.

O   **5.** Nothing makes you feel right at home like a good book, a purring cat, and a cup of tea.

F   **6.** Every rock contains clues about the environment in which it formed.

O   **7.** By 2010, e-books will be more popular than paperback books.

F   **8.** Some high-tech companies have more personal computers than telephones.

F   **9.** Adobe is an ancient building material.

O **10.** The simplest things always provide the most pleasure.

Exercise 2

Read each sentence. Decide if it is a statement of fact or an opinion. Mark it *F* if it is a fact or *O* if it is an opinion.

F   **1.** NBC's Sydney Olympics coverage drew the lowest national ratings for a Summer or Winter Games since 1968.

F   **2.** Job Corps is the nation's largest residential training program for men and women ages 16 to 24.

O   **3.** Nothing compares to the grand sights and sounds one can experience in Africa.

F   **4.** Wal-Mart Stores is the world's largest retailer.

F   **5.** Seventy percent of all automobile crashes happen at low speed and close to home.

O   **6.** In any recipe, fresh ingredients are always superior to frozen ingredients.

F   **7.** The Denver Broncos fans made it into the *Guinness Book of World Records* for the loudest cheer—128.7 decibels.

O   **8.** Attending a job fair is the best way to find a new job.

O   **9.** Willie Morris's autobiographical novel, *My Dog Skip,* is a perfect piece of bedtime reading for kids and their parents.

F **10.** In 1900, the average age of death was 46. Today, the average age is 78.

Of course, real writing is rarely this obvious. Authors, even textbook authors, often use a combination of facts, opinions, and reasoned judgments to support and explain their ideas. You may even find facts and opinions in the same sentence.

> ### Exercise 3

Answer the questions following each paragraph.

1. ¹In Salzburg, Austria, you can visit many of the places used in the movie version of *The Sound of Music*. ²You can walk through the Mirabell Gardens where Maria and the children danced around the statue of Pegasus, the winged horse, as they sang "Do-Re-Mi." ³You can visit the Leopoldskron Castle that was used as the setting for the von Trapp family home. ⁴You can also see the Mondsee Cathedral where scenes of the marriage of Maria to the Baron were filmed. ⁵Made in 1964, starring Julie Andrews and Christopher Plummer, it is one of the best movies of all time.

    a. Is sentence 1 fact, opinion, or a combination of fact and opinion? If it includes both, list which information is fact and which is opinion.

    F _____

    _____

    b. Is sentence 5 fact, opinion, or a combination of fact and opinion? If it includes both, list which information is fact and which is opinion.

    Combination: F—made in 1964, starring Julie Andrews and

    Christopher Plummer; O—one of the best movies of all time

2. ¹Downhill skiing and snowboarding, the flashiest winter sports, attract more than 11 million participants a year. ²But other cold-weather activities are getting their fair share of enthusiasts, too. ³For example, in 2002, 7.8 million Americans ice-skated, and 2.6 million Americans went cross-country skiing. (Doheny, "Winter Sports," *LA Times*)

    a. Is sentence 1 fact, opinion, or a combination of fact and opinion? If it includes both, list which information is fact and which is opinion.

    Combination: F—skiing and snowboarding attract more than

    11 million participants a year; O—the flashiest winter sports

    b. Is sentence 3 fact, opinion, or a combination of fact and opinion? If it includes both, list which information is fact and which is opinion.

    F _____

    _____

3. ¹The earliest device created to measure the passage of time was the sundial. ²It measured the sun's shadow. ³The water clock was an improvement over the sundial, since it didn't depend on the sun. ⁴Once the art of glass making was perfected, the hourglass was created to mark the passage of time with sand. ⁵However, none of these devices were as creative as the modern clock.

    a. Is sentence 1 fact, opinion, or a combination of fact and opinion? If it includes both, list which information is fact and which is opinion.

F
_____

_____

b. Is sentence 5 fact, opinion, or a combination of fact and opinion? If
it includes both, list which information is fact and which is opinion.

O
_____

_____

4. [1]The salt cedar, or tamarisk tree, is a serious threat to native plants and
wildlife across much of the Southwest. [2]One way it forces out other
plants and animals is by using large amounts of water. [3]For example,
one salt cedar alone can use 200 gallons of water a day, more than the
amount used by a small family. [4]It also adds large amounts of salt to
the soil and rivers. [5]The trees now cover more than 1 million acres.

a. Is sentence 3 fact, opinion, or a combination of fact and opinion? If
it includes both, list which information is fact and which is opinion.

F
_____

_____

b. Is sentence 5 fact, opinion, or a combination of fact and opinion? If
it includes both, list which information is fact and which is opinion.

F
_____

_____

5. [1]Science-fiction movies are fascinating. [2]If they are well produced, they
succeed in transporting us into unfamiliar worlds and making us feel
quite comfortable in them. [3]Often, after the initial wonderment at
where we are "taken," we settle in to follow the plot much as we would
with an old-fashioned "western" or situation comedy. [4]The unfamiliar
quickly becomes commonplace. [5]We begin to believe in the characters,
even those who are rather different from us humans. (Rose, Glazer, and
Glazer, *Sociology*)

a. Is sentence 1 fact, opinion, or a combination of fact and opinion? If
it includes both, list which information is fact and which is opinion.

O
_____

_____

b. Is sentence 5 fact, opinion, or a combination of fact and opinion? If
it includes both, list which information is fact and which is opinion.

O
_____

_____

6. [1]While there will always be exceptions, most good-paying jobs now require specialized education. [2]The earnings gap between college graduates and those without specialized skills continues to widen. [3]Family

income for high school dropouts fell 10 percent. [4]For college graduates, it has soared up to 28 percent, says Cleveland-based economist John Burke. [5]Clearly, workers with the best earning potential have specific marketable skills—skills learned and honed through a college education. (Adapted from Harris-Tuck, Price, and Robertson, *Career Patterns*)

a. Is sentence 2 fact, opinion, or a combination of fact and opinion? If it includes both, list which information is fact and which is opinion.

F _____

_____

b. Is sentence 5 fact, opinion, or a combination of fact and opinion? If it includes both, list which information is fact and which is opinion.

Combination: F—workers with the best earning potential have specific

marketable skills; O—skills learned and honed through a college education

7. [1]We first acquire the use of symbols and begin uttering sounds in infancy. [2]Gradually we acquire our first words, and from approximately two to six years of age, we increase our vocabularies from a few words to about 8,000. [3]As we continue to increase our vocabularies and build sentences, we gain the ability to handle complex language skills. [4]Our opportunity and ability to interact with other people are very important to this stage of language growth. (Bittner, *Each Other*)

a. Is sentence 2 fact, opinion, or a combination of fact and opinion? If it includes both, list which information is fact and which is opinion.

F _____

_____

b. Is sentence 4 fact, opinion, or a combination of fact and opinion? If it includes both, list which information is fact and which is opinion.

F _____

_____

8. [1]Human beings need some daily exercise or physical activity, not just for weight control but for optimal health. [2]The type and the amount of exercise that have been shown beneficial to health involve about half an hour a day of moderate exertion. [3]Many pleasant activities such as walking, bicycling, dancing, tennis, gardening, and even lovemaking are sufficient to satisfy this daily requirement. [4]Thus many experts agree that we do not need to push ourselves to the limit of endurance in order to benefit from exercise. (Adapted from Alexander, *Adjustment and Human Relations*)

a. Is sentence 1 fact, opinion, or a combination of fact and opinion? If it includes both, list which information is fact and which is opinion.

F _____

_____

b. Is sentence 4 fact, opinion, or a combination of fact and opinion? If
it includes both, list which information is fact and which is opinion.

O _____

_____

9. ¹As adults, we're often tempted to skip breakfast and start the day with
a cup of coffee on the run. ²But the old adage that "breakfast is the
most important meal of the day" is absolutely right; and it's even more
important for our kids than it is for us. ³It has been shown that children
who eat a healthy breakfast do better in school. ⁴They concentrate more
intently, and have more energy and stamina. ⁵They even score higher
on tests. ⁶In fact, students who participated in one school breakfast
program had significantly higher math grades than those who didn't.
(Kraft Foods, *Family Roundtable*)

a. Is sentence 1 fact, opinion, or a combination of fact and opinion? If
it includes both, list which information is fact and which is opinion.

O _____

_____

b. Is sentence 3 fact, opinion, or a combination of fact and opinion? If
it includes both, list which information is fact and which is opinion.

F _____

_____

10. ¹Generally speaking, supervisors create one of three climates, or working environments, for employees. ²Some supervisors are very controlling and strict. ³The direct opposite of a strict, structured climate is a
permissive atmosphere with few controls or restrictions. ⁴The third
type, a democratic climate, is one in which the supervisor maintains a
leadership role but creates a team feeling by keeping all employees involved. ⁵A permissive climate will always reduce productivity while a
democratic climate will always increase productivity.

a. Is sentence 4 fact, opinion, or a combination of fact and opinion? If
it includes both, list which information is fact and which is opinion.

F _____

_____

b. Is sentence 5 fact, opinion, or a combination of fact and opinion? If
it includes both, list which information is fact and which is opinion.

O _____

_____

TIPS FOR PREPARING FOR AND TAKING STANDARDIZED READING TESTS

Although many of these ideas may help you prepare for and take any type of test, they are specifically for standardized reading tests for which you cannot study specific content.

BEFORE THE TEST

Familiarize Yourself with the Test

Know how long it is and what kind of questions it contains. For example, a typical state standardized reading test consists of six to eight reading selections of 300 to 750 words each. The selections represent a variety of subject areas and are similar to material you are likely to read in college. After each selection, you answer five to six multiple-choice questions about the selection.

Each multiple-choice question consists of two parts:

1. The Stem—the statement or question. These test your ability to do things like (a) determine the meaning of words and phrases, (b) understand the main idea and supporting details, (c) identify an author's purpose and point of view, (d) analyze the relationships among ideas, (e) use critical reasoning skills to evaluate information, (f) organize and summarize information, and (g) interpret graphic information.
2. The Choices—also known as alternatives. From three or four possible answers, you select the option that best completes the thought expressed in the stem or answers the question posed in the stem. You may refer back to the selection to answer the questions.

Practice What You Will Be Doing on the Test

The single most effective way to prepare for any test is to practice what you will do on the test. Get sample test questions or a copy of a practice test from the testing center or on the Web. For example, the Texas Academic Skills Program (TASP) Web site at *http://www.tasp.nesinc.com/index.htm* includes a TASP Practice Test with typical readings and questions.

Be Prepared to Take the Test

Get adequate rest the night before the test. Eat and exercise on your regular schedule. Have all the supplies you need, such as pencils, erasers, and a watch, with you. Arrive at the test room early. Select a seat that has good lighting and where your view of students leaving the room is minimized. Be calm and alert. Plan to do well.

Listen to and Read All Directions Carefully Before Starting the Test

Know what you need to do, how to mark your answer sheet, and how long you have to complete the test. Calculate how much time you can allow for each selection and budget your time to allow yourself to complete all the selections.

Know How the Test Is Scored

If there is no penalty for guessing, answer every question. If, however, you are penalized for wrong answers, blind guessing will probably hurt your score.

DURING THE TEST

Read a Selection Before You Attempt to Answer the Questions

Although this point gets a lot of debate, I suggest you first read the passage to determine the main idea. Then, read and answer the questions, referring back to the passage as needed for specific details. Remember, however, that the order of information requested in the questions does not necessarily correspond to the order of information in the reading selection.

Read the Question and Answer It in Your Mind; Then Look for the Matching Answer

- Read the question—the stem.
- Think about a phrase that would answer the question.
- Compare each choice—alternative—to your answer.

By thinking of the answer first, you are less likely to be fooled by a wrong answer.

Look at All the Answers Before You Mark an Answer

It is important to read all the alternatives before you select one. Do not just take the first answer you think is correct.

Watch for Words Such as *always, never, every, absolutely,* and *only*

These absolute-type words make statements apply to everything all of the time, not just 99 percent of the time. Statements that use words like these are often incorrect because there are very few statements that have no exceptions (but there are a few).

Watch for Words Such as *sometimes, often, seldom, may,* and *generally*

Unlike the absolute words that make a statement true 100 percent of the time, qualifying words like these are so vague they often make an answer difficult to disprove. This means they may be included in a statement that is correct.

If the Question Is Difficult, Try to Make It Less Complex

Try the following tactics:

- Underline the subject and verb to focus your attention.
- Mark key words. To help find the key words, ask yourself what? who? where? when? and how?
- Restate the question in your own words, but be sure you don't change the meaning of the question.

Do Not Spend Too Much Time on Any One Question

Every minute counts. If you do not know the answer, make a guess, circle the question number, and go on to the next question. When you finish all the questions you do know, go back to your circled questions.

Mark Your Answer Sheet Carefully and Neatly

Make sure the number you are marking on your answer sheet corresponds to the number of the question you are answering. If you skip a question, be sure to leave the space for that question blank. Carefully fill in the entire answer space and completely erase any changes.

When You Don't Know the Answer, Make an Educated Guess

If there is no penalty for guessing, never leave an answer blank. Use strategies like these to help you analyze the answer choices and select the correct alternative.

- *Cross out any of the answers you know are wrong.* By carefully eliminating answers you know must be wrong, you can increase your chances of guessing correctly.
- *Look for the most general alternatives.* Since the most general alternative includes the most information, it is often the correct answer.
- *See if two alternatives mean the same.* If two alternatives mean the same thing, and there is only one correct answer, eliminate both of them. Neither will be correct. Make your choice from those remaining.
- *See if two alternatives are similar, but different.* If two alternatives mean almost the same thing, one of them will often be correct. Look for the word or concept that makes them different and determine which one is correct.

- *See if two alternatives state the opposite of each other.* The correct alternative is probably one of a pair of direct opposites. If you notice that two alternatives have opposite meanings, one of them is probably correct.

- *Check for singular and plural words in the stem.* If the stem uses the word *is*, then the correct alternative will most likely be a singular word. If the stem has the word *are*, look for an alternative with a plural, or a word that means more than one object.

Do Not Keep Changing Your Answer

Although this point also generates debate, I suggest that unless you have a serious reason to change, your first impression is likely to be the right one.

After You Finish the Test Go Back to Any Questions You Circled

When you reread a question you were unsure of, spend a moment thinking of the answer before you read any of the alternatives. If the answer does not come to mind, and none of the alternatives jog your memory, and there is no penalty for a wrong answer, use one of the strategies listed above and make an educated guess.

Use the Allotted Time

Unless you are sure you have answered every question correctly, never leave a test early.

Sample Reading

ADVICE TO BEGINNING WRITERS

Robert L. McGrath

[1]Countless successful writers—and some not so accomplished—have tried to unlock the secret of their triumphs to share it with others. Obviously, there is no patented method to achieve success. What works for one person may be a washout for others. But here's a method that works for me, and perhaps it will be helpful to you. I call it SWAP—a four-part approach to achievement in your writing efforts.

[2]S—Studying. Writing requires a lifetime of study. Your study may be concentrated at local colleges that offer writing courses at various levels, along with occasional seminars and local writers' groups. Or it may involve reading all the books about creative writing you can find. Constant review of magazines such as *Byline, Writer's Digest, The Writer,* and others will contribute immeasurably to your study program. Read the type of

material you aspire to write. Saturate yourself with it. Have at hand several basic tools: a good dictionary, a thesaurus, a market list, books on technique covering the categories you hope to sell. Use them!

[3]W—Writing. This, of course, is the only way to succeed. A writer must write; otherwise, he or she is not a writer and cannot lay claim to the appellation. Study courses, either in classroom situations or by correspondence, can be helpful, combining study with actual writing by requiring a certain amount of discipline—otherwise often elusive. I like an additional formula: SOP-2-SOC—seat of pants to seat of chair. So Hemingway stood at the mantel to write . . . do it your way, but do it. Pen, pencil, typewriter, word processor—they're all good tools. Use them! Form the habit of writing, every day if possible. Time and place do not matter. Just do it!

[4]A—Ambition. Set realistic goals for yourself. Be practical. Your first effort probably won't be the Great American Novel. But an expressive poem just might find print in an obscure journal and set you on your way. Or you might be a winner in one or more of the many *Byline* contests. You'll need a certain amount of self-confidence, for without it, you'll never reach those goals. Know that you have the native ability to put words on paper—words that will be worthwhile not only to you, but to others as well. Another formula comes to mind: SYI—scratch your itch. You have that urge to write. So write . . . write . . . write.

[5]P—Perseverance. Never give up on something you believe in. You can succeed, but only if you refuse to toss in the towel. My files contain irrefutable proof of the value of hanging in there. My short story, "Payment Received," won tenth place in the 1955 *Writer's Digest* contest. I figured it had to be a worthy piece. But on thirty-nine trips to various editors, it failed to make the grade. The fortieth submission was to a magazine that previously had rejected it. I goofed; otherwise, I probably wouldn't have resubmitted it to *Alfred Hitchcock's Mystery Magazine*. It was later published in a hardcover collection of Hitchcock yarns and reprinted in two separate paperback editions of the same anthology. It was read over a South African radio station (for which I was paid). It was the subject of a *Writer's Digest* experience report. Perseverance caused its sale. Other stories have parallel records. One sold to prestigious *Stories* magazine on its fifty-fifth trip out. The record for me is a sale on the eightieth trip to an editor's desk. Believe in yourself—persevere!

[6]Try the SWAP plan. Results aren't guaranteed, but it's worth a try.

Sample Reading Questions

1. Which of the following best expresses the main idea of the selection?

    a. No one really knows the keys to being a successful writer.

    (b.) Although it's not guaranteed, study, practice, self-confidence, and perseverance can help you become a successful writer.

    c. All successful writers write something every day.

    d. SWAP is a four-part approach that guarantees writing success.

2. The writer's main purpose in writing this selection is to do the following:

    a. Outline the steps you should use when writing an essay.

    b. Describe the writing process.

    (**c.**) Provide advice to writers who want to sell their work.

    d. Explain the differences between writing for pleasure and writing for publication.

3. In paragraph 5 the author writes, "You can succeed, but only if you refuse to toss in the towel." In this context, what does the author mean by <u>you refuse to toss in the towel</u>?

    (**a.**) You won't give up.

    b. You reject the idea of rewriting.

    c. You decline to listen to critics.

    d. You won't stop to do the laundry.

4. Which of the following sets of topics best organizes the information in the selection?

    a. **Advice**

        Study

        Write

        Never give up

    b. **Tips for Success**

        Read what you want to write

        Write every day

        Set realistic goals

        Believe in yourself

    (**c.**) **SWAP**

        Studying

        Writing

        Ambition

        Perseverance

5. In describing the story that sold on the eightieth trip to an editor's desk, the author wanted to illustrate which of the following ideas?

    (**a.**) A writer should never give up.

    b. Editors can never make up their mind.

    c. Some stories never sell.

    d. A good story always sells on the first try.

6. Which of the following best defines the word <u>appellation</u> as it is used in paragraph 3?

    a. money

    b. reward

    c. discipline

    (**d.**) title

7. Which of the following is a valid conclusion based on the information in paragraph 5?

   (a.) The author has sold more than one piece of writing.
   b. The author only writes mystery stories.
   c. The author has never sold any of his writings.
   d. The author has been writing for about ten years.

8. Which of the following statements from the selection is presented as a fact rather than an opinion?

   a. Writing requires a lifetime of study.
   b. Form the habit of writing, every day if possible.
   c. Your first effort probably won't be the Great American Novel.
   (d.) My files contain irrefutable proof of the value of hanging in there.

9. Which of the following is the best assessment of this writer's credibility?

   a. The author's enthusiasm for writing raises a serious question about his credibility.
   b. The considerable amount of factual detail the author presents inspires faith in his credibility.
   (c.) Because the writer is offering suggestions based on his own experience, his credibility is good.
   d. Although the selection provides useful information about writing, the writer's credibility is weakened by his failure to say how much he gets paid for his work.

USING TEXTBOOK DESIGN CLUES

The various styles of type and design used in a textbook aren't just decorations to make it visually appealing. These devices are selected to give the reader clues about the relative importance of the ideas. Using these clues can help you accurately and efficiently gather information.

TITLES AND HEADINGS

Although every textbook has its own way of displaying information, within a text there is a consistent visual pattern. This means you can use the size, style and placement of the titles and headings to identify different levels of information. Typical techniques include:

- *using different type fonts*—such as using a sans serif type font for one level of heading and a serif type font for another level;
- *varying the sizes of type*—such as using a large type size for the most important or broadest idea (such as the chapter title) and using smaller type sizes as headings become more specific;
- *using different type styles*—such as color, bold, italic, all capital letters, and underlining;
- *varying the amount of indentation from the margin*—such as putting the title of a chapter close to the left margin and using more indentation (white space) from the left margin as a heading becomes more specific, similar to an outlining technique.

Analyze the levels of headings in this example from *Government by the People* by Burns, Peltason, Cronin, Magleby, O'Brien, and Light. What is the organization scheme in your textbooks?

WHAT PARTIES DO FOR DEMOCRACY
Party Functions

Political parties are organizations that seek political power by electing people to office so that their positions and philosophy become public policy. American political parties serve a variety of political and social functions, some obvious and some not so obvious. They perform some functions well and others not so well, and how they perform them differs from place to place and time to time.

Organize the Competition   One of the most important functions of parties is to organize the competition by designating candidates to run under their label. For some races, parties recruit and nominate candidates for office; they register and activate voters; and they help candidates by training them, raising money for them, providing them with research and voter lists, and enlisting volunteers to work for them. For more visible contests, especially ones where there is a real chance of winning, multiple candidates often compete with each other for the nomination, often without party efforts to recruit them. Recently, campaign consultants rather than party officials have taken over some of these responsibilities; we explore this topic at some length in Chapter 10.[5]

Body Text

Authors use different type styles within paragraphs to direct you to important words and ideas. And, although putting words in boldface or italic type or underlining them are the most common styles used for emphasis, authors can use a vast array of clues. So again, your job is to analyze each of your textbooks, discover the patterns, and use those clues to help you understand the information you need.

Consider how Macionis's use of bold and italic type point out important terms and their definitions in this example from *Sociology*, ninth edition.

> Once measurements are made, investigators can pursue the real payoff: seeing how variables are related. The scientific ideal is **cause and effect,** *a relationship in which change in one variable causes change in another*. Cause-and-effect relationships occur around us every day, as when studying for an exam results in a high grade. *The variable that causes the change* (in this case, studying) is called the **independent variable.** *The variable that changes* (the exam grade) is called the **dependent variable.** In other words, the value of one variable depends on the value of another. Why is linking variables in terms of cause and effect important? Because this kind of relationship allows us to *predict* how one pattern of behavior will produce another.

White Space

White space on a page isn't accidental. White space is built into the design for a purpose such as directing the reader's eye to information or providing a rest stop. For example, authors can use white space to help a reader identify a new paragraph by indenting the first line of a paragraph or by leaving extra space between each paragraph.

Analyze how the authors of your texts use white space.

Graphic Elements

Authors can also use a variety of graphic elements such as boxes, bullets, and color-tinted boxes as cues to a specific kind or level of information. Often, they combine several design elements to more clearly communicate their message. See how Griffin and Ebert combine white space, color bullets, and italic type to cue important information in this example from *Business*, eleventh edition.

> The first step in developing the structure of any business, large or small, involves two activities:
>
> ■ *Specialization:* determining who will do what
> ■ *Departmentalization:* determining how people performing certain tasks can best be grouped together
>
> These two activities are the building blocks of all business organizations.[3]

OTHER FACTORS

Line length: Long lines of type are difficult to follow and may cause you to lose your place in the text. Although you cannot physically change the length of the lines of type in the books you read, you can reduce problems. To keep your place and encourage your eyes to move ahead, try sliding an index card over the line you have just finished.

Capital letters: Most people read by the shapes of words, not letter by letter. We use ascenders (the portions of letters that extend above a line of print in letters like b, d, t, and h) and descenders (the portions of letters that extend below a line of print in letters like y, p, g, and j) to help us quickly identify the shape of a word. Text printed in all capital letters—with no ascenders or descenders—forms uniform blockish shapes that make word identification difficult. You need to slow down when you have to read text in all capitals.

antonym   A word that means the opposite of another word.

appendix   A special section located toward the end of a book that contains supplemental information. The plural of *appendix* is *appendices*.

compare; comparison   Tell how two or more objects, places, events, people, or ideas are alike.

context   How words are used with other words in a sentence and surrounding sentences.

context clue   Information an author provides within the sentence or paragraph to help the reader understand important words.

contrast   Tell how two or more objects, places, events, people, or ideas are different.

controlling thought   What the author wants the reader to know or understand about the topic; the most important point the author makes about that topic.

directly stated main idea   The topic and controlling thought of a paragraph stated in a sentence; often called a topic sentence.

fact   An objective statement that can be proved true or false; when proven to be true, facts are reliable support for main ideas and good sources of information.

general   Broad, comprehensive, including everything.

glossary   An in-book dictionary that contains the meanings of important words used in the book.

implied main idea   When the author doesn't directly state the main idea and leaves it up to the reader to piece together the information from all the sentences and infer, or put together, the main idea.

imply   To express indirectly (an author implies; a reader infers).

infer   To reach a logical conclusion based on given information.

inference   A reasoned conclusion based on given information.

index   An alphabetical list of the topics covered in a book and their page numbers, located at the end of a book.

irrelevant information   Information that is interesting, and sometimes important, but does not support or develop the main idea in a paragraph.

main idea   The umbrella idea that unifies, or holds together, all the sentences of one paragraph; the primary thought the writer wants you to understand in a paragraph.

major supporting detail   A specific piece of information that directly supports and explains the main idea.

minor supporting detail   A very specific piece of information that supports and explains a major detail.

multiparagraph selection   A group of related paragraphs—such as an essay or text chapter—each with a main idea that supports and explains one thesis, or overall main idea.

opinion   A subjective statement that expresses a person's thoughts, feelings, beliefs, and attitudes. An opinion is not right or wrong, or good or bad, however, depending on the amount and type of evidence the author considered before forming the opinion, it can be valid or invalid.

outline   A type of graphic organizer that uses differing amounts of indentation to create a picture of the relationships among the ideas.

paragraph   A group of sentences that fit together to support and explain one main idea.

paraphrase   Restate information in your own words.

planning strategies   Techniques such as setting a purpose, previewing, activating your prior knowledge, and estimating the difficulty level of the material to help you become an active reader and give you a head start on good comprehension.

preface   An introductory letter from the author located in the first few pages of some textbooks.

prefix   A word part added to the beginning of a root word to change its meaning.

preview   To survey, or examine, reading material in an orderly way *before* you begin to read.

prior knowledge   What you know about a topic before you begin reading about it.

purpose for reading   Specific reasons for reading based on what you need to know when you finish reading.

reasoned judgment   Thoughtful, coherent evaluations that informed individuals make from the available evidence.

root word   The basic part of a word.

sentence   The basic unit of writing authors use to express their ideas.

signal word   Words, phrases, or punctuation that point out a particular type of information or move you in a specific direction of thought; also called directional words or transitions.

specific   Limited, individual, narrow in scope.

strategy   A tool or technique a reader consciously selects in order to complete a task accurately and efficiently.

structural organizers   Parts of an article or essay like titles and subtitles that you read during preview to give you an overview of the content.

suffix   A word part added to the end of a root word to change its meaning or the way it can be used in a sentence.

synonym   A word that means the same, or nearly the same, as another word.

table of contents   Located in the first few pages of a textbook, it lists the titles, and often the subtitles, of the chapters and the page number on which they begin.

text structures   How an author develops and supports the thesis or main ideas; the structure he or she gives the information. Six common methods of organizational structure are examples, comparison and/or contrast, cause and effect, sequence or process, classification, and definition. Also called rhetorical pattern.

thesaurus   A book of words and their synonyms.

thesis   The primary idea of a multiparagraph selection that combines the main ideas of all the paragraphs; the frame that holds the paragraphs of the essay or chapter together.

topic   The who or what the author is writing about.

transition sentence   Connects what you have just read with what you are about to read.

transition word   See *signal word*.

word analysis   Defining a word by defining its root and any prefixes and/or suffixes.

INDEX

A

C

D

E

F

G

U

Umbrella idea. See Main idea
Unstated main idea. See Implied main idea

W

Word parts, using to define words, 20
Words:
 how to remember, 39
 importance of understanding, 14

CREDITS

Excerpts from TOC, Preface, Index, etc. by Leshin. Student Resource Guide.

Webster's New World Dictionary, 3rd College Ed.

"Your Role as a Nursing Assistant" by Wolgin from *Being A Nursing Assistant* © 1999.

"Facts About Anxiety Disorders" by National Institute of Mental Health.

"Getting Organized" by Tricia Alexander from *Adjustment and Human Relations* © 2000.

"Causes of Cultural Change" by John Macionis from *Sociology* 8/e.

"When X-Cold Strikes" by Robert L. McGrath from *Young Americans*.

"Healthy Aging: A Lifelong Process" Excerpt pp. 530–532 from ACCESS TO HEALTH, 5th ed. By Rebecca J. Donatelle and Lorraine G Davis. Copyright © 1998 by Allyn & Bacon. Reprinted by permission of Pearson Education, Inc.

"Infancy Through Childhood" by Pruitt, Crumpler, Prothrow-Stith from *Prentice Hall Health Skills for Wellness* © 2001.

"Change Your Bad Habits to Good" by Dr. Robert Epstein from Dr. Epstein © 1998.

"How to Write Clearly" by Edward Thompson from International Paper Company.

"Improving Your Nonverbal Skills" Business Communication Today, 7/e by Bovee, Thill & Schatzman, © 2003. Reprinted by permission of Pearson Education, Inc., Upper Saddle River, NJ.

"The New Frontier" by Clayton, Perry, Reed, & Winkler from *America: Pathways to the Present* © 2000.

"Attitude" by Charles R. Swindoll, source *Strengthening Your Grip* 1982.

"It is Time for An Attitude Adjustment" by Barbara K. Bruce and Denise Foley, source *USA Today* Magazine September, 1998.

"Why Aren't We Happier?" by Neil Rosenthal source *Boulder Camera* June 23, 2002.

"Cheers" by Lise Funderburg, source O, *The Oprah Magazine* Feb. 2002. Reprinted by permission Lise Funderburg.

"Hold On To Your Positive Attitude", Ch 3 by Chapman and O'Neil, source *Your Attitude is Showing* 10/e 2002.

"Little Engine Holds a Valuable Lesson", by Ana Vaciana-Suarez. Reprinted by permission.

"A Healthy Environment", by Pruitt, Crumpler & Prothrow-Stith, source *Prentice Hall HEALTH Skills for Wellness* 2001.

"With Every Breath You Take", by Kimi Eisele, source *OnEarth Winter*, 2003 Reprinted by permission.

"NASA Plant Study" by NASA and Zone 10 reprinted by permission.

"The Oil Was Everywhere" by Bruce Gray, source MSNBC. Reprinted by permission.

"Noise Pollution—It's Everywhere and it's Worse than You Think" © 2001 reprinted with permission of Advanced Brain Technologies, LLC. *www.advancedbrain.com*, infro@advancedbrain.com

"Are You Big Foot?" by Kim Todd, source *Sierra Magazine* Jan/Feb 2003 Reprinted by permission.

"Butterflies In Formation" by Edwin Powell, source *OfficeSolutions* July-Aug. 2002 Reprinted by permission.

"Making a Winning Presentation or How to Think Like A Listener" by John R. Graham, source *American Salesman* Oct. 2001. Reprinted by permission of © National Research Bureau, 320 Valley Street, Burlington, Iowa 52601.

"Deliver Your Message with Effective Oral Presentations" *Business Communications* by Bienvenu & Timm, © 2002. Reprinted by permission of Pearson Education, Inc., Upper Saddle River, NJ.

"What You Can Say Without Speaking" by Kare Anderson © 2001 by JPM, The *Journal of Property Management*, published by the Institute of Real Estate Management. Reprinted with permission.

"VivaVoice", by Lisa Murphy, source *Chatelaine* June 2002.

Notes for Instructors

SYLLABUS SUGGESTION

As class size and student interests, maturity, and skill levels vary, so does the amount of time we spend on a particular chapter or theme. However, this is my typical approach for a sixteen-week semester: eight to ten weeks working through the six instructional chapters; about three weeks working on Theme 1; the last few weeks of the semester students select either Theme 2 or Theme 3 and work in smaller groups. I set some assignments and deadlines, and allow some flexibility for individual and group activities.

GENERAL PRINCIPLES TO GUIDE INSTRUCTION

This excerpt from the article "A Teacher's Dozen—Fourteen General, Research-Based Principles for Improving Higher Learning in Our Classrooms" by Thomas Anthony Angelo (AAHE Bulletin, April 1993) concisely presents many of the principles that guide my work with students. Dr. Angelo is senior vice president and provost at the University of Akron.

Before I share my current teacher's dozen, a final caveat is in order. Given the range of human variation, there are bound to be exceptions to nearly every generalization about learning. It's up to individual faculty members to determine which principles apply to whom, when, where, and how.

That said, for each of the fourteen principles listed below, I offer a very brief explanation and then suggest one or two implications for or applications to teaching and classroom assessment. These general implications and applications are meant merely as "pump-primers," to stimulate you to come up with more specific, appropriate ones.

1. Active learning is more effective than passive learning.

What I hear, I forget, what I see, I remember; what I do, I understand.

—Chinese proverb

Let the main object of this, our Didactic, be as follows: To seek and find a method by which teachers may teach less, but learners learn more.

—John Amos Comenius

As these quotations suggest, teachers have long known what researchers have only recently confirmed about the value of active learning: students do learn more and better by becoming actively involved. But activity in and of itself doesn't result in higher learning. Active learning occurs when students invest physical and mental energies in activities that help them make what they are learning meaningful and when they are aware of that meaning-making. As George Stoddard put it, "We learn to do neither by thinking nor by doing; we learn to do by thinking about what we are doing."

Implications/Applications.

Having students teach or explain something to others that they have just learned helps them learn it much more effectively, especially if they actively rehearse that "lesson" ahead of time and get feedback. To assess actively, ask students to paraphrase a central concept in a couple of sentences for one specific audience, and then to paraphrase the same explanation for a completely different audience. The two audiences might be parents and children, professionals and laypeople, novices and experts. Assess these directed paraphrases for both accuracy and appropriateness.

2. Learning requires focused attention and awareness of the importance of what is to be learned.

The true art of memory is the art of attention.

—Samuel Johnson

One of the most difficult tasks for novice learners in a field, whatever their age, is to figure out what to pay attention to and what to ignore. Students in introductory courses often cannot tell what is central from what is peripheral, foreground from background, superordinate from subordinate. Novices find these distinctions elusive, usually not because they lack intelligence but because they lack the experience needed to evaluate the data they encounter.

If you've ever found yourself lost and alone in a busy city in a country whose language, culture, and street signs are totally unintelligible (some of you are thinking Boston; others, New York), then you can imagine how many students feel when they encounter a "foreign" discipline for the first time in college.

Implications/Applications.

You can help novices by pointing out some of the major landmarks, by writing a list of the five key points in your lecture on the board before class, for example. You also can assess how well they are learning to read the "maps" that lectures or readings provide. Using a "minute paper" to find out what students thought were the most important points in a lecture or reading, and what questions they still have, can provide useful information on where they are getting lost and clues for getting back on track.

3. Learning is more effective and efficient when learners have explicit, reasonable, positive goals, and when their goals fit well with the teacher's goals.

> *If you don't know where you are going, you will probably end up somewhere else.*
>
> —Laurence J. Petei and Raymond Hul

When learners know what their educational goals are and figure out how they can best achieve them, they usually become much more efficient and effective. Adult learners often fit this bill. When learners know how—and how well—their goals fit the instructor's, they tend to learn more and get better grades.

Implications/Applications.

Early in the term, ask students to write down a few specific learning goals they hope to achieve through your course. Then involve them in comparing their learning goals with those of other students and with your teaching goals. Look for and build on areas of congruence, but don't gloss over potential conflicts or disconnects. Refer back to and assess progress toward shared goals throughout the semester.

4. To be remembered, new information must be meaningfully connected to prior knowledge, and it must be remembered in order to be learned.

> *Thinking means connecting things, and stops if they cannot be connected.*
>
> —G. K. Chesterton

The more meaningful and appropriate connections students make between what they know and what they are learning, the more permanently they will anchor new information in long-term memory and the easier it will be for them to access that information when it's needed.

Implications/Applications.

Provide many and varied examples, descriptions, drawings, images, metaphors, and analogies. But ask students to provide them as well, then give the students feedback on their usefulness and appropriateness. For instance, two simple ways to help students make connections, and to assess the connections they are making, are to ask them to compose a metaphor ("Learning is _____") or to complete an analogy ("Teaching is to learning as _____ is to _____").

5. Unlearning what is already known is often more difficult than learning new information.

It is what we think we know already that often prevents us from learning.

—Claude Bernard

Habits, preconceptions, and misconceptions can be formidable barriers to new learning, all the more treacherous because, like icebergs, this prior learning is usually 90 percent hidden from view. Before we can help students unlearn or correct prior learning, we need to know something about what is below the surface.

Implications/Applications.

Before you present new material, find out what students already believe and know, and what they can do about it. A quick diagnostic "probe," containing a few questions, often can help you locate dangerous "icebergs." By asking a few diagnostic questions, you might also find out that the shipping lanes are clear and that your students are more experienced navigators than you had assumed. Whatever you discover, it will help you and the students find more appropriate starting points for your work.

6. Information organized in personally meaningful ways is more likely to be retained, learned, and used.

Much goes on in the mind of the learner. Students interpret. They over-interpret. They actively struggle to impose meaning and structure upon new material being presented.

—Donald A. Norman

Humans are extraordinary pattern seekers. We seek regularity and meaning constantly, and we create them when they are not apparent. Witness our penchant for seeing dragons in clouds, for example. To be most useful, the ways learners organize knowledge in a given domain need to become ever more similar to the ways experts in that field organize knowledge. This requires making what is usually implicit, explicit.

Implications/Applications.

Show students a number of different, useful, and acceptable ways to organize the same information. Use prose, outlines, graphs, drawings, and models. Assess students' organizing schemas and skills by getting them to show you their "mental models" in a similar variety of ways.

7. Learners need feedback on their learning, early and often, to learn well; to become independent, they need to learn how to give themselves feedback.

Supposing is good but finding out is better.

—Mark Twain

Regular feedback helps learners efficiently direct their attention and energies, helps them avoid major errors and dead ends, and keeps them from learning things they later will have to unlearn at great cost. It also can serve as a motivating form of interaction between teacher and learner, and among learners. When students learn to internalize the voice of the "coach," they can begin to give themselves corrective feedback.

Implications/Applications.

Don't assume that students understand: ask. Try asking them to jot down what the "muddiest point" was in a particular reading, lab, or lecture, then respond to the most common muddy points in your next class. Find out what students are doing with the feedback you're already giving them. Do they read and use the comments you write on papers and exams? If so, how? If not, why not? Explicitly demonstrate how you get feedback on your work and what you do with it.

8. The ways in which learners are assessed and evaluated powerfully affect the ways they study and learn.

Let the tutor demand an account not only of the words of his lesson, but of their meaning and substance. . . . Let [the learner] show what he has just learned from a hundred points of view, and adapt it to as many different subjects, to see if he has rightly taken it in and made it his own.

—Michel de Montaign

Whether faculty "teach to the test" or not, most students try to "study to the test." For generations uncounted, students have annoyed their teachers with the question, "Will this be on the final?" One reason they persist is that most genuinely want to get good grades. But a second reason is that knowing what will be on the final, or on any upcoming test or quiz, helps students figure out where to focus their attention. In other words, they are looking for a roadmap. One way to improve learning, then, is to make sure our test questions require the kind of thinking and learning we wish to promote, and that students know—at least generally—what those questions will be.

Implications/Applications.

Once you're sure your questions are testing what you want students to learn, give them a sample exam or a list of study questions from which the exam questions will be selected. Give students regular opportunities to practice answering similar questions and to get feedback on their answers. If students work in study groups, that corrective feedback often can come from their peers.

9. Mastering a skill or body of knowledge takes great amounts of time and effort.

There are some things that cannot be learned quickly, and time, which is all we have, must be paid heavily for their acquiring.

—Ernest Hemingway

In a study of talented young adults who had achieved high levels of mastery in a variety of fields, Benjamin Bloom and his colleagues found that none had achieved mastery in less than a dozen years, and the average time to mastery was sixteen years at between twenty-five and fifty hours per week of practice and study. This means that at least 15,000 to 30,000 hours of time and intense practice were required to reach the highest levels of mastery. If we halve those figures to "guesstimate" the time needed to achieve an acceptable mastery level, we're still left with about 7,000 to 15,000 hours of preparation—the equivalent of forty-hour weeks, fifty weeks a year, for three-and-a-half to seven years.

Implications/Applications.

Unplug all the TVs. Seriously, though, students need to know how long it actually takes to attain mastery in their field. Then they need to find out how much time they actually are devoting to that task. Give students a simple form on which they can log all the times they study/practice for a week and indicate how productively they used each block of time. Discussing their findings with other students in a nonjudgmental way can help them become aware of and gain control over their time use.

10. Learning to transfer, to apply previous knowledge and skills to new contexts, requires a great deal of practice.

Research on learning to transfer generally is depressing. Most learning is highly context-bound, and few students become skilled at applying what they've learned in one context to another similar context. In fact, many students cannot recognize things they've already learned if the context is shifted at all. This is one of the reasons why students will point at questions that are only slightly altered versions of homework questions and protest, "We've never done problems like these before!" Those students who are being honest simply cannot see the similarities. They learned to solve problems involving giraffes, motorcycles, and Cincinnati; they never had to solve problems about wildebeest, cars, or Dayton.

Implications/Applications.

If you value transfer, teach transfer. Direct students' attention continually between the general and the specific. Give them many different examples of the same concepts or principles, and make sure they see where the similarities and the differences are. Challenge students to identify and then to create similar but different examples or problems.

11. High expectations encourage high achievement.

For some time now, we've known that younger students tend to achieve more by working with teachers who expect more of them. For the so-called Pygmalion effect to work well in college, however, the students must share the teacher's high expectations of themselves and perceive them as reasonable.

Implications/Applications.

Begin by finding out what your students expect of themselves in your class, letting them know what you expect, and discussing those expectations. Begin the course with assignments that diligent students can succeed in to build confidence. Have learners interview successful former students, or invite them to class, to illustrate in flesh and blood that high expectations can be realized.

12. To be most effective, teachers need to balance levels of intellectual challenge and instructional support.

In discussing the ways in which mothers help children acquire language by constantly adjusting their speech to stay slightly ahead of the child's, Jerome Bruner writes of "scaffolding." Scaffolding is a useful metaphor for college learning, as well. The weaker or smaller the student's foundation (preparation) in the subject, the stronger and larger the instructional scaffolding (structure and support) that is required. This is one of the many reasons that teaching a first-year course requires a different approach than teaching a third-year course in the same discipline. Students in the third year generally require less structure and direction, and benefit from more autonomy and responsibility. This also helps explain why students of lower ability or much weaker preparation often benefit from and appreciate highly structured courses. They need the scaffolding.

Implications/Applications.

Even when learner ability or preparation or both are weak, expectations should remain high. To reach those expectations, less-prepared students will need more explicit instructional scaffolding, such as tutoring, highly structured directions, and more personal contact with the instructor. Students who are better prepared or able can be encouraged to master their learning by serving as tutors, helping to create scaffolding for others, and to take more responsibility for their own learning through independent studies and special projects.

13. Motivation to learn is alterable; it can be positively or negatively affected by the task, the environment, the teacher, and the learner.

Though we tend to talk about students as being either motivated or not motivated, most of our students are very motivated to learn certain things and not at all motivated to learn others. Research suggests that you stand a good chance of increasing motivation to learn if you can positively influence your students' beliefs and expectations about one or more of the following: Students are likely to be more motivated to learn in your class if they see the value of what you're teaching; believe that learning it will help them achieve other important goals; believe that they are capable of learning it; and expect that they will succeed.

Implications/Applications.

Give students lots of specific examples of the value and usefulness of what they're learning and help them make connections between short-term course goals and their own long-term goals. Use simple, anonymous surveys to gauge students' expectations, beliefs, and self-confidence levels, then respond to that information with specific examples, suggestions, and, whenever possible, realistic encouragement.

14. Interaction between teachers and learners is one of the most powerful factors in promoting learning; interaction among learners is another.

As with activity, it isn't interaction in and of itself that promotes academic learning, it's structured interaction focused on achieving meaningful, shared learning tasks. As the professional world never tires of pointing out, our students need to learn to work more effectively in teams.

Implications/Applications.

Most students have to believe teachers know and care about them before they can benefit from interactions—or even interact. Learn students' names as a first step, then try to engage them in working with you to learn. Classroom assessment and classroom research projects can engage students and teachers in working together to solve meaningful problems, such as finding ways to ensure that *everyone* in class has a fair chance to master the course content. If you want students to cooperate effectively with other students, first, challenge them with assignments that groups can carry out more effectively than individuals can; second, provide guidelines and guidance for group work, especially for those who haven't had experience; and, third, de-emphasize competition among individuals for grades and approval. Meaningful and positive interactions require mutual trust.

Final Notes

Nothing is so useless as a general maxim.

—Lord Macaulay

Psychology is a science; teaching is an art, and sciences never generate arts directly out of themselves. An intermediary, inventive mind must make the application, by use of its originality.

—William James

I argued at the outset that mastery of an academic discipline is not sufficient for effective college teaching. But even disciplinary mastery complemented by familiarity with research on college learning is not sufficient. Truly effective teachers know their subjects, know something about the research that informs teaching, and also know how to adapt and apply relevant research findings to their own classrooms. Lord Macaulay was partially correct: Nothing is so useless as a general maxim that isn't properly applied to the particular. Like James, I'm convinced that we need inventive, original minds to make the applications of these or any other general principles of teaching. I'm also confident we have such intermediary, inventive teachers in abundance among our faculty.

IDEAS AND ACTIVITIES FOR INSTRUCTION

I hope these ideas and activities will complement your repertoire of instructional strategies. Of course, the events of the day and the interests of you and your students will yield a plethora of additional possibilities.

General

I find these two ideas adapted from K. Patricia Cross, *Teaching and Learning in the Next Century*, useful many times each semester.

- *The Minute Paper.* At the end of class, ask students to answer these two questions: (1) What is the most important thing you learned in class today? (2) What is the main, unanswered question you leave class with today?
- *Diagnostic Learning Log.* At the beginning of class, before you collect the homework, ask students to assess their learning process by answering these four questions about their homework assignment: (1) Briefly describe the assignment you just completed. What do you think was the purpose of this assignment? (2) Give an example of a question for

which you had a great answer. Why do you think you were so successful on that question/type of question? (3) Give an example of a question
that you had trouble answering. Why do you think this question/type of
question gave you trouble? (4) What is one thing you can do differently—one new strategy you can use—on your next assignment to be
more successful?

Chapter 1: Previewing Textbooks

■ Divide students into work groups. Give each group the unconnected
pieces of a jigsaw puzzle. Do not show students the box or give any
clues about the completed puzzles. Give five minutes to work on the
puzzle. Then, hand out the box tops that show the completed puzzle.
Give them five additional minutes to work on the puzzle. Discuss why
and how it's easier to complete a puzzle, or most any task, when you
have context and perspective. Segue into previewing texts.

■ Have students bring in their texts from other classes and/or borrow an
assortment of texts from the learning center. Working in small groups,
have students identify the features of each text. Compare and contrast
the various features across texts.

■ Stage a role play: "passive and active behavior." Ask students to demonstrate passive behavior such as a basketball player who stands around
and won't go after balls and a person watching television. Then ask
them to show active behaviors. Discuss the differences and the expected results of the behaviors. Discuss passive and active readers.

Chapter 2: Understanding Vocabulary

■ Compile a selection of paragraphs from various sources with words
that have one meaning in general usage and a different or more specialized meaning in the paragraph's context. Mark the words. As a class or
in smaller work groups, have students list the various definitions and
the contexts in which each is appropriate.

■ Group students by common academic interest: pre-nursing, automotive
technology, biology, and so on. Have each group develop a list of the
twenty-five words every student in this field should know. Encourage
students to work with knowledgeable resources, such as instructors in
that area or second-year students.

■ Develop a list of words that have interesting origins. Ask each student
to select a word from the list and trace its origin. Suggest traditional
library resources as well as Web resources such as *<http://www
.allwords.com>*. For example, it is believed that the word *book* goes
back to the early eighth-century Old English *boc*, which meant a writing tablet or document. Some scholars believe *boc* was derived from
the nearly identical Old English words for beech, *boc* or *bece*, supposing that early writings were carved into beechwood tablets.
Current spelling of the noun form dates from 1375; the verb form
dates from about 1380.

WEB Extra

Have students complete a puzzle from one of these crossword puzzle sites:

> Crossword Central at *<http://www.thinks.com/crosswords>*
>
> Crosswordsite at *<http://www.crosswordsite.com>*
>
> Ray Hamel's Crossword Puzzles at *<http://www.primate.wisc.edu/ people/hamel/cp.html>*

Chapter 3: Understanding Main Ideas

- Prepare a set of ten general sentences such as "Yesterday was a great day." Working as a class or in workgroups, ask students to rewrite each sentence to make it more specific, such as "Yesterday was sunny, and the temperature was perfect," or "I got an A on my math exam yesterday."

- Divide students into groups of three or four and number-off (numbered heads). Give each group a paragraph to read. Have students identify and write down the main idea independently. Then, give groups two minutes to discuss and reach consensus on the main idea. Call a number (1–4) and have that person report for the group. Repeat the process with more difficult paragraphs.

- Have a colleague give a presentation on plagiarism. Ask him or her to include why it's important to paraphrase and to show examples of how to paraphrase effectively.

WEB Extra

Have students (1) conduct a search and find an e-zine or online version of a print magazine that interests them, (2) read one or more short articles, (3) identify and print out one paragraph with a directly stated main idea, (4) underline the main idea, and (5) restate the main idea in their own words.

Chapter 4: Understanding Implied Main Ideas

- Ask two or three former students to present a brief skit that requires students to make inferences. The role play should demonstrate how easily we make inferences—valid and invalid—every day. After the skit, discuss ways to minimize making invalid inferences when we are reading, watching, and listening.

- Collect a selection of paragraphs, some with stated main ideas and some with implied main ideas. Photocopy or type each one onto a sheet of paper and onto a transparency (or into a computer presentation program you can project). Have students work in pairs on two or three paragraphs. Their task is to read the paragraphs and reach consensus on the main ideas. At the end of the time limit you have set, ask students to share their work as you project the paragraphs for the class to read.

- For additional instruction on how to make inferences, consider this slide show presentation from St. Cloud State University at *<http://alc .stcloudstate.edu/Presentations/120INFER/index.htm>*.

WEB Extra

Have students log on to one of these sites and complete an activity on making inferences.

- *<http://www.brocktonpublicschools.com/schools/high/english/inferences-characters.html>*

  This page, from Brockton Public Schools, provides a list of character traits and inferences that can be made about a character based on those traits.

- *<http://www.spjc.edu/webcentral/admit/Placement/reading.htm>*

  This page, from St. Petersburg College, explains what will be on a reading comprehension test. It then gives sample questions, some of which require making inferences.

- *<http://www.humanities-interactive.org/texas/wtw/wtw_student_la_inferences.htm>*

  This page, from Humanities-Interactive, requires students to make inferences after viewing a picture.

- *<http://www.sbcc.net/academic/esl/esl130/unit2main2.htm>*

  This page, from Santa Barbara City College, is from the ESL department, but works for first language students also. It provides a lesson on inferences, followed by a link to an online quiz.

Chapter 5: Identifying Supporting Details and Using Relationships among Ideas

- Work with freshman composition teachers to assemble a set of paragraphs with a clear main idea and a variety of major, minor, and irrelevant details to support it. Give student workgroups two paragraphs to read and then label the main idea and each detail. Project paragraphs as groups report their findings. As a class, discuss and reach consensus.

- Divide students into workgroups of six and have each member select one of the six common ways text authors organize information. Give students ten minutes to prepare a two- to three-minute explanation of the structure. Have students present their lessons to their groups.

- Ask students to bring a nonfiction library book to class. Ask them to briefly preview the book, then start reading the first chapter and continue reading until they reach the first signal word. Their assignment is to copy the sentence containing the word and explain what the word signals. Two primary purposes for this activity are to (1) get students into the library to select and check out a book, and (2) help students begin to see that what they are learning about reading doesn't apply just to textbooks.

WEB Extra

Have students log on to *<http://www.whitehouse.gov/history/firstladies/index.html>*, a site that contains biographies of all the First Ladies. Ask them to select a First Lady and read about her life. Have them print out her biography and mark the major details and the minor details.

Chapter 6: Reading Multiparagraph Selections

■ Want an unconventional way to open a discussion about the need to "set a purpose" when reading? Bring in several copies of a map—preferably of your city or state. Distribute the map and ask students to plan a trip using the most direct route. When they ask, "Where are we going?" respond that you don't know. As you can imagine, students quickly say that it's impossible to know the best way to get somewhere if you don't know where you're going. It doesn't take long for them to see the connection to setting a purpose for reading.

■ Remind students of the work they did in Chapter 1, "Previewing Textbooks." Review some of the advantages of knowing the big picture before you start with one of the pieces. Relate how the same previewing skills are useful for text chapters and articles. As an example, lead the class through a preview of Chapter 6, looking at titles, subtitles, and typographical clues such as sizes and styles of type.

■ Project an editorial from the college or local newspaper. As a group, identify the thesis and the main ideas. Then, give a general-interest article to smaller workgroups (all groups get the same article). Allow groups time to identify the thesis and main ideas and write them on poster paper. Have groups tape their findings to the walls. Discuss and work as a class to reach consensus.

WEB Extra

Have students log on to the index page for *USA Today* essays at <*http://www .usatoday.com/news/opinion/colindex.htm*> and read one essay by the columnist of their choice. Have students print out the essay and state the author's thesis.

Theme 1: It's All About Attitude

■ Read Alphonse Karr's quote that opens the theme. ("Some people are always grumbling because roses have thorns; I am thankful that thorns have roses.") Share a couple of additional "positive attitude" quotes, such as

Our greatest glory is not in never failing, but in rising up every time we fail.

—Ralph Waldo Emerson

If you can DREAM it, you can DO it.

—Walt Disney

Never let the fear of striking out get in your way.

—George Herman "Babe" Ruth

Have students find or create two additional attitude quotes to share with the class.

■ Before students tackle "'Little Engine' Holds a Valuable Life Lesson," read aloud Watty Piper's original *The Little Engine That Could*. In this classic children's story about the power of positive thinking, a little train carrying tons of toys to all the good boys and girls is confronted with a seemingly impassable mountain. The Shiny New Engine and the Big Strong Engine say "I cannot. I cannot." But, with the rallying mantra, "I think I can, I think I can," the Little Blue Engine overcomes insurmountable odds and pulls the train to the other side.

■ Have students conduct an experiment on the effects of smiles and frowns. On day 1, have them spend an hour walking around campus smiling and greeting everyone they meet. On day 2, they should be generally grumpy and frown at everyone for an hour. As a class, discuss how the different attitudes affected them and those they met.

WEB Extra

Have students log on to *<http://www.positiveinstitute.com/stories.html>*. The site usually has at least ten inspiring stories that students can choose from. Have them read one story and write the thesis (moral).

Theme 2: A Healthy Environment

■ Invite students and/or faculty involved in various college and community efforts to reduce pollution (recycling, bike to school and work, reducing pesticide use, etc.) to present information on how one person can make a difference.

■ Working individually or in small groups, have students write a letter to the editor of the campus or local newspaper encouraging people to take a particular action to create a healthier environment.

■ Drawing from current news stories, discuss how healthy our environment is. To be sure that a variety of views are discussed, you may need to assign students to research certain people, organizations, and viewpoints.

WEB Extra

Have students log on to a site that offers a broad range of information on Earth's environment, such as

> *<http://www.unep.org/>* (United Nations Environment Programme)
> *<http://www.epa.gov/>* (U.S. Environmental Protection Agency)
> *<http://www.NCSEonline.org/nle/index.cfm?&CFID=8638265&CFTOKEN=14364662>* (National Council for Science and the Environment's National Library for the Environment)

Have them select one aspect of the environment—water, air, ground, noise— and (1) compare the status of your local environment to another city in the world, or (2) describe how a clean-up measure used in another city could be replicated locally, or (3) give an example of a problem in another city that does not exist in your city and tell why you have escaped the problem, or (4) compile a list of problems and possible solutions.

Theme 3: Speaking with Confidence

- Arrange to take students (probably in groups of five or six) to a Toastmaster's meeting.

- Have students research and write the outline for a speech. Teach them (or have a colleague or computer lab assistant teach them) the basics of how to use a presentation software program such as PowerPoint to create visuals and handouts to support their speech.

- Show a video about nonverbal communication and discuss how our nonverbal language impacts our verbal language. (You might select one from the University of California video series on Nonverbal Communication produced by Dane Archer, a professor at the University of California at Santa Cruz [email: archer@cats.ucsc.edu]. Each video is about thirty minutes long and comes with a detailed instructor's guide. For example, the video *A World of Gestures: Culture and Nonverbal Communication* focuses on international differences in gestures and cultural differences in nonverbal communication generally. It examines angry gestures, obscene gestures, friendly gestures, warning gestures, the development of gestures in children, gang gestures, secret gestures, and embarrassing gestures. Throughout, the emphasis is on how this powerful form of nonverbal communication varies across cultural and national boundaries. For a full listing of the series, log on to *<http://nonverbal.ucsc.edu>*.)

WEB Extra

Have students log on to *<http://www.public-speaking.org/>*. The site is maintained by the Advanced Public Speaking Institute and offers about fifty concise articles on every aspect of public speaking. Have students read one article of their choice and identify the author's thesis. Have them print out the essay with the thesis identified or e-mail the information to you.

READABILITY

Readability formulas were created in the 1920s for science teachers and became popular with other educators in the 1940s after the publication of Rudolph Flesch's bestselling book *Why Johnny Can't Read*. Today, readability formulas are used by a variety of groups—from state legislatures to insurance companies—to make sure their documents are easy to read.

In this context, easy to read means short words in short sentences in short paragraphs. Thus, readability formulas count and calculate the average of such elements as the number of syllables per word, words per sentence, and sentences per paragraph.

However, as critics of readability formulas point out, such calculations overvalue condensed prose and undervalue elements such as content, complexity of thought, and tone. For example, the enigmatic Emily Dickinson poem, "I heard a Fly buzz when I died," scores as "very easy" to read on the Flesch Reading Ease scale.

Even so, many instructors tell me they find readability numbers useful as one variable to consider in judging an article's difficulty. Therefore, the accompanying chart displays the approximate number of words and the

Flesch-Kincaid readability calculation for the text's essays and articles. In the literature, the Flesch-Kincaid is listed as scoring passages in the midrange of all formulas.

LOCATION	ARTICLE	AUTHOR	FL-K	WDS
Chap. 6	Facts About Anxiety Disorders	National Institute of Mental Health and National Institutes of Health	10.5	585
Chap. 6	Getting Organized	Tricia Alexander	9.5	640
Chap. 6	Causes of Cultural Change	John J. Macionis	11.5	181
Chap. 6	When X-Cold Strikes	Robert McGrath	6.2	329
Chap. 6	Healthy Aging: A Lifelong Process	Rebecca Donatelle and Lorraine Davis	12.1	1,488
Chap. 6	Change Your Bad Habits to Good	Robert Epstein	9.8	1,000
Chap. 6	How to Write Clearly	Edward T. Thompson	5.6	1,032
Chap. 6	Improving Your Nonverbal Communication Skills	Courtland Bovée, John Thill, and Barbara Schatzman	11.0	1,090
Theme 1	Attitudes	Charles Swindoll	6.1	162
Theme 1	Is It Time for an Attitude Adjustment?	Barbara K. Bruce and Denise Foley	7.5	1,600
Theme 1	Why Aren't We Happier?	Neil Rosenthal	7.2	1,015
Theme 1	How to be an Optimist	Lise Funderburg	9.8	1,415
Theme 1	'Little Engine' Holds a Valuable Life Lesson	Ana Veciana-Suarez	6.1	696
Theme 2	With Every Breath You Take	Kimi Eisele	9.2	2,000
Theme 2	NASA Study—Shows Common Plants Help Reduce Indoor Air Pollution	Zone 10	13.0	950
Theme 2	The Oil Was Everywhere	Bruce Gray	5.7	840
Theme 2	Noise Pollution: It's Everywhere— and It's Worse Than You Think	Dorothy Lockhart Lawrence	9.8	1,040
Theme 2	Are You Big Foot?	Kim Todd	7.7	2,100
Theme 3	Butterflies in Formation	Edwin Powell	10.4	1,280
Theme 3	Making a Winning Presentation,— or How to Think Like a Listener	John Graham	8.5	2,000
Theme 3	What You Can Say Without Speaking	Kare Anderson	9.1	1,240
Theme 3	Viva Voice	Lisa Murphy	7.9	1,640
App	Advice to Beginning Writers	Robert McGrath	6.4	580

Answer Key

CHAPTER 1

Exercise 3

2. List two ways the Internet is a valuable tool (any two of the following):

   - Finding the latest information on a subject for research papers.
   - Collecting data from others online.
   - Collaborating with others who share your research interests.
   - Crosscultural exchanges with Netizens worldwide.
   - Meeting and learning from subject matter experts on virtually any topic.
   - Access to resources such as dictionaries, encyclopedias, and library catalogs worldwide.
   - Access to literature such as the classics and novels.
   - Access to news publications and electronic journals with resources for researching their databases for past articles.
   - Access to databases of diverse information at universities and government agencies.
   - Learning about companies by visiting their Web sites.

CHAPTER 5

Exercise 5

3. **b.** (1) Colonial West was the forested region just beyond the settled Atlantic coastal plain. (2) For the generation preceding the Civil War, it was the land between the Mississippi and the Missouri. (3) The "Last West" of 1865 to 1910 was the broad expanse of territory stretching from the Missouri River to the Pacific Ocean.

5. b. (1) Direct economic losses were estimated to be $40 billion. (2) Over 70 percent of the United States had suffered some socioeconomic losses. (3) Widespread crop damage occurred. (4) Fires raged in parts of the Northwest. (5) Reservoirs in many areas were dry or critically low. (6) Barge traffic on the Mississippi, Missouri, and Ohio rivers was disrupted.

8. b. (1) the end of group creativity, (2) a need for individual creativity, (3) a personality conflict, (4) family pressures, (5) legal complications, and (6) financial necessity.

CHAPTER 6

Exercise 1

2. Two things a reader will be able to do after completing the chapter include:

   - Display qualities that are desirable in a good patient/nursing assistant.
   - Identify duties and role functions of nursing assistants.
   - Practice good personal hygiene.
   - Behave ethically.
   - Keep confidences to themselves.
   - Work accurately.
   - Be dependable.
   - Follow rules and instructions.
   - Develop cooperative staff relationships.
   - Show respect for patients' rights.
   - Explain how laws affect them and the patients they care for.
   - Report incidents.

3. Two important ideas in the introduction could include:

   - A nursing assistant is an important member of the health care team.
   - Duties may include a variety of direct and indirect patient care tasks.
   - Specific job descriptions vary among institutions.
   - In addition to job duties, nursing assistants are expected to demonstrate good interpersonal and organizational skills.
   - A personal code of ethics and awareness of legal aspects of nursing are essential.

Exercise 3

1. Important ideas in the summary that were also in the introduction could include the following:

   ■ A nursing assistant is an important member of the health care team.

   ■ In addition to job duties, nursing assistants are expected to demonstrate good interpersonal and organizational skills and good hygiene.

   ■ A personal code of ethics and awareness of legal aspects of nursing are essential.

2. Important ideas in the summary that were not in the introduction could include the following:

   ■ Nursing assistants will be ensuring that patients do not suffer any extra pain and will be making their stay easier.

   ■ Always remember that patients are entitled to respect for their human rights.

   ■ Patients must be kept safe and properly cared for at all times.

   ■ Laws protect both the patients and the workers.

Exercise 5

4. The NIMH, National Institute of Mental Health, is part of the National Institutes of Health (NIH) under the direction of the U.S. Department of Health & Human Services. The mission of NIMH is to diminish the burden of mental illness through research.

Exercise 6

7. List any four of these warning signs of hypothermia:

   Chattering teeth and shivering.

   Slow, hard-to-understand speech.

   Forgetfulness, confusion.

   Fumbling hands.

   Stumbling, difficulty in walking.

   Sleepiness.

   Exhaustion (if the person can't get up after a brief rest, X-cold has taken over).

8. List any four of these positive actions:

   Find shelter.

   Build a fire.

Get the victim out of wind, rain, snow.

Strip off wet clothing and put on dry clothes or wrap up in a sleeping bag.

Give warm drinks.

Avoid medicines.

Exercise 7

9. Five types of "age":

Biological age refers to the relative age or condition of the person's organs and body systems.

Psychological age refers to a person's adaptive capacities, such as coping abilities and intelligence, and to the person's awareness of his or her individual capabilities, self-efficacy, and general ability to adapt to a given situation.

Social age refers to a person's habits and roles relative to society's expectations.

Legal age is based on chronological years.

Functional age refers to the ways in which people compare to others of a similar age.

10. The quality-of-life index (how much life a person has packed into the years a person has lived) combined with the inevitable chronological process appears to be the best indicator of the "aging gracefully" phenomenon.

THEME I

Selection 2

13. False. People with a gloomy outlook are <u>not</u> just as healthy as optimists. Or: Optimists are typically physically and mentally healthier than pessimists.

16. Examples of how being an optimist pays off:

do better at work, school, and in life

are healthier

recover from illness quicker

have energy and motivation to make things happen

Selection 3

"Secrets" for gathering riches in our daily life:

Look mindfully and deeply at the blessings in your life.

Train yourself to be appreciative of your life every day.

Revel in the incredible gifts inherent in our ordinary lives and ordinary experiences.

Learn the art of jumping for joy.

Don't hang on so tightly to the way it's "supposed" to be.

Focus your attention on your senses.

Selection 6

14. Examples of body language:

smiling

frowning

shrugging

shoulders

shaking or nodding head

shaking fist

15. Reasons a positive attitude is essential to career success:

It helps you be more energetic, motivated, productive, and alert.

When coworkers perceive you to be a positive person, they will be attracted to you.

You will contribute to the productivity of others.

Coworkers will like you.

You will be given greater consideration when special assignments and promotion opportunities come up.

THEME 2

Selection 1

1. landfill

2. ozone layer

3. sulfuric acid

4. environment

5. chlorofluorocarbons

6. pollutant

7. temperature inversion

8. carbon dioxide

9. radon

10. carbon monoxide

11. runoff

12. eutrophication

13. smog

14. high-energy radiation

15. ozone

16. recycling

17. carcinogens

18. asbestos

19. We are dependent on the environment for the air we breathe, the water we drink, the food we eat, and more.

20. Natural wastes are recycled as part of the cycle that helps to maintain homeostasis.

21. The level of carbon dioxide in the atmosphere is increasing because of widespread burning of coal, petroleum, and other fossil fuels.

22. Chlorofluorocarbons are considered a problem in the environment because they destroy the ozone layer.

23. Common particle forms of air pollution are dust, soot, and mold spores.

24. Sources of water pollution are sewage, industrial wastes, runoff, oil spills, household cleaners.

25. A landfill can cause water pollution because their hazardous wastes can leak into the groundwater/water supply.

26. A substance is considered hazardous to life when it has the potential to harm you or other living organisms.

27. X-rays are an artificial source of radiation.

28. Loud noise is harmful because prolonged exposure causes permanent hearing loss.

29. Answers will vary.

30. Answers will vary.

31. Answers will vary.

32. Answers will vary.

33. Answers will vary.

34. Answers will vary.

35. Answers will vary.

36. Answers will vary.

37. Answers will vary.

38. Answers will vary.

Selection 6

1. Examples of "chronically noisy environments" could include:
    video arcade

    living room with television playing

    car with radio blasting

    cafeteria with conversations and other noises

Selection 7

6. Examples of "decisions with the biggest impact" include:
    how much we drive and use other energy-expensive transportation

    what kind and how much energy we use in our home and office

    how much we eat

    how far the products we consume must be transported

    Examples of decisions that "loom large in the popular imagination" include:
    whether to take paper or plastic bags at the grocery store

    how much we recycle

    if the windows on envelopes are recyclable

10. The three specific ways to reduce their personal ecological footprint and the advice for friends and family will vary. (An increasing number of students suggest volunteer and political actions in addition to more typical drive less/walk more answers.)

THEME 3

Selection 1

2. Making your "butterflies fly in formation" means reducing the anxiety. ("Butterflies in my stomach" is a common expression conveying anxiety, fear, and nervousness about an impending activity. The origin of the term is unclear although the feeling approximates what it might feel like to have real butterflies ricocheting from stomach wall to stomach wall.)

7. Things you should be aware of as you deliver your speech include:
    eye contact

    volume

    rate

    tone

    gestures

    audible pauses

    duration

Selection 3

9. Things you can do to reduce your fear and anxiety include:

Reduce the number of unknowns you face.

Be well prepared.

Know that your audience wants you to succeed.

Have confidence in your ideas.

Use exercises to reduce symptoms of anxiety.

Relax.

Selection 6

8. Strategies that can help you to sound your best include:

Give your vocal cords some TLC.

Practice breathing from the diaphragm.

Sing to loosen the vocal cords.

Stretch your mouth, read aloud, and recite tongue twisters to improve articulation.

Smile and use your hands.

10. Students are usually amazed when they analyze their log—they speak with others much more than they think. Strategies for improving their voice vary tremendously.